GEORGE THE THIRD

of Mecklenburg-Strelitz
1744 - 1818

PRINCESS LEININGEN
Victoria Marie Louise
of Saxe-Coburg
1788 - 1862

Ernest
1771 - 1851
DUKE OF CUMBERLAND
KING OF HANOVER
married
Frederica
of Mecklenburg-Strelitz

Two Sons *who died in*
infancy and six daughters:
Charlotte Augusta Matilda,
Augusta, Elizabeth, Mary,
Sophia *and* Amelia.

Alexandrina) **Victoria**
1819 — 1901
QUEEN VICTORIA
married 1839
Albert
of Saxe-Coberg-Gotha
1819 - 1861
PRINCE CONSORT

Albert Edward
1841 — 1910
KING EDWARD VII
married 1863

Alexandra
of Denmark
1844 — 1925
Established the present
royal succession

II. *The* FITZCLARENCES

By his mistress, Dorothy Jordan, William, DUKE OF
CLARENCE, *had ten children: George,* EARL OF MUNSTER;
Henry; Sophia; Mary; Frederick; Elizabeth;
Adolphus; Augusta; Augustus and Amelia.

Allanson INV. et SCRIPS.

IV. *The* HOUSE *of* BRUNSWICK

CHARLES — *married* — Augusta
Duke of Brunswick   *daughter of*
1735 - 1806   Frederick
                             PRINCE OF WALES
                             and sister of
                             GEORGE III *of England*
                             1737 - 1813

FREDERICK   Caroline
Duke of Brunswick   *married*
married   George
Marie   PRINCE OF WALES
of Baden   GEORGE IV

CHARLES   WILLIAM
Duke of Brunswick   *Duke of Brunswick*
                             with whom the line
                             became extinct in 1884

The Youthful Queen Victoria

By DORMER CRESTON

Victoria, Queen at 18, was far from the dominating personality she later became. Vivacious and spirited, yet with a tendency still to cling to some older relative or adviser, she was an appealing figure. Miss Creston's singularly fascinating portrait shows how the young woman who was to be Europe's most formidable sovereign coped with the manifold problems of a new regime, a host of unruly and intriguing relatives, and a major scandal in her household, all in the space of the two-and-a-half years before she married Prince Albert. During this time she won her spurs as a ruler, with Lord Melbourne's help, and was unscathed by the wave of criticism that assailed her after Lady Flora Hastings, one of her Maids of Honor, was falsely accused of being pregnant.

Miss Creston's canvas adroitly includes entertaining glimpses of Victoria's childhood and education and of the Duchess of Kent and the eccentric uncles who were sons of George III. Here is a first rate biography, of particular interest at a moment when a young woman wears the crown of England for the first time since Victoria.

Dormer Creston is the author of *The Regent and His Daughter* and *Andromeda in Wimpole Street*. She recently received the Royal Society of Literature's award for *In Search of Two Characters* and she is a frequent contributor to *The Times Literary Supplement*.

With 24 pages of illustrations

The Youthful Queen Victoria

From the painting by Thomas Sully

" Such a little love of a Queen ! Lord Melbourne must take
care to throw a something paternal into his manner."

(From a letter by Lady Granville)

" Such a little vixen."

(From a letter by the Rev. Archer Clive)

The Youthful Queen Victoria

A Discursive Narrative

by

DORMER CRESTON, pseud.

Baynes, Dorothy Julia.

G. P. Putnam's Sons
New York

MANUFACTURED IN THE UNITED STATES OF AMERICA

VAN REES PRESS • NEW YORK

TO

MY FRIENDS

ACKNOWLEDGMENTS

It was by gracious permission of His Majesty King George VI that I included reproductions of the following pictures: *Charles, Prince of Leiningen,* by Wilkie; *The Prince of Wales's Phaeton,* by Stubbs; *The Prince Consort, 1840,* by Partridge; *Queen Victoria and the Duchesse de Nemours,* by Winterhalter; *The Duchess of Kent,* by Winterhalter; *The Duke of Wellington and Sir Robert Peel,* by Winterhalter; *Her Serene Highness Feodore, Princess of Hohenlohe-Langenburg;* and the *Concert at the Château d'Eu,* by Eugène Lami. My gratitude is due to Her Highness Princess Marie-Louise for allowing me to use information which she gave me.

I am indebted to Mrs. Henry Cust for permitting me to quote from the Journal of her mother, Victoria Stuart-Wortley (Maid of Honor to the Duchess of Kent), incorporated in Mrs. Cust's unpublished script, "The Poor Old Diary"; to Mrs. Wadman for allowing me to make liberal use of the letters of her grandmother, Mary Davys (Extra Woman of the Bedchamber to Queen Victoria); to the late Miss Henrietta Tayler for authorizing me to take what I wished from her unpublished script containing extracts from the letters of the Honorable Harriet Lister (Maid of Honor to Queen Victoria). During the five years that I have been writing this book two more have left us to whom I am indebted for information: Louisa, Countess of Antrim (Lady in Waiting to Queen Victoria); and the Honorable Maurice Baring. I am most grateful to the Marquis of Bute for so kindly sending me a photograph of the portrait of Lady Flora Hastings; and to Sir Edward Hanmer, Bart., for allowing me to reproduce the portrait of his ancestor, *Sir*

John Conroy, by Fowler. My warmest thanks are also due to a number of people who have given me private information or helped me in some other manner. The first I should mention is Mrs. Keating (Lady Housekeeper at Kensington Palace) who in the kindest way has given up so much of her time to assist me. Among others whom I would wish to thank are the Honorable Lady Reid (Maid of Honor to Queen Victoria); the Honorable Mrs. Hugh Wyndham, Lady Wingfield, Mrs. Eric Palmer, Miss Dorothy Margaret Stuart, Miss Murray Lawes, Lord Courtauld-Thomson, Sir Charles Wingfield, Mr. Roger Fulford, and Mr. Cecil Phillips.

As usual with my biographies, the generosity of Sir John Murray in allowing me to quote from a number of books published by him outruns all thanks. Those of which I have made the fullest use are *The Girlhood of Queen Victoria,* edited by Lord Esher, and *The Letters of Queen Victoria,* edited by Lord Esher and Mr. Arthur Benson, from both of which I am allowed to quote by permission. Regarding extracts I have taken from *The Creevey Papers,* edited by Sir Herbert Maxwell, and *Creevey's Life and Times,* edited by John Gore, I have to thank both Sir John Murray, and Mr. J. R. Blackett-Ord, owner of all the Creevey papers. Other books Sir John Murray has sanctioned me to quote from are *Lady Bessborough and Her Family Circle,* edited by the Earl of Bessborough; *The Queen Thanks Sir Howard,* by Mary Howard McClintock; *Recollections of a Long Life,* by Lord Broughton; *The Croker Papers,* edited by Louis J. Jennings; *Red Cross and Berlin Embassy,* by Viscountess D'Abernon; *Queen Adelaide,* by Mary Hopkirk; *Elizabeth Lady Holland to Her Son,* edited by the Earl of Ilchester; *Private Letters of Princess Lieven to Prince Metternich,* edited by Peter Quennell; *Correspondence of Princess Lieven and Earl Grey,* edited by Guy le Strange; *Correspondence of Sarah Spencer, Lady Lyttelton,* edited by the Honorable Mrs. Hugh Wyndham; *Mary Ponsonby,* edited by Magdalen Ponsonby; *Life and Correspondence of Arthur P. Stanley,* by Rowland E. Prothero; an article entitled *Character of Queen Victoria,* by Sir Edmund Gosse, that appeared in the *Quarterly Review;* and an article entitled *Tragedy of Claremont,* by Osbert Lancaster, published in the *Cornhill Magazine.* I have to thank the owners of the copyright in the edition of *The Greville Memoirs* edited by the late Lytton

Strachey and Roger Fulford, and published by Macmillan. My thanks are due to Messrs. J. W. Arrowsmith of Bristol for my quotations taken from *Victoria, Queen and Ruler,* by Emily Crawford. I should also like to acknowledge my indebtedness to various other authors and publishers from whose works I have quoted. All these appear in my list of Authorities.

I wish to emphasize that in this, as in all my biographies, even the smallest fact mentioned is authentic, as, too, are the spoken words of the characters. In my comments on persons or episodes I always make it clear that they are my comments only.

My recognition of kindness is above all due to Sir Edward Marsh for reading my typescript and giving me his invaluable comments.

My appreciative thanks go to my three typists, Mrs. Neave, Mrs. J. M. Lovell, and Miss Riddel for their patience and accuracy.

I warmly thank Mr. Cox of the London Library, and his assistant, Miss Bolton, for their generous and sympathetic help.

CONTENTS

xi

LIST OF ILLUSTRATIONS

List of Illustrations

The Youthful Queen Victoria

"Authors and commentators, then, must oftener than any others lose their time and their labour who will always be looking out for great causes to great events—by neglecting trifles they overlook truth."

LORD HERVEY

CHAPTER I
SOME APPROACHES TO A COMPLEX CHARACTER

Our past monarchs are all national possessions, but Queen Victoria is more; she has become a national treasure, such increasing interest has that small precise figure seated in the royal Valhalla drawn to herself. On the surface it is strange that this should be so when one considers that her whole behavior—duty bound, conventional, scrupulously moral, careful of tradition—is in direct antithesis to what is now commonly considered pleasing and worthy of attention. Possibly her undefeatable integrity and self-assurance act as a subconscious anchorage for the bewildered emotions, the sliding valuations, and general nervousness of our own sore-pressed epoch. Here is an ordered mind confronting disorder. As one listens back there is a kind of refreshment in hearing that silver voice remark in those beautifully enunciated tones, "I'm bored with the future altogether, and don't want to hear any more about it." There within the consciousness of the nation she remains as one of the most successful of monarchs; for she had what can only be described as a genius for queenship. Her deeply emotional nature coupled with her confiding simplicity in expecting everyone to participate in her feelings has obscured the fact that she was both an exceptionally intelligent woman and a unique being. She possessed little purely intellectual curiosity, and, further, though in her schoolroom her mind had been packed with information she had been initiated into no literary or aesthetic discernment. But as a ruler she came into her own, for her native shrewdness led her instinctively to train her very varied and subtle gifts to form *in toto* a remarkably efficient instrument of state. Another of the reasons for her power of survival, of becoming ever more instead of less vivid to posterity, may lie in the fact that no character in our history was so determinedly and, one might say, unconcernedly all of a piece as this prominent Queen: all of a piece, and yet, like a mosaic, of a most involved pattern. Her sense of rectitude was so paramount that she allowed her individuality to develop and densify as it would. It is this, combined with her sapience, that led her to give vent to those enchanting, at once bland and autocratic, Victorianisms. "Dear me," she remarked one day when, after some public man had been presented to her, one of her entourage was unwise enough to give voice to a surmise as to the impression he had received of the Queen, "Dear me, I did not give a thought to that. It is so beside the question. What really signifies is what I think of him." The same indifference to the effect on others of herself or her actions would lead her at times to do small things of the quaintest nature. Mr. Amherst Webber, the accompanist of many of the great singers of the day, used to relate how when he arrived in the royal precincts to perform before the Queen in her later years, everyone waiting for her in the concert room would instinctively only speak to each other in carefully hushed voices. Suddenly two emphatic knocks would bang through the tense atmosphere. On the instant there would be silence, and everyone would rise to their feet. Then that small but most individual figure in sober black, by some subtle process inducing around herself a positive aroma of majesty, would appear in the doorway and pass to her seat quite close to the performers. They found such intimate nearness of the royal presence alarming enough, but on occasion there was worse to come. As soon as the concert began, up would go the royal opera glasses, and thus they would remain, making the musicians feel as if they were specimens under a microscope. This habit of the Queen did not imply lack of consideration for the feelings of others—in general no one showed more exquisite and tactful kindness—but, accustomed herself to the steady stare from thousands of eyes, it would not have struck her that the effect of her opera glasses at such close quarters could be nerve racking. If a cat may look at a king, surely the king may look at the cat. This kind of unruffled, delightfully risible actions have all helped in building up what the English love: a character. England also instinctively approves of any well-known figure who lives a very long time. Both these demands Queen Victoria fully met; but to make her name stand out in such decisive lettering there must have been in the background a peculiar blending of forces other than are contained in the two obvious attractions named above. Condemnation of others is one of the commonest forms of self-praise, and to our satirical and agnostic age no character of the past has proved an easier prey for derision; but no one who is really conversant with her can fail to realize that at core she possessed some indefinable and most potent quality which, in her position, stood her in greater stead than if she had been merely an intellectual. One manifestation of this elusive quality was, when she chose to exert it, that of inscrutability: this being no doubt one of the reasons for her ascendancy over those who from their own outstanding position were used to the satisfaction of seeing others self-diffident in their presence. Bismarck was so nervous of her that when on one occasion she gave him an interview in Berlin he was discovered afterward mopping his forehead. "That was a woman!" he exclaimed. "One could do business with her." "*Très équilibrée et très sage*," remarked Prince Bülow after a long private talk with England's Queen. "Don't believe any of the nonsense now talked of the Queen being 'ordinary,' " said Lord Ronald Leveson-Gower —who had known her well from his childhood up—"she was a clever and an extremely original woman." As for Lord Salisbury, he had the profoundest admiration for her capacities. "It was," he said, "always a dangerous matter to press on her any course of the expediency of which she was not thoroughly convinced; and I may say with confidence that no Minister in her long reign ever disregarded her advice, or pressed her to disregard it, without afterwards feeling that he had incurred a dangerous responsibility." Lady Gwendolen Cecil, Lord Salisbury's daughter, declared that when her father returned after one of his lengthy talks with the Queen "there would be no shadow of condescension in his report of her opinion upon this or that vexed question"—as to, for example, a foreign statesman's secret intentions, or regarding "an Emperor's published point of view and his real one." "She knows what she is talking about," would exclaim Lord Salisbury.

Catherine the Great was the most voluptuously immoral of women; Victoria the Good the most moral. Yet, as one studies their two characters, Victoria seems like a reverberation in a more civilized age and country of that egregious Empress of Russia. Certain markedly divergent tastes must be admitted. Catherine, more intellectual than Victoria, delighted in philosophical discussions; Victoria detested them. Catherine was peculiarly indifferent to music; to Victoria, from a child up, it was a necessity of her being. Allowances, too, must be made for the disparity of surroundings and upbringing, and for the fact that one lived in the eighteenth century and the other in the nineteenth. Nevertheless, their likeness to each other is arresting.

Here are two emphatic and most determined characters, at once vehement and wise, both possessed of a fundamental breadth of being, a benign outlook, a marked sense of duty to their country and desire for its prestige. With both, once their affections were engaged, the chosen became paramount. Lord Ponsonby, who had every opportunity for an intimate knowledge of the living Victoria, writes that she "did not belong to any conceivable category of monarchs or of women." One might say, however, that she and Catherine were evidently members of some not yet categoried genus. In this connection it is interesting to note that by birth Catherine was wholly, and Victoria more than half, German. In becoming aware of how not only in their characteristics but also in certain factors in their lives the one mirrored the other, it is difficult entirely to disentangle what was peculiarly similar in incident from what arose from similarity of temperament. Ignoring this inevitable overlapping, it is noticeable that both were short, slight in girlhood, and in later life very stout, but in each case such an innate sense of their high position radiated from them that their lack of inches was no matter. Both suffered in early youth from difficult psychological situations arising from the elder people around them, which situations they grappled with in precisely the same manner: by an adroit outward show of submission that hid the resolute character forming within. Each of these two precocious children possessed an intriguing, ambitious, and not wholly affectionate mother, but received moral support from a devoted *gouvernante en titre*. Victoria had her Fräulein Lehzen; Catherine her Mademoiselle Cardel; in each case the governess markedly influencing her pupil's mind. A small detail, but yet one of interest, is that, as girls, Catherine and Victoria were equally enchanted with the letters of Madame de Sévigné. Each flung herself zealously into her lofty position, acquiring all the knowledge she could to fit herself for it. Here, too, is the same passion for dancing, for reckless riding, the same delight in playing games with children. Yet, in spite of this marked love of small children, they were again alike in that in neither of them was their maternal sentiment for their own offspring anything like in intensity what one would expect from such warmhearted beings. Catherine appears to have shown little interest in her illegitimate or her one possibly, but most improbably, legitimate offspring. Queen Victoria was an affectionate and most dutifully attentive parent, but—except while Prince Arthur was a boy—there seems to have been little real enthusiasm in her feeling for her children. She herself acknowledged this. "Even here, where Albert is often away all day long," she wrote from Balmoral in 1856, "I find no especial pleasure or compensation in the company of the elder children . . . only very occasionally do I find the rather intimate intercourse with them either agreeable or easy. . . . I only feel properly *à mon aise* and quite happy when Albert is with me." And again, the next year, writing to King Leopold, she cries out that when her husband is away, "*All* the numerous children are as *nothing* to me."

To continue the parallel between these two women monarchs, we note the same abundance of being, the same genius in the art of ruling, an independence and sureness of judgment, a most appealing kindness to all around them, a temper difficult for the owner to control, freedom from any petty jealousy or rancor, and above all—and there is no understanding of Queen Victoria unless one takes this into account—an intensely amorous nature. Catherine, within her half-barbaric setting, led a life of shameless libertinism; Victoria, gently bred and most Christian lady, was immersed from the age of twenty in an almost desperate attachment to one man, who, alive or dead, absorbed her feelings and motivated her mind. Notwithstanding this singleness of devotion, when she was bereft of the Prince Consort the near presence of some man always about her still remained a necessity of her being. It had been inevitable that Lord Melbourne should be the focal point for the tender emotions of her adolescence; and, once the Prince Consort was dead, in an entirely innocent and sublimated form, John Brown, and later, her Indian attendant, the Munshi,* gave her at least that solace of a masculine presence without which her nervous system could know no serenity.

In the Queen's emotional wreckage after losing her husband, Brown—already, in 1851, chosen by the Prince Consort to lead her pony at Balmoral—became indispensable. Instead of the dreadful void around her in her private rooms there was, now that she had raised Brown to be her indoor as well as her outdoor attendant, another male figure moving in and out; and within that stalwart Highlander a heart which she knew to be at once devoted and protective. If his usefulness to her in two aspects in particular had been generally realized, there would not have been so much misapprehension of her relations with him. When she lost the Prince Consort her sense of isolation afflicted her beyond anything that a private person can, without a stretch of imagination, understand. Even four years after his death we find her, when staying with Lord Dalhousie, writing in her Journal, "Lady Christian [Maule] took us upstairs. I had two nice small rooms. The two maids, Lenchen [Princess Helena] and Lady Churchill, and Brown were all in our passage, away from the rest of the house. I felt tired, sad and bewildered. For the first time in my life I was alone in a strange house without either mother or husband, and the thought overwhelmed and distressed me deeply. I had a dear child with me, but those loving ones above me were both gone,—their support taken away! It seemed so dreadful!" Was this a sense of spiritual loneliness only? Victoria was full of physical courage, but the number of murderous attacks, or threatened attacks, made on her could not but leave their impression. Before she had been on the throne six years she had seven times been the victim of alarming acts of hostility. In 1837 when out driving, she had received threats from a German baker. The same year she was again threatened, when out driving, by another man who, when taken before the Privy Council, said that "if he could but get hold" of her "he would tear her to

---

* Queen Victoria engaged some Indian servants in 1887, liking this "ceremonial reminder that she was Empress of India." Among them was Abdul Karim, who finally rose to be her Indian Secretary, generally known as "the Munshi." "A bungalow," writes Lord Ponsonby, "was built for him at Osborne, fully appointed with furniture and linen," and here he would have staying with him various Indian friends of a somewhat problematical character.

pieces." In 1839 a man got into Buckingham Palace who, on being arrested, said he "had come there for the sole purpose of killing Her Majesty." The same year two shots were fired at her as she sat in her carriage. In 1840, driving with Prince Albert, she was shot at in Constitution Hill. In 1842 she was shot at again, and two months later yet another pistol was aimed at her, but missed fire. During 1848 and the following year pistols were twice leveled at her. In 1850 as she drove away one day from Cambridge House, where she had been to inquire after the ill Duke of Cambridge, a colonel struck her across the forehead with a cane. In 1872 as her carriage one day drew up at the garden door of Buckingham Palace she suddenly found a pistol thrust in her face. Brown instantly threw himself on top of the man holding it, and flung him to the ground. Within ten years the Queen was again attacked, this time by a man firing at her as she sat in the carriage sent to meet her at Windsor Station. In a moment Brown had sprung from the rumble and rushed at the man amid roars of "Kill him!" from a crowd of Eton boys.* Is it surprising that she liked to have this watchful and protective St. Bernard constantly at her side? As an old lady, long after Brown's death, she confided in one of her ladies in waiting, Lady Antrim, how she dreaded further assaults.

Lady Antrim used to recount a small incident that occurred one day when she was in waiting. She was sitting by the Queen driving back from Paddington to Buckingham Palace. People who had collected outside the station began to cheer her, but one woman suddenly gave vent to some screeched-out hostilities. The Queen naturally took no notice at all, but quietly went on bowing; neither did she make any comment to Lady Antrim. But the moment they were alone together in the hall at Buckingham Palace, the Queen turned to her and exclaimed, *"Did you hear that woman?"*

* The assailant had put his arm actually inside the Queen's landau, and fired twice, the bullets going through the back of the carriage. Instantly two of the Eton boys beat him to the ground with their umbrellas. That evening the Queen asked that every Eton boy should come up to the castle at eleven o'clock the next morning. Eight hundred boys arrived and were placed in a semicircle in the quadrangle. Then the Queen walked out from the castle door, and stood with the arch entrance behind her. One of the head boys came forward and, first read, and then handed to her a short speech. She read out a reply, and handed it to him. Then the two who had struck down her attacker were brought forward amid a frenzy of cheers, and presented to her, and to each in turn she said, "When you are old enough I shall give you a commission in my Guards."

The other aspect of John Brown's relationship to her which is scarcely known was equally valuable. After the Prince Consort's death, in her despairing need still to feel in some way in touch with him, she used to hold spiritualistic séances. These were, naturally, of a most private character; but she always had one or two ladies with her. The first medium she used was the then well-known Mr. R. J. Lees. Besides being an outstanding medium, he was a writer on mysticism. Then it was discovered that John Brown had medium-istic powers; and he was often used by the Queen in this capacity. As for the suggestion that he was her lover, or that he was even privately married to her, such commonplace guesses are, to anyone who has closely studied her character, beyond the bounds of the most extravagant supposition. She regrettably allowed him to ad-dress her as "womman," much as monarchs in the past allowed their court jester any verbal intimacies. Here again Catherine re-appears, going even further in permitting familiarity, for in her stirring philosophical discussions with Diderot he would seize her hands, shake her by the arm, and in his excitement become so rough that she took to having a table placed between them to save herself from bruises.

At one time Catherine took to lighting her own fire in the early morning rather than disturb her servants. With England's Queen there was the same domestic tenderness. It is said she would never have a servant dismissed. At Balmoral one of the footmen was so often the worse for drink when waiting at breakfast that he could scarcely get round the table. It may have been this particular foot-man or some other manservant on whom the Queen was sent a written report, from the master of the Household, complaining of his drunkenness. But this report merely received in the margin the comment, "Poor man." In State or Court functions Catherine de-manded barbaric display; Victoria the extreme of correctitude and etiquette; but again, both possessed a very different facet from that of the ceremonial. Catherine's evenings of hilarity with her friends in the part of the palace called The Hermitage are well known, but not so Victoria's positive delight in gaiety. For make no doubt of it, by instinct Queen Victoria was a merry monarch. "If those of her ladies who have seen her at the little purely feminine dinners in Scotland or at Mentone would but speak [declared one who knew her well and was referring to her in later life], they would give us charming studies of Her Majesty in the *allegro* vein." On these occasions the Queen would be amused "almost beyond her own endurance till she was simply breathless and could bear no more. Her rather prominent blue eyes would positively beam." * Indeed, lascivious Catherine and chaste Victoria both reveled in *"le fou rire."* But Prince Albert was not by nature lighthearted; the calls of overbearing necessity were always present to his mind. True, as a young man, he was full of mimicry and practical jokes, and of a rather laborious kind of humor, but all this faded out as his intensities worked to the surface; and the Queen, in her ever-increasing adoration, attuned her behavior as closely as she could to his. Business activity was what his nature craved, therefore she too became ever more immersed in public affairs. On summer nights at Windsor, at the changing of the guard on the terrace, the officer in command would be aware, in the dark façade of the castle, of a lighted window, and within this bright parallelogram would be visible two intently occupied figures, the whole making as it were a *tableau vivant* afloat in the surrounding dimness—the Queen and Prince Albert sitting one on either side of a writing table, each with a reading lamp shining on the documents over which they leaned. This shared burden of State was dear to the Queen as intensifying their intimacy; intellectually it became for her a further avenue of eroticism. Our tough epoch has but a caustic glance for her perpetual grief over losing the Prince Consort, for those who are only capable of shallow feeling naturally scold those whose emotions are deep seated. But a lately published biography of the Prince Consort † throws such a revealing light on him that the Queen's anguish at being bereft of a man of such rarity exalts her as it does him. Only those of mankind whose emotions have their source in depths unknown to the majority can understand the true nature of grief:

* From Sir Edmund Gosse's article, "The Character of Queen Victoria," published in the *Quarterly Review,* 1901. The material for this was in part provided by Lady Ponsonby, wife of Sir Henry Ponsonby, the Queen's secretary. Before her marriage Lady Ponsonby was a maid of honor to the Queen, and remained a close friend for life.

† *The Prince Consort,* by Roger Fulford, published 1949.

that in essence it is holy, and one of the most searching of man's spiritual initiations. "To me and to the state of my great grief Let kings assemble."

At first sight it appears startling that Oscar Wilde—that writer whose brilliance is so lamentably offset by the lush and the superficial—should have had "an immense respect and admiration for Queen Victoria." It is only in certain passages in *De Profundis,* those passages of anguished sincerity written when he was in prison, that we become aware of the possible meeting place between two such alien natures as his and the Queen's. In Wilde's days of triumph the Prince of Wales was often a guest at his house in Tite Street, and this fact perhaps emboldened Wilde in 1888 to write asking for leave "to copy some of the poems written by the Queen when young." Actually, she had never written one line of poetry. "Really what will people not say and invent," ran her comment on the minute to be returned to her secretary. Oscar Wilde had been released from prison scarcely a month when, in his hiding place at Berneval, he gave a village fete to the French children in honor of Queen Victoria's Jubilee, spending his exiguous money on, as he writes, "strawberries and cream, apricots, chocolates, cakes and *sirop de grenadine* . . . a huge iced cake with Jubilee de la Reine Victoire in pink sugar, just rosetted with green, and a wreath of red roses round it all."

Victoria thought to impress her husband on the mind of the nation as the great being that in reality he was by placing his effigy with all its supporting pomp and circumstance in Kensington Gardens. But, alas for her intentions, that memorial has emphasized him in exactly the opposite manner to that which she desired. When, once unveiled, the treasured figure was revealed in all its flash of gilding, a sardonic whisper crept from one London drawing room to another—"*the golden calf!*" Must one believe that this dreadful murmur reached the ears of the Queen herself? Whatever the reason, the day came when workmen clambered up the monument, and the image received a darkening wash. But derision and laughter still linger around that Gothic extravaganza. The query as to what book it is that the sculptured hand grasps has become a stock catch question. The truth is that the nation in general disliked the Prince Consort when alive, and like him no better now that he is dead. There is something about that lofty mind which the English metabolism cannot digest. Neither men nor women can forgive him: the men his lack of vices; the women his lack of charm.

Prince Leopold, in his efforts to turn his niece into a successful Queen, has, in a peculiar way, injured her reputation for being the intelligent woman that she was. Belgium's King could not resist a constant underlining of words in letters to Victoria and, in his excited indignation over certain members of the English royal family, he would at times underscore whole sentences. It seems that she, devoted proselyte of her Uncle Leopold, caught the trick from him. Her vehement nature carried it to yet further lengths, and now in any of her writings that deal with public affairs, their worth, at a casual reading, is nullified by this habit. If one rereads them, ignoring these italics, her wisdom and shrewdness become apparent. As far as her sophisticated acumen is concerned, it is, moreover, regrettable that those *Leaves from the Journal of Our Life in the Highlands* and *More Leaves,* that were received by her subjects with such enthusiasm, were made public. Was it necessary, the satirical may well ask, that the Queen should announce to the world that, on a threatening morning, "my dear Albert always said we could not alter it, but must leave it as it was"? That which is written by a saddened heart in secret should remain secret. Once disclosed, nothing stands more naked before laughter. But if in one sense it would have been better that her *Leaves* had not been published, in another the second volume accomplished something that has proved of inestimable benefit to the country. They revealed to the people at large, in a way that had never before been done, that royal hearts are in their capacity for suffering the same as hearts which are not royal; and in this realization the feelings of sovereign and people became fused. Gratitude for sympathy on the one side, and understanding and respect on the other drew Queen and country together, and was to draw the succeeding monarchs and their subjects together, in an emotion akin to love. Those coarse lampoons, those foul cartoons on the royal family were annihilated. The nation would no longer suffer them, for a new and rare plant of human relationship, and one dear to the people, had grown up in their midst.*

In general the Queen's Journal was, on her own saying, merely a jotted-down memorandum by a tired hand and brain at the end of a long, over-occupied day. These duties, these ceaseless calls on her mind, her energies, and her sympathies impart at times a charmingly Lewis Carroll atmosphere to certain of her instructions. "Pray telegraph whenever you arrive ANYWHERE," † ran a wire which Sir Howard Elphinstone, Prince Arthur's tutor, received when he was traveling on the Continent with this, her favorite son.

It is irresistible here not to give another quick lift of the royal curtain. A dinner, at which the Kaiser (the Queen's grandson) is present, is in progress at St. George's Hall. "The Queen . . . after a prolonged silence, beckoned across the table to the Kaiser and said, 'I hope you liked the fish, William?'

"The Kaiser with *empressement*: 'Oh immensely, Grandmama.'

" 'I am very glad, lieber Wilhelm.' Renewed silence."

No sooner had the Queen died in 1901 than the inevitable hagiologies appeared in which sycophancy reduced that salient being to a model monarch of the most tedious quality. If she had been alive to read these outpoured paragraphs she would have made as short work of them as she did of some divine when, in his letter of condolence over the Prince Consort's death, he said she must now look on Christ as her husband. *"That is what I call twaddle!"* exclaimed the Queen.

While on the subject of writing it is not important but of a slight amusement to record that in their later years both Catherine and Victoria were continuously, ceaselessly, to be seen writing letters; in each case the writer being surrounded by beloved dogs. Two final parallels must be drawn. They both maintained a reserved attitude

---

* In 1923 there was an exhibition of Sir Max Beerbohm's caricatures at the Leicester Galleries, among them being some suggested illustrations for Sir Sidney Lee's biography of the late Edward VII—these including a cartoon on the then Prince of Wales (Edward VIII). Far though the cool elegance and pizzicato wit of these fantasies were from the boorishness of the old type of royal travesty, two of these drawings—one of those of Edward VII and the one of the Prince of Wales—raised such an outcry that, two days after the opening of the exhibition, they were withdrawn. Curiously enough the caption on the one of the Prince of Wales prophetically referred to him as "Mr. Edward Windsor."

† In earlier days of telegraphy the post-office clerk would add "underlined" after a word underlined by the sender.

to the son who was to be their successor, and in neither case was the heir allowed any political power while his mother was alive. Secondly, each of these monarchs had a notable flatterer: Catherine her Voltaire, who acted as advertising agent to spread her fame across Europe; Victoria her Disraeli with his whimsical little spoonfuls of sirup. Did Catherine really believe Voltaire sincere when he cried out that she was "equal to the Mother of God," "wiser than all the Academies," "above nature, history, philosophy itself"! I doubt if Catherine was Voltaire's dupe to that extent. As for Victoria, one of her daughters, Princess Louise, said that her mother was not taken in by Disraeli's extravagances, but that they amused her.

2

Queen Victoria undoubtedly possessed creative gifts that the arduousness of her life prevented from coming to fruition. Even as a child she showed a feeling for draftsmanship that might, if she had had intelligent instead of mistaken tuition, have developed far; for she appears instinctively to have realized Henry Tonks's maxim, "A drawing should be a document." She gives as well every indication that she had it in her to have become an outstanding actress, for not only did she always evince an absorbing and highly critical interest in every posture, gesture, or delivery on the stage, but she possessed in herself "a distinct theatrical sense," and "was unrivalled in her sense of the proper *mise en scène* of a formal ceremonial." "Perhaps," continues Edmund Gosse's narrative, "the most salient of all her native, as distinguished from her acquired characteristics," was "her strongly-defined dramatic instinct": she "possessed, to a degree shared with her by certain distinguished actors only, the genius of movement." It is the unqualifiable in anyone that finally counts, and these aesthetic elements that lay more or less dormant within the Queen may possibly have had some connection with the undeniably strong influences that issued from her.

One of the aspects of her that might be said to come under the heading of the delightful—delightful, that is to say, to those who are charmed by, and not contemptuous of, her peculiar character, at once transparent and yet mysteriously powerful—is that with the general outlook and tempo of life changing during her reign with

unusual rapidity she refused to change either her tempo or her outlook. Baroness Lehzen, Lord Melbourne, and the Prince Consort
were her three paramount modelers—in so far as such a closely
knit disposition could be manipulated. What she had come to be
when the Prince Consort died—and she was then only forty-two—
she continued to be—complacently, undefeatably, to the end. In her
youth she had been, so it is recorded, indelibly impressed by "the
stately *tenue* of Lord Melbourne and of Lord Conyngham," and
in consequence she "retained not a little of the air of a bygone
age . . . her scheme of manner was distinctly more *vieille-cour* than
that of anyone else in Europe. In itself beautifully finished, it
offered positively an antiquarian interest." And this air of a bygone
age remained not only in her manner but in her mind. At the end
of the long walk at Windsor there is an equestrian statue of George
III, commonly known as the Copper Horse. One evening at dinner
at the castle, the Queen, aware that an important guest staying with
her had been tramping the countryside that afternoon, solicitously
remarked, "I hope you were not tired by your long walk?"

"Oh, not at all, thank you, Ma'am. I got a lift back as far as the
Copper Horse."

A horrid surmise stamped itself on the Queen's face. "As far as
what?"

"Oh, the Copper Horse, at the end of the Long Walk."

The prominent blue eyes transfixed him. "That's not a copper
horse. That's my grandfather."

Precisely. According to *vieille-cour* standards the guest had committed an impertinence. He had to be rebuked. But diners at the
castle occasionally received sterner censure. One evening Mrs.
Montgomery (one of Sir Henry Ponsonby's daughters) and Sir
William Harcourt were sitting next to each other, and though conversing in normal tones were certainly laughing a great deal. The
Queen, while watching them, wrote a note, and had it given to one
of the footmen to take to Sir William Harcourt. Opening it he read,
"Will Sir William kindly remember his manners, and where he is."
Meanwhile, those seated near the Queen heard her repeatedly
muttering to herself, "*Das ist schrecklich . . . schrecklich . . .*" *

* "Really dreadful . . . dreadful. . . ."

When the Prince of Wales was nineteen he too came under the Queen's ban regarding his behavior at meals. She decided she must write to him on the subject, he being then at Cambridge University.

Buckingham Palace, June 2nd 1861

My Dearest Bertie,

...I had not an opportunity of saying something to you the other day, which I meant to do. As I may be prevented seeing you quietly when we meet next time, I will just write it in this letter. It is, dear, about your manner of sitting, and at meals in general. It is not like dress, a matter of taste (you know I leave you quite to your own taste in that respect, and feel sure that you never would do anything extravagant or slangish). But you forget and have got into a habit of sitting quite bent, on one side, or lolling on the table with your elbows and wrists while you eat, and leaning back as if you were eating in your *own* room after a great fatigue. This, dear child, will NOT do for *any* person in your position, or any gentleman, and still less I am sure you never see it, even at your *own* table. While I look round at dear Uncle, Papa, Philip, Louis and indeed any of your relations or of our visitors, I *never* see anything of the sort, and I feel quite *pained* at what has the effect of ill breeding, or *nonchalance,* which I am *sure* is the very thing you would *not* intend or wish....

"I am of course very thankful to receive any advice from you," the Prince wrote back. "I certainly was not aware that my manners at meals were not good, and I am very sorry that such is the case ..." and so on, in the politest and most soothing of veins.

But when the Queen was dealing with political matters there was none of that cautious approach which she exercised with her eldest son. Now and then we catch her incisive voice as she raps out a few retorts to her secretary, Henry Ponsonby. It is 1886, and he is warning her "that the feeling against the House of Lords is increasing and that some reform must take place if the Institution was to remain."

She asked him "who wanted to touch it."

"Lord Elgin's brother."

"Everyone knows he is a radical."

"Lord W[illiam?] Compton."

"He is the same."

"Lord Wolmer."

"Really! I wonder what Lord Salisbury says."

"Albert Grey."

"Albert Grey! Impossible."

The generally accepted idea that Queen Victoria allowed her personal feelings to influence her in questions of policy is erroneous. Her antipathy to Gladstone ("that dangerous old fanatic," "this half crazy . . . old man") arose precisely from the fact that she considered his politics fanatical and crazy. "She is dead against Home Rule as calamitous for Ireland, hazardous for England and tending towards separation," wrote Sir Henry Ponsonby, "but she says she is convinced Mr. Gladstone undertook the work from the highest motives . . . and if he is right and she is wrong so much the better." The principle of "if he is right and she is wrong so much the better" was, in spite of her vehement feelings on any subject, the check she was broad-minded enough always to impose on herself. Her duty as she saw it was to keep intact the great Empire which, to use her own words, had been "confided to her care and which she wishes to hand down unimpaired to her children and their children's children."

Apropos of her letter to the Prince of Wales, if it gives the impression that the Queen had a dreary cast of mind, let us again go back into the royal past and listen and observe. A maid of honor, Miss Aline Majendie, had been having lessons in skirt dancing, and one day when she was wearing her accordion-pleated skirt and passing through the hall of Buckingham Palace she caught sight of one or two members of the Household waiting to accompany the Queen on her drive. Gaily she held out her skirt and began to twist and to twirl. Suddenly she became aware that the Queen had arrived on the scene, and was watching her. Embarrassed, she came to a stop. The Queen, however, told her to finish her dance, and, when it was over, remarked, "It is customary I believe in these cases to offer the dancer a present. What would you like me to give?" It was at the time when the Queen was incensed with Gladstone for what she believed to be his disintegrating policy, and now, at her question, Aline Majendie exclaimed, "I should like Mr. Gladstone's head on a charger, Ma'am." "That is a request," replied the Great Lady, "which will require some consideration," and passed on to her carriage. The next morning a note was brought to the maid of honor from the Queen. It ran, "I regret I cannot give you the first part of your request, but the charger is waiting for you in the stables."

Though I have shown how in Queen Victoria we see the reflection of Catherine the Great, and have emphasized some of the Queen's creative instincts that lay behind her visible capacities, I have not revealed, and I do not believe it ever clearly can be, how, again to quote Lord Ponsonby, "partly from circumstances but chiefly from her specially original personality" she had "created for herself one of the strangest positions any monarch has held." In later years when she could walk but little, Prince Bülow described how, at the great dinner in St. George's Hall already mentioned, he saw her carried in "by the Indian attendants on a gilt First Empire chair" which gave the impression of *"une espèce de trône."* This appearance, almost as of an idol, of the now aged Queen, "and the suggestion of oriental Empire and dominion had fired his imagination," writes Lady D'Abernon, to whom Bülow related the incident. And if in her physical appearance she at times gave this impression, spiritually she had undoubtedly grown into an idol in the mind of the nation. She had developed into such a mysterious being, so apart from, and considered so elevated above, the rest of mankind that it is no exaggeration to say that she came at last to be regarded as positively sacrosanct. Her beautiful candor and sincerity flowed from her like light across the country for whose weal she ceaselessly worked.

The following pages do not present her when she had evolved into this ameliorated and incontestable personality, but reveal her nature displaying itself with all the fervor and overemphasis of youth. Here are recorded the peculiar conditions that surrounded her as she grew up; and her first years of power before her marriage, when she astounded everyone by her verve and aplomb.

Before going back to her in those early years, we will take one final glance at her as the now veteran Queen when her end is not far off. Often she would work on late into the evening with her private secretaries,* and at times it would be past twelve o'clock before she had conclusively dealt with her business. But, at last, the secretaries would be dismissed, and the Queen, and, possibly, Princess Beatrice, now her constant companion, would be left together in that withdrawn and quiet sitting room, suffused by the light of candles only, for the Queen would allow nothing else. And then (and it was the same every night), before she went to her bed, Queen Victoria would pick up long strands of—what exactly? as far as we can see they are strands of something like braid or long strips of paper—and placing these before her she would start methodically plaiting them together. During the day—and for her at her age it was a remarkably extended day, as every morning up to the last week of her life she was down to breakfast by half-past nine—all these hours she had been distracted by a thousand duties and urgencies. And this was the same not only on one day but on every day of a life that had been crowded with overmuch—too many responsibilities and decisions, too many strains and stresses, too many deaths. She had discovered that each evening before she went to sleep the necessary folding back of her spirit upon itself, this suggestion to her mind as of the knitting-up of the raveled sleave of care, could be soothingly induced by this repetitive monotonous movement of her fingers.

And there, her face quietly bending over her occupation—that face so affecting with its air at once of distinction and sadness—we leave her, while outside around the palace walls the night silence deepens.

---

* Several of her ladies acted in this capacity. The "two ladies most closely attached to the Queen were Lady Ely and Miss Stopford who shared the secretarial labours between them."

CHAPTER II
THE DUKE OF KENT AND THE
PREDICTIONS

THE end of April, 1819. Down the Continental roads leading from Amorbach to Calais there is blundering along one of those great carriages that to our eyes, accustomed to the relentlessly shaved outline of the modern car, seem, with their spaciousness, their touching little adornments, and aesthetic value in line and bulk, to emphasize how far apart in general sentiment of outlook are we and the people of those days. This particular carriage, too, either because of its specially antique build, or from its being stuffed to bursting with the occupants and their possessions, appears to have impressed the onlookers as having a most peculiar effect. On the box sat a plethoric man of about fifty, as powerfully built as the vehicle he drove. This self-appointed coachman was one of George III's sons, Edward Augustus, Duke of Kent and Strathearn. He had deliberately chosen to drive this heavily loaded conveyance from the Castle of Amorbach to Calais himself, for within sat his wife, perilously near her confinement, and he was convinced that if he held the reins she would be less shaken than if anyone else were driving. Within the frowsty depths of the carriage the Duchess had, joggling along with her, her lady in waiting, Fräulein Späth; a lovely featured little girl of twelve called Feodore (the Duchess' daughter by a former marriage); the child's Hanoverian governess, Louise Lehzen; two maidservants; a couple of Russian lap dogs; and cages of waxbills and canaries. Behind her, the Duchess was leaving her home, and her son; a boy who, if Wilkie's portrait of him as a young man—a sketch hastily flung together as if in a burst of admiration—is to be believed, was made of the same godlike substance as Feodore. The Duchess was no doubt helped to endure

the tedium of this seemingly endless drive by the companionship
of the intelligent, still youngish governess in addition to that of her
devoted old Späth; but to us, who can look into their future, it is
curious to see the Duchess complacently sitting there cheek by jowl
with Louise Lehzen whom, by her own choice, she is bringing to
England, both unaware that a warfare of the bitterest nature is for
some sixteen years going to be waged between them for possession
of the spirit of the yet unborn Victoria.

The Duke had a strong-hewn but fleshy face. In his portraits the
spring of his nose, and his black, relentless eyes are suggestive of a
bird of prey, and the firmness of the thick, protruding lips is formidable. Here is a man of grim stuff; dogmatic, pompous, im-
placable, respectable, dignified, rigid. His voice, in keeping with
his appearance, was slow and deliberate; his manner solemnly
courteous. His whiskers and the sparse fringe of hair at the back
were dyed a dark brown. Indubitably a bore. A conclusion shared
by the Duke of Wellington, for Creevey tells us how, on one of his
sojourns on the Continent, he caught sight of the Iron Duke's
coach and six coming full tilt along the Valenciennes road, and,
later, learned that this precipitancy was due to Wellington's determination to escape a threatened visit from the royal Duke. Certainly
this particular son of George III is a most perplexing man in that,
although the description of him as "the greatest rascal that ever
went unhung" is one of Charles Greville's occasional lurches into
overstatement, he did yet undeniably possess, alongside of his
bustling efforts for the good of the public, a strain of domineering
brutality which he exercised on such members of that public as
came within his grasp.

Queen Victoria was fond of referring to herself as "a soldier's
daughter," and, cherishing this designation to the last, gave directions that after her death her body was to be borne to the mausoleum
at Frogmore on a gun carriage. But her attitude to her army, maternal and grateful, was the very opposite to that which her father,
with his fierce, German-trained eye, had had toward the men under
his command. His daughter's affection for him arose from the
romantic sentiment for an early-lost parent. In her case strongly
reinforced by the consideration that it was through her father alone
that she inherited the blood, not only of the Hanoverian kings of

England, but also of the Stuart monarchs who had sat on the English throne. "I am far more proud of my Stuart than of my Hanoverian ancestors," she would remark.

As one gazes at the Duke of Kent's portrait by Dawe—even in this captured moment of immobility, sitting there at his most serene and harmless, left elbow jauntily stuck out, little muslin bow spruce and neat beneath his chin—as one closely studies this passive rendering-up of a personality to an artist's faithfulness in transcribing, there seems gradually to emanate from that massively molded face a bullet force that is positively repellent. One feels assailed as if by the implacability of a machine. And the more one gazes the more acute the impression becomes.

2

Within twenty-one years Queen Charlotte and George III had fifteen children, of whom Edward, born in 1767, was the fourth son, and the fifth child. This family, arriving in the world on each other's heels, formed in their upbringing almost an adumbration of the modern mixed schooling, so intimately interwoven were their lives. To the brothers and sisters in those early days at Kew and Windsor, the boys in their satin suits, the girls in their panniered muslins, all of them joyously mixed together, tomboying, laughing, hilariously playing cricket, life was fresh and sweet as new-mown hay. The result of their intermixing was a lifelong tender affection between the group of lovely sisters and the group of hefty brothers, an affection that, increased by the intense vitality of the boys, and the exceptional beauty of the girls, at times seems almost, though innocently enough, to have approached the amatory. Innocent though it was, years later, as will appear, it was to give rise to scandal of the most salacious nature.

At a year and a half Edward had thoroughly acquired the art of talking, and as he turned from boy into man discovered the knack of dealing out all those sonorous platitudes that for forty-odd years were to be the delight of sycophants and the derision of the intelligent. His life was to be curiously interwoven with prophecies that came true, and, unfortunately, while he was a child, a gypsy murmured to him that it was his line, and not that of an elder brother, that would succeed to the Crown. The delighted boy (for him power and happiness were always to be synonymous) could not resist harping on this theme, to the annoyance of his father. Edward's tutor, Bishop Fisher, declared that it was his boyish tactlessness on this subject that during his early years made George III begin to take a definite dislike to him. King George was an assiduous, typically eighteenth-century parent, but no psychologist, and when one day his fourth son secretly and deliberately smashed to smithereens a certain clock for which his father had a particular affection, the King saw in this apparently unaccountable action nothing but another proof of Edward's general horridness. Actually, the more his father pushed him away from him the more his son craved his affection, and there is genuine pathos in a remark the boy made one day when his tutor happened to read out to him what the Duke of Ormonde had said on the death of his son, "that he would not change his dead son Ossory for the best living son in Europe." Tears came to the boy's eyes, and he asked if, supposing he should die, his parents would say the same of him, and then, before his tutor could answer, he added, "As I am a child I suppose not, but if I live to grow up perhaps they would say the same."

George III was in advance of the period in his belief in the benefit for the young of fresh air, exercise, plenty of vegetables, and no overeating. The effect of this regime on his elder sons had proved almost too rewarding, such dynamos of health, energy, insubordination, and debauchery had they become. Confronted with their turbulence, the King stood aghast at what his methods had brought to fruition. Hourly fussed over by his dovelike group of daughters, and used to being called "the Dear," he had considered it in the natural order of things that his sons would at least treat him, and treat his opinions, with respect. While his eldest, George, was still a boy he had opened the King's eyes to the fallacy of any such supposition. Finding that his father had been criticized by Wilkes in the forty-fifth number of the *North Briton*, George rushed to the door of the King's bedroom, and, beating on the panels, kept yelling "Wilkes for ever! No. 45 for ever!"

Frederick, the second son, though for six years of his youth he had been in Germany for his military training, in general enthusiastically followed his elder brother's social technique. Derided by both of them, George III determined to take no further chances, and when his third son, William, was fourteen, he sent him to sea. Then came the unpopular Edward. He, too, the King decided, should at seventeen be sent out of the country, and in Hanover, under the ceaselessly vigilant eye of a governor, should be thoroughly chastened and subdued by German military discipline. For this post of governor the King chose a Baron Wangenheim, a man as unpleasing in appearance as he was in disposition. Doubtless the King's satisfaction at finding in him all the marks of a man who could be relied on to be tyrannical to youth deterred him from investigating further into his character. Actually, his behavior to the boy given into his charge turned out to be intolerable.

Though Edward was not liked by either of his parents, he had not been stinted of the ample upbringing of all King George's sons, and from twelve years old had had his own house and separate establishment on Kew Green, with his governor, tutors, pages, porters, nightwatchman, housekeeper, and domestic servants. Two thousand pounds a year had been allocated for his food alone. His long, carefully brushed curls fell on to the shoulders of a luxurious succession of satin coats, "six suits of full dress clothes a year"; and every fortnight he inserted his feet into a new pair of shoes. All these attentions and appurtenances were dear to him. Self-importance was, and was to remain, the dearest of his possessions—no doubt a compensatory sentiment to the knowledge of how low he stood in his father's opinion. But in Hanover, Wangenheim, securely hidden from George III's eye, saw in this post of governor to his son an opportunity of filling his own pocket at the boy's expense, and out of the six thousand pounds a year that he was given for his pupil, Wangenheim only allowed him thirty shillings a week pocket money, and refused him either a horse or a carriage. During these early years of his military training, first at Lüneburg, and later at Geneva, the young man was already impregnated with a lively sense of what was due to him as a son of the King of England, and now, his sense of manhood burgeoning daily, he naturally wanted to live the social life, not only of an officer, but of a prince. Intolerably cramped by Wangenheim's niggardly pocket money, he began to borrow, and to run up debts. This was the beginning. These debts were to increase and multiply every year of his life, and, in the end, only to be finally settled by Queen Victoria the year she came to the throne. But in Germany, in addition to acquiring the habit of living on credit, Edward eagerly, and most fatally, with all the impressionability of adolescence, imbibed the harsh principles of German militarism. Within a few years this boy with his quiet, courteous manner, fresh from the gentle family life of Kew Green, had been taught that no extremes of coercive brutality were to be condemned if they turned a regiment into an efficient weapon. These principles linked themselves in his mind with a craving for that super-exactness in all the material minutiae of life so often noticeable in those who have a sense of failure in other directions. This instinct and his German training were soon reinforcing each other only too succesfully.

Wangenheim had a double grip on his victim: he not only confiscated his money, but through the Prince's valet, a man called Rymers, was kept informed of all the young man's private doings. In addition, Wangenheim intercepted his letters to King George, and complained to the father of his son's extravagance. Naturally the King became increasingly annoyed both at the paucity of letters from Edward, and at his behavior as viewed through Wangenheim's complaints. The boy, unaware of what was going on behind his back, was puzzled and hurt at the lack of affection in King George's letters, but realized only too well that he was becoming still more unpopular at home. So much so that when he hoped, by an appeal to his father, to get permission to keep a couple of horses, he wrote sadly to a friend, "*I have so seldom found a gracious answer to any of the little trifling requests that I have made him, that I am now very shy of asking.*"

For five years the young man submitted and endured, but by the time he was twenty-two he felt he could bear this tyranny no longer, and one winter's day he and a friend, having managed secretly to get hold of some sort of open carriage, made a frantic seven-hundred-miles dash to the coast. In the middle of January, 1790, he suddenly appeared in London, to the stupefaction of his eldest brother, who was the first member of his family with whom the young man got in touch. However, the splash of the whole thing exactly coincided with George's own views as to how an awkward situation should be dealt with, and he bore Edward off in triumph to Carlton House, delighted at this chance of giving a slap to their father and his parental admonishments.

When the King heard that Edward, placed by him on the Continent, had, unauthorized, returned to England, his anger blazed. For twelve days the situation remained stationary, but then Edward was informed that he had been given the command of the Royal Fusiliers, and was to set sail for Gibraltar within twenty-four hours. Peremptory as was the order, he must have felt all the same that his effort at emancipation had borne worth-while fruit.

Before he sailed he was permitted, but for a few minutes only, a view of that heavy-featured, kingly countenance—that face which could be so benign, which could be so condemnatory. The powerfully built young man stood there pierced by the chill gleam from the pale, protruding eyes that surveyed him with such distaste. He received a few words of parting, but words unwarmed by any affection. Then father and son separated, not to meet again for eight years.

3

Here, on the Rock, where the newly appointed Colonel's regiment arrived in August, came not only the young soldier's opportunity to put into action those German principles with which his mind was now saturated, but, by doing so, to impress his father; of gaining a little of that parental affection for which, in spite of King George's persistent hostility, his son continued to crave.

Unfortunately, his newly acquired position of authority went to his head. He became an unreasonable martinet. Every morning he rose exultantly from his bed to order parades, drills, inspections, floggings. But this attempt to put German militarism into British soldiers met with fierce resentment: the discontent and grumbling of both officers and men became known at home. The inadvisability of having a markedly unpopular officer at such an important military center as Gibraltar became evident, and within nine months of having assumed command the Prince and his regiment were ordered to Canada.

But he did not leave Gibraltar without enjoying a farewell fanfare. A spectacular ball was given in his honor by the garrison officers at the Hotel de l'Europe. In the supper room the Prince's chair was canopied in pink silk and silver, and, in an attempt to counteract his sense of dismissal, in niches on either side and above, were figures of Victory, Fame, and Minerva—for the gods and goddesses still haunted the minds of men to the enhancement of many forms of art; they and their attendant cupids not yet having become *vieux jeu*. A huge rising sun had also been inserted into the decorative scheme. Thus enheartened, the Prince set out on his two months' journey across the Atlantic.

Naturally there was no reason why Edward should behave differently on one side of the Atlantic from what he had on the other, and he did not. If anything, his harshness increased. The military punishments he ordered were barbarous: for a small fault in dress a hundred lashes; for graver misdemeanors five hundred. Before long the men under him came to the conclusion that existence as arranged for them by the Prince was insufferable, and they began to desert. There was an outstanding character in the regiment, a Frenchman called Rose, whose behavior and courage had originally gained encomiums from the Prince, but he too in time found his Colonel's brutal and senseless overdiscipline intolerable, and the day came when his name too was down as a deserter. The Prince saw in this prize soldier's defection a chance, by making him an example, to put a conclusive end to these desertions. The difficulty was first to catch the culprit. The Prince himself led the search party, and finally Rose was discovered having a meal in an inn in Pointe aux Trembles. Seeing the Prince, he got up, and remarked, "You are fortunate, Sire, that I am unarmed, for if I had a pistol, by Heaven, I would shoot you where you stand."

At the court martial that followed, Rose was sentenced to nine hundred and ninety-nine lashes. The Prince came to watch the deserter receive his punishment. The two men, onlooker and victim, stood there confronting each other, each stiff with masculine pride: the one at seeing this man who had dared to disobey and threaten him now humiliated and tortured, the other, strung with determination that the Prince should not have the satisfaction of hearing a single groan escape him. The stamina of the Frenchman was as incredible as his courage, for when the terrible ordeal was over he refused any help in dragging his coat over his lacerated body, and then, swaying over to where the Prince stood, he snapped his fingers in his face, exclaiming, "That's that. It is the bullet that should punish, my lord. No whip can cow a French soldier."

About two years after his arrival in Canada a serious regimental conspiracy was discovered, the plot being to seize the Prince and other officers, and under threat of murder to demand concessions. One of the men concerned received seven hundred lashes, and the ringleader, Joseph Draper, was condemned to death. On an April morning a fantastic cavalcade set off for the place of execution. It was headed by the Prince himself on foot. Behind him came a detachment of troops. Then the pall-covered coffin of the condemned man, while, behind it, walked Draper himself ready dressed in his grave clothes. He was followed by the regimental band playing dirges. It took nearly an hour for this macabre procession to reach the cemetery. The firing party and their victim faced each other, but instead of the Prince giving the order to fire, he stepped up to Draper and told him that though he had "now reached the awful moment when a few minutes would carry him into the immediate presence of the Supreme Being," he, his Colonel, "was happy to be authorized to inform you" that having applied to the King's Canadian representative for his pardon he had obtained it. The procession then returned to barracks.

Unlike the men in the Prince's regiment, the Canadians themselves were much enamored of this son of King George, for they had discovered him to be a lamb in wolf's clothing. Once the military wolfskins were flung aside there stepped forth the most amiable royal sheep imaginable. In private life, says an officer who served under him, he was "the affable prince and the polished gentleman." His affability, be it understood, always just slightly stiffened with the consciousness of his royal blood, but this consciousness gave the Canadians as much pleasure in the receiving as it did him in its bestowing.

It is while he is in Canada that the Duke's character, which when he was a growing boy was understandable, and, certainly in part, deserving of sympathy, begins, as it were, to go underground, and finally to become perplexing in the extreme. One thing is evident: his father's treatment had soured him; his sense of having been the victim of injustice was to be both a deep-seated and a treasured grievance for the rest of his life. Henceforward, feeling that he must rely on his own acumen and push his own way through the world, he began to bring to perfection a particular social technique: superficially urbane to a degree, beneath—at least, so in later life, his family decided—sly to a degree. "Joseph Surface," the Regent once sneeringly tossed off; and, its appositeness acclaimed by his family, the name clung. Stockmar, that acute reader of character, on one occasion watching the Prince conversing when he was a middle-aged man, noted how the smoothly benign expression suited the well-chosen words, but also noted the calculating look that at the same time was sliding over his features.

But now, in Canada, the inhabitants were far from having any complaints to make against this courteous young man who with his impressive person was such an outstanding figure wherever he appeared; and when he took as his mistress *en titre* a well-born French widow living in Canada (who certainly had enough names to act as pedestal—Alphonsine Thérèse-Bernadine-Julie de Montgenet de St Laurent, Baronne de Fortisson), the Canadians were all pleased approval.

For nearly thirty years Julie de St Laurent was to live with Edward in all but name as his wife. As if to counteract his own monumental personality, he had chosen a companion of the greatest verbal gaiety, and it says much for her ebullient nature that in spite of his constant companionship she could yet write to a friend on the birth of this friend's baby, "Hurrah! Hurrah! Hurrah! A thousand rounds in honor of the charming Souris and the new-born. In truth my head is so full of joy and my hand trembles so much I can hardly hold my pen. . . . I embrace the whole household without distinction of age or sex."

In 1793 the Prince was ordered to join the British troops fighting the French in the West Indies. Here his bravery was such that he was thanked by the English Parliament. All the same he had by now such a fixed sense of his family's hostility against himself that, referring later to this expedition, he remarked in his heavy way, "The wish entertained about me in certain quarters when serving there was that I might fall."

The next year he was given command of the British troops in Nova Scotia and New Brunswick, and built himself a house overlooking Halifax harbor. This country place that grew up under his directions, with its rotunda in the park, its bell-hung Chinese pagoda for his band to play in, its multiplicity of paths suddenly debouching upon a view of the far-stretching Atlantic, possessed a touch of that Eldorado atmosphere that George IV later induced both at the Pavilion and among his royal barges and tents at Virginia Water. It is curious how both brothers possessed within their extremely material minds this leaning to the fantastic.

Debauchery made no appeal to Edward. What he enjoyed was organizing, improving, and disciplining his fellow men; to be instituting systems and imposing regulations. He was essentially one of life's manipulators, and at times he organized to good purpose. Nova Scotia found itself for the first time the possessor of reasonable roads, old forts were repaired, new ones built, a military hospital arose in Halifax, new barracks in Charlottetown; while the commissariat the Prince introduced for the troops was so excellent that it remains to this day the basis of the British army supply system.

After several years in Canada, a fall from his horse made an excuse for him to go to Bath for treatment, and in 1798 he and "Edward's French lady" (as his family called her) sailed for England. The next year he was raised to the peerage as Duke of Kent and Strathearn, and Earl of Dublin; given a Parliamentary grant of twelve thousand pounds a year; and received the appointment of Commander in Chief of the forces in British North America. He returned to his house at Halifax, but soon a series of bilious attacks made an excuse for returning home permanently, which he did in 1800. "It is with no small degree of pride that I perceive the many beneficial effects which you are so good as to ascribe to my residence among you," ran his final gift of verbiage to the Canadians, "but I have not vanity enough to flatter myself that my absence will be so severely felt as you have the kindness to intimate." Then, a uniformed figure, made to appear still more gigantic by his Fusilier's plume, he strode down the streets between crowds of citizens come to take a last glance at their royal Duke as he walked to the quay. He and Julie stepped up the gangway of the fifty-gun man-of-war, H.M.S. *Assistance*, which had been sent to fetch them, and as she glided out into the Atlantic, the Canadian chapter of his life came to a conclusive end.

4

Strange as it seems after his failure at Gibraltar eleven years before, in 1802 the Duke of Kent was gazetted as Governor-General and Commandant of that outpost. In spite of his being one of the most hard-working and respectable of their sons, some unnamable quality that he possessed, or, possibly, merely prejudice on their part, made King George and Queen Charlotte still view him askance, and as the King said good-by to him on the eve of his departure to take up his new post, he remarked, chillingly enough, "Now, Sir, when you go to Gibraltar, do not make such a trade of it as when you went to Halifax." All the same it appears that, in principle, the military authorities considered the Duke's methods exactly the corrective needed at the moment by the Gibraltar troops; the lack of discipline among them at the time being scandalous. But the young man's irresistible impulse for overdriving, his refusal to allow the necessary margin for human frailty, were again his undoing.

His elder brother Frederick, then Commander in Chief, had warned him before he sailed to practice only "a moderate exercise" of his authority, but the exhortation left no impress on that rigid mind. The relentless systems that he applied to the troops resulted in a plot not only to seize his person but actually to fling him from the Rock into the sea. He was warned in time, and when at Christmas the mutineers began to get to work their Commandant was ready. There was a court martial. Three of the mutineers were shot; seven transported for life. In March, 1803, the Duke was recalled, and a new Governor nominated. The Duke wrote to Frederick demanding a court of inquiry regarding his conduct. Frederick got out of what was an extremely awkward position by telling his brother that "to adjudicate on the acts of an officer of his rank was manifestly inexpedient. No Court of Enquiry could be granted."

That rising sun which, some twelve years before, his brother officers had so optimistically depicted behind his gala chair, had, as far as his military career was concerned, set forever. Though he was only thirty-five, he was now faced with a future that, officially, was, and was to remain, empty. But, owing to the very peculiarities of his nature, he had at hand ways of filling what would otherwise have been a vacuum. Also from this, his Gibraltar disaster, he had at least brought back with him a certain possession, if one of only a decidedly immaterial character. While there he had visited a gypsy renowned for her powers of second sight, and she had announced to him, "You will have a daughter, and she will become a great Queen."

There followed some fifteen years of retirement from public life: long years during which he ruminated on the injury done to his career by his recall from Gibraltar, and the unfairness of the Government in showing no alacrity in raising his allowance so that he could pay the debts which it was one of his chief occupations to accumulate. The King had given him a suite of rooms in Kensington Palace, but though he used them only as his official headquarters— preferring to be with Julie de St Laurent at her house in Knightsbridge—he had spent eleven thousand pounds on furniture for these rooms, buying among other things a set of beautiful gold and crimson-seated Empire chairs that, through a part they were to play in Queen Victoria's career, have crept into history, for these appear to be the chairs in the often-reproduced picture by Wells of Queen Victoria as a girl in her dressing gown receiving the news that William IV is dead. The bill for these Empire chairs was merely one item among his debts that, by 1806, had reached the sum of £108,200. He had, too, a house at Ealing, Castle Hill Lodge, where he indulged himself in bringing efficiency in domestic matters to a point that was inhuman. In this house, too, there again appeared his leaning to the fantastic. It was almost as if, concealed somewhere within that abnormal rigidity of nature, was a craving to touch a more ethereal state of mind, which at Castle Hill he tried to induce by means of unusual lighting effects, softly splashing water, and the singing of artificial birds.

Judge Hardinge, one of the justices of the grand sessions for Brecon, stayed for a night at the Duke's Lodge in 1811, and wrote afterward of "all the mazes of my enchantment." As he drove along the winding approach to the door he marveled at the lamps that flanked it on either side, "the most brilliant I ever saw." Once inside, "I was," he says, "all astonishment accompanied with dismay at the awful silence which reigned, as well as the unexampled

brilliance of all colours. . . . Opening by accident one of the doors of
the bedchamber, painted with treillage in green and gold, I discovered in an adjoining closet a running stream and a fountain. I
began to think I was in the fields of Elysian." "The bed was only to
be ascended by a ladder of steps, and they were dressed in flowered
velvet." His surprised eyes gazed at the varying colored lights that
were thrown on every passage and staircase "as if a masquerade
were in train." The library opened on a succession of other rooms,
and by "a contrivance in the management of the light, it seemed as
if the distance had no end." As for the Judge's bedroom, "such a
room was that bedchamber as no Loves and Graces ever thought
of showing to *a hermit.*" While at breakfast the next morning, he
noticed in the room a remarkably "ornamental glass door." The
Duke poured out his guest's tea, then opened this door, and gave
an order in German. Just as the Judge was lifting his cup to his lips,
there came the sound of thirty wind instruments playing a march
"with a delicacy of tone, as well as precision for which I have no
words equal to the charm of its effect." But when this was followed
by "the dirge upon our *naval hero,*" "It threw me into a burst of
tears." Whereupon his host, taking his hand, remarked, "Those are
tears which do none of us any harm."

The Judge was enchanted at this observation. He was the perfect
companion for the Duke, always reacting just in the manner intended. Before he left, his host told him that he had "for *two
months been putting a little circuit horse in train*" for the Judge's
use. "It was," exclaimed the Duke, "a pet of the dear King . . . and
you will ride it with more pleasure for both our sakes." This was
affecting indeed, but his host's parting words overcame the Judge
completely.

"You see," cried the Duke, "that we are not formidable. Do
come to see us again. Come soon and come very often."

"*May* I not, *must* I not love this man?" cries Judge Hardinge.
Time has not yet removed that query.

At Castle Hill Lodge the servants were forced to function with
the same metallic precision as did all the busy mechanical objects
with which the Duke had now surrounded himself—indoor fountains, cages filled with toy birds, organs with dancing horses, and a

multiplicity of clocks. On every side he was beset with tickings and chimings, alarums and strikings, rhythmic plashings, and sharp, self-induced bell ringings followed by a waiting servant tearing to answer the summons: the Duke having a system of bell ropes in his study, at the other end of each rope being a servant perpetually at attention. It was the duty of another of these harassed creatures to sit up all night to ensure that the Duke's fire was alight by five o'clock, and each morning the whole staff had to parade before the royal martinet for inspection. Visitors who were granted an interview in the Duke's study would be exasperated at the way the passing of every quarter of an hour would be briskly commented on by, not one, but two chiming clocks. A small Canadian goddaughter of the Duke had neatly summed up one side of her godfather, *"Notre parrain est réglé comme du papier à musique et il veut que nous ayons autant d'ordre que lui."*

But all this curriculum at Castle Hill Lodge was to the Duke the mere background to a life of incessant, self-inflicted work. His craving both to manipulate humanity and to impose himself was now turned from the military sphere to the civilian. In politics a Liberal with definite Left tendencies, he trod heavily in pursuit of new movements and lost causes, inevitably placing himself under those two sensational human banners of the Liberal party, the Princess of Wales and Princess Charlotte. He even took up with that strange personality, Olivia of Cumberland, who insisted that the second son of George II, the then Duke of Cumberland, was her father. Her days were spent in trying to persuade the royal family to agree with her on this point: a conclusion they were loath to come to. The Duke of Sussex (King George's youngest son but one) used at times (as he said, "for fun's sake") to indulge this problematical lady with an interview, at one of which, says Creevey, "being rather off her guard from temper or liquor, she smacked off her wig all at once, and said—'Why, did you ever in your life see such a likeness to yourself'?" "No one," exclaims Creevey, on another occasion, "can have any doubts of the royalty of *her* birth. She is the very image of our Royal Family. Her person is upon the model of the Princess Elizabeth, only at least three times her size. She wore the most brilliant rose-coloured satin gown you ever saw, with fancy shawls (more than one) flung in different forms over her shoulders, after the manner of the late Lady Hamilton. Then she had diamonds in profusion hung from every part of her head but her nose, and the whole was covered with feathers that would have done credit to any hearse."

But the Duke of Kent took this *soi-disant* princess more seriously than did his brother or Creevey, and she became added to the ranks of the many people who optimistically fastened themselves on to him. He loved to be fastened on to. He possessed enough nourishment in the way of patronage, effusion, and professed affection for everyone. He had, says Stockmar, "an extraordinary love of patronising and concerning himself in the affairs of others." From genuine benevolence? Or that it pleased him to pretend to himself that he possessed more influence than he actually did? Whatever the motive, the various ministerial departments received from him such an avalanche of forwarded petitions that, says a contemporary, "his name was never uttered without a sigh by the functionaries of every public office." The several secretaries he employed, however energetically they drove their quills, could scarcely grapple with all the correspondence involved. England appeared to be chiefly populated with persons who needed help from this responsive Duke. He became a regular bureau of advice and philanthropy. "I work eighteen hours a day!" he exclaimed in triumphant self-pity. He was the treasured supporter of nearly every charitable organization in the Kingdom: heathens, invalids, Jews, workmen, Philanthropic Harmonists, expectant mothers, distressed authors—it was all one to him. His largesse was flung helter-skelter. In a sense these charities cost him nothing; they merely increased his debts: this in turn giving opportunities for further correspondence in demanding financial relief from the Regent, the government, personal friends, or, in fact, from anyone from whom he could possibly hope to extract a loan. Clerically, it was a busy, bustling life. Or he would write to Halford—doctor to, and confidant of, nearly all the royal family—to find out details as to the health of his relations; though at times himself adding to their ills by his interfering habits (Edward *"would* force himself into Sophy's room to have this conversation with Frederick," exasperatedly wrote Princess Mary on one occasion; the result being that, later, Sophy was "taken with one of her worst spasms"). But to Halford himself the Duke wrote of Sophy in devoted strain as "my poor little suffering favourite."

This doctor, Sir Henry Halford, was like a soothing psychological fluid interpenetrating the minds and feelings of nearly every member of the royal family, so eagerly and constantly, in addition to his medical ministrations, did they demand his sympathy and his counsels. In all the family disputes, in any situation that needed a messenger of tact, a coaxing of one or a suggestion to another, a reassurance that had to be applied, or a sweet reasonableness induced—in all this, as in all physical ills, Halford was the person applied to. In life and in death he was the royal family's support. And they indeed needed support, for the state of emotional upheaval and mental stress they lived in was extreme: disputes, financial crises, hostilities, quarrels, amorous intrigues, circuitous plottings, jealousies, misunderstandings, illegal marriages, political divergences kept the family pot seething. The sisters, in continuous repercussion to all this turmoil—shedding tears, dispensing sympathy, falling into "spasms"—tried, in as far as they were able, to soothe the protagonists, and disentangle the situations, at the same time endeavoring (aided by their brothers but discouraged by the King) to escape by matrimony into some normal life of their own, or even, constricted and thwarted as they were, contracting—such is the strong supposition—secret marriages. This family commotion was all the time intensified by the King's recurrent insanity, the Queen's inclement temper,* and the sons' practice of expressing their mutually opposed political views at the top of their voice in the House of Lords with all the outspokenness and vigor of their factious minds. It is not to be wondered at that the demands for Henry Halford were incessant. A mundane and very practical use the royal family made of their doctor was to treat him as a perambulating post office for taking messages one to another, or applying to him as to where at the moment any particular member of the family or their entourage might be found. Perpetually galloping in his carriage-and-four from one royal pillow to another, he was

---

* The Queen's third son, Prince William, was uncommonly outspoken as to his mother's character. One day at Weymouth Mrs. Harcourt remarked to him how sorry she was that the Queen had had such bad weather for her "water expedition." "I only wish the accursed bitch would have spewed her soul up," cried William, "and then we should have had some peace in the house."

always peculiarly well informed as to the movements of any given individual of the Court.

Naturally, all this physical and mental activity on behalf of the House of Hanover was very remunerative; Halford's bills ran into thousands, and his private life was of the most luxurious. Medically, he is of great interest, being one of the first, and the most successful, of English exponents of the theory that the mind of an invalid requires as much attention as his body. Desirous, even in his physical gestures, of striking exactly the right note, he developed an almost too courtly manner, and on one occasion, when called in to attend on Lord Liverpool who had fallen into a coma, the physician as he crossed the room was seen three times to make a profound bow to the unconscious figure on the sofa.

On yet another occasion his behavior was peculiar. In 1813 the Prince Regent had had Charles I's coffin opened before him, and Halford had been standing by his side. There before them was undoubtedly the identical King who lives on Vandyke's canvasses; and in such a state of preservation that one of the eyes was still "open and full, though it vanished almost immediately." Before the lid of the coffin was replaced Halford could not resist appropriating for himself a little snippet from the King's auburn beard, one of his teeth, and a piece of the cervical vertebra that had been cut across by the executioner's knife.* Some seventy years afterward the then Prince of Wales (Edward VII) received from a grandson of Henry Halford an ebony box containing these very objects. What should be done with them? The Prince appears to have felt little relish for this gruesome present and it was decided that it should be passed on to Charles I himself. The slightly risible aspect of this restitution of bits of his person was, very properly, countered by carrying it out with all solemnity. The incident took place in December of 1888. After evensong on the thirteenth three workmen came to St. George's Chapel, and, under the eye of a Dean, two Canons, and the Chapel Surveyor, removed six small squares of the black-and-white marble that covers the vault in

---

* It is possible that the Regent had himself given these relics to Halford, for he had had Charles's head held up for his inspection. "The complexion was dark and discoloured. . . . The shape of the face was a long oval. The hair was thick at the back of the head . . . of a beautiful dark brown colour, that of the beard was a redder brown."

which lie the bodies of Charles I, Henry VIII, and two others. An aperture was thus made directly over the center of Charles's coffin. After this the three workmen quietly scuffled out. "The Prince of Wales then came to the Chapel. It was just past seven o'clock and the choir was wrapped in darkness on the winter evening. Only a long coil of magnesium wire served to light the narrow chamber in which the Martyr King and his royal companions lay." Amid a profound silence the Prince stooped down, lowered the little box, and placed it on King Charles's coffin. This accomplished, he left the Chapel. The workmen returned. "The marble pavement was relaid, and by half-past nine that night all had departed."

A minute piece of King Charles's beard was, however, still missing. It was coiled up in a ring belonging to Sir Walter Scott; the hair, needless to say, having been a present from Henry Halford.

5

The Duke of Kent's benevolence flowed continuously to one family in particular, the De Salaberrys. Why this family were treated as if they, in especial, had a justified claim on him is not known, but the general opinion is that they were probably connected in some way with Julie de St Laurent. Whatever the fundamental reason, his kindness to them was unceasing; as, indeed, it seems to have been to most people so long as the question of discipline was not involved.

At times, leaving his study and his secretaries, the Duke would mount his horse and go for a ride. "He liked," says a contemporary, to go at "a full swinging trot of nine miles an hour." How those words "a full swinging trot" bring the man before one with a rush: that great royal torso briskly rising and falling on the back of the powerful, slickly groomed horse as it goes spanking along between the hedgerows; the Duke's relentless eye noting every detail of the passing country scene around him: the efficiency, or lack of it, as shown in the hang of a gate, the condition of a ditch, the thatching of a barn. But, on the contrary, it it possible his thoughts may have been entirely concentrated on his saddle; for one saddle maker after another had succumbed before his preliminary instructions, his final condemnations.

6

It was during these years of civilian life that the Duke became involved with Robert Owen the socialist. Owen was a man of the finest caliber, aflame with spiritual fire; his one desire to benefit mankind. He has left behind him an absorbing autobiography, the early part of which has an almost Dickensian flavor in its descriptions of working-class life, though here the life is of the late eighteenth century. At the age of twelve or thirteen Owen wrote a letter to the Prime Minister on the subject of the desecration of the Sabbath at Stamford, where Owen was then living.

"After I had sent it through the post-office Mr. and Mrs. McGuffog asked me what I had been so interested about.

"I have been writing a letter to Mr. Pitt.

"To Mr. Pitt! ... What could you have to say to Mr. Pitt?"

In about ten days, "Here," said Mr. McGuffog, bringing in a London newspaper, "here is an answer to your letter to Mr. Pitt," and there, printed on the sheet, was actually "a long proclamation from the government, recommending all parties to keep the Sabbath more strictly."

This, as it appeared, rapid responsiveness of governments to the dictates of children was a foretaste of the ease with which the difficulties of any project seemed always to melt away at Owen's approach. But meanwhile he had his living to earn; and, when about fifteen or sixteen, he served as a boy shop assistant in a poorish sort of haberdasher's that stood on London Bridge. Here he lived in. Even when he had been working sixteen hours on end, he had the next morning to be in the shop by eight o'clock, and, before this, "Boy as I was then, I had to wait my turn for the hairdresser to powder, and pomatum, and curl my hair, for I had two large curls on each side, and a stiff pigtail, and until all this was very nicely and systematically done, no one could think of appearing before a customer."

The New Lanark cotton mills, outside Glasgow, were the scene of Owen's grown-up activities. He became manager and partner, starting "a new system of management on principles of justice and kindness," while at the same time, to use his own words, bringing "one of the most difficult manufactures to a high degree of propriety over all competitors." This young man was as competent as he was original. He embodied his theories in a book entitled *New Views of Society*. To the modern mind it seems curious that this book should have had such a startling effect on the world, for it merely put forward one of the hundreds of systems of thought and education that have since been devised for the improvement of mankind. But Owen was of the race of forerunners: the freshness of the originator lay on his brow, and the serious-minded of his day were profoundly stirred. Was it, they asked themselves, and well they may have asked, conceivable, as Owen affirmed, that if his views were put into practice there would be achieved "fullformed men and women, physically and mentally, who would always think and act consistently and rationally"? Throughout England, in studies, in libraries, in schools, in episcopal palaces, all over the Continent and America, men read and wondered. A copy even reached Napoleon at Elba. He was impressed, and wished to know more of Owen. Wilberforce, Godwin, Malthus, and Mill each had his copy; Jeremy Benthem and William Allen gave their support; the Archbishop of Canterbury grew warm with enthusiasm; the Archbishop of Armagh asked Owen to call. The Austrian Ambassador, Prince Esterházy, demanded that the author should be introduced; the American Minister asked for a sufficient number of copies to give to the governor of each state in the Union; the Czar's sister, the Grand Duchess of Oldenburg, on a visit to England had Owen sit by her on the sofa for two hours; the Liverpools gave him an interview in their drawing room. Gradually it became as fashionable to visit the Lanark Mills as it is now to go to Hollywood. It was startling to that generation to see Owen's schools for children run on kindergarten principles and the infants treated "with kindness and confidence, and altogether without fear." The Grand Duke Nicholas stayed two nights with Owen; the Archdukes John, and Maximilian of Austria, ambassadors, peers, bishops, innumerable clergymen, and "wealthy travellers for pleasure and knowledge," arrived one after another at the Mills "to investigate."

The genial Duke of York sent for Owen, and they had, from the socialist's point of view, an extremely puzzling interview. "I could never discover," wrote the reformer (unaware of Frederick's fundamental flippancy), "the object which his Royal Highness had in view; for our communication was very commonplace, and without interest to me." But his contacts with the Duke of Kent, and with the Duke of Sussex, too, were far more satisfactory. Owen gave a party in Bedford Square to display an exhibit of his own invention intended to impress the onlooker with "the proportionate amount of the different classes of society." This was effected by superimposed colored cubes which Owen placed one after another on a table, starting with an extremely large cube representing the pauper and working classes, and so on up to a minute one for the royal family. The Duke of Sussex was so startled at seeing his family reduced by this relentless statistical method to a minute block of matter that he gave the Duke of Kent a dig, exclaiming, "Edward, do you see that?"

"The whole party," remarks Owen with some satisfaction, "for the moment seemed confused."

Kent and Sussex were at this time, writes Owen, "much united in affection and pursuits," and together they now set out to investigate this socialist will-o'-the-wisp, often sending for him to come to Kensington Palace for long discussions; or the Duke of Kent would take the chair at his friend's lectures. When Owen went to Paris, the Duke gave him an introduction to King Louis Philippe.

One looks on with slightly quizzical interest at Owen and the Duke in juxtaposition: the mind of the one as guileless and transparent as the other's was devious and obscure. Each saw the other in the light that issued from his own character. To Owen's charitable heart Kent appeared to possess "all the essential qualities for a great and successful reformer without violence." Kent accepted this flashing spirit and his theories as forces that would strengthen his own political position. Moreover, Owen's idea of a fresh manipulation of the minds of men, of regimenting mankind by a moral system struck the note that above all appealed to the Duke. Here was another opening for imposing order and perfection around him. Taking the chair at one of Owen's meetings, the Duke remarked, "It may be doubted whether the permanent safety of the British Empire does not depend upon the measures which may be speedily adopted to ameliorate the condition of the working classes." Certainly a different approach to the subject from Owen's, which was based on religious mysticism. "This essence," so he described the universal religion that he preached, "is the spirit of pure undefiled universal love and charity for man, applied to daily practice in voice, manner, and act; and love for that energy and power which composes, decomposes, and recomposes perpetually the elements of the universe, and which is called God. . . ." But again the Duke's firm tones come tramping, "The public must therefore feel that Mr. Owen has employed his talents in a useful direction, with what success will afterwards appear."

The Duke of Sussex was Grand Master of the Freemasons of England, and, bemused with his own jumble of religion, skepticism, and erudition, conceived the idea that Owen ought to become a member. But the astute Kent saw the indiscretion of such a step. "No," he exclaimed, "no, by all that is good, were he to witness our ceremonies he would make us all to appear fools. His objects are of a character too serious and extended for him to be occupied with our trifling amusements."

Owen was convinced that the Duke of Kent, his eyes opened by his teaching, intended in future to curb his extravagance. Needless to say, the Duke had no such intention, but all the time he was at pains to impress his socialist friend with the fact of his own "limited means," and there now arose the most curious feature in their relationship. The Duke is seen extracting loan after loan from Owen; not, be it noted, for himself, but for the self-named Princess Olive of Cumberland. On one occasion the Duke asked him "to advance on his account" to this lady three hundred pounds; on another five hundred, at other dates a hundred, and further unspecified sums. Owen accepted this boisterous princess with the gentle benevolence with which he accepted any member of mankind, and did not even intend to ask for the return of these loans unless, so he wrote, "I should myself feel the want of it." To Kent's credit it must be recorded that a month or two before his death he "even pressed me," wrote Owen, "to receive his note of hand for six months, when he proposed to pay me." However, Owen "resolutely declined doing so, having the fullest confidence in his word."

Only the death of the Duke, a few months after his offer, put an end to this incongruous friendship, and left these debts, like his others, unpaid.

7

In the autumn of 1817 the Duke and Madame de St Laurent were living in Brussels, ostensibly to economize. But, needless to say, ostensibly only; the Duke having established himself and his mistress in "a superb mansion in the *Place Royale*." "The Duke's taste for architecture," writes Lockhart Gordon in his memoirs, "embellishing, and adorning, was well known, and no one was surprised when a host of carpenters was put into requisition; and in a few months the house was so altered and ornamented (and of course improved), that the young count (Count de Maldegham), when invited to see what the Royal Duke had done, could hardly recognize his late abode. The extensive gardens next attracted his royal highness's attention, and were new-modeled and replanted with the choicest flowers and rarest shrubs which the Kingdom could produce. The stables and *remises* were furnished with stalls and mangers, and pavements and ventilators, according to the most approved plans in England; and his royal highness's stud became the admiration of the public.... His large establishment of servants and his stable were his chief expenses."

All this did not deter the Duke from writing to Mrs. Fitzherbert that he was living "in the full spirit of my plan of economy and retrenchment."

On a Sunday morning early in the November of this year Creevey and his friend Lockhart Gordon were strolling along together under the autumn leaves in the park when they received from some passer-by the astounding information that at eleven o'clock that morning a courier had arrived in Brussels with the news of the death of Princess Charlotte. Filled with surmises, Creevey and his companion at once set off for the Duke's house. Here the news was confirmed, and accordingly Creevey "wrote his name in the book," and the two friends then continued their stroll. But they had not gone far before a messenger came scurrying up to Creevey saying that his Royal Highness requested his "immediate presence." The delighted Creevey, called thus to the fountainhead of information, hurried back. An hour had not passed before Lockhart Gordon, still idling along the paths in the park, found Creevey again at his side, and in a most exalted condition. "I have," he exclaimed, "had a most curious conversation with the Duke, and so interesting, that I shall go home immediately and put it in writing while it is fresh in my memory, and if you will call on me in a couple of hours I will show you my minute."

When the time came, Lockhart Gordon appeared at Creevey's house. "He had," writes Gordon, "just finished this document ... and he read it to me." But before he started he imparted to his friend the agitation the Duke had shown when he saw Creevey entering his room. And he may well have been agitated; for in that meticulously arranged study, immersed in the Sunday quiet of the autumn morning, expectancy was on tiptoe. Whatever carefully molded phrases of sympathy would shortly come from the Duke's pen, whatever heavy-footed expressions of grief, there was no grief in his heart. Here at last, after all these years of delay, was the prophecy of his boyhood come startlingly near, taking on an actual flavor of probability. Before his excited mind a door swung wide. Princess Charlotte had been King George III's only legitimate grandchild. Now she had gone, another English heir must be provided.

Of Kent's elder brothers, apart from the Regent, the Duke of York, though married, was childless; the Duke of Clarence had a large but illegitimate family by the actress Mrs. Jordan. Of his younger brothers, the Duke of Cumberland had had one child which had died at birth. The Duke of Sussex had two children by Lady Augusta Murray, to whom he was married, but this marriage, as it violated the Royal Marriage Act, had been declared void, and the offspring barred from succession. King George's daughters were either unmarried, or had no children.

At the time of Charlotte's death, as matters then stood, after the deaths of her uncles, aunts, and two middle-aged cousins, the Duke of Brunswick, then a boy of thirteen, would have succeeded to the English throne. He was nephew to the Regent's hated wife, Caroline, and a first cousin once removed of the Regent himself. His father had been that Duke of Brunswick who "Rushed into the field and foremost fighting fell." This boy and his younger brother spent some years in London, the Regent acting as their guardian. In response they adopted the Regency dandyism both in their dress and their habits, the elder showing a reckless wildness that almost amounted to insanity. At the beginning of our own century there would still have been people living who, if they had happened to be in the Paris Opera House during Queen Victoria's reign, might have seen seated in one of the boxes a man "with a brilliantly-painted face, a black wig, and a shirt-front and fingers blazing with diamonds." Charles, Duke of Brunswick,* whom Providence saved the English from having to accept as their king.

As Creevey sat down for a talk with the Duke, his host's mind was already bristling with plans of action. It is usual for historians of the period to quote extracts only of all that he now confided to Creevey, but considering what an incomparable dish of unction, humbug, calculation, acumen, and mock-modesty is set before us, it seems a pity to withhold any of it.

When Creevey made his bow on entering the study, the Duke was talking to one of his secretaries, but he instantly left the room, and the Duke, writes Creevey, "began, to my great surprise, a conversation upon the death of the Princess Charlotte, and upon an observation from me upon the derangement of the succession to the throne by this event, and of the necessity of the unmarried Princes becoming married, if the crown was to be kept in their family; and having in addition asked him, I believe, what he thought the Regent would do on the subject of a divorce, and whether he thought the Duke of Clarence would marry, the Duke of Kent... I would almost say word for word, spoke to me as follows.†

" 'My opinion is the Regent will not attempt a divorce: I know persons in the Cabinet who will never consent to such a measure. Then, was he to attempt it, his conduct would be exposed to such recriminations as to make him unpopular, beyond all measure, throughout the country. No: he will never attempt it. Besides, the crime of adultery on her part must be proved in an English court of justice, and if found guilty she must be executed for high treason.

* He was deposed from Brunswick in 1831, and succeeded by his brother William, who lived till 1884. Charles died in 1873.

† It is evident that when Creevey wrote down what the Duke of Kent said to him he had had two conversations with the Duke, which he then combined in one narrative.

No: the Regent will never try for a divorce. As for the Duke of York, at his time of life and that of the Duchess, all issue, of course, is out of the question. The Duke of Clarence, I have no doubt, will marry if he can; but the terms he asks from the Ministers are such as they can never comply with. Besides a settlement such as is proper for a Prince who marries expressly for a succession to the throne, the Duke of Clarence demands the payment of all his debts, which are very great, and a handsome provision for each of his ten children. These are terms that no Ministers can accede to. Should the Duke of Clarence not marry, the next prince in succession is myself; and altho' I trust I shall be at all times ready to obey any call my country may make upon me, God only knows the sacrifice it will be to make, whenever I shall think it my duty to become a married man. It is now seven-and-twenty years that Madame de St Laurent and I have lived together: we are of the same age, and have been in all climates, and in all difficulties together; and you may well imagine, Mr. Creevey, the pang it will occasion me to part with her. I put it to your own feeling in the event of any separation between you and Mrs. Creevey.... As for Madame de St Laurent herself, I protest I don't know what is to become of her if a marriage is to be forced upon me; her feelings are already so agitated upon the subject. You saw, no doubt, that unfortunate paragraph in the *Morning Chronicle*, which appeared within a day or two after the Princess Charlotte's death; and in which my marry-ing was alluded to. Upon receiving the paper containing that article at the same time as my private letters, I did as is my constant prac-tice, I threw the newspaper across the table to Madame de St Laurent, and began to open and read my letters. I had not done so but a very short time, when my attention was called to an extra-ordinary noise and a strong convulsive movement in Madame de St Laurent's throat. For a short time I entertained serious appre-hensions for her safety; and when, upon her recovery, I enquired into the occasion of this attack, she pointed to the article in the *Morning Chronicle* relating to my marriage.

" 'From that day to this I am compelled to be in the practice of daily dissimulation with Madame de St Laurent, to keep this sub-ject from her thoughts. I am fortunately acquainted with the gentlemen in Bruxelles who conduct the Liberal and Oracle newspapers; they have promised me to keep all articles upon the subject of my marriage out of their papers, and I hope my friends in England will be equally prudent. My brother the Duke of Clarence is the elder brother, and has certainly the right to marry if he chooses, and I would not interfere with him on any account. If he wishes to be King—to be married and have children, poor man— God help him! Let him do so. For myself—I am a man of no ambition, and wish only to remain as I am. . . . Easter, you know, falls very early this year, the 22nd of March. If the Duke of Clarence does not take any step before that time I must find some pretext to reconcile Madame de St Laurent to my going to England for a short time. St. George's day is the day now fixed for keeping the birthday, and my paying my respects to the Regent on that day will be a sufficient excuse for my appearing in England. When once there, it will be easy for me to consult with my friends as to the proper steps to be taken. Should the Duke of Clarence do nothing before that time as to marrying, it will become my duty, no doubt, to take some measures upon the subject myself.

" 'You have heard the names of the Princess of Baden and the Princess of Saxe-Coburg sister to [Prince Leopold] mentioned. The latter connection would perhaps be the better of the two, from the circumstance of Prince Leopold being so popular with the nation; but before anything is proceeded with in this matter, I shall hope and expect to see justice done by the Nation and the Ministers to Madame de St Laurent. She is of very good family, and has never been an actress, and I am the first and only person who ever lived with her. Her disinterestedness, too, has been equal to her fidelity. When she first came to me it was upon £100 a year. That sum was afterwards raised to £400, and finally to £1000; but when my debts made it necessary for me to sacrifice a great part of my income, Madame de St Laurent insisted upon again returning to her income of £400 a year. If Madame de St Laurent is to return to live amongst her friends, it must be in such a state of independence as to command their respect. I shall not require very much, but a certain number of servants and a carriage are essentials.' "

He went prating on a little longer, but suddenly, writes Creevey, "a clock striking in the room where we were seemed to remind the

QUEEN VICTORIA AND PRINCE ALBERT

EDWARD AUGUSTUS
DUKE OF KENT
From the painting by Dawe

" Picture Post " Library

THE DUCHESS OF KENT
From the painting by
R. Rothwell

Duke he was exceeding his time, and he came to a conclusion almost instantly, and I retired."

The Duke was hoodwinking Creevey when he said, "God only knows the sacrifice it will be to make, whenever I shall think it my duty to become a married man," for we know from a letter written by Prince Leopold of Saxe-Coburg to his sister, Countess Mensdorff-Pouilly, which has lately been published, that in 1817, while Princess Charlotte was still alive, the Duke of Kent and another of Prince Leopold's sisters, the young widow Victoire, Princess of Leninen, had already, so it appears, decided on marriage.

"I am very pleased with her [Victoire]," runs Leopold's letter; "everything she says to me in her last letter was most reasonable. I fear, however, that no marriage will take place this year ... but in an affair of this sort a move at the wrong time would ruin everything. Poor Vicky is very afraid that she will be somewhat ridiculed over here [in England], but the poor little thing will have some difficulty in avoiding this sort of annoyance, for here everyone is caricatured and even the most popular figures are forced to submit."

8

The vivacious Victoire, who was to take the place, legitimately, that for twenty-seven years Julie de St Laurent had filled illegitimately, was now about thirty. Charlotte, happily married to Leopold, had wished that her Uncle Kent should be equally happy married to Leopold's sister. This wish may have been prompted partly by gratitude, as at the time when her father would not hear of her marrying Leopold, and was practically holding her prisoner at Windsor, the Duke of Kent had kept the lovers in touch by employing one of his equerries to go to and fro between Windsor and the Continent with their letters. This time the Duke's behavior does most certainly seem to have arisen entirely from benevolence, and from sympathy with his bullied niece, for in helping on her marriage, and thus encouraging the continuance of another branch of the royal family, he was acting directly against his own interests.

This young widow who was to become Duchess of Kent had, many years before, when she was a girl of about sixteen, figured in a list of German princesses that one of Napoleon's agents had submitted to him as a possible wife to take the place of Joséphine, whom, even as early as this—in 1802—he had thoughts of repudiating. However, just about that time Victoire had married the sporting, hard-drinking, far from agreeable Prince of Leiningen-Dachsburg-Hadenburgh, a man nearly thirty years older than herself. His property on the left bank of the Rhine was taken by the French, but he was given compensatory lands in Lower Franconia. In 1814 the Prince died, and his widow of twenty-eight found herself left with two children, a boy and a girl. She was now Regent of the Principality. It was fortunate for Victoire that she was full of vitality and capability, for she had often already been faced with problems that might have proved overwhelming to a less resolute young woman. Even while her husband was alive, it was she who had had chiefly to deal with all the stray soldiers who, sick from typhus or wounds, would turn up anywhere, and who, living or dead, were equally a problem, for, even when they were dead, there were still their corpses to be buried. Fire destroyed some of the Leiningens' valuable pinewoods; army surgeons took their household linen; money difficulties faced the family on every side. But Victoire grappled with everything, and would startle her friends by "her accounts of how she managed officers sent to requisition"; an observation intended, apparently, only to imply her shrewdness. Naturally, this marriage of the Duke of Kent and Victoire meant the conclusive dismissal of Madame de St Laurent. Poor Julie's days of verbal gaiety, of Hurrah, Hurrah, were over. In the Duke's talk with Creevey we hear the echo of her one desolate cry as she received the impact of destiny, but after that there is no sound.

9

The Duke of Kent's newly acquired wife was now in that rich tract of life that lies between youth and maturity, when the sense of nascent power tingles through the mind and before disillusionment, grief, bewilderment, remorse have had much time to worm their way in. She was well trained to endure a boring husband: after the disagreeableness of the first, the heavy courtesy of the second appeared to her charming, and as the months went on, she was to become genuinely and deeply attached to him. She was a bright, very fashionably dressed, conventionally minded young woman; her successful accomplishment in the art of pleasing counterbalanced a solid sense of the importance of doing one's duty, and of seeing that others did theirs. At the bottom of what was on occasion a kind and sympathetic heart lay a good deal of hardness. She was eager for all the glamorous presents that life has to offer: in her case social position and Paris clothes making a special appeal. Rather tall, full-bodied, full-blooded, she made a rich feminine figure that filled the eye and the senses, her physical allurement heightened by her preference for bright silks that swept and rustled, and great hats crowded with ostrich plumes.

Her actual character is as bewildering to assess, as full of discrepancies, as the Duke's. As one gazes at her in her portrait by Rothwell of about this date, one receives an impression of young piquant contours, of dark-eyed glancings, of easily smiling lips—and whether a suspicion of cunning, of callousness, really lurks among those charming features, or whether one imagines them there because one is aware of her later developments, it is hard to say. Hidden within was something slightly, but undeniably, commonplace; at present scarcely noticeable, it was gradually to manifest itself both in her appearance and in her behavior. Barring this quality, she was a fit vis-à-vis for the emphatic character she was about to marry, and the Duke was fully satisfied. She, too, must have been well satisfied with the Duke, considering how much she was giving up in order to marry him: her Regency, her annuity that amounted to five thousand, and (taking into account the probability of her living in England) her home, her relations, her friends, her son. In fact her whole past was flung into the scales so as to obtain the extremely doubtful chance that she might one day be Queen of England; and to gain the lifelong companionship of another middle-aged man: the unpleasantness of the first replaced by the tedium of the second. But she was still of that age when only the delightful possibilities of a change of situation are foreseen, and not the inevitable undertow.

In May, 1818, Victoire and the Duke were married. That year two of the Duke's brothers also hurried into matrimony, as anxious as was Kent to father the future heir to the hrone. The Duke of Clarence was united to Princess Adelaide of Saxe-Meiningen, and the Duke of Cambridge to Princess Augusta of Hesse-Cassel.

In the summer of this year the Duke of Kent and his Duchess came over to England and were remarried at Kew; the Duke of Clarence and his bride being married there at the same time. This double wedding took place in the drawing room of what is now called Kew Palace. The lovely upstairs drawing room, with its theatrically pillared fireplace and recessed windows giving on to the trees in the gardens, had been turned that afternoon into the semblance of a chapel. Four crimson velvet cushions had been placed on the floor near the altar for the royal couples, and around these officiating clergy and relations were crowded. Considering the moderate size of the room, everyone must indeed have been closely wedged to his neighbor—the Duke of Sussex, velvet skullcap on head, of such height and width that he was like a man of another race, towering above everyone in the room as he does in all the contemporary paintings of royal ceremonies.

In the beginning of September the Kents boarded the yacht *Royal Sovereign,* to cross the Channel once more. It was hateful to the Regent to have to contemplate these three new potential fathers of England's future sovereign, and he asked at least that, to save his pride from injury, they should live out of England.

The Kents, returning to the Continent, found Creevey still prying about, passing on to the Duke of Wellington any absurdities he could discover regarding their fellow creatures; and Wellington, now in command of a joint army of occupation, found the monotony of military life a good deal brightened by the arrival of the Kents, such nourishment did they supply for his and Creevey's laughter. Wellington had a very different opinion of Kent from what that royal peer had of himself, and, discussing with Creevey the refusal of Parliament to augment the establishments of the three brothers, the Dukes of Clarence, Kent, and Cambridge, on their marriages, he exclaimed, "By God! there is a great deal to be said about that. They ... are the damnedest mill-stones about the necks of any Government that can be imagined. They have insulted—*personally* insulted—two-thirds of the gentlemen of England, and how can it be wondered at that they take their revenge upon them when they get them in the House of Commons? It is their only opportunity, and I think, by God! they are quite right to use it."

Creevey had passed on to Wellington the details of Kent's conversation with him at Brussels about his marrying to provide an heir, the result of which was, says Creevey, "The Duke of Wellington's constant joking with me about the Duke of Kent." When one evening they all found themselves, the Kents, Wellington, and Creevey, at a ball given by Count Woronzow, "The Duchess of Kent waltzed a little, and the Duke of Kent put his hand upon her cheek to feel if she was not too hot." Wellington, apparently as a comment on this bourgeois gesture, turned suddenly to Creevey and said, "Well, Creevey, what has passed between you and *the Corporal* since you have met this time?"

Creevey had his news ready, and recounted how, a few days before, when arriving late at a dinner party of sixty he had purposely obliterated himself in the background, but the Duke of Kent, who was one of the guests, saw him immediately and "forced his way through the crowded room" to reach him. "You may probably be surprised, Mr. Creevey," exclaimed the Duke, "at seeing me here considering the illness of my poor mother, but the Queen is a person of the greatest possible firmness of mind ... she would not listen to any offers of mine to remain with her, and indeed nothing but her pressing me to come abroad could have made me do so."

This confidence of Kent's ("not omitting, of course," titters Creevey, "the *pathetic* part about the Queen") he now passed on to Wellington, who "laid hold of my button and said, 'God damme! d'ye know what his sisters call him? By God! they call him Joseph Surface,' " and at this he gave such a shriek of laughter that "made everyone turn about to the right and left to see what was the matter."

The next morning the whole party were breakfasting at Count Woronzow's, but instead of letting them sit down to their breakfast, their host insisted on their first inspecting his military school where the men were taught to read and to write. Creevey, extremely hungry, began to get bored and peevish at the whole thing, and especially over the Duke of Kent, who was "to the last degree tiresome in examining all the details of this establishment, and asked questions without end." At last Creevey could contain his hunger and his impatience no longer and gave voice to his craving for some food. Wellington overheard him. "I recommend you," he said, much amused, "whenever you start with any of the royal family in a morning, and particularly with the Corporal, always to breakfast first."

Having on this occasion taken the precaution to do so himself, he now kept on pointing at Creevey, delightedly exclaiming, "*Voilà le monsieur qui n'a pas déjeuné!*"

10

Once settled with his wife at Amorbach the Duke of Kent inevitably turned to the castle's improvement, he having brought English artisans with him for the purpose. Urged on by the Duke, there "rose like magic," first, temporary stabling, and, finally, permanent, up-to-date stables and coach houses to accommodate his thirty-six horses and nearly twenty carriages. These activities cost him ten thousand pounds. Fortunately Amorbach was situated far from Robert Owen's eyes and ears.

Meanwhile Victoire was with child. Husband and wife had accomplished the object of their marriage, and shared ambitions and plans now bound them closely together. The Duke had a firm intention that his child should be born in England, and had written to the Regent saying that he wished to bring Victoire over for her accouchement. The Regent had written back saying that he saw no necessity for it. Actually, the Clarences were also expecting a baby, but, though they, like the Kents, would have preferred that their child should be born in England, they did not struggle against the Regent's foibles, and remained quietly in Hanover. Flouted by the Regent, the Duke of Kent applied to Prince Leopold—now living at Claremont—for the necessary funds for the journey he still had every intention of taking. But Leopold knew that the Regent wished Kent to remain in Germany, and no help was forthcoming from Claremont. In spite of the fact that on Kent's marriage an additional grant of six thousand a year had been added to his income, he was now reduced to his usual state of insolvency, which, considering those luxurious new stables at Amorbach, is quite understandable. But nothing ever deterred him from a course of action he had decided on, and now he was resolved to push himself, his wife, and his coming child into England. From the Duke of Devonshire, Lord Fitzwilliam, Robert Owen, Alderman Wood, and others he managed to extract money to pay his Brussels debts, and so make the journey feasible.* He then decided that his dignity required a Royal yacht to transport himself and Victoire across the Channel. There was little hope that if he applied direct to the Regent his brother would supply him with the means of coming to the country it was his one wish to keep him out of. The approach must be circuitous. Princess Mary therefore received a letter from her absent brother asking if she would do her best with the obstinate Regent . . . exert pressure . . . persuade. Victoire, so he pointed out, was now in her sixth month. The Duke threatened that if he was not lent the yacht he would transport his wife on the *Packet*, an extremely rough steam-and-rail cross-Channel ship. "I fear," wrote Princess Mary to the Regent apropos of this move, "I fear it is a *deep*—a *very* deep-layed plan"; while his eldest sister, Princess Augusta, exclaimed, "I am outrageous with Edward, for he is behaving like a fool and a madman." The Regent was exasperated. Why should Edward, younger than Clarence, make such a fuss and to-do about himself and his wife: push themselves forward in this undesirable manner? However, he did concede the yacht.

Once the Kents were on their way, some sort of preparation had to be made for their arrival, and the Regent bestirred himself on their behalf so far as to drive out to Kensington Palace and choose the rooms they were to have. He settled, possibly with sardonic intent—as Edward had upheld the cause of the Princess of Wales—on the rooms where she had groaned through many an endless day. Then the Regent climbed into his carriage, and returned to Carlton House.

Buckingham Palace
April 7th 1838
   * The Queen having been informed that the late Earl Fitzwilliam, about the year 1818, advanced the sum of Two Thousand Five Hundred Pounds to His late Royal Highness the Duke of Kent, which was never repaid to that Nobleman, Her Majesty avails herself of the earliest opportunity to return that sum to the present Earl, and at the same time the Queen begs to offer the accompanying waiter for His Lordship's acceptance as a token of Her Majesty's sense of the liberal manner in which the money was granted to Her late revered Father.   Victoria R.

I I

The Kents' great coach was brought across with them to Dover, and there the Duke again climbed on to the box seat, picked up the reins, and headed the horses for Kensington Palace. As he and his wife drove along the Kentish roads, where the light spring green of the hedgerows shone shrill against the tender sky, their aspirations glowed brightly. The only cause of uneasiness was the Duchess of Clarence, for, though a baby she had given birth to a month before had died, if she had had one baby she might have another, and any offspring of hers would take precedence of the Kents'. This very April, too, the Cambridges had had a child, a boy: also the Duchess of Cumberland was with child. The Kents, however, could view these Cumberland and Cambridge babies with equanimity. The danger point was any increase in the Clarence family. But if their hopes for the succession were radiant they were not so at all regarding their reception in England. They were well aware they were coming uninvited and unwanted, were forcing themselves on a host whose feelings for them were definitely hostile.

In the Regent's mind, resentment against Edward had been sizzling for years. One of the unforgivable counts he had against his brother dated from about fifteen years before, when the Princess of Wales had sent an obscene drawing to her hitherto friend, Sir John Douglas, depicting Sir John's wife in bed with another man. Douglas had consulted the Duke of Kent, who had advised him to ignore the incident. It was not till the following year that the matter reached the ears of the Regent, who became incensed at his brother having acted on his own initiative, and without saying a word to him on the subject. It was, the Regent considered, and rightly, both a slight to himself and a gesture of protection to Caroline. It was then that he began sneeringly to refer to his brother as Joseph Surface, and to regard him as a treacherous character. Again, several years later, there had been the military scandal connected with the Regent's favorite brother, the Duke of York, whose mistress, Mary Ann Clarke, wrote a book entitled *The Rival Princes*, in which she stated that Kent had promised her an annuity if she would bring such evidence of corruption on the Duke's part as would turn him out of his office of Commander in Chief, with a view to the Duke of Kent supplanting him. There is no conclusive evidence that Kent had made any such promise to his brother's mistress, and in both Houses he denied these allegations, asserting them to be "foul and unmerited aspersions."

What the Regent's own opinion of the business was, and what sediment the episode had left in his mind, is not known, any more than it is known whether Mrs. Clarke's allegations were true or false. But there is little doubt it had hardened the Regent's already prejudiced mind against Edward. In addition there had been his ceaseless extravagances and his equally ceaseless demands for financial relief. The Regent had quite enough to do grappling with the results of his own extravagance without being perpetually teased by Edward's. But it is doubtful whether all these causes of resentment put together equalled in force the personal one of the moment: the fact that this disliked brother, and not the Regent himself, was about to provide a possible heir to the throne. All these royal babies arriving with the spring crocuses were to him so many irritants. This appearance in England of Edward, thus stressing his own family's importance, emphasized to the Regent his own broken line of descent. It was intolerable to his vanity that the eyes of the country should be drawn from him to one of his brothers. Beneath his bright brown wig his thoughts moved about angrily. Very sore must he have felt when he realized that Edward, his wife, and household would by now have arrived at Dover and were actually on their way to Kensington Palace.

12

Kensington Palace,* that great red-brick, stone-mullioned house, with its row of classic vases on the Wren façade outlining themselves against the sky, was then a dreaming old place gently enbosomed in what was still the country. Beech and chestnut trees spread their branches over a far wilder parkland than now; nuthatches, and even the sensitive blue of the jay, were to be seen

* Originally known as Nottingham House. It had been bought from the Earl of Nottingham by William III for £18,000.

among the leaves; and in the dwindling light of evening rooks
made their dissolving spirals above the palace roof. At the foot of
the palace garden was the then quiet old High Street, in which the
little houses were not even high enough to overlook the palace
gardens. William III had had an affection for all garden conceits,
and the royal gardeners at the palace were kept busy in "the transforming of evergreens into the shapes of birds, beasts, and mon-
sters"; on every side, too, were to be seen "slopes, labyrinths; trees
trimmed with gigantic dumb-waiters; long alleys of alternate box
and apple-trees, with obelisks peeping between," while "the walks
became longer and straighter like canals." After William's death
Queen Anne, who, like him "in trim gardens took her pleasure,"
brought into submission still more of nature's untidiness, to the
exasperation of a contemporary writer who cried out that "The
measured walk, the quincunx, and the étoile imposed their unsatisfactory sameness." But so charmed was Queen Anne with the combined efforts of her brother-in-law and herself that on summer
evenings she would take her supper in the spacious and beautiful
Wren orangery that she had had built, and, seated there, would let
her gaze dwell on her surrounding world of leafy fantasy.

Within this palace that was to be the background to Queen Victoria's childhood are vast rooms and galleries: the galleries' immense length made bearable by the plenitude of light flooding in
through the serried rows of high windows that reach to the ceiling.
The effulgence from these windows had fallen on to the perukes
and brocaded shoulders, the panniered petticoats and stomachers
of the reigning sovereigns and their consorts from William and
Mary to George II. No house in England was fuller of memories
and legends, of notable or fantastic figures of the past, now living
only in the printed word, in tradition, or in painting. In one small
paneled room looking out on the park had taken place that final
lacerating parting between Queen Anne and the Duchess of Marlborough, when to the Duchess' pleadings for some explanation of
the Queen's hostility she only received the retort, and one that she
merited, "You desired no answer, and you shall have none." It was
in Kensington Palace that Queen Caroline, poking about one day
in a bureau, had come across between eighty and ninety of Holbein's

original drawings for portraits of Court notabilities in the reign of Henry VIII. Through these limitless rooms had constantly passed and repassed the figure of Lord Hervey bearing that countenance so ethereally whittled by sensibility . . . and, suddenly, in the quiet air we hear voices speaking. Soon we get their meaning. Queen Caroline, a lover of good pictures, has, in George II's absence, had some remarkably bad ones removed from "the great drawing-room," and replaced by others indubitably superior. The returned King, discovering what has been done in his absence, has ordered Hervey, as Vice-Chamberlain, "to have every new picture taken away and every old one replaced."

Lord Hervey, tender for the Queen's happiness, is asking "if his Majesty would not give leave for the two Vandykes, at least, on each side of the chimney to remain, instead of those two sign-posts, done by nobody knew who, that had been removed to make room for them."

"My Lord . . ." answers the King, "I suppose you assisted the Queen with your fine advice when she was pulling my house to pieces and spoiling all my furniture: thank God, at least she has left the walls standing! As for the Vandykes, I do not care whether they are changed or no; but for the picture with the dirty frame over the door, and the three nasty little children, I will have them taken away, and the old ones restored; I will have it done too to-morrow morning before I go to London, or else I know it will not be done at all."

"Would your Majesty . . . have the gigantic fat Venus restored too?"

"Yes, my Lord; I am not so nice as your Lordship. I like my fat Venus much better than anything you have given me instead of her."

Hervey carried this unwelcome news to the Queen next morning at breakfast. While they were discussing together, "the King came in, but, by good luck, said not one word of the pictures: his Majesty stayed about five minutes in the gallery, snubbed the Queen, who was drinking chocolate, for being always stuffing; the Princess Emily for not hearing him; the Princess Caroline for having grown fat, the Duke [of Cumberland] for standing awkwardly; Lord

Hervey for not knowing what relation the Prince of Sultzbach was to the Elector Palatine: and then carried the Queen to walk and be resnubbed in the garden."

One of the rooms looking eastward over the trees had often reverberated to the sounds issuing from "a wonderful and gigantic musical box" belonging to the early Georges: the great brass rollers studded with pins that fed its mechanism being housed in ornamental cabinets between the windows. Here, too, at the palace, in one of the smaller rooms, Frederick Prince of Wales would give his little intimate dinner and supper parties—possibly in the very room where now hangs a picture by Laroon depicting just such a party. There is, in fact, a strong supposition that the host in this intriguing conversation piece is the Prince himself. The youthful giver of the party is seated at the head of the table, the blue ribbon of the Garter aslant across his gala suit of white satin, fine lace falling back from beneath his cuff, as, from the decanter in his right hand, held high above his head, he pours an arching stream of wine into the glass extended in his left hand near the ground. In the exquisite performance of this feat, as of a god pouring forth a stream of lifeblood to enhance the vitality and joyfulness of his guests, there is about him a kind of royal grace mingled with the casual assurance of a professional cocktail shaker. At his side, holding a tray of glasses brimmed with the ruby wine that has already been so dramatically poured into them, stands a veritable little coxcomb of a boy page, he, too, tricked out in a satin coat, in color a dark raspberry, with knee breeches, waistcoat, and sash of gold brocade. His face, turned away from the guests, gazes out of the canvas at any chance spectator with an air of the most accomplished arrogance. A success child. Behind this satin and brocade little showpiece a small greyhound stands delicately upreared on its brittle legs to be fondled by one of the guests. There are, among these, more men than women, and a something too forthcoming about these ladies' faces, and the way one of the male guests is leering at the rounded cheek nearest him makes one suspicious as to what kind of ladies the host invited when he and his friends were out for a flaring evening. Among the standing figures behind the diners—attendants, servants, and others—is a cleric in cassock and cravat, his cherry cheeks positively about to burst with too good living and general hilarity. The whole canvas is instinct with shared, unashamed delight; filled with an almost childlike party excitement, that, even now, seems to exude a pagan warmth into the chill of that empty room.

Peering back into the tenebrous past, we discern, threading their way in and out of these great galleries of Kensington Palace, some most unexpected and improbable figures. Two Turks come stepping out of the shadows, who, with their twisted turbans and eastern dress of soft, colored silks, must have given the same bizarre touch to the scene around them as do the oriental figures in an occidental tapestry. These two Turks, named Mustapha and Mahomet, originally taken prisoner by the Imperialists in Hungary, were said to have saved George I's life in the siege of Vienna in 1685. Whether they had actually played such a spectacular part in the career of the then Electoral Prince of Hanover or not, he brought them to England with him in his suite, and at Kensington Palace, vaguely designated as pages of the backstairs, they gradually became persons of secret importance and influence, into whose hands it was believed that much money was covertly pushed by those anxious to obtain posts at Court. Mahomet finally stands out in a beneficent light, passing on his either well- or ill-gotten wealth in releasing debtors from prison. But a still stranger figure than the Turks was Peter the Wild Boy. This werewolf child, running on all fours, was discovered in 1725 in the woods near Hanover, then a boy, so it was guessed, of about thirteen. In his frenzied attempts to escape from his would-be captors he rushed up trees with the rapidity of a squirrel. However, they caught him, and while George I, then in Hanover, was at dinner, the terror-stricken creature was dragged in for his inspection. The King, acting as genial host, kept blandly offering him the various foods on the table, and gave orders he should be given whatever he liked best. But, actually, what he liked best was grass and moss; and, incidentally, his freedom. One day he managed to escape, and, a hurriedly galloping object on all fours, disappeared once more into the woods. He was caught again, and, this time, sent over to England "and once more was brought before his majesty and many of the nobility." Kensington Palace now became the bewildered boy's house of misery; for a misery of the most tormenting kind his life must have been, so determined were his captors to force him to become a civilized being, so piteous were his efforts to remain what he was. A bed was hateful to him, so were clothes, but he was compelled to submit to both, and was decked out in "gaudy habiliments." He was pulled up off the floor and taught that he must balance and walk on his legs alone. Subdued at last, he "often sat quietly for his picture"; an action, or rather a lack of it, that appears for some reason to have been considered by his instructors as a great moral victory. It was thought that "the philosophical Dr. Arbuthnot" might induce him to speak, and he was placed in the doctor's charge. But in this, the final assault of civilization, the Wild Boy came off victorious. The compliment of Swift writing a satire on his person; his becoming a subject for the pen of Lord Monboddo; and the Bishop of St. David's unbending so far as to describe him in one of his letters, never so much as reached the locked mind of the Wild Boy. To the last he "resisted all instructions," lived on pensions granted him by George I, George II, and George III, and was finally given into the care of a farmer at Berkhampstead. He lived on and on, and died at about seventy.

In one part of the palace, placed between two windows, gleams the bust of a Negro in various colored marbles: an object of aesthetic beauty. The black face, full of awareness, is raised alertly, as if perpetually listening for some summons: an impression intensified when one learns that he was an old servant of the royal family. Except for this one fact nothing appears to be known about him. But that he was slave as well as servant is only too evident from the heavily padlocked collar around his neck: insignia of what unguessed humiliation, nostalgia, despair; an arresting face forever gazing into the shadows of the old place: mute, but yet speaking with the overwhelming power of silence.

The wall at the side of the chief staircase is frescoed by William Kent with life-sized figures all crowded together behind a painted balcony. This medley of persons were all well-known figures in the reign of George II, habitués of the palace, and, represented in this way on the staircase, are "supposed to be spectators of the company on court days." Mustapha and Mahomet are among them, so is the

Wild Boy; also a young man in Polish dress, "Mr. Ulric," a royal page "admired by the court for the elegance and beauty of his person." Another page is there too, a young man who was in attendance on Lady Suffolk. Though all the other figures are depicted behind the balcony, this svelte boy stands outside, as if he had leaped over the balustrade in his eagerness to quit the company of the dead and to return to the humming life of the palace as he had known it.

But as the Kent family drew near their future home it was not only forms half-lost in the recesses of the past that awaited them. The living were there too. Certainly most of the figures moving about those trancelike rooms were old themselves: "fogey officers" filling various posts, ancient servants who tottered about pushing at the heavy paneled shutters, drawing up or pulling down the blinds, dusting the tiers of pictures or, doubtless, to be seen on warm days sunning themselves like pigeons on enclosed grassplot or courtyard.

In a suite of rooms on the ground floor lived the youngest but one of the sons of George III, Augustus, Duke of Sussex. He, too, was no longer young. He was nearing fifty, and from adolescence had been a victim to asthma. He was a solidly built giant of six foot three inches. At twenty, while in Rome, he fell in love with all the frenzy of emotion usual with the sons of George III. For the time being he lived only for Lady Augusta Murray—daughter of Lord Dunmore—and persuaded her to agree to a private marriage in Rome. Later, when they came to England, they were remarried at St. George's, Hanover Square. They had two children, whom they named Augustus Frederick and Augusta Emma. However, King George's consent to his son's marriage—which consent, under the Royal Marriage Act, was obligatory—had not been asked, and in 1794 the King had the marriage annulled by the Dean of Arches. The Prince, notwithstanding, remained faithful to his Augusta; faithful, that is to say, till 1801, when he was created Duke of Sussex and given a Parliamentary grant of twelve thousand pounds. For reasons known only to himself, he immediately deserted her, but gave her a yearly allowance amounting to four thousand. A year or two later Lord Dunmore, incensed at various financial misbehaviors on the part of his son-in-law (such as leaving the deserted Augusta to settle with his creditors for furniture bought by him when they were living together), demanded an audience of the

King. Lord Dunmore complained to him bitterly of the circumstances in which the Duke had left his wife, and of "his unfeeling conduct to his children in leaving them in such a state of destitution."

At this the King lost his temper. "Bastards! Bastards!" he cried out "in a rage."

"Yes, Sire, just such bastards as yours are!" retorted Lord Dunmore.

The King "became as red as a Turkey-cock, and going up to him repeated, 'What, what, what's that you say, my Lord?'"

"I say, Sire, that my daughter was legally married to your son, and that her children are just such bastards as your Majesty's are."

At that "the King stared at him—as if in a violent passion, and then without a word retired into another room."

The Duke of Sussex was a scholar and a Whig, and lived snugly enough in his pleasant, ground-floor, low-ceilinged rooms that looked on to what was left of the Dutch garden of William III and Queen Anne. Around him was the library he had collected of fifty thousand books: Hebrew, Latin, and Greek MSS; a unique collection of the manuscripts of Italian operas; and a thousand Bibles. In a glass case lay eighteen watches. One had, on its back, according to the unpleasing custom of the day, the painting of a single eye: the eye in this case being that of his dead niece, Princess Charlotte. Numbers of birds hopped and twittered in their cages. Like his brother Edward, the Duke was much occupied with the passage of time, and, whether to salute this passage, or in an endeavor to dominate and regiment it, he, too, lived surrounded with clocks. The striking of every hour would be greeted with an accompanying outburst of the national anthem and martial tunes. Following a fashion not then altogether departed, the Duke owned a small Negro page, a living *objet d'art* among all his static possessions, who, a little figure of exquisite aesthetic value, would be seen threading his way through the rooms. He was always referred to by his master as Mr. Blackman.

The Duke, dressed in a violet satin dressing gown, embroidered waistcoat, and black velvet skullcap, would sit absorbed in his books; at times with immense care, drawing a hand in the margin that pointed to some particular passage: in approval, or derision? Or, heaving his massive person from his chair, we see him in our imagination strolling out to gaze at the garden that was another of his treasures, and where flower or shrub, each displaying its own meticulous perfection, was in no need of a critically pointing finger.

CHAPTER III
ALEXANDRINA VICTORIA ARRIVES
IN THE WORLD

Soon after four o'clock on the morning of the twenty-fourth of May, 1819, in a large bedroom at Kensington Palace, through the windows of which could be seen the Round Pond lying like a great mirror of light, the Duchess of Kent gave birth to her baby: a girl. The Duke, forestalling every contingency, taking no risks, had seen to it that the Duke of Wellington, the Archbishop of Canterbury, the Bishop of London, the Chancellor of the Exchequer, Lord Lansdowne, Lord Bathurst, and Mr. Canning were all safely closeted within the walls of the palace for the birth. The Duke of Sussex, too, had come walking through his rooms for the event.

When the Regent heard of this carefully prearranged pomp and circumstance for the arrival of Edward's baby as if it were the unquestioned heir to the throne, his exasperation with the Kents intensified. He did, however, a month later, consent to be one of the infant's godparents. The others were the Emperor Alexander (represented by the Duke of York), the Queen Dowager of Württemberg (represented by Princess Augusta), and the Duchess of Kent's mother, the Dowager Duchess of Coburg (represented by the Duchess of Gloucester).

Again, for the christening, the Duke exerted himself to make the occasion as spectacular as possible, and succeeded in acquiring a gold font from the Tower of London, which was brought over to the palace in a cart, and in borrowing some crimson draperies from the Chapel Royal at St. James'.

On June 24 the christening party, collected in the Cupola Room at the palace, awaited the arrival of the Regent. This room with its marble-pillared doorways, its painted and gilded walls, and domed ceiling of blue and gold is a tour de force of William Kent. In their high-up niches on the walls, life-size gilt figures of Ceres, Mercury, Venus, Minerva, Bacchus, and Apollo mutely surveyed the crowd of uniformed men and gaily dressed women who were collected around the royal baby. Among them was the saddened figure of Prince Leopold. "A painful task" it was, so he said, to attend the christening of this baby who had been called into existence to replace his own stillborn child, but all the same, he "thought it right to come." Little did he think as he glanced at the tiny flushed lump displayed in all its baptismal froufrou what a vital part it was going to play in his life.

The appearance of the women at this christening party, in their newest dresses, as they moved about the great room talking to each other, is clearly seen by us through Ackermann's colored fashion plates. The exquisite restraint of the Empire style of dress has suffered a decline: those long white muslins, clinging so seductively, and given character by bright-hued picturesque wrap jackets often edged with fur that would have about them now a Cossack, now an oriental touch—all this is rapidly disintegrating into an anarchy of tasteless and pointless dressmaker ornamentation. Though the guests still have their waists under their armpits, their muslins are made, not to cling, but to stick out stiffly at the foot by means of complicated trimmings: ribbons, ruchings, trellisings, writhe over them everywhere. Poke bonnets, often with an indoor lace cap peeping from beneath, are heavily massed with ostrich plumes or flowers.*

The Duke of Sussex did not form one of the christening party: he was in hiding in his rooms till his eldest brother should have come and gone, for he and the Regent were immersed in one of the usual family disputes, and at the moment would not speak to each other. However, as soon as the Regent should have driven

* It is noticeable that at this time, after the Napoleonic wars, women's hats had taken on a remarkably truculent air. So in the same way, toward the end of the 1939-45 war, feminine millinery shot up into monstrous, almost diabolical edifices. These distortions first appeared on the heads of the *midinettes* in Paris during the German occupation, and were recognized as being purposely worn as a symbol of defiance and contempt. As the war drew to a close this astounding fashion crossed the Channel, and appeared for a time on the heads of the more sartorially adventurous Englishwomen.

away it had been arranged that Sussex should quietly emerge and join the Kents for their dinner party at four o'clock.

The question in the minds of all the guests was whether now, at the crucial moment, the Regent would actually appear, for already there had been unpleasantness over the name to be given to the baby. The Duke of Kent, past prophecies glistening ever more brightly in his mind, had aspired to Elizabeth, but his brother, detecting the inference, would not hear of it. The final list submitted to him by the Kents had been Alexandrina Georgiana Augusta Victoria. Even over the name Alexandrina there had been a commotion, the Regent becoming restive at this gesture toward the Russian Emperor whose personality had unfortunately quite eclipsed his own in the London peace celebrations of 1814. The Duke of York had shrewdly advised Kent to leave the question of this particular name unsettled, and then that he should "suddenly bring it out at the christening." Another scheme was to include it in a list of names only to be whisked out and given at the final moment to the officiating Archbishop of Canterbury. Even when the actual christening day had arrived this question of names was still in confusion.

At last the sounds of the arrival of the most important of the carriages were heard in the courtyard, and within a few moments the ponderous figure of the Regent within the doorway dominated the room. His puffed, florid face was redder than usual, and his expression, as everyone noticed, was far from agreeable. The greetings over, the Regent turned to the officiating clergy. "My Lords," he said, "I suppose the ceremony may now begin?"

There arrived the moment for naming the baby. The Archbishop, the foamy bundle lying in his arms, asked, "By what name does it please your Royal Highness to call this child?"

No answer. There came a long pause.

But something had to be done. Gazing at the Royal godfather, the Archbishop gave voice to "Georgiana?"

Still silence.

"Shall she be called Georgiana?" repeated the Archbishop.

"On no account," rapped out the Regent.

"Charlotte, after your Royal Mother, and the child's Royal Aunt?"

"Certainly not."

But the Duchess, still weak from her lying-in, could bear the strain no longer: all her husband's careful preparations, the golden font, the crimson drapings, the crowding guests—all was being brought to nothing by this muddled indecision over the names: she could endure no more, and suddenly the taut atmosphere was broken by the sound of sobs.

The Archbishop became more definite. "What name is it your Royal Highness's pleasure to command?"

"What is her mother's name?"

"Victoria," answered the Duke of Kent.

The Duke of York now pushed forward a suggestion—"Alexandrina Victoria." This was accepted, and the christening continued its course.

The baby once christened, the Regent's idea was that its parents should take it to Amorbach as rapidly as possible: but the Duke of Kent thought otherwise. Ever since he had known Victoire was going to have a baby, excitement had been growing within his massive frame. How miraculously both the prophecy of his boyhood and the prediction of that gypsy at Gibraltar seemed to be fulfilling themselves . . . this child once arrived, what before had glimmered in his mind as a hope now shone almost as a certainty. He was so filled with the sense of security that he could not keep his satisfaction to himself. "My brothers," he would constantly remark, "are not as strong as I am. I have lived a regular life. I shall outlive them all. The crown will come to me and my children." The Regent might give up his hopes as to his brother Edward returning to Germany. It was only with the greatest difficulty that the Duke had transplanted himself and his family to England, and he had not the slightest intention now of being removed. Another, if minor, satisfaction to him was that the Duchess was herself nursing the baby. "I shall only observe," he wrote to a friend, "I shall only observe that parental feeling and a just sense of duty were the motives that actuated her in the line she has taken."

He and the Duchess—carrying out when possible his policy of striking a democratic note—would go driving about Hyde Park in an open carriage with their little Drina so as to display her, or would hold her up at the windows of the palace to please inquisitive passers-by who were now always peering at their apartments to spy what they could. Even at a review at Hounslow Heath the Duke and Duchess and the inevitable baby—now getting on for four months old—were to be seen. The Regent's roving eye caught sight of it.

"What business has that infant there?" he snapped.

It was at Hounslow Heath that yet another fortuneteller made the Duke a further prediction, telling him that the next year, in 1820, there would be two deaths in the royal family. A wise woman, she then came to a stop, and mentioned no names.

The Kent ménage was now progressing as satisfactorily as possible. The corn-haired, blooming-faced baby was the most thriving, energetic little creature imaginable. As for the parents, their natures dovetailed perfectly: neither of them an entirely sincere character, their mutual insincerities the more easily accommodated themselves to each other. The Duke had in his Duchess an agreeable woman and an effective showpiece. She, at his side, was enveloped with social prestige, and his kindness and carefully polite manner had awakened in her a real warmth of affection. She had none of the perspicacity of a Wellington or a Creevey to pierce through her husband's grandiose edifice and discover the vacuum within. Nor would she have been disturbed if she had. He gave her all she required. Her concern was for the surfaces of life only. Also, to her, ignorant of her husband's language, his pompous phrases doubtless seemed merely the natural idiom in which an Englishman expressed himself. So, too, his eagerness to attend funerals, and his deathday book which matched his birthday book, would not have struck her as peculiar. And it was not only Victoire who responded so contentedly to the Duke. Her little Feodore appears to have loved her towering, benevolent stepfather. He was included in a serenade the pretty creature gave for her mother's birthday this August. Early that morning, as the Kents still lay in bed, "God Save the King" suddenly burst from the room next door—Feodore, her music master, and all the servants being the warblers. The Kents would not have been surprised, for at this date parents were accustomed to being serenaded on special occasions by their children; these often falling on their knees as they piped out their salutations.

One consideration alone fretted the peace of the Kent household:

the usual one of the Duke's debts, of the unaccommodating nature of his creditors. It is probable that it was these awkward debts more than, as the Duke gave out, that his wife needed a change of air, that decided him to leave Kensington Palace for a time, and settle at the seaside. This view is strengthened by the fact that about now he used to give The Palace, Salisbury, as his address, it being that of his old tutor, Bishop Fisher, who acted thus as a slight screen to protect his former pupil from too frontal attacks.

The Regent was fussed at the idea that this exasperating Kent trio might invade his own specially adopted Brighton, but the Duke took a small house, Woolbrook Cottage, outside Sidmouth, a snug, much-verandaed, and creeper-hung little place. For funds for the journey he had this time to fall back on his equerry, Captain Conroy, the young Irishman who has been, but, it seems, wrongly, credited with having formerly gone to and fro between England and the Continent bearing letters from Princess Charlotte and Prince Leopold.

Owing to various arrangements the Kents did not arrive in Devonshire till the Christmas Eve of 1819. After the spaciousness of Kensington Palace they must have felt excessively cramped in this cottage, also they discovered that a musty smell hung about the small rooms. The Duke must indeed have been incommoded by his debts to suffer such a contraction in his surroundings. Then, to add to petty annoyances, they had not been there a week or two before the baby was all but killed by a boy, carelessly shooting at birds outside the cottage, who inadvertently sent a bullet into the nursery, which so nearly struck the infant that its sleeve was torn. The Duke had heard the shot; and on the instant, his mind still busy with the prediction regarding the death of two members of the family, he believed his child to have been killed. Even when reassured, the shock—so Princess Feodore maintained in after years—had been so great that it affected even his magnificent health. Actually, regarding the succession to the throne, the horizon of the Kents' ambitions was at present most satisfactorily clear. Clearer, indeed, than it had been for some time. For though, several months back, the Duchess of Clarence, that dangerous woman, had been again with child, she had had a miscarriage in September. All, from the Kents' point of view, was again serene. So confident, in such a state of exaltation did the Duke now feel over the situation, that when visitors came to Woolbrook Cottage he would show them the baby, exclaiming, "Look well at her for she is to be your Queen." Or at other times he might be seen walking about Sidmouth beach, himself holding the precious bundle in his arms.

In between writing letters to his creditors, it must have been interesting for him and Victoire to speculate as to which two of his relations, among such an abundant family, would, according to the Hounslow gypsy's prediction, die during this newly arrived year, 1820. George III, the Regent, and the Duchess of York, for instance, were all in a bad state of health. Nor were several other members of the Royal Family in particularly good condition. And always for the Duke there was that satisfying reflection; "My brothers are not as strong as I am. . . ."

And then the most unforeseen, the most undreamed-of disaster occurred in the Sidmouth cottage. It was a bitter, hostile winter. One afternoon, only a few weeks after they had arrived, the Duke and Captain Conroy went for a long walk, and came home with their feet wet and frozen from the slush they had been tramping through. Before going to his room to change, the Duke dawdled about in his wet socks and caught a chill. Pleurisy set in, and by the end of January he was dead.

That that powerful presence, that incessant busybody, only such a short time ago so loquacious, so pervasive, should now be lying there extinct and silent, not functioning in the slightest particular. Even to read of such abrupt cessation of such amplitude seems incredible. And yet, against Victoire's exhausted and grief-torn mind there pressed the stark, undeniable fact. Hourly now she had to accustom herself to the realization that the man for whom she had cut herself off so completely from her past had left her forever. Fortunately for her, still comparatively a stranger to England, she had at her side, not only her husband's equerries, but her brother Prince Leopold.

He was at Lord Craven's, in Berkshire, when the news came to him of the dangerous condition the Duke was in, and he had at once come posting across England, through such torturing cold that he could never even speak of the journey afterward without a shudder. Behind the fine-cut face, a face possessing that rarity, significance and beauty combined, there functioned one of the astutest minds of any young man in Europe. Calculating every step with the shrewdest precision, he had raised himself from the position of penniless German prince to that of husband to the Regent's daughter, Princess Charlotte. His nature was one difficult to define. With his remarkable capacity for responding brilliantly to all the contacts of life, he was yet weighed down by some leaden quality: his inclinations dulled by a pervasive melancholy. Though possessing a sly, cutting wit, and a certain charming whimsicality fashionable among the cultured society men of the day, he could at times be coldly, inhumanly prim. Charlotte, with that slight hesitation in her voice which was so attractive, with her exuberance, her luxuriously developed young body, and the gift of high position she had bestowed on him by marriage, had raised him to an exhilaration of mind, an apotheosis of being that before, in the strain of his early career-making days, he had never known, and, after her death, was never to recapture. She had, too, assured him that, when she succeeded to the throne, she would have him made king. With the loss of her, a blight fell on him. A latent stiffness of mind, that her bursting gaiety had dispersed, returned, gradually corroding his nature, and intensifying his egoism.

Now, while he sat back hour after hour muffled up in the corner of his chaise as it went racketing along, many memories, many threads of thought, many subtle calculations must indubitably have been interweaving within his brooding mind. It was evident that his brother-in-law was on the point of death. Given this certainty, a most unforeseen situation, what might almost be called a replica of the past, hung before Leopold's eyes. Here, most peculiarly, were nearly the same elements, the same constituents as had formerly been combined. The same, and yet, not the same. Before, he had been husband to the heir presumptive of the English throne, and father to her coming child: that child which had been born dead. Here, as then, were a mother and—this time a living—baby, close to the throne, to whom he was nearly, though differently, related. As in the past he had been upraised by his marriage to Charlotte, so now the more nearly he associated himself with Victoire and her baby, so much the more would he be lit with their prestige, so much the stronger would be his own position. To his scrutinizing, circumspect mind it was impossible but that these considerations must have been clearly apparent. But if the implications of this shifting of the royal scene were inevitably present to his mind, his later behavior shows that within him at this moment were also emotions of a more gentle and more tender nature. He was an affectionate brother, and no one was more aware than he of the difficulties his widowed sister would now have to face, left alone in the very center of the miserable confusions caused by the royal squabbles, all of these carried on in a language with which she was not yet familiar. She would need his support. Moreover, foreseeing the little Kent creature left fatherless, a quasi-parental emotion crept into his heart. His sister's buxom infant was gradually to turn for him from a reminder of what he had lost, into a substitute.

The Duke once dead, Leopold applied himself to his sister's affairs. And they indeed required the attention of an energetic mind. A widow in a foreign country with a young baby, and now bearing the burden of her husband's unpaid debts. Even without these debts, the six thousand pounds a year allowed her by the English Government would not be sufficient to support her position as the widow of a Royal Duke. Her wish was to escape from it all back in her familiar Amorbach. But Leopold envisaged the situation otherwise. With his usual acumen he foresaw the advisability of her remaining in England, and finally persuaded her to stay, himself giving her three thousand pounds a year to make this feasible. This was generous; but the English Government had been generous to him, as he was still drawing fifty thousand a year, besides the pay of a field marshal.

At the moment, as was usual with the Kent household, there was a lack of ready money. Victoire had not even the wherewithal for the journey back to London. From some source or other twelve thousand pounds were now hurriedly borrowed to cover mourning and other necessaries. The fact that Leopold had urged his sister to stay on in England proves that he must have considered—in spite of the possibility of the Clarences providing an heir to the throne— that the advantages for her of remaining in the country were overwhelming, for he was well aware of the disadvantages. He knew from personal experience the circumspection required by any foreigner who married into the royal family and wished to remain on good terms with all its members, while being at the same time conscious that the country in general was scrutinizing the newcomer's every action. All this gave the new arrival the sensation of being balanced on a tightrope.

My position politically is endlessly difficult [Leopold had written to Countess Mensdorff-Pouilly, several months after embarking on his married life in England], and in order to emerge unscathed and as far as possible unsullied, I am forced to watch every step. Here nothing is considered insignificant, and owing to a publicity which makes it quite impossible to keep any kind of secret one must carefully consider the slightest move before making it. You people on the continent can have no conception of English life, where publicity is mixed up in everything; and all is dominated by the party spirit. No noble or upper-class family can do anything which is of the remotest interest without its being known and straightway published in the newspapers with comments favourable or otherwise. Consider how much worse is the position of people situated as we are who excite the interest of the whole nation? I am in the middle of all these people, and, what was hardest of all at first, of a family whose members hate one another with an inconceivable bitterness. In trying to reconcile so many different points of view and interests and at the same time to do what is right and to escape scandal—"il y a de quoi être un peu pensif" I can assure you! ... I could write you pages and pages on this subject.

And now again, more than ever, but this time for his sister, it was one of those situations in which *il y a de quoi être un peu pensif*. However, as before at Claremont, so now at Woolbrook Cottage, where the Duke of Kent lay in state, illumined by candles, Leopold had at his side to help him in his decisions the man who had become his alter ego, Stockmar. Originally Leopold's doctor, this man, with his rough features, his expression of an exceptionally alert, perspicacious terrier, had gradually developed into the young Prince's supporter, adviser, and most intimate confidant.

Six days had not passed since the Duke's death before the disturbed atmosphere was made still further so by news of a most unsettling nature. George III had died. At once the whole outlook at Woolbrook Cottage had to be readjusted to this event. The Duke's unreliable—and to Victoire and her child most inimical—

brother, the Prince Regent, was now King, and his say in the order-ing of the lives of his sister-in-law and child would be all the more potent. Even now Leopold did not waver. To his mind, without a doubt, his sister must remain in England. The only question at the moment was, in these changed circumstances would the new King allow her to return to Kensington Palace? As usual it was thought best to approach that explosive character in a circuitous manner. His sister, Princess Mary, was applied to. In response, her ink flowed; and to good purpose. The permission was granted.

Now, everything at last arranged, on a January morning the dis-mal return procession to London set out on its way. Not only were the occupants of the coaches in deepest mourning, but even the postilions were in black; there were black cockades beneath the horses' ears, and black fringes on the hammercloths. But amid all this recognition of death one tiny person spoke of budding life, of vitality at its gayest: a gurgling, fidgeting baby whom the Duchess —already trained to please the British public—held up to the shut window of the carriage, on which the sturdy infant perpetually thumped and banged.

Meanwhile, a letter had been galloped across Europe, written by Princess Lieven * to her lover, Metternich.

I was astonished [she writes] to hear yesterday of the Duke of Kent's death. That Hercules of a man is no more.... No one in England will mourn the Duke. He was false, hard and greedy. His so-called good qualities were only for show, and his last public appeal to the charity of the nation had lost him the support of the only friends he had—prisoners and City men. His wife kills all her husbands though. She would cut an interesting figure now if she had it in her to do so; but, whatever you may say, she is the most mediocre person it would be possible to meet.

2

Empty indeed must Kensington Palace have seemed to the Duchess of Kent during those first winter weeks after her return: cruelly desolate those vast rooms now that Edward's substantial presence was no longer there to fill them. The new King's sisters

* Wife of the Russian Ambassador in England, 1812-34.

were all compassion, all sympathy, while his brother, the Duke of Clarence, typical boisterous sailor of his era, was so saddened at the thought of Victoire's isolated position that he asked his wife to go to her every day. And in these kind of situations that called for tenderness of heart no one was more suitable than that gentle, and, historically speaking, faint color-wash figure, Adelaide of Saxe-Meiningen. In her portraits her peaky little face peers out shrinkingly from all the piled-up showiness of sausage-roll curls, diamond hair slides, and lace veils that was the fashion; her general air as if she apologized for the royal state thrust upon her. But on looking closer, one discerns behind all the timorousness an underlying expression of exceptional sweetness. Her look of apprehension is explained by Creevey, who writes that her "fixed impression is that an English revolution is rapidly approaching and that her own fate is to be that of Marie-Antoinette." * Meanwhile, the poor lady, awaiting the guillotine, showered kindnesses on every side, stitched assiduously at her embroidery, or cut out silhouettes in black paper. Her love of flowers made her push little bunches of them, "posies of cowslips, violets, roses and mignonettes," into her waist belt, creating a fashion that, when it was long past, was carried on by old ladies who, pointing to their nosegay, would murmur "like Queen Adelaide."

Each day now the Clarence carriage turned in at the iron gates that led to Kensington Palace, drew up at the door in the courtyard, and Adelaide stepped down. One young German princess in a foreign country come to support and console another. They would read prayers together in their own language. The friendship ripening, they gradually became on such easy terms that when Adelaide arrived she would go familiarly through the rooms calling out for Victoire till she discovered her. There must, however, have been during these daily visits a curious—and with Victoire an inevitably slightly hostile—undercurrent of feeling between the two young women, for Adelaide was again *enceinte*. Again the possibility of

---

* As one reads what Croker wrote in 1832 one is not surprised at Adelaide's fears. "The King, the Queen, and the Royal Family are libelled, caricatured, lampooned and balladed by itinerant singers, hired for the purpose, to a degree not credible. They [William IV and Queen Adelaide] are constantly compared to Charles and Henrietta, and to Louis and Antoinette, and menaced with their fate.... Depend upon it, our Revolution is in a sure, and not slow, progress."

her coming offspring supplanting Victoire's baby had to be reckoned with.

3

When the Duchess of Kent had returned to Kensington Palace she had found in addition to the Duke of Sussex yet another member of the royal family ensconced in a set of apartments within those all-embracing walls: a daughter of George III, Princess Sophia. Once one of the lovely group of sisters who gossiped as their embroidery needles and little paint brushes flicked to and fro in the drawing rooms of Windsor Castle and Buckingham Palace, she was now a rather pathetic, emotionally battered, and already aging woman of between forty and fifty. We can still see her in Gainsborough's child portrait: the most enchanting little *amore* possible, buttercup nursery curls dangling beneath a broad hat with a great pink bow, a black lace fichu drawn tightly round her minute shoulders.

Her life as she grew up had, like that of all the sisters, been compressed into an unnatural shape by their custodian mother. One way of escape had, however, offered itself to this sensitive and delicate girl, and rashly and secretly she had snatched at it. George III had an elderly, and, in the eyes of most people, a far from attractive equerry, Colonel Garth, but Princess Sophia's emotions, allowed so little outlet, had tremulously hovered around this Court figure. Colonel Garth, on his side, was not insensible to being adored by a little being who was at once young, royal, and most lovely. Whether they were privately married, or whether he was her lover only, is not certain, but it is known that by the end of August 1800 she had had a baby by him. Except for this indubitable fact the whole episode is obscure. A scandal of the most cruel nature, however, spluttered for a year or two around this baby. It was whispered that Princess Sophia's brother, the besmirched Duke of Cumberland, was in reality the child's father. This unfounded and brutal libel—said to have emanated from the fly-away brain of the then Princess of Wales—died down for the time, but, as will be seen, for the time only.

In general, George IV was a monument of egoism in his human relationships, and yet, where his sisters were concerned, he was the most devoted of brothers. He sympathized with their distresses; disentangled their financial muddles; encouraged their marriages; sent them letters, presents, love, hats, trinkets; attended to shopping commissions when they were ill; calmed down the inevitable discords between them and their mother. "I do love you *de cœur et d'âme*," exclaimed Princess Sophia in one of her letters; and, again, "my heart *overflows* with gratitude." So now, here she was, another of his guests at Kensington Palace, which appears to have been used at present chiefly as a refuge for those members of the royal family whose lives might be described as "difficult": the Duke of Sussex himself at the moment being in a hiatus between two morganatic marriages.

To the Duchess of Kent and her growing baby, Princess Sophia was to become a permanent and most familiar figure in the background of their palace life. To a great extent a muted figure, her mind turned in on itself, secretly tethered to that hidden side of her life which must never be referred to, must always remain concealed. Did her son, now a young man of about eighteen, come, unknown to the rest of the palace, and visit her? Was it in order that these visits should be as much unobserved as possible that she had asked to be given rooms in this secluded sleepy place? Was it for the same reason, though ostensibly she gave a different one, that she refused to have any permanent lady in waiting but, instead, had readers who came at arranged hours? Hers was a situation that could not but give vent to every kind of surmise.

Entirely withdrawn from life's stage, health and sight already beginning to go, we see her patiently sitting in her silent room, clicking a pair of steel needles as she makes one of the fashionable netted purses, or embroidering a piece of thick cream-colored silk that would finally be framed as a pole screen. There she leads her solitary existence; a spirit who in one desperate bid had endeavored to escape stultification, and who, shamed, maligned, and bespattered, now sits with bowed head in gentle resignation.

But if in her corner of the palace there lay a sense of inanition and decay, an atmosphere as of the dispersal of all vitality, in the Kent quarters an azure-eyed, vigorous little creature gave the elder people around her a feeling of springtide, of oncoming life. To the Duchess of Kent, her frolicsome baby was not only a living legacy from her husband, it was her justification for continuing to stay on in England, to draw that six thousand a year from the Government, and have rooms in Kensington Palace. She was always eager to be in the forefront of the social stage, and through this nursery infant she might one day secure a great position for herself, might even attain to being Regent of England. Therefore a little scene given us by Lady Granville is quite in character.

One August morning she happened to be paying a visit to the Duchess of Gloucester, George IV's sister, Mary. The Duchess of Kent and her baby were also there, and Lady Granville found Victoire "very pleasing indeed," and adds that she was "raving of her baby." *"C'est mon bonheur, mes délices, mon existence. C'est l'image du feu roi!"* she cried out to the other ladies. This final exclamation raises a smile, as she could scarcely have wished that flower-petal face to resemble the ponderous, heavy-jowled countenance of the mad King. All the same, the Duchess' determined hitching of her baby on to the royal line is understandable. From now on it was her wisely chosen line of action.

As for the baby itself ("so fat it can scarcely waddle"), it was in a state of continuous explosion of energy and bad temper. That superabundant vitality that later, thrusting on through eight of her nine children, was to people half of Europe with monarchs, now vented itself in the Kensington nursery by making an inconceivable din. The governess, Louise Lehzen, presumably experienced in youthful hullabaloos, said she had "never seen such a passionate and naughty child." It seems that the Duke of Kent's daughter positively took a pride in her power of raising these cyclones. When she was a year or two older her mother on one occasion admitted to a visitor that that day there had definitely been "a little storm."

"Yes, one at dressing and one at washing," corroborated a small voice.

Neither could the Duchess successfully impose on her the usual twisted philosophy of the nursery. "When you are naughty you make *both me and yourself* very unhappy," she one day hazarded. But the producer of scenes was not going to hide her satisfaction in her own prowess. "No, Mamma, not *me*, not *myself*, but you."

There is an interesting aspect to these convulsions of temper. One notices that they leaped up especially when her elders tried to

KENSINGTON PALACE
By W. Westall, R.A.

QUEEN ADELAIDE

From the portrait by Sir William Beechey, R.A.

shackle her with such civilized disciplines as washing, putting on clothes, fixing her attention on matters for which she felt no interest. Within her was an untamed creature, frantically struggling for freedom, endeavoring to reach some kind of existence quite other than the one her nursery jailers were determined to impose. It was almost as if the spirit of Peter the Wild Boy, still lurking in the palace, had taken the possession of the child. But the interesting point is that though for years this hunger for freedom was to be driven underground, it always remained, and in later life was to reappear in different forms. The first recurrence, as we shall see, being when she was about sixteen, then again going into hiding and, in later life, reappearing most markedly in various idiosyncrasies. As this small person grew bigger she would, when in a benign mood, stagger along in Kensington Gardens, upheld on either side by her mother and her half sister Feodore: nods, smiles, "good mornings," bursting from her cherubic face equally to those she knew and those she did not. From the careful pens of onlookers the most enchanting little scenes in Kensington Gardens re-form themselves before our eyes. We become aware of a group progressing in desultory manner beneath the trees: several ladies—a manservant in attendance—surrounding a white donkey decked with blue ribbons led by an old soldier who had served under the Duke of Kent, and on the back of the donkey its complacent owner. But did one of the group dare suggest the rider should dismount and run about at a moment it was not the lady's pleasure to do so? On the very instant it would become evident that the Duke of Kent's indomitable will was not lying quiescent within the royal vault at Windsor, but was still living, vibrant and explosive, behind a pair of infantile, furious blue eyes.

Or an indoor scene. A piece of yellow carpet laid down in the Kensington drawing room especially for the little Drina to disport herself upon; these gambolings watched by the Duchess of Kent and by a black-clothed figure, of precise and formal manner, Dr. Fisher, Bishop of Salisbury. The gold and crimson of the set of Empire chairs and this piece of yellow carpet with the corn-haired baby tumbling about on top would have made a charming synthesis of color, as the Duchess, with her decorative sense, would have been well aware. But the Bishop was not concerned with the blend of colors before him. It was the social aspect that he found soothing and warming in the highest degree. For he had not always been so snugly welcome in royal drawing rooms. A painstaking snob, he was always trotting after royalty like a boy after a brass band. The "Kingfisher," so, with a snigger, George III's family had dubbed him. He had been tutor to the Duke of Kent, and later attached to Princess Charlotte's household at Warwick House. There he made every endeavor to become cosy with Charlotte and her governesses, but Charlotte would have none of the pedantic fellow. "The Great U.P." she would exclaim disgustedly behind his back in derision of the way he mouthed "Bish*up*." But revolving time had been generous to this tedious old sycophant. His niece had married Captain Conroy. So now, as uncle to the wife of the Comptroller at Kensington Palace, as former tutor to the Duchess' dead husband, as visiting divine to his pupil's newly bereaved widow, the Bishop found himself very cosy indeed in the Kensington drawing room; and often his dismal person would come bowing in at the door. On this particular occasion, only too ready to ingratiate himself with the Kent baby, he had become humanized so far as to kneel down beside her so that she could play with the Garter badge * that he wore on a ribbon round his neck. As a grown woman Queen Victoria would relate how, as she fiddled with this little object, at that instant consciousness of her surroundings smote her with extraordinary clarity—the yellow carpet, the feel of the badge beneath her exploring fingers, the presence of the Bishop—the whole scene was to remain imprinted on her mind for the rest of her life. A further vignette of her nursery days never became obliterated. Her third daughter, Princess Helene, once asked her what was her very first recollection. The Queen considered for a few moments, and then, "My earliest remembrance," she said, "is going to Carlton House Terrace to watch Sir Thomas Lawrence paint the Duchess of Gloucester."

Yet another scene: this time in an engraving of the period. Now the trees in Kensington Gardens reveal their pencilings against the colorless winter sky. Impinging on the quiet air is heard an approaching soft scuffle of sound, the quick trotting of tiny hoofs, the

* As Chancellor of the Order of the Garter he was entitled to this badge.

slight scrunch of small carriage wheels; and then, out from the trees comes a minute phaeton, a boy postilion bumping up and down on the back of one of the two long-tailed ponies, and seated within this absurd but enchanting little carriage a fair-haired child, her smiling face aureoled by a great bonnet. But even as we look at it, neatly, swiftly the whole deliciously contrived little affair trots by, trots away again into the frosty mist beneath the trees, back again into the past from which for one instant it has been resuscitated.

4

While bringing up her baby the Duchess had to continue accustoming herself to life without her husband. It was a heart-rending task. She ached for that ponderous presence. "She quite adored poor Edward," wrote Princess Augusta. Victoire tried to find what consolation she could in writing down in a notebook her longings to be reunited with him. Years later, after her death, Queen Victoria came across these notes. She was surprised at the warmth that arose from the pages. "*Such* love and affection," commented the Queen. "I hardly knew it was to *that* extent."

During these first months of the Duchess' widowhood she must have been constantly fretted with an unsettling sense of apprehension, for if Adelaide's coming baby did successfully arrive, and did successfully live, what would happen to herself and her treasured Drina? In that case, would there be any further reason for remaining in England? Actually, Adelaide's offspring arrived without mishap in the December of that year, 1820. "We are all on the kick and go," wrote Conroy in his jaunty way, "our little woman's nose has been put out of joint"; but Princess Elizabeth Georgiana Adelaide only blocked Drina's path for four months. Then a royal effigy was ordered, a very small one indeed, of a recumbent baby. "My children are dead," wrote poor Adelaide to the Duchess of Kent, "but yours lives, and she is mine too."

The disappointment to Adelaide was overwhelming, but the world was remarkably little concerned over the disappearance of this second of her vanishing babies. "Nobody troubles about her," commented Conroy. For at the moment something far more sensational was titillating the public mind: the coming coronation of

George IV. The year before, the rearrival in England of his wife, followed by his unsuccessful efforts to divorce her, had thrown the whole country into "a state of incredible excitement." Now in the King's determination that at his coronation his Queen should not be crowned, and in her equal determination to force an entrance into the Abbey and to insist on being crowned, there was indeed every kind of anticipatory thrill for the whole of England. Leaving that impossible but pathetic creature, Caroline of Brunswick, unsuccessfully trying on the day of the coronation itself to force her way through the shut and guarded doors of Westminster Hall, we return to the quiet of Kensington Palace, and the transforming of a screaming baby into the young Victoria.

5

As if by the law of compensatory balance, as opposed to the incisive Captain Conroy there appeared one spring morning at the palace, as English reader to the Duchess, a clergyman of the mildest disposition, Mr. Davys, later to become successively Dean of Chester and Bishop of Peterborough. He possessed, so we are told, "a poetical mind"; had an instinct for quietly circumventing the perplexities of life; enjoyed "writing for the poor," and in this activity was said to have become "eminent." This, considering the conditions in which the poor then lived, thousands of them half naked, and living only on potatoes or turnips, was indeed a feat of ingenuity, and must have taxed the inventiveness of the most competent writer.

Mr. Davys was already familiar by sight to the Kensington group, as he took the services in the palace chapel. The Duchess had now asked him to come to read English with her, feeling that she needed some further initiation into the language. So much tact did he show in being at once deferential and tutorial, in softening those too emphatic German gutturals into the more slippery English locution, that after a few weeks the Duchess exclaimed, "You teach me so well that I wish you would teach my little daughter." Lessons were agreed on. Confronted by this determined infant of four, Davys, forestalling kindergarten methods, approached his pupil with all the cautious adroitness that he did the London poor.

A box of letters was produced. He wrote words on bits of cardboard, placed them about the room, called out one of the chosen words and told the child to run and find the correct card. Drina was intrigued. There came to the fore a trait that was to be apparent all her life: her delight at being brought in contact with an original mind. Perplexing as it must have seemed to the exhausted victims of those nursery tornadoes, her tutor pronounced her to be "a sweet-tempered child" and as possessing "great feeling." He also noticed her generosity in giving or lending her toys to other children. But there were moments when this public generosity was not so apparent. When she was six years old, another little girl of the same age, Lady Jane Ellice, was brought one afternoon to Kensington Palace by her grandmother. The two children were put to play together. The small visitor was delighted with all the grand toys of her royal friend—that white satin dolls' sofa; those three little dancing figures; those orientals, richly robed, mechanically strolling in and out of their bell-hung pavilions. Enchanted, little Jane began to fiddle and explore—but she was soon made to realize her mistake. "You must not touch those, they are mine; and I may call you Jane, but you must not call me Victoria." Not altogether a pleasant afternoon visit for little Jane.

CHAPTER IV
CAPTAIN CONROY HAS HIS DESIGNS

THREE or four years later. The scene, Kensington Palace in the dawn of a certain summer's day. It was still so early that a passing workman noticed as he walked through the gardens that "the sun was scarcely high enough to have dried up the dew of Kensington's green alleys." As Charles Knight, for such was the workman's name, pursued his way, his eye was caught by a little group on the lawn of the palace's private garden, a group which, so he exclaims, "was to my mind a vision of loveliness." Just outside the Duchess of Kent's suite of rooms she and the small Victoria were having breakfast, an attendant page hovering. Though they are not mentioned, it may be assumed that Louise Lehzen, Feodore, and old Madame de Späth would also have been seated round that early morning breakfast table. Victoria's still cherubic face was, we are told, "bright with smiles."

Nothing, to read of, could sound more sylvan, more secure from harm than this matutinal scene, and yet, nevertheless across it lay the shadow of an unseen but most sinister figure, a man whose character was believed to be so vile that he would not flinch from having poison secretly inserted into the bowl of bread and milk that each morning the small Victoria absorbed so complacently. The possibility of these machinations so possessed the Duchess' mind that she never allowed the child to begin her breakfast until someone had first tasted what she was going to eat. Whether it was the Duchess herself, the governess, the nurse, or some specially detailed attendant who thus offered herself to meet death at eight o'clock each morning, we do not know. This human vulture that the Duchess believed always to be hovering over Kensington Palace was her husband's brother, Ernest, Duke of Cumberland. The Duke of York was now dead. Therefore, as the position then stood, if it had not been for Victoria the Duke of Cumberland would have come next in succession to the throne after his brother the Duke of Clarence. At that time Hanover was an appanage of Great Britain. But though Victoria could succeed to the English throne she could not, on account of the Salic law, succeed to that of Hanover. If neither George IV nor the Duke of Clarence had direct male heirs, the Kingdom * of Hanover would automatically fall to the Duke of Cumberland. But this Royal Duke possessed not only a particularly virile intelligence, and was capable of filling any throne with distinction, he was as well a rigid Tory, and his political supporters would definitely have preferred that the English crown should pass to him rather than to that small limb of the Whig party, his niece Victoria. In addition, Cumberland made no secret of his extreme annoyance at the probability of his being supplanted by his brother Edward's daughter. These considerations, coupled with the baleful reputation the Duke had acquired, had given rise to a suspicion, vaguely afloat, that he wished to clear his niece from his path.

The Duke of Cumberland has come down to us surrounded with such a fog of opprobrium that it is difficult to discern the real man, but it is clear that everything about this markedly individual son of George III was vehemently contentious. He hurled himself at life with the violence of a prize fighter. So that his appearance should be in keeping with the hatred he was to incur, fate had seen to it that during his military career one side of his face had been mutilated, thus giving the conclusive villainous touch to his personality. Unlike his portly brothers with their chubby limbs, the Duke was unusually tall and lean. "A more magnificent frame of man was never seen," commented John Hobhouse to himself on an occasion at Strelitz when, at two o'clock in the morning, the Duke leaped from his bed to receive some dispatches Hobhouse had brought. And at this exclamation, with his gaunt height and impressive air, his ghastly eye socket, and tangle of whisker and mustache drawn across his scarred cheek, the "wicked Duke" springs to life again

* In 1815 the Electorate of Hanover had become a kingdom.

before us like some horrific figure out of a drawing by Gillray or Rowlandson. In one respect he was as cruel as the Duke of Kent, for his regiment, the Fifteenth Dragoons, was the only one in which the punishment of picketing was still practiced: the victim being forced to balance himself on one foot, for long periods, on the end of a stake driven into the ground.

Cumberland was undeniably a disagreeable, quarrelsome, revengeful, bitter, mischief-making man. The Duke of Wellington said "that there never was a husband and wife, nor father and son, nor brother and sister, that he did not strive to set against one another." To those he despised, and enjoyed sneering at, he behaved like a bullying schoolboy. Walking one day down Piccadilly with Sir Charles Wyke he caught sight of his cousin, the family butt, known as Silly Billy, coming out of Gloucester House. "Duke of Gloucester, Duke of Gloucester," yelled Cumberland. "Stop a minute, I want to speak to you." Silly Billy, pleased at being noticed by this towering personality, "ambled up, smiling." "Who's your tailor?" "Stultz." "Thank you, I only wanted to know because he ought to be avoided like the pestilence."

Cumberland and the Regent were far the most amusing of George III's sons, and the Regent's admiration for Ernest's brains and fear of his scorching wit may have been the reason for a curious ascendancy that Cumberland seemed to exercise over his eldest brother. Ernest's friendship for him, needless to say, was not without its stabs, such as his remark about the Regent's gout that the trouble "was higher than the foot, a blister on the head would be more efficacious." The Regent, in a burst of indignation, said he would never see Ernest again except in public. Cumberland's riposte was at once not only to force his way into Carlton House, but into the Regent's private rooms. Once inside, the brothers' voices, each screaming at the other, could be heard all over the house. Nevertheless, within a few minutes they emerged together, to all seeming as good friends as ever.

This obstreperous Duke married his cousin, the widowed Princess of Salms-Braunfels, a most amiable woman but undeniably *un peu légère*. This, added to the fact that she had before been engaged to, but had jilted, Cumberland's popular younger brother, the Duke of Cambridge, incensed not only the English nation but the royal family; Queen Charlotte and her daughters refusing even to receive Cumberland's Duchess. Needless to say, at this, further bitter family feelings were engendered, further disputes, further quarrels.

The Duke was Grand Master of those Tory hotbeds, the Orange Lodges, which comprised thousands of members in both England and Ireland, and this gave him, in the eyes of the Whigs, the aspect of a general backed by a powerful and hostile force. There is no doubt there were political intrigues still sizzling on within the "Salic Set," a party that had been active when Princess Charlotte was heir presumptive, and was strongly opposed to a woman occupying the English throne and so causing a severance between the kingdoms of England and Hanover. As already said, these ultra-Tories would infinitely have preferred Cumberland as King to the Duke of Kent's daughter as Queen. How much real danger lurked in these Lodges, how much it consisted merely of tendentious talk, it is impossible to say; but this seething underground hostility to the child Victoria would have been known both to the Duke of Kent, and to Prince Leopold, who would undoubtedly have warned the Duchess.

It is evident that Cumberland himself had no personal designs on the Kensington innocent. But the Duchess, bewildered, as well she might be, by the whole situation, and confronted with a specimen of that character so difficult for a foreigner to understand, the fire-breathing Englishman, considered it quite possible that her treasure might any moment be the victim of villainy, and not only at breakfast but at every meal the tasting rite was performed.

A young equerry of the Duke of Sussex, Major Keppel, would on these early summer mornings, while waiting for the Duke to come down to breakfast, occupy himself by looking out into the garden where, her own breakfast over, Victoria would be seen with her watering can briskly bespattering the flowers just beneath the Duke's windows. The waiting equerry says it amused him to see how indifferently this little figure in the broad-brimmed hat and white cotton frock flung the water helter-skelter on to either the flowers or her own feet. But, so he writes, "My chief was the essence of punctuality. We breakfasted precisely at nine," and leaving his window he would, as the hour drew near, go to the foot of the staircase to wait for the Duke. He tells us how, as he heard the clock in the courtyard strike the hour, on the instant "from every nook and corner of the Duke's suite of apartments" there burst forth the inevitable cacophony of national anthem, martial airs, and chiming timepieces, while at the same moment would come hurtling down the staircase a whole avalanche of little dogs yapping with morning excitement at finding themselves yet again freshly alive. Behind them appeared the minute Negro page—doubtless in the scarlet and gold of the royal livery—and towering above this diminutive creature there came, heavily stepping, the gigantic Duke himself, who, black skullcap on head, the folds of his violet satin dressing gown revealing his embroidered waistcoat, fanciful slippers on his feet, must have had almost the appearance of some Eastern potentate.

2

As the Duke and his aide-de-camp sat down to breakfast, his niece Victoria, in one of the Kent rooms round the corner, sat down to her lessons. The gentle Davys had been succeeded as general instructor by Fräulein Lehzen, though Davys still came to teach her Latin. The little girl gradually acquired in addition a whole list of special instructors for different subjects; Monsieur Grandineau brought the accent of the French tongue to her ear; a Mrs. Steward initiated her into the labyrinths of arithmetic; the famous Lablache trained her voice; Madame Bourdin showed her how to point her toes; Westall, the Academician, how to draw. Each path to knowledge and accomplishment had its appointed guide. The Duke of Sussex, too, by far the most cultured of George III's sons, would, in his *grand-seigneur* manner, throw a glance over her education, and occasionally toss a few grains of Hebrew into her mind. But, even when she grew older, among her many instructors we do not find that the Duchess thought it necessary to have one who would teach her "the exercise of the fan, how to express the passions by it, and, above all, how to throw it," all of which was at that time a recognized and subtle art among the fashionables who frequented Carlton House and Brighton Pavilion. It seems that besides teaching her arithmetic Davys led Victoria toward the secluded groves of poetry; but as, by the time she was seven or eight, the only volumes of verse he had opened before her were *The Infant Minstrel, Poetry Without Friction* by a Mother, *The Keepsake,* and *The Literary Box,* it is doubtful whether Mr. Davys' "poetical mind" was of the highest order.

Mrs. Trimmer's little educational books for the young were much in evidence in the Kensington schoolroom, her instructions on Nature being not without their sensational side: an ill-advised boy, for instance, eats some unripe gooseberries, "by which means, his stomach being filled with nasty trash, he entirely lost his appetite; and his rosy cheeks became as pale as death; at last worms, live worms, came into his bowels." In those days the hours of instruction imposed on the children of the well-to-do were mitigated by the presence of enormous globes, one terrestrial, one celestial, balanced on brass and mahogany stands. Whirling those huge revolving balls round on their pivots, their curving polished contours so exquisitely smooth and cool to the fingers, must have eased many otherwise dreary scholastic moments. When Victoria was nine years old she had a special book to instruct her on the use of these fascinating objects—*The Introduction to Astronomy, Geography, and the Use of the Globes,* by John Sharman. John Sharman did not spare the nascent intelligence; sharply demanding, for instance, "At what hour will the morning twilight begin, and the evening twilight end, on the 10th of February, also on the 27th of August, in Dublin?" The child reader was also supposed to be able "To find the sun's oblique ascension, his eastern amplitude and azimuth, with the time of rising on any particular day." But the youthful Victoria's mind would soon have grasped amplitudes and azimuths, for even though occasionally her protests at having such a quantity of information pushed into her were so emphatic that they could be heard two rooms away, her mind was already exceptionally quick both to receive and to retain. She was also preternaturally observant. When only a very small child, toddling along by the side of her nurse and Feodore, their "dear Bobby" one day heard a tiny voice demanding, "Why do all the gentlemen raise their hats to me, and not to Feodore?"

Not only did Fräulein Lehzen become governess to Victoria, she gradually became her closest companion, friend, and supporter. This last word may strike strangely, for, it may well be thought, what support could have been necessary for this little person, round whom, because of her important future, the whole household revolved? Truth to tell, within the Duchess of Kent's household with all its visible orderliness and decorum, each day and hour among this group of closely linked-together people, conflicting and hostile feelings were being engendered that later were to manifest themselves in the most far-reaching manner, and with a vehemence and searing of spirit to be experienced in all its bitterness by the actors. As the child grew into a little girl she inevitably became aware of, and involved in, this emotional entanglement that made a strain at the very center of the palace life. Possibly it was in part this awareness that was so soon to turn her goldilocks little countenance into one of those grave, thin-featured, rather bare-looking faces that even at twelve or thirteen already hint at maturity—in her case a locked, passionless face, curiously at variance with the intensely emotional nature that lay beneath.

3

The moment has come for a close scrutiny of this nucleus of people at the palace who in their forced daily collisions of temperament were to become so intimately and in some cases so painfully aware of each other. Apart from the Duchess, the figure that stands out the most emphatically is that of John Conroy; a personality with whom everyone had to reckon. He came of an old Irish family. His grandfather, who had a flair for society, wrote of himself, "Jonny Conroy is a rollicking boy"—a phrase equally applicable to his grandson, who, as a social virtuoso, was a more efficient edition of the grandfather. The Duke of Kent gone, a whole field of action of the most extended and exhilarating kind opened before this intensely ambitious and competent young man, who had now become comptroller of the household to the Duke's widow. He was a determined career monger, impudent, undefeatably shrewd, quickly contemptuous, and with a violent temper; but all that was detrimental in his disposition was overlaid by the most accomplished technique. Among the group of women at the Palace—the widowed and saddened Victoire; her unprepossessing lady in waiting, Madame Späth; the pale-faced governess, Louise Lehzen—among these uprooted German women, pursuing in the brooding quiet of the old place their repetitive, daily occupations, Conroy moved about, the purposeful male, an upstanding six-foot figure in gold-braided artillery uniform, glimpsed now, perhaps, in the courtyard, flinging his leg across his horse's saddle, or now appearing in a doorway, passing through a room, creating movement in a too static atmosphere, bringing with him a sense of masculine efficiency —psychologically supplying to at least one of these women in their sexless lives a subconscious need. His portrait by Fowler is an epitome of the man: at one glance it is evident that here is a man who would be a swift glider into the minds of others; ostensibly a giver, but in reality a plotter; one who would be the recipient of close confidences; whose powers of pleasing, especially with women, would be so effective that the fact that at heart he was not far from a cad would for some time pass unobserved. The figure in Fowler's portrait holds itself so arrogantly that it is all but bent backward from the hips; the face, consciously self-satisfied, but masked and secret, just flicked over by a half-amused sneer. The strength of the cleft chin is remarkable. This Irishman possessed a whole assortment of drop curtains behind which to conceal himself, one suitable for each person he had to deal with; and the list of his conquests, from tradesmen to royalties, was continually being extended. He even, for a time—and this may be considered the apex of his powers of deception—succeeded in hoodwinking Melbourne. It could be said of Conroy as was said by Lord Hervey of Robert Walpole: "No man ever knew better among those he had to deal with who was to be had, on what terms, by what methods, and how the acquisition would answer." But if he supplied a psychological need for the Duchess—and one must remember that at this time they were two vivacious people of about forty—his effect on Lehzen and Späth was before long to be exactly the opposite of soothing. He seems to have carelessly amused himself by wounding them with any weapon in his well-stocked mental armory that came to hand, and soon their faces will be turned from him in indignant antipathy; their cries of distress will arise in the air.

Louise Lehzen now lives chiefly in the eyes of the world as a Lytton Strachey burlesque, and as an opponent of the Prince Consort, whom he successfully felled. All the same, one cannot but suspect that history has maligned this sensitive and intelligent being. A woman of deep feeling, she had an intuitive wisdom in human contacts that was lacking in her employer, who would rustle in and out of the schoolroom in clothes of the latest fashion in merely an effective pretense of superintending Victoria's education. This royal governess was obviously in many ways an admirable, gifted, and finally a much-to-be-pitied woman. Queen Victoria, when a child, did a little pen-and-ink sketch of her, and, so carefully accurate was this amateur draftswoman in all her efforts, one may feel assured that the governess' salient characteristics have all been captured. The dark lustrous eyes are brimmed with tenderness; and the long, slender, curiously concave nose, and sensitive lips form a whole that is as markedly individual as it is appealing. Here is the face of a gentle, ruminative spirit, which it is difficult to associate with the intriguing nature that time has foisted upon her. As with all normal humanity, Louise Lehzen felt the need both to give and to receive love. Cut off entirely from her Hanover home and relations—Feodore, on whom she had bestowed years of care and affection, now grown beyond the need of her tuition—the governess' whole being turned to, and gradually became entirely concentrated upon, that small, lively tempered little creature, the budding Victoria. For thirteen years, without the break of a single day, everything of value in the pastor's daughter—and there was much—flowed without stint into the mind of the child. If Louise Lehzen was of a thoughtful disposition, she was at the same time undoubtedly a woman of a forceful nature. It was Victoria's destiny from her earliest days to have always at her elbow one remarkable character or another, and here, in her governess, steps forward the first of the series. Lehzen, conscientious to the point of severity in lesson time, yet succeeded, by appealing to Victoria's affections, in grappling with those infant tempers in a way the Duchess had failed to do. In her governess the child sensed a something indefinable but of inestimable value that was missing in her mother, and she succumbed to it. All her life she was to feel the necessity of having someone who was not only close to her in person but also close to her in spirit and affection. Her abounding, warm-blooded nature could not otherwise be satisfied. The Duchess of Kent, so prodigal to the world of smiling gleams from those hazel eyes, appears to have imbued the educational atmosphere of her two daughters with inexpressible dreariness: "not one cheerful thought in that dismal existence of ours," wrote Feodore many years later to Queen Victoria, looking back on what she called the "imprisonment" of their childhood days.

In between schoolroom hours Lehzen softened the edges of the Duchess' discipline for the young by finding occupations for her latest pupil. She induced an atmosphere of easiness; she gave understanding, wisdom, sympathy; and as the years passed the relationship between these two gradually approximated more and more to that of mother and child. One of her holds over Victoria when she was small was her cleverness in dressing dolls for her and in teaching her to do the same. But in looking at many of these tiny dolls, that are not so much dolls as figurines, one is convinced that it was chiefly grown-up fingers that had accomplished that astute manipulation. These tiny creatures of only a few inches high display in the most intriguing manner, not only the physical, but almost the mental characteristics of the originals, for they are all portraits of various society women of the day, and when exhibited in the present century at Lancaster House each had its name attached. In spite of their, to our eyes, out-of-date clothes, Lehzen's talent manages clearly enough to convey which were the dowds, and which the *bien mises*. Visitors to Kensington Palace, as they first curtsied to, and then chatted away with, their royal hostess, would have seen the quiet, half-blotted-out figure of the governess in the background, always in attendance when Princess Victoria appeared. But they little realized that every detail, not only of their dress, but of their figure, their whole individuality, was being noted, docketed, and memorized; how, once they were gone, sooner or later, out would come a little naked doll and some garnered scraps of material, and beneath those neat fingers of the Hanoverian pastor's daughter they would be brought to life in miniature. Victoria became absorbed with these puppets—with this curious reproduction of well-known people of the day, many of whom would come to her mother's parties. These were far from being the only kind of doll Victoria possessed. In all she had well over a hundred, entering all their names in a book as if they were a pack of hounds.

Adroit as Lehzen was in grappling with Drina's spluttering rages, there were yet moments when that minute person succeeded in dominating the entire household, days when having, as she herself said in later years, "set pretty well *all* at defiance," she would be led by her exhausted elders, with what vociferation on her part can be imagined, to her bedroom. This room contained the most charming set of what from their description were obviously Hepplewhite chairs, painted green and white, with cane backs. On their wide seats lay cushions of ivory Chinese silk embroidered with leaves. And in this bedroom, in solitude behind the locked door, her small face congested with temper, Drina would be left to the contemplation of the Hepplewhite chairs and the Round Pond.

Then there was Lehzen's natural companion, and almost colleague, the Duchess' adoring lady, Madame Späth ("poor old Späth" as Feodore called her), a woman known to us only by other people's reactions to her; never by hers to them. And from the reactions of others to her we get a sense of fussy futility. Summed up at a glance by the Duke of Wellington as a woman no man could possibly want to take in to supper at a party; described by Creevey as an "old ugly German female companion"; despised by Conroy; treated with great friendliness by Lehzen, but all the same incurring her disapproval by her silly habit of kneeling on the carpet in adulation before the infant Victoria—old Späth clucks about in the background of the palace life like some vague, fluttering hen, and, for posterity, never quite materializes into three-dimensional life.

Finally, the pivot of the group, the Duchess herself. So far we have seen her as the pliable, successful young wife of the man who had gratified her by lifting her out of a smaller position into a greater. She was successful too in impressing the ladies of the royal family with her devotion to Edward, in pleasing them with all her pretty graciosities of manner. Then she had become engulfed in widowhood and mourning. But now she is emerging again into daylight, being, as we have already seen, still a young woman of great attractions, full of appetite for life, aware of her own fascinations, and eager for a more extended field in which to display them. It obviously fretted her to be merely duenna to an important little daughter, and to be living in this secluded place belonging to a brother-in-law who paid scarcely any attention to her. She and Conroy being the same age—she the elder by two months—both materialists, both ambitious, their outlook on the world was much the same. Conroy being comptroller of her household, this young man and this young woman could meet at any moment with perfect propriety. That a close intimacy should evolve between these two ardent personalities, both primed with their individual charms, was inevitable. As will be seen, their manner to each other was gradually to become inadvisedly flirtatious. In later years Queen Victoria said that Conroy "was devoted" to his wife, and although he and the Duchess delighted in their shared jokes and laughter, he with his emphatic character very likely found his delicate, less vivid wife the more appealing as a woman. But whenever this young Irishman passed up the flight of stairs that led to the Duchess' rooms, he was drawing near to the person who was to him the richest purveyor of opportunity that life had yet offered—an opportunity that, manipulated with all his astuteness, might, if events proved favorable, place him, as her intimate friend and adviser, in a position of prominence and influence enough to make any covetous young man catch his breath. Compared with the Duchess, all the other figures at Kensington Palace were to him of very secondary importance: obsequious Späth, merely a piece of old rubbish; Lehzen, ridiculous with her habit of scattering caraway seeds over all her food; his reactions to Feodore we do not know; as for the Duchess' smaller child, he seems at first to have treated her much as he did his own little daughter Victoire, godchild to the Duchess, who constantly came running into the Kents' part of the palace so as to companion Drina. Conroy, feeling each year more certain of his grip on the whole situation, did not hesitate, when he felt in the mood, to say things to annoy Victoria. Noting her carefulness in parting with her pocket money, for instance, he would "chaff her about her closeness," and ask her "if she wished to resemble old Queen Charlotte," well knowing how teasing, to the child, would be any comparison of herself to that acid figure of the past.

Captain Conroy had so many to cajole, so much legerdemain to be practiced on those who mattered, that no doubt he often felt the need to ease off with those who did not. Apart from the Duchess, the two who at the moment were of salient consequence to him, and

over whom he was therefore occupied in casting his nets, were
George IV himself and his inamorata, Lady Conyngham. He had
also taken the precaution of making friends with Macmahon, the
King's disreputable factotum in all his more shady transactions.

The Duchess, the perpetual guest of George IV at Kensington
Palace, was well aware that she and Victoria lived at his disposal.
His dislike for Edward he extended to Edward's widow; and, with
his splenetic disposition, his vindictive hates, what more probable,
if she annoyed him in any particular, than that the whole Kensington party would find themselves dispatched back to Amorbach?
And there were still more dangerous aspects of the King's mind to
be taken into account. Considering Conroy's intimacy with Lady
Conyngham, he and the Duchess of Kent must have been well
aware that George IV was constantly playing with the idea of taking
Victoria away from her mother and bringing her up himself. His
inimical feeling for the Duchess being such he would have thought
nothing of appropriating his child. It was, it seems, chiefly owing
to the Duke of Wellington that Victoria was saved from such a
disaster as being imbued during her most impressionable years with
the evaluations of George IV and Lady Conyngham, for when the
King would start fidgeting with the idea, Wellington would slyly
circumvent him, "not by opposing him . . . but by putting the thing
off as well as he could." One has only to listen to some of George
IV's gamboling, inconsequent, fatuous chatterings with, for example, Princess Lieven, to realize the disintegrating effect which
daily companionship with him would have had on such a virile-
natured, quick little creature as was Victoria. We hear him gossiping
away one evening at dinner at the Pavilion, the intimately small
group around the table companioned on every side by representa-
tions of pagodas, Chinese, palm trees, and dragons, while above
them blazes a gargantuan chandelier. [This chandelier was of such
a terrifying size, thirty feet in height alone, that when William IV
and his wife came to inhabit the Pavilion, Adelaide one night had a
shuddering dream in which she saw it crash on to the table and the
guests around it. This dream so scared William IV that he had the
chandelier removed.] Next the King sits Princess Lieven. Her
little gazelle face—but a face imprinted with acuteness—is fixed in
mock admiration upon the scabrous *bon viveur* countenance as he

goes booming on above her; and their two voices, clearly trans-
mitted by her, float to us as easily as if we were in the room.

His Majesty: "My dear, I'm no ordinary man; and—as for you—
you've more intelligence in your little finger than all my subjects put
together. I said 'little finger' because I did not want to say 'thumb.' Now
you, my dear, who are so intelligent, you must admit that I am not a
fool."

Myself: "Indeed, Sir, I wish I could tell you what I think without
descending to commonplace flattery. Obviously, your Majesty is a very
remarkable man."

His Majesty: "That's true. You have no conception of the ideas which
sometimes go through my head. I have seen everything in a flash. I'm no
mystery-monger; but I am a philosopher.... Lieven knows very well
whom the Bourbons owe their throne to. It was all due to a dispatch that
he wrote on my behalf in 1814. Without that dispatch, there would have
been a M. le Comte de Lille, but no King of France."

[Then, turning to English politics of the moment, he scampers on]
"My dear, what have you been saying about those people who were
almost in power—whom I almost begged to form a government—and
who, then and there, by a series of most unbelievable stupidities, went and
slammed the door in their own faces? My Ministers are imbeciles; the
Opposition—dolts. And here am I in the middle—a pretty position for
me to occupy!"

"I have done extravagant things, and I'm not ashamed of it; but I've
always had my principles, and my principles have always been the same—
gallant to every woman, faithful to one. I'm not going to make you a
speech; I have no intention of imitating that mystery-monger (*in the
King's vocabulary, this word is equivalent to 'mystic'*) Capo d' Istria.*
(*Aloud*) Lieven, I've just been saying that Capo d' Istria is a rascal; but
(*sotto voce to me*) one of these days soon I shall be sending the Emperor
a certain document—something really memorable—*quite* unprecedented
—a document that will make a tremendous effect. I composed it myself;
but I shall not tell you what it is. No good making those charming eyes at
me; you won't discover! My dear, if I had a difficult negotiation in
hand, I should entrust it to you in preference to anybody else. (*To the*

---

* Count Capo d' Istria, in the Russian diplomatic service, and said to have been at this
time "one of the directors of Russian foreign policy."

Princess Augusta) Sister, I drink to your health. Long live wine, I say, long live women! Long live wine, long live men, you will retort. Gentlemen (*addressing the whole company*), the firmest support of my throne, the one man ... (*Here the King stops short, joins his hands, lifts his eyes to heaven and moves his lips as if he were reciting a prayer. Then, to Princess Esterházy*) My dear child, do you know the story of the tailor who was perpetually dropping his wife into the Seine? Very well, I'm the tailor. You don't understand me, but Madame de Lieven does—I can see that from the corner of her mouth."

Myself: "I understand the moral of the story, Sir. (*What story on what moral I had no idea. But it didn't matter: he had no more idea than I had.*)"

His Majesty: "That's right—the moral of the story. (*Angrily*) *Damn it, she takes the words out of my mouth!* My dear, as I have already told you, you're more intelligent than anybody else at table. (*Thus, from being more intelligent than all his subjects, I was reduced to being more intelligent than all his guests, and, as I looked round the table, that seemed to me no difficult matter.*) Gentlemen (*with unction*), the firmest support of my throne, the one man who has taken it upon himself to defend the honour of my crown, the man I shall honour to my dying day, behold him—the Duke of Montrose! After him, I count on Ireland. I shall go to Ireland. Long live Ireland! My dear, you should come with me to Dublin, then to Hanover, then to Vienna. At the frontier, I should put on the white uniform; and once I had put it on I should no longer be King. I am a general of the Austrian army: I intend to pay homage to my master. Paul (*to Esterházy*), you will go ahead to announce me and ask the Emperor to give me only one day of festivities. I shall be merely a general. Then from Vienna, I shall go to Spa and Paris; and we will laugh and enjoy ourselves."

Myself (*turning towards my neighbour, Saint-Aulaire*): "Eh Seigneur, dès ce jour sans sortir de l'Épire, du matin jus-qu'au soir qui vous défend de rire?"

His Majesty: "What's that you're saying, my dear?"

Myself: "Sir, I am comparing your Majesty to Pyrrhus."

His Majesty: "Yes, indeed, he was a great man; but, personally, I prefer Henry IV, whom I admire almost to the point of extravagance. He shouldn't have kept Sully, though. Sully was a rascal, wasn't he?"

Myself: "I am sorry to disagree with you, Sir; but I should never have thought that of Sully."

His Majesty: "My dear, I assure you that I am well up in the subject; I have read the memoirs of the period, M. de la Fayette, Madame de Sévigné, Madame de Bavière. (*At this juncture, he nods at me and we get up from table.*)"

As for Lady Conyngham, George IV's latest and final adored, "Love which allows nothing to interfere with it is all very fine," comments Princess Lieven, "but how extraordinary when its object is Lady Conyngham! Not an idea in her head; not a word to say for herself; nothing but a hand to accept pearls and diamonds with, and an enormous balcony to wear them on."

It greatly amused Princess Lieven to watch the stupefaction of any new arrivals when they first found themselves confronted with the Pavilion *mise en scène*. "You cannot imagine how astonished the Duke of Wellington is," she wrote to Metternich. "He had not been here before, and I thoroughly enjoy noting the kind of remark and the kind of surprise that the whole household evokes in a new-comer. I do not believe that since the days of Heliogabalus there have been such magnificence and such luxury. There is something effeminate in it which is disgusting. One spends the evening half lying on cushions; the lights are dazzling; there are perfumes, music, liqueurs." The Duke's eagle face, now so quiet with age, turned here, turned there, as he took it all in. As the various scents assailed his nostrils—scents straying around the life-size Chinese figures ensconced in niches, scents drifting around Indian cabinets and across fringed draperies—"Devil take me, I think I must have got into bad company" came *sotto voce* to Princess Lieven's ear.

Yes, the atmosphere at secluded Kensington Palace may have been vitiated with ill feeling and duplicity, and, in the schoolroom, with overdiscipline, but all the same it contained more moral ozone for Victoria than was to be found in the Brighton Pavilion.

Apart from the fear that she might at any moment be carried off to the King's hothouse, there was yet another very present anxiety at Kensington Palace regarding that most incalculable of monarchs: the fear, now that his wife was dead, that he might take another. All the commotions of his mind were by now made more enigmatic by his attacks of gout. When one of these descended upon him no one could tell in what direction his thoughts might jump. Princess Lieven relates that during one of these attacks she was given an interview. "I must say that I have never seen a man dressed more oddly. He was lying at full length in a lilac silk dressing-gown, a velvet night cap on his head, his huge bare feet (for he had gout) covered with a piece of pink silk net. I spent an hour and a half *tête à tête* with this get-up. We talked love, religion, tittle-tattle, politics. . . . At the end of this itinerary I got two smacking kisses."

Regarding this particular fear of the Duchess of Kent that he might consider a successor to his dead wife, it must be borne in mind that when the Duchess had returned to Kensington Palace as a widow George IV was only fifty-eight. Always exasperated at the thought that his brother Edward's line should inherit the throne, what more likely than that he would remarry? It was said that Feodore was "always much in favour" with him and some people thought that as she grew into girlhood he even went so far in his mind as to consider marriage with that modest and lovely young creature. Within a few years of his death, everything in his blurred mind and diseased body falling into confusion except concupiscence, it is just within the bounds of possibility that he did at times contemplate such a version of Beauty and the Beast. However, not only is it unthinkable that the Duchess would ever have agreed that Feodore should be pushed into his arms, but any marriage of George IV would be against her own and her younger daughter's interests; these being, from the Duchess' point of view, identical. The probability of Adelaide having another baby had become so remote that the Kensington Palace group were gradually beginning to act as if this danger did not exist. It was to Lady Conyngham's interest, too, that her royal acquisition should not remarry. Any nuptials in that quarter would have been as disastrous to her as they would have been unwelcome to the Duchess of Kent and her comptroller. Also, for reasons not known to us, Sir William Knighton— that mysterious figure who, a kind of domestic king at Windsor, was yet detested by his royal master—he, too, did not wish George IV to remarry. It is said that through the combined persuasions of Lady Conyngham, Conroy, and Knighton, the King was finally induced to give up any such intention. So much we know, but as to the methods employed by those three wary characters, as to their mutual consultations, schemes, and confidences, alas, as we endeavor to draw near, we meet a shut door through which not so much as a whisper exudes.

To return to Fräulein Lehzen. Where among this chance assortment of people at Kensington Palace—the Duchess, with that hard underlining to her seductive manners; Conroy with his crafty nature; Madame Späth, that conventionally subservient lady in waiting—could the German pastor's daughter, the owner of those soft intelligent eyes, find the nourishment she needed for her spirit and her affections? If the Duchess had had more perception, more insight into the needs of other hearts than her own, she would have realized both the inevitability and the closeness of the tie that would before long be binding Lehzen and her pupil. Indeed, by the Duchess' daily arrangements the two were thrown together almost every moment of the day. Victoria was never, such were her mother's commands, to be left in a room with a servant; never to be allowed to walk downstairs without someone holding her hand; a watchful figure must be in attendance while the maid did her hair night and morning, the same for dressing and undressing; and even, once she was in bed, guard had to be kept until the Duchess, who slept in the same room, came up to undress. It was unavoidable that this role of domestic sentinel should devolve almost entirely on the governess. In truth, this holding of Victoria's hand on going downstairs, which was continued till she came to the throne and which sounds so ridiculous—this, if it referred, as it appears to have, to the narrow staircase leading directly from the Kent bedrooms to the drawing rooms below, was a most necessary precaution, for undoubtedly it is the most dangerous staircase in England. Having corners, but no landings, the steps narrow at one side to vanishing point, and the bannister rail suddenly shoots down away from the hand in the most unnerving manner. Any child would immediately fall headlong. It is difficult to imagine how the Kent servants carrying trays of food, when Victoria, as she often did, would have her dinner upstairs with Lehzen, ever circumvented those treacherous steps without crashing to the bottom.

It is easy, with the knowledge that we have, to reconstruct the evening scene in the Duchess' bedroom when Victoria lay already asleep in her "little French bed with its pretty chintz hangings" which always stood by the side of her mother's larger one. Let us visit the room on a winter's evening when, in the generous grate, the flames of a piled-up fire would be snugly blobbing, sending out over the ceiling undulating veils of light and shadow. This wavering light, more fluid than water, is quivering over the whole room, over the drawn curtains of the three great windows, over the various chairs and tables, over the turned-back sheets on Drina's bed, over Drina's sleeping face, over the big tortoise-shell watch that used to belong to the Duke, and now always hangs suspended in its case near his daughter's bed. We can see Lehzen sitting there near the fire, the light from candles or shaded lamp falling on that comely, rather plump little figure; on the pale quiet face beneath, perhaps, one of those enchanting tossed-up muslin headdresses as shown in one of Victoria's drawings of her—for the studied elegance of the eighteenth century has not yet quite passed away. What Lehzen is occupying herself with we do not know, but she is not the character to sit vacuously doing nothing. Possibly, if our vision were clearer, we should see a tiny doll lying on the table and a scatter of those oddments of silk and ribbon that her adroit fingers are about to manipulate into one of her figurines, or perhaps at intervals she softly turns another page of a book she is reading. As Victoria slid to sleep in a silence filled only by the blurred licking of flames and the ticktock of the tortoise-shell watch, the last thing she would have seen would have been that reassuring presence seated in a pool of light against the darkling shadows of the big room.

But for us, having seen all that we can see, the whole picture fluctuates, becomes dimmer, fades, and is gone.

4

Curious to the modern mind as must seem this ceaseless surveillance of the Duke of Kent's daughter, the whole political panorama the Duchess found herself surrounded with made it not only understandable but reasonable. At the present day our municipally minded, well-ordered population expresses its passing disgruntlements in picketed strikes and not in savage uprisings, but the England of the early nineteenth century was composed of very inflammable material: the whole country then possessed far more the spirit of the Continental nations, and those surplus emotions that now find vent at moving pictures or sports arenas were then lying loosely about unco-ordinated, and ready at any moment to be heaped up in a frenzy on the head of any individual who, in the opinion of the masses, did not fall in with their views, political or otherwise. From the French Revolution had blown over ideas of the most subversive kind, and hitherto undreamed possibilities were knocking about in the minds of England's half-naked, half-starved, and wretchedly housed proletariat.

The world is so accustomed to the historical picture of Queen Victoria following on in smooth dynastic succession to her uncle, William IV, that it is not generally realized how cloudy and uncertain, even apart from the possibility of Adelaide having further offspring, were her beginnings, how inimical to her succession were the powerful Orange Lodges with their thousands of adherents ready at a word to back their Grand Master, the Tory Duke of Cumberland, in opposition to the little Whig princess; their desires strengthened by the consideration that a male sovereign would not necessitate the separation of the Kingdom of Hanover from that of England. Though it is evident that Cumberland had a deep jealousy of his niece, standing as she did between him and the English throne, he must, as already stated, be exonerated personally from ever having the slightest intention of allowing any injury to be done to her. When in 1836 the radical, Hume, suggested in the House that on the death of William IV the Orange Lodges were ready to rise for the Duke of Cumberland and declare him King in the place of Victoria, the Duke dramatically assured the House of Lords that if necessary he was prepared to fight to the death in defense of "that innocent person." But the gutter press delighted to hint that Victoria might meet death in the same way as had the Duke's valet (whom the Duke had been accused, but wrongly, of having murdered), and hints of intrigues, made more sinister by the uncertainty and mystery that surrounded them, must often have found their way to Kensington Palace. The Duke of Cumberland's reputation was such that anything vile could be and, if opportunity arose, invariably was, imputed to him. Kensington Palace, that rambling place in which a dozen people could hide without detection, was then far out of London and very casually guarded, and in the scrimmage and the lawlessness of any political agitation Victoria might easily, if not carefully watched, have been kidnaped by some hostile faction.

Endless must have been the discussions between the Duchess and Conroy when, after an excursion into the outside world, he came riding or driving back beneath the clock belfry into that drowsy courtyard with its numerous windows, bringing to the waiting Duchess in her drawing room now a snippet of news, now a disquieting rumor, now a warning of a hitherto unlooked-for development that might affect the lives of their group. One fact after another of the situation, royal or political, would become apparent to their vigilant eyes. There were so many aspects to be considered, so many members of the royal family whose actions might affect theirs. Above all did they have to reckon with that egregious figure at Carlton House, known to be pliable to the influence of the Duke of Cumberland, whose razor tongue of ridicule he dreaded above all things. The knowledge of how, when George IV was Regent, he had worked to get even his own daughter out of the country by marrying her to William of Orange must always have been in the Duchess' mind, cautioning her not to exasperate him, to be on her guard against ever putting a fuse to that uncertain temper. The success or failure of her plans for the future meant the success or failure of Conroy's; and these shared interests and anxieties were every day intertwining their minds more closely.

Among the dark instincts smoldering within the fetid stews and alleys of that unkempt London of the early nineteenth century was the desire for some public figure to act as a focus for a venomous hate: a desire now slow to be aroused in a people whose varied private interests so occupy their minds that their reactions regarding public individuals have become comparatively temperate. But in the period of which I write this was far from the case. In times of stirred public emotion, out from some side street would come racketing a roaring mob with Hogarthian faces imprinted with every bestial instinct. In the midst of this pandemonium of macabre, cursing humanity would be jerked along, carried on a chair placed on poles, a rough effigy, on its way to be burned, of the man who was at the moment the central point of this macabre mob's fury; a scapegoat of imagination for all the unspeakable misery of their own lives. In the ill-treatment of this stuffed manikin they momentarily received a kind of frenzied compensation. It was a satisfactory orgy of paying back. What a full-blooded evening of delight it was for them, leaping round their object of hate, slashing at it with sticks, spitting, hooting, yelling, screaming....

Apart from the nauseous disgust that any respectable passer-by must have experienced on suddenly finding himself a witness of one of these explosions from the gutters, the aesthetic aspect, lit as the whole scene was by the spasmodic flare of torches tossing about at every angle, must have possessed a dramatic element now entirely absent in our too mechanically dominated existence. With the departure of torches, bringing to birth each evening as darkness fell a fitful, mysterious world within world, displaying not only scenes of horror such as we have just witnessed, but efflorescences of sudden beauty and enchantment—with the vanishing of these leaping tongues of fire our streets have had to sacrifice to utility incomparable visual delights. Cleaving their way through these transformation night scenes would be not only the beautifully painted and emblazoned carriages of the day with four horses and jigging postilions, but still occasionally a "sedan," attended, if the occupant was a person of importance, by eight footmen, their torches lighting up the figure within its luxurious cage. When this luminous procession arrived at its destination the footmen, separating and reforming like figures in a ballet, would place themselves in two rows on each side of the steps of the house, holding their torches aloft to guide the arriving guest. Defunct reminders left to us of all this wild night beauty are here and there visible standing up above the wrought-iron railings by the doorsteps of houses in Bloomsbury, Soho, and elsewhere—the rusty extinguishers into which footmen or linkmen would thrust their torches when they wished to put them out. But if beauty has fled our hours of darkness, many aspects of gruesomeness that accompanied it have departed as well. Not only in the early years, but up to the middle of the nineteenth century, dinner guests would often have their carriages deflected from one street to another by finding the road blocked by a mob surrounding a street fight, often of two women, who, having torn off most of each other's clothing, would continue their clawing and screeching insensible to the fact that they were all but naked.

This was the kind of night London, savage, undisciplined, unpredictable, through which Victoria, as she grew a little older, would often be driven with the Duchess and Lehzen on their way to the opera; a London of which, as they drove along, quickly vanishing vignettes of interest or excitement were visible to them, momentarily brought into being by the gleam from the great oil lamps fixed to the front of the carriage. Inside this roomy vehicle Victoria would be ensconced with her mother and Lehzen. Conroy and old Späth would certainly have been in attendance, and sometimes Lady Conroy, deserting her bed, would come too. Victoria, her thoughts on all the coming pleasure of the luster-lit opera house, of the soaring voices that would soon enchant her ear, would probably have been indifferent to the confused London night through which they were driving, but to the Duchess, these streets of loose disorder, those ill-omened, scarcely human faces that would occasionally surge through the darkness and be for a moment discernable through the carriage windows, must have made apparent what human fuel lay close at hand, ready if circumspectly lit by the Tory party, to flare up in menace to all her desires for herself and Victoria.

5

If on one side of the Duchess of Kent stood as her supporter the figure of Conroy, on the other side his vis-à-vis, and, as far as gaining an ascendancy over her was concerned, his rival, the Duchess' brother, Leopold. Through the Dowager Lady Ilchester's reactions when she first met this young man at the Pavilion, it is apparent that he well knew how to impress with his Coburg charm, his beautiful features, "Enchanting as far as appearance and manners," Lady Ilchester exclaimed in a letter to a friend, "and imagination cannot picture a countenance more justifiable of love at first sight. There is a particularly soft and gentle expression blended with positive manliness of cast." Lady Ilchester would have been surprised if it had been revealed to her what a remarkable amount of chicanery that soft and gentle expression concealed. During these early years of both Leopold and his sister's widowhood he was so constantly with her and his niece that he may almost be considered as one of the Kensington group. As the years went on, however, Leopold was to discover that not even all that positive manliness which had so impressed Lady Ilchester was sufficient to counteract Conroy's insidious, ever-growing influence over his sister Victoire.

Leopold enjoyed giving direction to other people's lives, and most particularly to those of the House of Coburg. Having by his acumen and graceful manners so successfully hoisted himself into the world's saddle, he considered himself especially competent to advise, warn, and instruct. Also for this "craftiest of men," as Princess Lieven dubbed him, there was his own advantage to consider. Now that his own career as future consort to an English Queen had abruptly terminated—"fallen from a height of happiness and grandeur seldom equalled" as he rather naïvely expressed it—he was scouring the horizon for another opening that would give him a further opportunity to display his exceptional faculties. At first, after Charlotte's death, the policy of his bruised mind had been chiefly to keep alive in the English people the remembrance of the intimate relationship to their country that he, Prince Leopold of Coburg, had all but attained. "Do you think the bustle of this life has already effaced Charlotte's memory in the minds of the people?" he wrote after his wife's death to Mrs. Campbell, one of Charlotte's governesses. "It is my pride," he went on, "that I am a living monument of those happy days that offered the country such bright prospects; and so I trust it will be made difficult for them to forget Charlotte as long as they see me," and, further, one might add, that in remembering Charlotte they would still contrive to feel an interest in Charlotte's widowed husband.

After dining with him at Marlborough House, Mrs. Campbell wrote to Lady Ilchester, "He asked me over and over if I thought that 'Charlotte' was still thought of and remembered in Dorsetshire." Continuing about her evening, "There were," she writes, "no ladies, so that I was there as one of the family. The B[ishop] of Salisbury and a Sir Lewis Somebody . . ." and so on. "The Prince was so kind, it was very gratifying. I sat by him, and after dinner he showed me the house, and sat on the sofa by me all the evening, and, except to the Bishop, spoke to no one but me. He said he had many things for me to assist him in, and that he should send Stocky to me very often as his little spy upon me.... The Prince has laid out a great deal of money on Marlborough House in painting and cleaning it, very handsome carpets to the whole range of apartments, and silk furniture, and on my asking if the silk on one sofa was foreign, he seemed quite to reproach me, and said I should never see anything that was not English in his house that he could avoid. I could not help wishing that Mrs. Williams had been with us to judge of the sum that Prince Leopold must have expended in the last three months on English manufactures—magnificent glass lustres in all the rooms. He has also purchased a large collection of fine paintings which are coming over."

Everything in Leopold of human value had been given to Charlotte, that tragic, ebullient girl who, with her loud voice and gawky postures, her whole roystering personality, sounds so peculiarly unattractive. But to Leopold she was without parallel. "What a feeling of love and tranquillity and happiness filled my breast when in the evening we came back home, and she slept with her head gently resting on my heart, and I said to myself: Your strong arm now holds your All, your delight and your treasure!" So he had written to his sister, Countess Mensdorff-Pouilly, after Charlotte's death. And again, "I have had experience of happiness and attained it in the highest degree possible to man." Charlotte had several times prevailed on Lord Liverpool to help save women condemned to death for theft. Among these was a seamstress whom she had set up in some small business. Out of gratitude, her protégée, on every anniversary of Charlotte's death, brought to Claremont "an ornamental composition of dried field flowers." Leopold was so touched by these delicately manipulated offerings, which amounted to over thirty, that he preserved every one of them in his palace at Laeken.

Such residue of affection as there was left over in a character naturally compressed and self-centered, he now bestowed on his niece Victoria, who, so some people thought, had a fugitive look of Charlotte. Every Wednesday evening his carriage would come driving into the Kensington Palace courtyard, and then there would be a family concert around the drawing-room piano. He acted too as yet another of Drina's cohort of instructors, and had a weekly record sent him of her educational progress; and she, with all the eager warmth of her child's heart, became almost romantically devoted to that pale melancholy face that would bend over hers with such tenderness. She would often stay at Claremont with her mother, where she would spring over the flower beds, listen to Uncle Leopold telling her the names of the wild flowers, and be most satisfactorily cosseted by the Claremont housekeeper, old Mrs. Louis, who used to be dresser to Charlotte. Indeed everything at Uncle Leopold's was so altogether delightful to Victoria that when the time came to return to the daily curriculum of Kensington Palace she would dissolve in tears, and in after years wrote to Leopold that at Claremont were spent "the happiest days of my otherwise dull childhood, when I experienced such kindness from you dearest Uncle." However, the reactions of some of Leopold's contemporaries were not so appreciative. "Humbug Leopold," sniggered Creevey. "A damned humbug," jeered Victoria's cousin, Frederick Fitzclarence. "Wearying . . . with his slow speech and his bad reasoning. Leopold is a Jesuit and a bore," opined Princess Lieven.

Though death had mulcted Leopold of his happiness, there was left him, to a certain extent, his position, and at times he liked, in his own lugubrious fashion, to display his still grand plumage by filling the rooms at Marlborough House with a party. "In the evening," writes Lady Granville in the summer of 1819, "we went to Marlborough House. The Regent was there, but in the midst of fat and thin women, and the heat was so great that I never went beyond the first two rooms. Prince Leopold was extremely civil to everybody, and looked pleased at having so many people."

Besides going frequently to Ramsgate, the Kensington party would at times take a change of air at Tunbridge Wells, Malvern, or Broadstairs. At these places, as well as at Claremont, Victoria sat and did her lessons, stuffily enough, in Lehzen's bedroom. Sometimes at these seaside places Leopold would be seen walking along the front in the blowy air with his sister, a little girl at their side in a "plain straw bonnet with a white ribbon round it," while all about them, in the fresh, salty atmosphere, was that gay confusion of nurses and children; bathing machines with their splash-

ing horses; seaside riffraff; rotund bathing women; and lovely or
grotesque bathers in ankle-length swim suits that, a few decades
later, was through Leech's pencil to appear so enchantingly on the
pages of *Punch*.

6

The Duchess naturally continued her acquiescence to the Whig
principles with which the Duke of Kent had imbued her, and not
long after his death invited Wilberforce to visit her one morning
at the palace. But we do not hear of her attempting to keep up to
the level of that enthusiastic attitude toward Robert Owen that her
husband had displayed. The truth is that that vigorous lady was
far too much occupied with the present situation that surrounded
her, and the future possibilities that lay ahead of her, to concern
herself with the education of workers in cotton mills, or the vaster
problem of the regeneration of the entire human race. She did,
however, go with Leopold when he laid the foundation stone of a
new school at Oxshott, and managed to present herself with a slight
panache by saying she would like it to be named the Royal Kent
School. What, naturally, would be of far closer interest to her was
the fact of George IV sending his niece Victoria a present for her
fourth birthday, he having so far paid remarkably little attention
either to her or to her mother. It was, besides, a present of value:
a miniature of himself surrounded with brilliants.* It looks as if,
in bestowing this on her, Victoria's uncle was making her a member
of a very private and intimate order, for ladies only, that he had
evolved a year or two before. "The King is in a good temper,"
Princess Lieven had written from the Pavilion. "He has just insti-
tuted an order with which I find I am the first to be invested. He
has given me his portrait to wear on a blue ribbon. Here is the
explanation of this favour. Lady Conyngham wants to wear it; but
it must be started by someone else; and the public must amuse itself
at the expense of that someone; then Lady Conyngham will wear
it when the joke is stale. I am the person considered suitable. You
see how submissive I am."

* In Mr. Davys' diary is the entry on May 24, 1823, "The King sent his picture set in
diamonds." Quoted from *Queen Victoria and Her Life and Empire*, by the Marquis of
Lorne, 1901.

THE PRINCESS VICTORIA
From the painting by R. Westall, R.A.

SIR JOHN CONROY IN 1827
From the portrait by Fowler
By courtesy of Sir Edward Hanmer, Bt.

Not only did Victoria receive a present from George IV on this particular birthday but also she was taken by her mother to Carlton House to thank him. Exceptionally observant child that she was, the romantically upholstered atmosphere of Carlton House—rose brocade swirling over the walls and festooning round the windows with their inner curtains of white taffeta; pictures suspended by golden cords and tassels; ceilings amorphous with blue skies and clouds—all this, if only subconsciously, would have mirrored itself within her mind.

We are told that she "always seems to have contrived to highly amuse her 'Uncle King'" who had his own, most successful, technique for children. The Duchess, in coaching Victoria to address George IV as "Uncle King" (for presumably it was the Duchess), displayed the most tactful shrewdness, the appellation being at once a reminder to the King of his close relationship to his niece, and at the same time including a little curtsy to his exalted position. Accustomed to the monumental size of her Uncle Sussex, Victoria would have accepted the bulk of this far more important Uncle as quite normal. To the Duchess, his getup at this party, if the same as that in which he had appeared not so very long ago at one of the Ancient Music Concerts, would have certainly seemed remarkable. "The King," so Mr. Wollaston, one of the audience at this particular concert, observed, "makes himself a strange figure by drawing-in his great body with a broad belt, and by the close buttoning of a kind of uniform jacket more than dress coat . . . and hiding the lower part of his face with a large black neck-cloth, and then swelling his shoulders and the upper part of his person with tags and embroidery, and covering it with orders, instead of the simple Star and Garter worn by his father, and yet for a man of near 60 he contrives to look young by the help of a wig without powder; and his air and manners were as graceful as they used to be."

Not only did Victoria have these two excitements of George IV's dinner and present for her birthday, but in the evening she gave a children's party "to whom she showed her many presents spread out on a table." At once a Kate Greenaway picture springs to the eye of a roomful of little boys and girls: small, silky heads above long muslin frocks; little boys in white-duck trousers and pea-green coats, their hair, as was the fashion, curled for the occasion; all of them tiptoeing round the table, peering, envying, longing to finger and play with those most desirable toys, but not, apparently, encouraged to do so. We are told of these white ducks and pea-green coats gracing a children's ball given by Victoria's Uncle Clarence at his house at Bushey. These parties given by the Clarences were not parties that Victoria attended, for that most genial of men, and his wife, Adelaide, that most complaisant and agreeable of women, lived surrounded by numerous illegitimate offspring of the Duke by the actress Mrs. Jordan. It was hardly to be expected that the Duchess of Kent, who insisted on the stiffest moral hedge round Victoria, would allow her to become intimate in a house where not only were Mrs. Jordan's theatrical friends made welcome, but where, over one of the mantelpieces, hung a portrait of this former mistress of the host. A portrait incidentally that, on his marriage, the Duke had had taken down, but which Adelaide, when she heard what he had done, had had replaced, saying, "it was the picture of the mother of your children, and it was not fit it should be displaced. You must gratify me and let it remain."

7

Though the actual possibility of Adelaide having a further child was to remain up to the death of her husband—in 1837—and for some months after, the probability grew ever more remote, and, in consequence, the dynastic importance of the schoolroom Victoria increased. It may have been this fact that induced George IV to invite his sister-in-law, Feodore, and Victoria, then a child of seven, for a three days' visit to Windsor, where they were to stay at Cumberland Lodge. Victoria's Aunt Mary of Gloucester was at the moment staying there too, the King himself being, not at the Castle, but nearby at the Royal Lodge. When the Kensington Palace group arrived Victoria was taken to make her curtsy to George IV. "Give me your little paw," he said; and the picture of this handshake between the rouged, upholstered old satyr and the fresh little nursery child, whose long future lay before her like a rolled-up scroll, has become one of the heirlooms of history. Then the great flaccid face was lowered for her to kiss, and all her life she was to remember her revulsion as her lips touched that heavily enameled skin.

All the same, already phenomenally quick at noticing nuances of personality, this child of seven always remembered too her Uncle's "wonderful dignity and charm of manner."

During this visit Lehzen and her pupil, Lady Conyngham's daughter Maria, and Lord Graves, one day all crowded into a pony carriage drawn by four gray ponies, to take Victoria to the Sandpit Gate to see the King's collection of gazelles and chamois. Another day the drive was to Virginia Water, this time the Duchess and Feodore being of the party. The lake and the grounds around it were enclosed to form a secluded garden of pleasure for the King and his friends, where, with his Chinese Pagoda, Fishing Temples, marquees, and pavilions; ambrosial food provided by the Windsor Castle chef; royal barges; swans afloat on the silk-smooth water of the lake, and music filling in the air, George IV had induced an atmosphere of celestial ease in which to tuck himself away from the frets of life. He would have himself conveyed there in a closely shuttered carriage, apprehensive, if seen, of the filth, stones, carrots, or other objects that might come hurtling against the panels accompanied by the foulest abuse from his unloving subjects. Then, after suffering temporary burial within that confined and stuffy darkness, this eclipse from a too outspoken world, he would, once safely within the guarded precincts of Virginia Water, emerge as if born again into a brighter sphere, assured that within the leafy seclusion of this place, rocked with music, cosseted and flattered by his friends, he would enter into all the sweet illusions of popularity and well-being.

As the carriage with the Cumberland Lodge party went trotting along through this Elysium they met a grander equipage, a phaeton which the King himself was driving, his sister Mary by his side. His eye fell on Victoria. "Pop her in," he exclaimed, and she was lifted up and squeezed in between him and Aunt Gloucester, who gripped her around the waist. "Mamma was much frightened," wrote Queen Victoria in later life. In a print of George IV as Prince of Wales, driving to the races, he is depicted in a phaeton with a team of six horses, a postilion on one of the leaders. This phaeton is a cockle-shaped affair, swung up to an extreme height above its curving springs. If this phaeton that day at Virginia Water was built at all on the same lines, it is quite understandable that the

Duchess trembled at seeing Victoria, in every sense her one *point d'appui* in life, recklessly borne away from her in such a tippety vehicle. But Victoria herself was "greatly pleased," especially at the splendid scarlet and blue of the liveries of the King's grooms; the quieter crimson and green being the colors for the rest of the royal family. It is curious—but typical of a daughter of the Duke of Kent—that a child of seven should have especially noticed this sartorial detail. The King drew up at the Fishing Temple. The excited child got the impression of there being "numbers of great people there, amongst whom was the Duke of Dorset, then Master of the Horse." Floating on the lake by the Temple was an enormous barge, on which this colorful company now placed themselves, and started to fish. Close by, too, was another barge from which a band was tossing its gay and flashing notes into the air. Delightfully in keeping with the general fantasia of the whole scene were the oarsmen in striped jackets of white and blue, white trousers, and straw hats. However, the King today had more than either music or fishing. The Venus-faced Feodore was by his side, and that day he "paid great attention to my sister," wrote Queen Victoria in after years, "and some people fancied he might marry her!! She was very lovely then—about eighteen—and had charming manners, about which the King was extremely particular." It is indeed quite possible that it was to have Feodore in his vicinity for a few days that had originally made the King ask the Kensington party to come and stay.

The day in any case was certainly providing the watchful Duchess of Kent with experiences she had not foreseen. First, that reckless drive for Victoria; now all this attention to Feodore from England's great man, which attentions must have raised in her mother's mind every kind of speculation of the most worrying nature.

For Victoria, on the contrary, the visit was providing a succession of felicities: and the sum of these joys was not yet complete. She was taken one evening after dinner to the royal Lodge, and in after years she still remembered the conservatory, with lit colored globes making velvet shadows beneath whatever ferns or flowers spread themselves below; and Uncle King, the royal family, and others "sitting in a corner of the large saloon." The King came up to her, and taking her hand, said, with his unerring flair for charming when he wished to charm, "Now, Victoria, the band is in the next room, and shall play any tune you please. What shall it be?"

"Oh, Uncle King, I should like 'God Save the King.' "

And again, when these halcyon three days were nearing their end, and he asked her "what she had most enjoyed during her visit," pat came the small voice, "The drive with you."

Was this, in such a young child, a case of almost incredible tact, or was she on both occasions simply telling the truth? That impromptu drive in Uncle King's swiftly moving phaeton probably was what she had most enjoyed; and such an observant child no doubt did delight in seeing the whole grand Windsor party—the men in their romantic uniforms, the women like exotic birds—all rising simultaneously to their feet in homage to her Uncle when "God Save the King" was played.

From her corner Princess Lieven had been noting every phase in this *rapprochement* between England's present and future monarchs. "In spite of the caresses the King lavished on her, I could see," she remarks, "that he did not like dandling on his sixty-four knee this little bit of the future, aged 7."

Curiously different from each other must have been the thoughts of the three, the Duchess, Feodore, and Victoria, as finally they drove along the country roads back to Kensington Palace. Everything points to the probability that it was on this visit that the Duchess was made aware of the dangerous interest that George IV was beginning to show in Feodore, and it is quite probable that his undisguised attentions to her at Virginia Water and the Duchess' fear of any preposterous developments in that direction were the reasons for the decided step that she took a few months later regarding this lovely girl; whose life she had always saddened by relentless overdiscipline.

The whole position of the Duchess in relation to her two daughters, their different destinies ever present in her mind, is too full of complications to be entirely unraveled, but it is a question whether her harshness to Feodore arose from personal jealousy of her young allurement, or from jealousy for the sake of Victoria, whose bright but rather birdy little countenance forecasted each day more clearly that any definite beauty was going to pass her by. Feodore's misery till, at twenty, by marrying Prince Ernest of

Hohenlohe-Langenburg, she at last escaped from her mother, hardens one's heart against the author of it. This elder daughter's visits with the rest of the party to Claremont were remembered by her as being "the few pleasant days I spent during my youth. I always left Claremont with tears for Kensington Palace." Again, referring in later years in a letter to Victoria, to her own life from fourteen to twenty, she wrote, "Not to have enjoyed the pleasures of youth is nothing, but to have been deprived of all intercourse, and not one cheerful thought in that dismal existence of ours was very hard. My only happy time was going or driving out with you and Lehzen; then I could speak and look as I liked. I escaped some years of imprisonment, which you, my poor darling sister, had to endure after I was married." "Those years of trial," she goes on, reacting to the moral values in which her browbeating mother had trained her, "were, I am sure, very useful to us both, though certainly not pleasant. Thank God they are over!" But now, though she was about eighteen, those incredibly dreary days were not yet over, and to this intimidated girl, after the realization at Windsor of her own powers of pleasing, and of all the sweets of admiration, this return to Kensington must have seemed like being crushed back into a dark box.

About a year before this she had become involved in a secret episode. The Duke of Sussex's son, Augustus D'Este—by then just over thirty, and a Lieutenant Colonel in a Dragoon regiment— had precipitately and passionately fallen in love with her: and, to our surprise, Baroness Späth, that usually dim and always most correct figure, suddenly steps into the foreground briskly encouraging Augustus' suit. Her activities, needless to say, were circumspectly hidden from the Duchess. We see the lady in waiting, like a benign if elderly fairy, skipping to and fro between lover and inamorata with their letters; arranging their meetings; and in her unwise zeal even going so far as to hint that she saw "no reason why the Duchess of Kent should refuse her consent." But when one day Feodore found Späth slipping into her hand two gold rings sent by Augustus, she took fright and refused to put them on. "Further pressed," she decided to reveal the whole affair to her mother. Inevitably, she received "a severe reprimand," after which the Duchess went to Augustus' father to enlighten him as to what had been happening; while Späth scurried the rings back to Augustus with a covering note "to the effect that all was over." The Duke of Sussex then wrote him a letter, the intention of which, according to Augustus, was "to insult, to torture, and to outrage every sentiment of Honor, of moral principle and of integrity in his son."

After this, Augustus D'Este and his grandiloquent phrases fade out of the Kensington scene, and, doubtless, Feodore was kept in stricter purdah than ever. The Duchess seems to have shown less austerity to her younger than she did to her elder daughter, as, after her death, Feodore wrote to Victoria, "I was often jealous of you, and told dear Mama she loved you more," on which the Duchess would give "one of her sad smiles" and say, "*Ich liebe euch beide gleich.*" *

As for the residue of the Windsor visit left in Victoria's mind, the Fishing Temple and the Pagoda, the phaeton and the scarlet-and-blue liveries, the Conservatory and the colored lamps, and that gay bewildering company of people, all presided over by Uncle King with his brown wig and raddled cheeks, the whole picture was as we know from herself to remain in her mind for life: a confused but enchanting scene, forever slightly vibrating to the rhythmic thudding of the royal band.

One thing Feodore's quoted letter makes markedly clear. The Duchess did not wish her elder daughter to be taken notice of, had no intention, if she could prevent it, of allowing her, seductive young creature that she was, to come to the fore in England within the frame of a successful marriage. She was to be prevented from any possibility of it by being "deprived of all intercourse." The Duchess had a clear plan before her: to place her younger daughter on the English throne and, before doing so, to draw to herself all the prestige and position that she possibly could. For some reason, on which one cannot exactly put one's finger, there was in this scheme no place for Feodore. The upshot of the situation was that it was arranged that this far too attractive girl should, for a time, be removed to Germany, and, whether by accident or design, not long after the Windsor visit, Victoria's grandmother, the old

---

* "I love you both just the same."

Dowager Duchess of Saxe-Saalfeld-Coburg, came to England, bringing with her Charles, the young Prince of Leiningen, Victoria's half-brother, whom so far she had never seen. The Kensington party was staying at Claremont at the time, and Victoria was on the doorstep in welcome when the traveling party's carriage drove up. "I recollect," wrote Queen Victoria in later years, "the excitement and anxiety I was in at this event—going down the great flight of steps to meet her when she got out of the carriage."

A bent old woman emerged, and laboriously climbed the steps with the aid of her stick. This accomplished, and once in her room, she sat down, and at once her gaze was turned on this grandchild of whom through her mother she had heard so much. The "fine clear blue eyes" took in the eager little girl in front of her. "A fine child," she remarked. The verdict had been given, and given satisfactorily. Many thoughts, many schemes were evolving behind that timeworn but intelligent old face. Those two small Coburg cousins of Victoria, Ernest and Albert, were constantly under her care at the Coburgs' country home, The Rosenau, and certain weavings for the future had already begun in their grandmother's mind. Those weavings closely concerned Victoria and Albert, and, as this old lady and the child confronted each other, it was as if, within the quiet air of that Claremont room, those two names to be linked together in futurity, momentarily sounded for the first time.

It was not long before Victoria's enthusiasm over the arrival of these new relations began to evaporate, for she found herself constantly compelled to take long and extremely tedious drives seated by the side of her grandmother, probably because the Duchess could not herself endure the boredom of these endless trottings along the lanes around Claremont. But in November the Coburg group departed, and Feodore went with them.

8

The grounds on which, in the year following the visit of Victoria's grandmother, George IV raised Fräulein Lehzen to the rank of a Hanoverian Baroness are open to speculation. We do know, however, that it was Princess Sophia who had asked the King to give this honor to the governess, and unless she had had a high opinion of Lehzen she certainly would not have suggested it. Possibly it may have been simply to please Sophia that George IV, that most good-natured of brothers, as far as his sisters were concerned, acquiesced. About the same time he created Conroy a Knight Commander of the Hanoverian Order. With Conroy's two friends at Court, Lady Conyngham and Sir William Knighton, one on each side to nudge the now often confused-minded old libertine, it would be easy to guess the impulsion behind Conroy's knighthood. On the other hand, it was natural enough that, with the contingency of Edward's daughter succeeding to the throne becoming each year more probable, George IV thought it only suitable that his sister-in-law's comptroller should be given a little gilding.

The Windsor visit, and, later, this upraising of her household, appear to have given the Duchess the conviction that she could now venture to bring herself and her child a shade more into the open, that that "unobtrusive tenour of her life" which Canning had on one occasion praised in the House could now be revealed more clearly to the British public; and that it should be impressed on them, and most especially on the Salic group with their predilection for that extreme Tory, the Duke of Cumberland, what a perfect little Whig sovereign was being prepared for them behind the Wren façade of Kensington Palace. She and her daughter would, so she decided, quietly slide into the consciousness of the country under the aegis of religion. Sitting down, she composed a long letter, to be sent to both the Bishop of London and the Bishop of Lincoln. In this she said that Victoria would be eleven in May, and that she felt the time had now come for "some test" of her education, and that she would like the bishops to come and personally examine her daughter.

The concluding sentence of his letter ran, "When she was at a proper age she commenced attending Divine Service regularly with me, and I have every feeling that she has religion at Her heart, that she is morally impressed with it to that degree that she is less liable to err by its application to Her feelings as a Child capable of reflection."

As the involutions of this final phrase tormented the bishops' ears they may well have thought it advisable that someone fully acquainted with English syntax should overlook the education that was being given to the Duke of Kent's daughter. Flattered by the Duchess' request, they arrived at the palace for this viva voce as required. The bowing divines and the tiny, ten-year-old curtsying figure confronted each other. "A great variety of questions were put": history, scripture, chronology, geography, arithmetic, Latin followed each other. In none did Lehzen's pupil flounder, or, if she occasionally did, the bishops were too gallant to record it. In their final report they affirmed that her answers on every subject were "equally satisfactory," and they could do not better, so they assured the Duchess, than urge her to continue her daughter's education on the same lines on which she had begun.

At intervals suspicions arose in the country that the Duchess was a papist; the idea was strengthened by the fact that some of her German relations were Catholics, and it is probable that this Kensington schoolroom examination by the bishops, taking place the year after the passing of the Bill for Catholic Emancipation, was at bottom a political gesture on the part of the Duchess and Conroy. Into such a tornado of emotion had the country been flung over the Catholic question, such apprehension had it raised in the minds of the Tories who saw in the Bill an adumbration of the Pope's triple tiara, that it is understandable that the two who daily confabulated together at Kensington wished publicly to emphasize that though the young Princess Victoria was being imbued with Whig principles, her education, religious and secular, was thoroughly approved by the Church of England, and that no faintest tincture of heresy tainted the Kensington Palace schoolroom.

It seems to have been when Victoria was about eleven or twelve that she gradually, and not suddenly, according to the wellworn legend, became aware that hers was not to be the usual flower-decked path of a royal cousin of the throne but that herself was the victim—for so she envisaged it—destined, once her Uncle Clarence had died, to mount the throne in his place. Those who surrounded her all gave different accounts as to how the realization of the unparalleled position she was to occupy first dawned on her. Lehzen put forward one version, Mr. Davys another, the Duchess of Kent a third. One thing is clear. If, as it seems, she had for some time had suspicions, these became a certainty through her one day pondering over a genealogical tree of her father's side of the family. It was Lehzen who said that when the full import of the genealogical tree became clear to her, the child exclaimed, "I will be good." But in later years Queen Victoria declared that she had never said anything of the sort. Had she forgotten, and Lehzen remembered? Whichever of them was right, those four simple but conclusive words have bestowed on her a kind of signature phrase that one would not lightly take from her.

When she was Queen, she said not only that the realization of her position filtered into her mind gradually, but that the knowledge "made her very unhappy." And in these words the child's character, so far only visible in snatches, and chiefly in moments of temper and screaming rebellion, begins to lie open to our view. She was only a little girl when the landscape of her future life became indubitably revealed to her—a little girl who, we are told, enjoyed covering small boxes with tinsel under Späth's supervision, making the snapdragons in the Kensington flower beds go pop, and who went eagerly jolting on her pony round "old Fozzy's" then fashionable riding school. To her the realization of this coming glory that would have fluffed up the mind of any ordinary child with a glamour of self-importance only brought a sense of apprehension, of inescapable responsibility that henceforth lay over her future like a somber cloud. Her naturally extremely gay disposition had been, though for the time only, too heavily tutored by her evangelical upbringing for her to be able to view such a future in any other light.

9

All these years Princess Sophia, that lonely occupant of her group of rooms in Kensington Palace, had been in the habit of constantly coming across the courtyard to visit the Kents, and great must have been the Duchess' perturbation when, about 1829, a horrible rumor gathered around this saddened daughter of George III. It began at first to be whispered, and then to be openly asserted, that her secret son by General Garth, now grown up and in the army, was in reality, not the General's offspring, but that of the Duke of Cumberland, whose character in the eyes of the world was such that he was now believed to have been capable of seducing his sister.

Princess Sophia, unable to come forward and defend herself or her brother from this scurrilous and unfounded scandal, tortured by this hideous twist given to her early romance with her father's old equerry, sat in her rooms at Kensington Palace, and suffered. "The poor woman has always said this business would be her death," wrote Creevey. If she opened the pages of *The Times*, the *Morning Chronicle*, the *Globe*, the *Examiner*, there, staring at her, were references to the topic that she knew only too well now filled every mind.

If Cumberland had before appeared in a bad light, his enemies now regarded him as Satan himself. But accustomed to calumnies, he stiffened himself to meet this latest one; and the accusation now sank into its proper place, with the equally false one of his having murdered his valet. Scarcely, however, had the commotion over this *canard* died down when he was accused of having attempted to assault Lady Lyndhurst when paying a call on her. He protested that, on the contrary, it was Lady Lyndhurst who had made advances to him; and this new scandal ended in a blur of confusion, for it was never conclusively proved who had made overtures to whom. Unbelievably, six months had scarcely passed before yet again a smell of brimstone surrounded the Duke. It now was reported that he was having a liaison with Lady Graves, who, incidentally, was a bespectacled woman of between fifty and sixty, and the mother of fifteen children. Lord Graves, a lord of the bedchamber to the King, was living apart from his wife, and he wrote her a letter saying he did not believe the rumors. However, a few hours later, he cut his throat. *The Times* published an article entitled, "Melancholy Suicide in High Life," in which the inference was that the Duke of Cumberland had not only murdered his valet but had now, in addition, murdered Lord Graves.

10

In the autumn of 1830 the market place of Devizes, that sunny stretch around which sprawl its little Georgian and Queen Anne buildings, received a disturbance in the sudden arrival of the whole Kensington party. They were on their way to stay with the Watson Taylors at Erlestoke Park, a few miles farther on; but when they arrived at the market-place inn, its name emphasized by a large model of a bear standing on the roof of the portico, the Kensington postilions drew up. The Bear Inn was the birthplace of Sir Thomas Lawrence, who was so immensely in vogue at that time that the Duchess, finding herself at the house where he had been born, asked if any of his portraits were "still extant in the town." Yes, there was one of a Miss White of the Castle Inn at Marlborough, and it belonged to Mr. Burrough Smith of Devizes. The question was, would the owner lend it for a few days to the Duchess of Kent? Mr. Burrough Smith was approached. He was all acquiescence. The picture came hurrying. It was stuffed into one of the carriages, and, having acquired this awkward addition to their luggage, off galloped the cortege, leaving Mr. Burrough Smith to cogitate on the peculiar habits of traveling royalty.

Diminutive Tom Moore, who, softly singing his own mellifluous verses, had fluttered into the hearts of peers and royalties, highbrows and nostalgically minded ladies, lived in a *cottage orné* not far from Devizes. George IV's favorite sister, Princess Augusta, had set some of Irish Tom's verses to music; and, incidentally, he was a close friend of Byron. All things considered, the Watson Taylors must have felt they ran few risks in trying the effect of him on the Duchess of Kent's sensibilities, and had asked him to stay at Erlestoke for the week end when the Kensington party would be there. He tells us how on an October Saturday he walked into Erlestoke about four o'clock, and was "amused at being behind the scenes to see the fuss and preparation for a royal reception." Dinner once over, the Duchess and Moore were soon at the piano chirruping away to each other with equal satisfaction to both. This satisfaction, however, does not seem to have been shared by everyone in the room, as Moore complains that he and the Duchess would have gone on "much longer if there had not been rather premature preparations for bed." The next day there was a big dinner party and, afterward, "Great anxiety for music" expressed by the company in general, "but," writes Moore, "the Duchess very prudently (it being Sunday) and very much to my satisfaction, protested against it." However, the following morning, once having eaten her breakfast, she was crying out for piano and song. The eleven-year-old Victoria also uplifted her voice. With the knowledge in our minds of the Duchess' consuming desire for the regency, it is delightful to hear her on this occasion singing, not once, so remarks Moore, but three or four times, "Go where Glory waits Thee."

Meanwhile Victoria, industrious child, had found time, during this brief week-end visit, to make a copy of Lawrence's picture.

CHAPTER V

ENTANGLEMENTS AT KENSINGTON PALACE

Except for the Duchess of Kent's successful affair with Victoria and the prelates of the Church, she and Conroy did not venture, while George IV was still alive, to push her own and her daughter's claims for recognition. The reactions of that burlesque King, dawdling out his last years at Windsor, were too unpredictable. While he still lived discretion alone warned the Duchess to remain an unobtrusive figure in the background. But during those early months of 1830, when it was evident the King could not last much longer, the minds of both her and her brother Leopold began to stretch themselves, to look about in anticipation of what changes might be forthcomnig, what fortuitous pickings there might be for themselves. Princess Lieven's assiduous eye noted this awakening. They were both, so she wrote, "holding themselves very high, as if the throne were to be theirs to-morrow." "Leopold," she further observed, "does not show himself, but works silently underground."

On the twenty-sixth of June in 1830, George IV lay dead: and when that former royal admiral, the Duke of Clarence, drove up from Bushey Park on his way to St. James's, a long crape veil blowing back from his white hat as he bowed from side to side, an entirely new prospect opened before the watchful eyes at Kensington Palace.

At first the new King was in such a froth of excitement at finding himself on the throne. His nautical gaiety of mind blew away all the cloying, oriental-potentate atmosphere of George IV's Court, and England found herself possessed of a stubby, red-faced sailor-King, the most well-intentioned of rulers, whose desire to be genial to the subjects that Providence had bestowed on him made him at times ignore the Court forms and formulas in what was certainly a surprising manner. His "This is a damned bad pen you have given me" on the day of his accession, as he signed the declarations, still enlivens the page of history; and when on a certain occasion the Freemasons filed into the royal presence expecting a ceremonious audience, "Gentlemen," exclaimed King William, "if my love for you equalled my ignorance of everything concerning you, it would be boundless."

William IV's one wish regarding his brother Cumberland was that "he would live out of the country." He could not force him to decamp, but he took from him the Gold Stick, in virtue of which Cumberland had, by remarkably shrewd management, "usurped the functions of all the other colonels of the regiments of the Guards, and put himself always about the late King." William IV tactfully gave as his reason for this move that "the Duke's rank is too high to perform those functions." Cumberland, who had made a habit of keeping his horses in the part of the royal stables allotted to the use of the King's consort, was now clearly told that his horses must go to make room for those of Queen Adelaide. At once came a splutter of damns and refusals. However, on being informed that if his grooms did not remove them, the King's grooms would, Cumberland gave in. Though William clipped his brother's claws, it was noticeable that at the same time he "began immediately," writes Greville, "to do good-natured things, to provide for old guards and professional adherents." He had no doubt plenty of impecunious hangers-on, for, till he came to the throne, his life had been spent not with the socially important but with a heterogeneous circle much besprinkled with his mistress' theatrical friends. "His life," wrote a contemporary, "has been hitherto passed in obscurity and neglect in miserable poverty." He was made "ridiculous from his grotesque ways and little meddling curiosity . . . nobody ever invited him into their house, or thought it necessary to honour him with any mark of attention or respect."

Such was the man—odd, bluff, lovable, absurd, both simple and shrewd, who was now the final obstacle in the path of the Duchess and Conroy's shared ambition: the final obstacle in the sense that, unless he had the grace to die before Victoria came of age in 1837, her mother would have no chance of becoming Regent; and to attain that position had now become her fixed idea. Hers and Conroy's, for if she rose to be Regent, he, in his own orbit, would rise too. The moment the Duke of Clarence became King, all his and his wife's years of steadfast kindness to Victoire dropped from her mind. From now on her chief occupation was to be the endeavor to acquire for herself as much prestige as she possibly could, and, incidentally, to flout and tease that most good-natured of royal couples. No more was to be bestowed on them that once sweet foreign smile of Victoire's; lost forever to Adelaide were those German prayers that she and Edward's widow used to sigh out together.

Conroy's investigating, perspicacious mind was all around the new monarch's in a moment: summing him up, discounting, in the manner of those who are themselves of little worth, what was of worth in him, gleefully fastening on his clownish quality as providing a splendid Aunt Sally for himself and his royal Duchess. For even Conroy had his blind spot. He misjudged both William IV and the child Victoria; ignoring the fact that the seemingly absurd and the seemingly defenseless often possess hidden forces that may suddenly manifest in the most surprising and inconvenient manner.

2

The Duchess' first gesture in the new reign was to write to the Duke of Wellington expressing her view that she might now be treated as Dowager Princess of Wales, with an income for herself and Victoria in proportion to that title, and for it to be entirely under her control. As the Duke of Kent never had been, and it was out of the question that he ever would have been, created Prince of Wales, her demand was ridiculous, and it is surprising that her crafty Irishman should have allowed her to take such a false step. Naturally, the Duke replied that her requests were "inadmissible." The Duchess, and it is proof of her captious nature, took umbrage at this sensible answer, and for a long time refused even to speak to Wellington. This childish suggestion shown up for what it was worth, Victoire must have been puzzled for the moment in what direction to move. But suddenly her horizon cleared. Lord Grey emphasized in the House of Lords the advisability of passing a

Regency Bill. He pointed out the possibility that, before Parliament again met, their present King might have died (my "memento mori," commented William IV), and then, "continuing to give his reasons for a Regency, hinted at the dark intrigues of which the succession was the object. He said that in the event of the demise of the Crown before the assembling of the next House of Commons the utmost confusion might prevail."

Lord Eldon pointed out the possibility that after William IV's death a child of his might yet be born, and that arrangements ought to be made for an *ad interim* sovereign. Later, Lord Grey framed the Regency Bill in which Princess Victoria was named, apart from possible offspring of William IV, as heir to the throne. Further provisions in the Bill were that if William IV left an heir Queen Adelaide should be Regent, but if Victoria succeeded to the throne the Duchess of Kent was to be Regent during her minority. If, however, William died leaving Queen Adelaide *enceinte*, Princess Victoria, if of age, would occupy the throne till her uncle's heir arrived. Strange as was this Box and Cox arrangement, in the circumstances it was the only feasible one that could be devised.

After the Bill had been carried the Duchess was granted an additional £10,000 a year for the household and education of Princess Victoria. When the delightful news was given to Victoire of her own and her daughter's now securely recognized position, when she saw that longed-for idea of herself as Regent thus made a possibility, she burst into tears, and sobbed out, "This is the first really happy day I have spent since I lost the Duke of Kent."

Extremely gratified at these attentions, the Duchess of Kent accompanied the King, the Queen, and the King's sister, Princess Augusta, to the House of Lords. As the royal group appeared in Palace Yard, cheers were called for by the onlookers for the Duchess of Kent and Princess Victoria. Devoted, even tenderly devoted, as Queen Adelaide was to her little Kent niece, this particular visit to the House of Lords, emphasizing, by bringing into the glare of daylight, her own failure to provide an heir to the throne, reminding her that the only child she possessed was that small marble effigy in her sitting room at Windsor—all this bringing forward of Victoria must have been to poor Adelaide painful to a degree. Sir James Hudson, who was watching her from among the crowd, noticed, as the cheers tore the air, the piteously sad look that passed across her features; a "more refined or thoughtful face one could not imagine." At her side, the very antithesis of herself, was displayed the upstanding figure of the Duchess, at the moment positively abloom with triumph. It was, however, noticeable that the almost too exultant getup which she had thought suitable for the occasion could not conceal "a certain German homeliness," a something a shade crude that was already beginning to work to the surface of the seductive creature whom, some twelve years ago, the Duke of Kent had married. However, apparent as well to James Hudson's scrutinizing eye was her "air of character and mental strength." Compared with her, Adelaide at this moment in Palace Yard, her face not only "disfigured by a scorbutic affection" but congested by a cough that every moment shook her body, seemed a mere nothing by the side of her acclaimed sister-in-law. So quietly did this veritable *ange du ciel* play her part in life, so lacking was she in any kind of worldly glamour, that history has treated her slightingly enough; but when she was alive those close to her recognized at least some of her qualities. "A far cleverer woman," wrote Princess Lieven, "than they generally give her credit for."

3

The new King's hilarity on first coming into power was soon dispersed by constitutional worries. In 1831 the country was in upheaval over the Reform Bill, and the bitter feelings engendered, the acrimonious tussles between Whigs and Tories, were such that William IV was even opposed to having a coronation for fear of political hostilities being brought too much to the fore. He went so far as to take legal advice as to whether he could dispense altogether with this ceremony which to his mind was merely theatrical and expensive nonsense. Eventually, however, he did submit, but stipulated that the cost to the country should be only one tenth of all that the sensational fanfare of George IV's coronation had cost. The Tory peers, shocked at this royal economy, began murmuring that they would not attend. William was not disturbed; merely remarking, "I anticipate from that, greater convenience of room and less heat."

Meanwhile, opportunity had come to Leopold. This year he was made King of the Belgians, having previously been offered the Greek crown, which, after infinite discussions and divagations, advances and withdrawals, he had refused.

This figure who softly trod through life shrouded in circumspection had by now, though only forty, become so hypochondriacal, that he was almost a case for a pathologist. He wore a wig for fear of catching cold; rode a pony instead of a horse because the movement was less violent; and for some reason propped his mouth ajar, before going to sleep, with gold wedges. His air of melancholy too was deepening.

His acceptance of the Belgian crown had necessitated a good deal of adjustment: he had to leave forever the place of his marriage happiness; to stifle his memories of Charlotte by taking a new wife—Princess Louise, daughter of Louis Philippe—and to settle up his financial affairs in England, which by now were in a sad mess. His debts amounted to eighty thousand pounds, but not only did Britain compassionately agree to paying these for him, but it was also arranged he should be given ten thousand a year for the upkeep of Claremont. The produce of the Claremont gardens he arranged to have sold in the markets, in this way continuing to draw a yearly income from England up to the day of his death. This financial tenderness to a man whose one connection with Britain was that he had, if indirectly and unintentionally, been the means of the death of the heir to the throne, can only be accounted for by a belief in his exceptional capacities for assiduity in the right quarters.

But to a little girl in Kensington Palace all these public arrangements spelled only one lacerating fact: that her dear, dear Uncle Leopold would no longer be one of the intimates about her but a distant figure on a throne; not so distant, indeed, as if he had accepted the Greek crown (and on learning how many miles lay between Greece and England she had shed tears), but still, farther than when he was at Claremont. First, Feodore had disappeared, and now Uncle Leopold. At eleven or twelve certain traits in the little girl were becoming evident, and one of the most noticeable was a convolvulus-like clinging to those who showed her kindness. Lehzen had discovered that, once these affectionate feelings were stirred, they, and they alone, could be played on to deflect her from her often tempestuous determination to get her own way. With these warm affections went a strong sense of loyalty. As the years went winding on, Lehzen found refuge from what must have been for her a cold and lonely atmosphere in the growing companionship of this emphatic and most interesting little creature under her care, and gradually began to confide in her all sorts of personal and private matters. But even in schoolroom dust-ups—and scuffles between them there were, when, annoyed with Lehzen, a lesser child would have snatched at those easy revenges of betrayal that lay in her hand—Victoria remained staunch and said nothing.

It appears that up to his departure for Belgium Leopold had had a good deal of influence of a steadying kind on his sister, but, once he was gone, Conroy was left in possession of the Duchess of Kent's mind: a mind that unfortunately was to become ever more responsive to every ill-conceived notion that came skipping into her comptroller's head. It is obvious he took a sniggering pleasure in egging her on to exasperate that "little, old, red-nosed, weather-beaten, jolly-looking person"—as one of his subjects described him—who from his throne was so earnestly trying to do his best for the country. Already, in 1830, while the Kent group had been staying at Ramsgate, a small opportunity had occurred for flouting King William. The Duchess had announced the presence of herself and Victoria in a house on the East Cliff by running up the royal standard, which flapped away in the coastal breezes for all both on land and sea to contemplate. This preliminary impertinence in the new King's reign, the royal standard being his prerogative, was, however, allowed to pass without comment. Soon another chance for the Duchess and Conroy to tease him arose. As the coronation approached the Duchess gathered that she was not to be given what she considered her rightful position at the ceremony. Authorities vary as to her precise cause of annoyance, but it certainly hinged on the question of precedence. One account says that she had heard it had been arranged that the King's brothers were to walk in front of the Duke of Kent's widow; another, that Victoria was to take precedence of her mother, led by the hand by her new show-governess, the Duchess of Northumberland, whom her Uncle William had bestowed on Victoria as a kind of schoolroom ornament. This dignified lady in no way interfered with Lehzen's monopoly. In fact she was never once permitted to see Victoria alone, but she inspected her copybooks and her drawings, and listened to her playing the piano or reciting. Afterward she recorded her own reactions to these efforts of Victoria, and then sent off her comments to the King.

Whatever the Duchess of Kent's precise cause of umbrage over the coronation, when Lord Howe wrote, by order of the King, to inquire whom she wished to carry her coronet, he received no reply. He tried again. Kensington Palace remained silent.

"I will get you an answer," exclaimed the King, and, telling Howe to write a further letter, himself signed it "Wm. R." At this Conroy bestirred himself so far as to write on the Duchess' behalf, saying that, "if she attended at all," Lord Morpeth was her choice.

This insolence came to Charles Greville's ears, and his irate quill transfixed Victoire on the page. She "chuses to set herself in opposition to the King on all occasions, and behave to him with all possible impertinence. The King and Queen are however both determined not to quarrel with her, and take no notice of her misbehaviour.... I should like to have to deal with her impertinence for a little while." In all these impertinences the hand of Conroy is evident, and his delight in twisting the royal lion's tail. He felt himself, with his compact jaunty mind, more than a match for the old sailor with his inopportune remarks and bubbling speeches.

Over this affair or another a quite chance word of the Duke of Wellington to Greville gave rise to the supposition, still current today, that Conroy was the Duchess of Kent's lover. Greville had been talking to Wellington about her behavior, and said he imagined that she and Conroy were lovers. The Duke said he, too, "supposed so." The Duke's "supposed so" was, in fact, simply a guess drawn from experience. Such appears to have been the chief origin of the rumor that, as the years went on, turned into a legend.

In the Queen's later life it came to her ears that the unpublished parts of Greville's Diaries contained allusions to this scandal. Filled with "disgust and horror," she sent for the Duchess of Abercorn, and asked her whether her own known dislike of her mother's comptroller was generally attributed to this imaginary intimacy.

The Duchess had to admit that it was.

The Queen, much agitated, then explained that she had been put against Conroy by having been told "by two people whom she trusted" that he had used his position as comptroller to enrich himself, but, later, she had discovered that this was not so, and that his acquired wealth was due to a fortune left to Lady Conroy. Further, the Queen impressed on the Duchess that "apart from the fact that her mother was one of the purest and most religious women, Sir John Conroy was devoted to his wife." Such was the Queen's defense of her mother. But if Conroy was not her lover, his influence over her was as potent as if he had been. In each of her two elderly husbands Victoire had had to deal with an intensive masculine type, and to both she had had to genuflect in spirit, hourly to adapt herself. With Conroy she experienced, probably for the first time, a really congenial and intimate companionship with a man of her own age, and one who, with every assiduity of his seductive nature, wooed, if not her body, her mind and her susceptibilities. In this case it was the man who did the adapting, and she the letting loose of her natural inclinations. As we have already seen, this loosening had not been altogether felicitous, and it was to become still less so. Curiously enough, her intimacy with Conroy had its justification, because, in a sense, it might be said to have had its counterpart in Queen Adelaide's friendship with her Chamberlain, Lord Howe. The first thing that strikes one in Lord Howe's portrait is his remarkable resemblance to Adelaide. They look like brother and sister. Whether his admiration for her arose partly from the contrast between her invariably gentle behavior and that of his own wife (who, when on one occasion driving with the King and Queen, chose to sit with her feet outside the carriage window) or from whatever other cause, his devotion to her, open and innocent as daylight, was known to everyone. His pondering eyes were invariably drawn to Adelaide's face, that most sensitive face, with something piteous about it like an exposed heart. "He never is out of the Pavilion," writes Greville, "dines there almost every evening, rides with her, never quitting her side, and never takes his eyes off her." "He is like a boy in love with this frightful spotted Majesty," giggles the diarist.

. . . .

Regarding Lady Howe pushing her feet out of the royal carriage window, this incident of past manners can be matched with others equally surprising. To mention only three.... When in 1832, William IV, then unpopular in connection with the Reform Bill, drove through the crowds on his way to dissolve Parliament, not a cheer nor a raised hat greeted him. To show his disgust he spat out of the window. ("George the Fourth would not have done that!" screamed a voice.) From William IV we turn to Lady Holland. At meals she had a Negro page behind her chair, and, as she ate, she would at intervals reverse her well-loaded fork over her shoulder, and the Negro, opening wide his mouth, would receive of her bounty. Finally, Queen Victoria herself. When the Prince Consort died she had all her young daughters' long hair cut off and placed in his coffin.*

As for William IV's coronation, the Duchess now decided on a spectacular move. She would not attend it at all; neither should Victoria. Having taken a house in the Isle of Wight, she swept the whole party across The Solent, and from her address of Norris Castle dispatched a letter to the King announcing that Victoria had injured her knee by a fall, and that therefore neither of them could come to see him crowned.

4

Victoria was thirteen when Leopold suggested to her mother that she and her daughter should go on a round of visits to the big country houses. Therefore, in the summer of 1832 the whole Kensington Palace party set off, driving through the sweet August weather on the start of their tour. For the occasion Victoria was supplied with a succession of "Journal books." These little manuscript volumes—the same size as a novel—with their dark leather backs and snuff-colored marbled sides still exist; the scribbled pencil writing clearly visible beneath the final inking-in.

As the several carriages conveying the Kents and their entourage went briskly along the country roads, the little girl inside the most important of them led an almost more strenuous life than if she had

---

* This would hardly have applied to Princess Victoria who had married the Crown Prince of Germany.

been doing lessons in her Kensington schoolroom. It was her task not only accurately to observe the scene on either side as they drove through it, but then and there to describe it in her Journal book, while at the same time she had to keep glancing at the traveling clock so as to record the precise moment of arrival or departure from a village, or a change of horses. The strain of simultaneously recording and clocking in ("5 minutes past ½ past 9" runs one entry, "19 minutes to 1," "1 minute to 4," and so on incessantly) must a good deal have spoiled the painstaking child's pleasure in all the changing aspects about her. And how lovely the country scene was to the traveler at that time as compared with now. Bypass roads had not then spawned their bald and hideous length across the land, no whisper had as yet arisen of telegraph pole, of motor car, pylon, roadside garage, hooter, and sudden death. This country through which the Kent party drove was a green and bosky landscape, full of all the freshness and charm of the accidental and the random, of luxuriously sprawling hedgerows, of twisty roads, and great trees dangling their branches undeterred. It was still the world of Morland and Gainsborough. In those days of summer the silence of the heat-drowsed villages, where, in the cottage gardens, the bees hummed round their domed hives, was stirred by nothing more strident than the urgent galloping hoofs of the horses of a road coach and the shrill toot of the guard's horn as he clung swaying in his beaver hat. Great, covered country wagons, with melodious sets of bells chiming on the team of horses, would go creaking by, or perhaps an open wagon decorated with boughs, through the leaves of which might be seen the sunburned faces of a whole family on their way to fair or cricket match. Pony carriages drawn by fat, long-tailed ponies; a doctor's gig; every kind of rider would be trotting along between the hedges. Or, passing the Kents' cortege might at times come a string of other carriages, almost an entire household driving from country house to country house, or on the preliminary stages of their journey to the Continent. Thus we read of the Granvilles setting off with courier, children, attendants, and servants on their way to The Hague. "Mr. Jones and Ralph will go in the britschka every morning to air the inns for us. Granville and I in the Chariot with Georgey Codkin, as she is sick, in the coach. Mademoiselle, Edward, Susy and Marie in the Landau, a housemaid and the children's maid on the box. We shall besides have a courier, one cook, Samuel and James, so that at the inns we shall feel at home."

Victoria's slightly prominent blue eyes eagerly glancing here, glancing there, might have glimpsed a country fair with its booths, the stalls piled high with gingerbreads and bunches of colored ribands; or a company of wandering acrobats, a Punch and Judy show, a clown, tired out with his mimings, asleep in the grass by the roadside, a great open umbrella stuck upside down with cheap prints for sale displayed between the ribs. Moving through the spattered sunlight of orchard or lane there would be, now a countryman in his linen smock; now a freckle-faced dairymaid, milk pails dangling each side from her wooden yoke; or, outside an inn, seated drinking at a table, a soldier in uniform, or a sailor in marine-blue jacket, white trousers, and glistening black hat. To our eyes a collection of Staffordshire china figures come to life, but, to the Kent party, an ordinary, everyday spectacle.

After changing horses at Birmingham, Victoria peered out through the window of her safe nest into a hitherto undreamed-of world where huge flames writhed within shifting smoke. Grasping her pencil and Journal book, the excited child alternately looked and scribbled. "The men, women, children, country and houses are all black. But I can not by any description give an idea of its strange and extraordinary appearance. The country is very desolate everywhere; there is coal about, and the grass is quite blasted and black. I just now see an extraordinary building flaming with fire. The country continues black, engines flaming, coals in abundance, everywhere smoking and burning coal-heaps, intermingled with wretched huts and carts and little ragged children."

The vision to her may well have appeared extraordinary, but what strikes the reader as peculiar is that a child of thirteen, while being rapidly driven through this scene, could at the same time describe it with such vividness. On went the royal horses ("Just now we go at a *tremendous* rate") bearing them away and away out of this nightmare world, and soon they were enveloped again in the far more familiar atmosphere of welcoming "arches, flowers, branches, flags, ribbons." The gay curvetings of a band fell on their ears, and then the whole party were unpacking themselves from the carriage at the door of Powis Castle, and there was Lord Powis bowing a greeting. Later, we see them at the Menai bridge. The cutter *Emerald* is there ready to take them for a sail around Puffin Island, the Duchess' sense of self-importance enhanced by the saluting coming from cannon placed on the bridge itself. They paid a several hours' visit to Sir Richard Bulkeley at Baron Hill. Though it was only four o'clock when they arrived, Lady Bulkeley, waiting to receive them, was dressed in white satin showered over with peridots and diamonds, while a wreath of orange flowers clasped her head. Then, when they went upstairs, there was their hostess' toilet table to astonish them, all covered "with pink, with white muslin over it trimmed with beautiful lace, and her things on the toilet table were gold." This thrusting of furniture into petticoats was a startlingly new idea to eyes accustomed to the legs of Chippendale and Sheraton tables left bare.

In all this traveling about Victoria not only had with her her own little French bed from Kensington, but when they got to Plas Newydd, her and the Duchess' riding horses appear in the Journal. ("We galloped over a green field. . . . Rosa went an enormous rate; she literally *flew*.") Now they have arrived as guests at Eaton Hall. Both here and in all the other houses they stayed at, Victoria's roving eyes might have been those of a decorator, so minutely did the child observe and appraise. Were they in a large room or gallery, up went the little chin as she gazed at moldings or cornice. "The ceiling joins in a round gilt with great taste and richness, while the sides arch towards the top." "The dining-room is a fine room beautifully worked at the ceiling." "Pillars arching to the top and gilt in parts rise from the sides," and so on and so on. At Eaton Hall she was well rewarded for this ceiling gazing by finding that a certain "magnificent lustre of gold and glass" had attached to it "a coronet of velvet and pearls." While at breakfast "a crown of gold with precious stones contained the bread."

Arrived at Chatsworth, the pages of her diary become choked with her attempts at an inventory of all the gilded, carved, woven, chiseled, painted, and molded beauty with which she found herself surrounded. Carpets as well as ceilings were patronized by her industrious eye, and in the room set apart for the traveling party to breakfast by themselves, having dealt with the ceiling ("painted, and represents some mythology"), her blue eyes explored the carpet beneath her feet, and the Journal was informed that it was "splendid." But Chatsworth proved too much even for her pen, and she gave it up. "It would take me days, were I to describe minutely the whole," and she turns her eyes from the house to the stables, where they discovered a Russian coachman, and four horses that reared at his command to greet her. What fun it all was! and how like dear Uncle Leopold to have been the originator of this scheme that was giving them such varied delights. Now, at Chatsworth, she could walk through conservatory after conservatory where exotic flower, fern, and tendril delicately outspread themselves in the heat-stuffed air. Then, indoors again, "a beautiful collection of minerals" received her young approbation: for fashionable society had lately developed a passion for the inorganic world, and when returning home from traveling on the Continent would add to their already bursting baggage piled on the post chaise, cases of chunks of minerals. After dinner at Chatsworth fireworks began to leap and quiver through the darkness outside the windows. Even the cascade, as it shivered downward, shone with illumination, as did the tossed water of the fountains. After this plethora of beauty, there were charades; and the big house party, under the scrutinizing eyes of that remarkably observant little Princess, did their best in scenes out of *Kenilworth* and *Bluebeard* and *Tom Thumb*. "When it was over at ¼ to 12 I went to bed." Either during this summer tour (or, possibly, on a later one) Lord Anglesey lent his house in Wales to the Duchess and Victoria. The clergyman who preached on Sunday would be asked to come to luncheon, and his descendants related how, during the meal, the Duchess, exclaiming, "We always try to save the servants on Sunday!" would make everyone turn his or her plate upside down, and then eat the next course off the bottom of it.

5

One day of this November of 1832, the royal party found themselves driving again into the familiar Kensington Palace courtyard, and went indoors, and "We resumed our old rooms." The trunks were unpacked, and dinner was ordered for seven o'clock, and everything went back with a click into the familiar routine. The inevitable Sir John Conroy appeared at dinner, also his daughters, Jane and Victoire, and Lord Liverpool as well; and afterwards "Aunt Sophia" (who, one cannot but think, might have been asked to dinner itself) came trotting in to hear the great all there was to tell.

If life seemed a little flat at Kensington Palace after that successful country-house tour, soon there were all the Christmas preparations to occupy the minds of everyone. The present giving took place on Christmas Eve. "At ¼ to seven we dined with the whole Conroy family and Mr. Hore downstairs," while amenable Aunt Sophia, as usual, only came in later. Then arrived the moment up to which all the weeks of preparation had led. Everyone collected in the drawing room near the dining room. Then the Duchess rang a bell, once, twice, thrice. Then, entrance of the whole party into the dining room, where, lovely to behold, two Christmas trees glimmered with their little candles, the dark branches hung with "sugar ornaments." Beneath each tree was a small table covered with presents. One table was for Victoria; the other for the Conroy family. Near by was another, but treeless, little table for Lehzen. "Mamma," writes Victoria, "gave me a little lovely pink bag which she had worked with a little sachet likewise done by her; a beautiful little opal brooch and earrings, books, some lovely prints, a pink satin dress and a cloak lined with fur. Aunt Sophia gave me a dress which she had worked herself. . . . Lehzen a lovely music-book. Victoire a very pretty white bag worked by herself, and Sir John a silver brush. I gave Lehzen some little things and Mamma gave her a writing-table."

After the exclamations and the admirations there was a move "to my room where I had arranged Mamma's table."

The Duchess' thought-out placing of the tables is full of interest. The obvious arrangement would have been for hers and Victoria's to be the two most important, those that bore the Christmas trees, but, by giving up her rightful table so as to place the Conroy family on an equal footing with Victoria, the Duchess paid a delicate compliment to the man who at present dominated her life. Victoria's "dear Lehzen" was accommodated near her pupil, but with a treeless table, thus placing her in an inferior position to Conroy. Then came the question of the Duchess herself. She, above all, must not in these arrangements be in the slightest degree diminished. So, having given up her rightful position to the Conroy family, she could not remain with less prestige in the same room, and therefore had appropriated an entire room to herself elsewhere. All very significant. On the Duchess' table lay, writes Victoria, "a white bag which I had worked, a collar and a steel chain for Flora [a dog], and an Annual; Aunt Sophia a pair of turquoise ear-rings; Lehzen a little white and gold pincushion and a pin with two little gold hearts hanging to it; Sir John, Flora, a book-holder and an Annual." No doubt it was a subconscious instinct that prompted Lehzen to give the Duchess "a pin with two little gold hearts hanging to it," and its implication probably passed unnoticed by either of them. When all this present giving was over, there was still something more delightful to come. Victoria's enthusiasm over Lady Bulkeley's tricked-out toilet table had not passed unnoticed by the Duchess, so now "Mamma then took me up into my bedroom with all the ladies. There was my new toilet-table with a white muslin cover over pink, and all my silver things standing on it with a fine new looking-glass." Conroy's present of a silver brush is explained. Then, at the end of everything, old Mrs. Louis appeared—perhaps staying at Kensington Palace so that, with Leopold now in Belgium, she should not be left to her Christmas all alone at Claremont—and gave the little Kensington princess, who to her was such an aching reminder of Princess Charlotte, "a lovely little wooden box with bottles."

Considering how historically emblazoned the name "Victoria" has become, it is curious to read that about this time there arose in political circles a strong inclination to change the name of the Duke of Kent's daughter to that of her dead cousin, Charlotte, "to which the King willingly consented." When Victoria was told of the possibility she was extremely upset, but, finally, Lord Grey and the Archbishop of Canterbury announced to her mother that the idea had been given up.

It is peculiar how, in later life, Queen Victoria referred to her childhood as "dull," for, as almost constant companion, she had little Victoire Conroy. By the time Victoria herself was thirteen or fourteen the whole party would often be driving off to the play or opera, forms of amusement that filled her with pleasure. Her country-house visits had further awakened her already quick mind. The tempo of her whole being now seems accelerated, impressions crowding in till her little Journal books can scarcely deal with the life that is pulsating within her. For the Journal was still kept daily, and was to be for the rest of her life. Its pages, the day after an evening at the opera, are alive with the Thespian scene: the ballets, the arias, the acting, the appearance and dress of the performers. All is noted with enthusiastic acumen, and during spare moments between her lessons she would make drawing after drawing of these operatic figures, efforts so full of observation and character that it is understandable that her drawing master, Westall, said that she could, if she had gone on studying, have become one of the best women artists of her day. When she was about ten, and her drafts-manship more shaky, she had copied a drawing by him of a little girl approaching a butterfly on a flower. She had then presented this effort to George IV. He was so touched by this childish atten-tion that, picking up his quill, he wrote on the back of it, "Drawn by the Princess Victoria, and given to me by her, August 12th 1829." If the rather haggard child in the drawing was supposed to be a portrait of Victoria herself, it had obviously suffered a good deal in the transference from Westall's pencil to her own.

In addition to plays and operas, riding parties would be made up of the various occupants of the palace, Lehzen and Lady Conroy at times adding themselves to the female figures in their floating veils and long mermaidlike habits. "At 12 we went out riding in the park with Victoire, Lehzen and Sir John" runs one entry. "It was a *delightful* ride. We cantered a good deal. Sweet little Rosy went beautifully!!" Now the celebrated underlinings and double un-derlinings have begun, and will continue to the end. Only by these energetic scorings could her nature express its delight at the increasing impact of life. Certain impacts the Duchess permitted, but not those of novels, though, later, Victoria was allowed to read *Ivanhoe* and *Rasselas*. One may be certain that the monthly maga-zine, *La Belle Assemblée*, that casket of Paris fashions, would have arrived regularly at Kensington Palace for the Duchess, and one may be equally certain that Victoria's eye was never allowed to wander through those pages where, interspersed with exquisite water-color fashion plates, were stories of the most romantic and melodramatic nature: dreams, shrieks, claps of thunder, kindling eyes, fevers, daggers, piercing yells, blood-curdled veins, unearthly voices issuing from icebergs, and oriental diseases, intermingling with ghosts, counts, bards, Turks, captives, brigands, astrologers, corpses, knights, and friars. On hearing of the faithlessness of her lover one heroine "shrieked, kicked, and fainted—salts, hartshorn and cold water were plentifully applied, and at length the fair deceived recovered, to rail eternally against the perfidy and inconstancy of man, and the fond credulity of woman." Not on such pabulum was the young Victoria being reared. Neither would the Duchess have considered the male cry, "Ah, me! what power hath made you such a beautiful annoyance," a suitable phrase for Victoria to ponder over.

La Belle Assemblée had several pages of advertisements, and in one number of 1812 is recommended an "Asiatic Tooth Powder Patronized and Used by their Royal Highnesses the Dukes of Clarence and Kent," while another entry runs, "An Hymn of the Resurrection by Charles Wesley, Organ Performer to his Royal Highness the Prince Regent. N.B. Wanted two or three good Clarinet Performers for the Duke of Kent's Band, whose abilities and characters will bear the strictest investigation."

Attention is drawn to: "Delicate amusements for Ladies of distinction who wish to plait their own Hats, Bonnets etc.: J. Palin, 76 Holborn Bridge, most respectfully informs these Ladies, who have so liberally patronized his Manufacturing of the Universally admired WILLOW SHAVINGS, that he is the *only person* appointed for the sale of WHALE FIN SHAVINGS—an article of the most translucent whiteness." Other advertisements are for "Sympathetic Dining Tables with removable leaves" and "Patent Elastic India Cotton invisible Petticoats, Opera drawers, Waistcoats, and Dresses all in one."

6

While Victoria entered in her Journal accounts of operas and riding parties, her mother's thoughts were otherwise occupied. As acknowledged possible future Regent she was now so inflated by the sense of her own importance that she considered she should

PRINCESS LIEVEN

From the portrait by Sir Thomas
Lawrence, P.R.A.

*By courtesy of the Trustees of the
Tate Gallery*

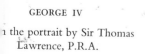

GEORGE IV

1 the portrait by Sir Thomas
Lawrence, P.R.A.

*permission of the Trustees of the
Wallace Collection*

have a more impressive setting, and, the year after this tour of country houses, she began to demand every kind of improvement and alteration to her part of Kensington Palace. Lord Duncannon, who was at the Board of Works, became exasperated at this clamor for expensive attentions. "He had," wrote Creevey, "the devil's own trouble with the Duchess of Kent, who bothers his and Lord Grey's and the King's life out with the perpetual demands she makes for alterations, additions, furniture etc. etc. for her Royal Residence. In short there is no end of her bother." In addition to dealing with her, Lord Duncannon was occupied with choosing furnishing materials for Buckingham Palace, into which the King and Queen, much against their inclination, were intending to move, leaving Clarence House where they were then living. Creevey, turning up now here now there, happened to be with the Duncannons one day when they were choosing from a collection of patterns of materials to cover the furniture of Queen Adelaide's rooms at the Palace: "Lady Duncannon and I were quite agreed about which she should have, but Duncannon would not hear of it as being much too dear; he would not go beyond six shillings a yard."

As for the Duchess of Kent, in all her wasplike activities in the autumn of 1833 she received an enthusiastic backing from Lord Durham, who, hostile to Lord Grey's Government, used the Duchess as a useful irritant, backing her in all her schemes. And never was such an importunate widow. "She is the most restless persevering troublesome devil possible," exclaims Creevey, "neither the King nor Lord Grey will answer her applications any more, and everything is referred to Duncannon. In return, through Conroy to Duncannon, she expresses the most violent indignation both against the King and Grey, considers and states that as Mother to the Princess Victoria she is entitled as *matter of right* to everything she asks, that she will receive nothing as matter of favour etc., and Conroy upon more than one occasion has had the folly to add that her Royal Highness having consulted the Earl of Durham had the entire sanction of his opinion in her favour. Was there ever?"

In spite of all this the King and Queen were, on their side, behaving in the most long-suffering manner, showing every kindness to her and Victoria. They were anxious to see more than they were allowed to of their niece, who, in her turn, had the warmest affection for them, but the Duchess' disgruntlements being continually on the increase, Victoria was constantly prevented from seeing her uncle and aunt. Before long, even Adelaide found, when she came to see her Kensington sister-in-law, that instead of as in old days being allowed to wander in friendly fashion through the rooms till she found her, she was now, as she confided to her friend Lady Bedingfield, "made to stop in some particular room" till the Duchess chose to appear.

All the Kensington discords and dissensions flew, as indeed everything, sooner or later, always did fly, into the ears of Princess Lieven. "The squabbles that have been going on at Kensington Palace do not surprise me," she wrote to Lord Grey. "The cause is that German *morgue* and little-mindedness which is rampant in that quarter; those people are wrong-headed to the utmost possible degree, all of which, however, is a great pity, for, after all, the future of England is placed in their hands." To the Duchess herself, without doubt, her own behavior seemed invariably estimable: was she not a most correctly religious woman, visible every Sunday in Kensington Palace Chapel, sweeping along into her pew in her latest trickeries from Paris, kneeling, singing, responding with pious decorum; was she not doing her utmost to bring Victoria up successfully to fill the stupendous position that lay before her, closing her in on every side with experts to train, teach, instruct, and inform; in her own tussles with the King and Lord Duncannon for what she considered her due, was it not—so, no doubt she persuaded herself—for Victoria's sake as well as her own; and, indeed, was she not, in making a stand for what she considered right, acting as her husband would have wished, showing loyalty to that impressive figure who still lived at the back of her mind?

In Winterhalter's portrait of the Duchess, a portrait instinct with life, there is not a suspicion of self-censure. On the contrary, the expression on those peculiarly brown-skinned, emphatic but comely features is triumphantly self-complacent; there hovers about them the same suggestion of a not altogether pleasant smirk that lies across Conroy's face. Their minds occupied with the same thoughts, their features developed the same expression. There is no doubt that their constant aspiration for what, in the end, they knew they might not get, was not having a happy effect on the character of either.

Very peculiar sometimes must have been their inward thoughts as their eyes fell on Victoria, her childish body earnestly bent over some work she was fiddling at—possibly one of her opera drawings, or at times she would paint fans, or be ornamenting her little boxes —for on that small, absorbed figure depended all the Duchess and Conroy's power and prestige, to both of them so inexpressibly dear. Such was the child's bestowal, and yet, contrarily, by the very fact of her inevitably growing older each day, she was to, or, to be more accurate, she might (if William IV did not die in time), snatch from them all the more she might have bestowed—herself be, in power and prestige, immeasurably their superior. Every day that now came and went was to them a day of import, for at its going Victoria was one day nearer her eighteenth birthday. That once attained, good-by regency.

Somewhere close by, in this scene drawn from the past, would inevitably have been Lehzen, her eyes following the child "with her usual half-anxious, smiling, fixed look." Lehzen who could not but have been half, if not wholly, aware of what was going on in the Duchess' mind, of what in Conroy's; and, herself, in consequence, full of ambushed thoughts. Seldom, in any close group of people, could one find combatant affections and jealousies, desires and motives, more inextricably mixed.

Incidentally, Victoria's efforts at drawing, needlework, or any other occupation must have been at times a good deal frustrated by the Duchess' habit of pinning a spray of holly under her daughter's chin to prevent her stooping. This was a mild corrective compared to the iron collar that for long had been, and for many decades was still to be, clamped round the necks of growing girls. Mrs. Sherwood, the author of *The Fairchild Family*, describes how she was forced to wear one of these collars fastened to a backboard strapped round her shoulders. To this, she writes, "I was subjected from my sixth to my thirteenth year. It was put on in the morning and seldom taken off till late in the evening: and I generally did all my lessons standing in stocks.... I never sat on a chair in my mother's presence ... even before I was twelve I was obliged to translate fifty lines of Virgil every morning, standing in these same stocks with the iron collar pressing on my throat."

There were no iron collars in the Kensington schoolroom, but the Duchess and Conroy's daily sight of Victoria, the realization of the cloud of inevitable glory each hour drawing nearer to her, roused in them lightly malicious feelings, and "they" (it appears that this refers to her mother and Conroy) would deliberately, so Queen Victoria asserted when older, try to annoy her, to make her "angry" by telling her, for instance, that her face resembled the unpleasing countenance of her middle-aged cousin Silly Billy. (This so distressed her that when she came to the throne she asked Lord Melbourne if he "saw any likeness in me to the Duke of Gloucester." "None whatever," came the prompt reply.)

What must have added fuel to the jealous feelings Victoria occasionally aroused in her mother was that, try as she might, she could not make her daughter confide in her what she felt about her coming queenship. The Duchess told a friend that she had not the slightest idea whether the child viewed her future "with satisfaction or with anxiety."

7

Time revolved, and it was Victoria's fourteenth birthday. "I am to-day fourteen years old! How *very old*!!"

Even before breakfast the presents began to collect. Kensington Palace was gradually becoming a perfect warehouse in which were piling up all the most expensive bric-a-brac from the London and Paris shops. Curiously enough, on her birthdays, Victoria herself pressed gifts into the hands of her mother and Lehzen, as a return for theirs to her. But these early-morning givings were a mere foreshadowing of what was to come. "After breakfast we went into the room where my table was arranged. Mamma gave me a lovely bag of her own work, a beautiful bracelet, two lovely *féronières*, one of pink topaz, the other turquoises; two dresses, some prints, some books, some handkerchiefs, and an apron. From Lehzen, a beautiful print of the Russell Trial." For it was then the fashion to collect prints within those large marbled-cardboard portfolios that, worn and faded, are still to be found hidden away in old country houses, and Victoria's portfolio had to be filled: though Lehzen's choice of a subject seems peculiar. Letters were given Victoria from the absent Leopold and Feodore. Then Conroy and his three sons arrived. The Conroy presents, mostly made of sandalwood or enamel, were soon submerged by offerings of a far grander nature from all the royal family, including the problematical Cumberland and his wife, who gave her a turquoise bracelet. Some of the presents that arrived sound a long-vanished note: "an ivory basket filled with the work of her nieces" from the Duchess of Northumberland; "a blue topaz watch-hook" from another giver; and from yet another "a beautiful album with a painting on it." "A brooch in the shape of a lily of the valley"—the flower that was just now being patronized as the fashionable one for ornamentation, and that would even appear in garden seats made of iron—is of special interest as being given her by her cousin, Prince George, a boy the same age as herself. His father, the Duke of Cambridge, was settled in Hanover as Viceroy, and his son now lived in England with the King and his wife almost as an adopted child. This Adonis boy, much cosseted by his kind Aunt Adelaide, always moved about with the Court, having his own tutor. The Duke of Cambridge himself, George III's youngest son, was a "stone-deaf old gentleman who wore a fair wig," and whose conversation consisted chiefly of a succession of shouted questions. He lived an agreeable enough life in Hanover, shooting over the Crown heaths and forests, and riding the splendid horses from his stud, said to be the finest in Germany. But once Victoria came to the throne all these amenities would pass to Hanover's future king, his brother, Cumberland; and the Cambridge family, deprived and dispossessed, would have to return to England. We read that the Viceroy's mind was beginning to hover round a possible marriage between his son and Victoria.

On this, her fourteenth birthday, the King and his Queen, invariably doing the kind thing, gave a "Juvenile Ball" at St. James's especially for their niece. It was then the fashion to chalk over ballroom floors with every kind of fantastic device to catch the eyes of the arrivals the moment they entered the room. This had been done for the child guests, and baskets of cherries and pineapples had been brought in by the royal gardeners. To keep the big company of excited children in proper order, the dancing mistress, Madame

Bourdin, was in attendance. When the ballroom doors were flung wide, the rosy-cheeked King led in Victoria as the guest of honor, and when the hour for supper came round, she was conducted to the supper room by her attentive uncle.

Quadrille after quadrille was pranced through by this small but most energetic dancer, her partner for one of them being the morning's giver of the lily-of-the-valley brooch, George Cambridge, that boy who, burnished with position as royal pet of William and Adelaide, wore his star and ribbon with a kind of romantic grace. During these lightly spun hours at the ball, when the music and Victoria's emotions became so exquisitely united, she could forget the thoughts that in quieter, more slow-moving hours sometimes lay on her so heavily—her threatened future, that looming queenship, the dread that she would not be equal to her responsibilities. But now, pointing her alert neat toes, caressingly impelled this way and that by the swaying cadences, she could gaily give vent to all the little-girl tol-de-rol of spirit that was natural to her. "We came home at half past twelve. I was *very* much amused."

8

During Victoria's West-of-England and Welsh progress with her mother she had got accustomed to such activities as presenting prizes to Welsh poets, standing godmother, inspecting factories, or herself receiving civic presents: the townships' ideas as to what was suitable running the gamut between an enormous doll and a Bible. But delightful as it all was, this year a new revelation of the sweets life has to offer opened before her. Two Württemberg men cousins came to stay. Though both much older than she, they entered most excitingly into the consciousness of their child cousin: "so amiable and so pleasant to have in the house; they were *always satisfied, always good-humoured*," runs the Journal.

The Queen at once gave another ball at St. James's, to which the whole Kensington party were invited. Victoria this time spent the evening sitting on one of the gilt chairs beneath the canopy that spread itself over her Aunt Adelaide and other members of the royal family. At this ball the Duchess of Kent's behavior passed all bounds. When Adelaide, in her usual charming way, asked that the Duchess' Württemberg nephews also should be invited to sit by her on the gilt chairs so that she could talk to them, Victoire refused; an invitation was then given that they should come to stay at Windsor, this too was refused. In conclusion, the Duchess swept Victoria off long before the ball was over, saying the child was fatigued. Adelaide put in a plea that at least the Württemberg nephews might be left behind, but no, they too, so Adelaide heard no doubt to her surprise, were fatigued and must return to their beds; and the entire Kensington party incontinently disappeared.

A few weeks later, on a July morning, everyone in Kensington Palace was early astir. The quiet of a diaphanous summer dawn lay over everything, over the palace, the gardens, the courtyard. "At half-past six we all breakfasted," and by seven o'clock the whole party, including the Württemberg cousins, were clambering into their chaises, "Sir John going in a post-chaise before us, then our post-chaise, then Lehzen's landau, then my Cousins' [the Württembergs] carriage, then Charles's [her half brother, who was also staying with them], then Lady Conroy's, and then our maid's." Thus surrounded and supported, the Duchess and Victoria were off again to the island and Norris Castle. As before, William IV had put one of his yachts at their disposal, the *Emerald*, now grown into *"the dear little Emerald."* For Victoria, the delight of being again at Norris Castle was enhanced by the chivalrous attentions of the Württemberg cousins. "Alexander took such care of me in geting out of the boat, and rode next to me; so did Ernst." And then, too, they "talked about *such interesting things,* about their Turkish Campaign, about Russia, etc. etc." It was her first realization, not only of the charms of male companionship, but of the enlargement of outlook that comes from contact with the male mind. But alas, before a fortnight had passed, these desirable cousins had to return home. "We saw them get into the barge, and watched them sailing away for some time on the beach . . . we shall miss them at *breakfast,* at *luncheon,* at *dinner, riding, sailing, driving, walking, in fact everywhere."* Alexander and Ernest Württemberg certainly knew the art of being successful guests.

During this Isle of Wight visit the Duchess and Victoria were immersed in an adulatory civic atmosphere of addresses, speeches,

luncheons, and reviews. One feature, however, that had been remarkably to the fore when the Kensington party had formerly been
to the island was lacking: royal salutes. The islanders, gratified by
the presence of their palace guests, had seized on every opportunity
as an excuse for the discharge of more and yet more gunpowder.
The sounds of these constant explosions reached the King's ears.
Even his immense good nature was, as regards his sister-in-law, beginning to turn sour, and this noisy method of drawing attention to
her was too much. He decided that "this continual popping" must
stop. Lord Hill and Sir James Graham, hoping to arrange the
matter quietly and agreeably, suggested to the Duchess that when
she next went to the island she should "send word that as she was
sailing about for her amusement she had rather they did not salute
her whenever she appeared." But the Duchess was certainly not
going to forgo any self-aggrandizement. Those slammings borne to
her on the fresh-blowing sea air had been most delightful, and now,
egged on by the sense of the islanders' loyalty, and by Conroy's
giggles over William IV—whom he referred to as "an angry
turkey-cock whose nerves were upset with green tea"—thus encouraged, she allowed Conroy the effrontery of saying "that as
Her Royal Highness's *confidential adviser* he could not recommend
her to give way on this point."

Then the King took action. By an Order of Council the regulations regarding salutes were altered. It was laid down that only
when the King or the Queen were on board was a vessel to be
saluted.

9

During this stay of the Kents at Norris Castle an incident occurred that, slight as it was in itself, throws a most revealing light
on the Duchess, and on what Victoria at times had to endure from
her mother's behavior.

On this summer visit to the island, Victoria's youthful hair, in
color pale brown, that had before hung in charming corkscrew curls,
was braided and twisted on top, two curls only being left to dangle
one on each side of her smooth little Hanoverian countenance.
Conroy, in a letter to a friend, remarked how pretty the effect was,
and said she seemed suddenly to have developed into "a young

lady." She had, too, grown a little, her wardrobe had been improved, and altogether she made quite an impression on the islanders. She was aware of it herself, and the watchful Conroy, noting the cygnet's first signs of swanhood, said that this awareness of her success "lighted her up wonderfully."

One day the Duchess and Victoria were going to cross The Solent to take part in a small ceremony. A pier was to be opened, and Princess Victoria had been asked to be the opener. The Kents and their attendants set off from Norris Castle in the royal carriages. The warmth of the islanders' appreciation had awakened in Victoria a self-realization that had not been there before, and during this expedition her mother became subtly aware of it, "annoyed," so we are told, "by something in the manner of the Princess." Immediately, within the closely seated-together group in the carriage, there was engendered "a state of nervous tension."

The Kensington party arrived at Southampton, but the mayor and town councilors received the Duchess far too unwarily. Filled with pride at having secured their future Queen to open the pier, they made no attempt to conceal their enthusiasm, and treated Victoria's mother merely as "the secondary personage." At this the Duchess' already simmering annoyance seethed over. Turning to the mayor, she "bluntly stated that she had decided not to let her daughter come forward at so public a ceremony, and would open the pier herself."

To the mayor this was a dreadful announcement. The Princess had already laid the foundation stones of a bridge and a church: if a bridge and a church had received her patronage, why not a pier? The distraught man hastily put forward all the soothing sentences he could think of to persuade the Duchess to relent, "but she cut him short, asking him to proceed to business." The poor little Princess, wincing at both the snub and the disappointment, yet "managed all through the ceremony to keep her round young face inanimate as a block of wood."

An important feature in the arrangements was a gala luncheon in a marquee, which the Duchess had already accepted. But now, so she informed the mayor, she must ask to be excused: "crossing the Solent," so she informed him, "had disagreed with her." What must have made it still more mortifying to the mayor was that, as soon as the irate lady and her party had repacked themselves into the royal carriages, they drove off to an hotel and had their luncheon there.

Here, in this slight Southampton incident, we see the minds of mother and daughter suddenly laid open for our inspection. All puzzlement as to their mutual relationship, both in the past and in the future, is cleared. In this vignette of what happened on the pier, the Duchess' restless jealousy, her unkindness to Victoria, her indifference to the feelings of the mayor and townspeople, not only reveal the superficial quality of that graciousness of manner which charmed so many, but prove that this exhibition of bad behavior must have been far from being an isolated one. Otherwise Victoria's face would not at once have automatically turned into "a block of wood." Few things teach self-control so effectively as living by the side of the uncontrolled. That this child, herself so full of hot emotions, had learned from dealings with her mother such self-restraint that she could practice it at a moment of acute disappointment is remarkable.

Another small incident, one that took place at Gloucester House, at what was then called a "child's ball," is yet another proof of how aware Victoria was that not only herself but everyone else had to tread gingerly when dealing with her mother. Victoria's Uncle Sussex was at this party, and when she saw him leaving, she ran over to him and said, "Won't you give me a kiss before you go?" And then, as he bent down, she whispered, "You have forgotten to say Good-night to Mamma." The implications of that child whisper are easy to decipher—the early-learned knowledge that her mother was always on the *qui vive* for slights to her self-esteem, and that if such took place outside the palace it was those inside who would receive the repercussion.

Incidents such as that at Southampton could not but have been discussed by Victoria and her governess over the schoolroom inkpot. Lehzen's disapproval, however loyal she may have tried outwardly to be to her employer, must have been apparent to the child. Thus, inevitably, a psychological scaffolding began to build itself round Victoria's adolescent mind. Invisible scaffolding, formed in part by Lehzen's protective sympathy, in part by the child's own forced reservations and restraints on account both of her mother's disposition and her close collusion with Conroy. For there was something in the very texture of that protean Irishman from which her young susceptibilities shrank back, something unaccountable but hurtful. Thus, from early childhood, she had undergone intensive emotional training. "I was extremely crushed and kept under and hardly dared say a word." Flinching away from Conroy; shut out from intimacy with her mother because of her mother's nearness to her comptroller; forced to witness the Duchess' ever-growing impertinence to her, Victoria's, dear Aunt Adelaide and Uncle William; made to submit to a ceaseless fretting surveillance; overtutored; overdisciplined; a whole delicate apparatus of inward self-preservation had necessarily to come into being. Outwardly, she was all compliance and submission; inwardly, a precocious maturity was strengthening every hour. Unnatural and bitter as the training was, it explains how, when she reached the throne, she was able to glide into her position with a composure and aplomb for which her surprised, middle-aged ministers could not account. They did not know that the human entanglements around her at Kensington Palace had been such that, even as a child, she had learned how to wipe all expression from her face; how practiced she was in the art of showing acquiescence, while, inwardly, she kept her own counsel. At the time of the Southampton incident Conroy, writing of her in his cheap way as the "Little Woman" (and of the Duchess as the "Little Woman's Mamma"), says that Victoria was at the same time "arch, sly, and artless." Archness and artlessness in conjunction sound charming. As for Conroy dubbing her sly, it is evident he had been brought up short against that scaffolding behind which she successfully hid.

The young Victoria is now at last beginning to stand out clearly before us: a definite, curiously intriguing personality. We see her, a small, girlish figure slipping quietly from room to room at Kensington; a demure, inscrutable, palace-bred character; nothing whatever in her all but prim demeanor to hint of the hidden forces within; of the amazingly tough determinations that were beginning to gather behind that composed, smooth-skinned little face.

The crosscurrents of domestic politics at Kensington Palace were proving too much for poor fluttery old Späth. To her feather-soft mind her position must have been the most bewildering and agi-

tating possible. How could she be loyal to her beloved Victoria, and
at the same time to her dear, dear Duchess, when mother and
daughter were in opposing camps? Out of honesty, or from lack
of circumspection, or, probably, from a mixture of both, she became
embroiled with the Conroy family. There were verbal passes between her and the child Victoire Conroy—the child, we may well
believe, urged on by her father to flout the elderly lady in waiting—
and Späth, so it seems, tried to put Victoire in her place. But
there was another and a more potent cause of enmity between
Späth and the Duchess' comptroller. The Duke of Wellington
told Charles Greville that Victoria's dislike of Conroy "was un-
questionably owing to her having witnessed some familiarities"
between him and her mother. "What she had seen she repeated to
the Baroness Spaeth [*sic*], and Spaeth not only did not hold her
tongue but," so the Duke believed, "remonstrated with the Duchess
herself. The consequence was that they got rid of Spaeth, and they
would have got rid of Letzen [*sic*] too if they had been able; but
Letzen, who knew very well what was going on, was prudent
enough not to commit herself, and she was besides powerfully
protected by George IV and William IV so that they did not dare
to attempt to expel her."

Greville says that regarding the Duke one could have "the certainty that every syllable" he said "was strictly true," and this
information which he passed on to Greville is of moment in clarify-
ing the tense situation within the walls of Kensington Palace.
George IV's, and William IV's, stalwart attitude to Lehzen proves
that they realized her value, and the necessity of her remaining on
to keep things steady in that tippety Kensington ménage. As for the
familiarities between the Duchess and Conroy which the startled
and horrified little Victoria happened to witness—and, considering
her prim upbringing, she must indeed have been startled and horrified—the probability seems to be that they were not lovers, but,
taking into account their natures, both lively, both gay, it is understandable that not only their propinquity, but their collusion over
their mutual ambition had induced a familiarity, a flirtatious easiness
of behavior that, considering the Duchess' position, and their official
relationship to each other, was certainly unsuitable.

To return to the complications at Kensington Palace: whether

Späth actually reprimanded the Duchess or not, she and Conroy decided to get rid of the old faithful; and the day came when the deposed woman bundled herself, with what inner heart-rendings can be imagined, into a carriage and was driven off on the first stage of her long journey to Germany, where she was to enter the service of Feodore.* Behind her Lehzen was left sitting in the palace, bitterly indignant at this treatment of her old friend, and with Conroy for the part he had taken in it; foreseeing, clearly enough that the same fate might be hers if she did not exercise every caution.

In all these collisions of personalities, and outbursts of temperament, what actual role did Lehzen take on herself to play? We may ask, but there is no answer. To us she is like a partially erased sentence, a not clearly heard observation. Yet, if the attempt to establish contact with her is like groping for someone in the dark, all the same we are aware that an extremely forceful figure is there, and that from it issue vital impulses; that in impregnating Victoria's mind with her own she is staking a fire which within a few years is to flare up with startling vehemence. Did the governess make too much of the unpleasant aspects of the Duchess and Conroy in a craving to center her pupil's affection on herself? Here is a question impossible to answer. What is clear is that hers was a nature that could find fulfillment only in a personal devotion; and Victoria was the one being she had to love.

10

While the Kensington party were at Norris Castle, seaweed was much to the fore in the youthful Victoria's life. The place for seaweed is sea water, where, its fronds afloat, it undeniably has a charm, but Victoria thought otherwise. Seaweed was busily collected, brought back to the castle, then, probably by the combined efforts of Lehzen and Victoria, forcibly flattened. Finally these glutinous objects were made to adhere to the pages of an album: the whole forming in Victoria's eyes such an object of worth and beauty that she considered it grand enough to be given as a present to the little Queen of Portugal, Maria da Gloria, a sophisticated-

---

* In 1828 Feodore had married Prince Ernest Christian Charles of Hohenlohe-Langenburg.

looking child, only a few months older than Victoria herself, who this year, while crossing from Havre to Portsmouth, had a meeting with the Kents in The Solent: the present of the album being perhaps in exchange for one given to Victoria by the child Portuguese monarch, a herbarium of Brazilian plants.

But during this visit to the Island, Victoria in her spare moments was not entirely occupied with seaweed. She started making a present for Uncle Leopold, a watch cover of "thick yellow silk ... ornamented with pansies in floss silks of other shades." It was not till December that she sent it him. The letter she wrote with it being in its gracefulness a remarkable production for a child of fourteen.

Kindly accept, dear uncle, this little article of my handiwork. I began it at Norris Castle. So you see, dear uncle, that I often thought of you there. I know you are fond of flowers, and hope you will like them on a watch-case. They are not copied from garden flowers, but from a painting. Pansies are sometimes called two-faces-under-a-hood. The Baroness says this might render them an appropriate gift for some statesmen, but not for you. I prefer the French name *pensée*, and I do hope that you and Aunt Louise will kindly overlook all shortcomings, and only see in the birthday present I venture to send *une pensée très affectuese.*

Your loving niece,

VICTORIA

Baroness Lehzen's care that Leopold should not think she considered him double faced is delightful. The two were good friends, and he would show his approval of her in his letters to Victoria. "My best regards to Lehzen." "Say everything that is kind to good Lehzen."

This winter it appears to have struck the Duchess of Kent that a smattering of physics must be added to Victoria's stock of information, and on two occasions lecturers were summoned to Kensington Palace. Not only Victoria and the Duchess but "Lehzen, Lady Conroy, Victoire, the Dean, and Sir John" likewise sat ready to receive enlightenment on such matters as the elixir of life, the universal solvent, results of chemical action, nature of flame, properties of matter, defect of wheel carriages, "Magnetic attraction, etc., etc.,—Repulsion exhibited in various ways, as counteracting the preceding influences"—a subject more apposite to various members of his Kensington Palace audience than the lecturer realized.

I I

To fill the place vacated by the dismissed Späth, one day a quite new figure drove up to Kensington Palace, Lady Flora Hastings, a young woman between twenty and thirty who had come as lady of the bedchamber to the Duchess. Youth and gaiety, and wit entered with her. But as she passed through the double doors beneath the portico, destiny gave a most ill-omened movement to her weaving shuttle. However, at the moment nothing could have seemed further from this blithe young person than disaster of any kind. The atmosphere of Kensington Palace no doubt received refreshment from the advent of this eldest sister of Lord Hastings, as she is said to have possessed "elegance of manners" and "vivacity." Refreshment, that is to say, for the Duchess and Conroy, as the new arrival inevitably ranged herself on their side. Her wit and Conroy's mingled like two drops of water run together, and before long they were convulsed over Lehzen and her caraway seeds that would arrive for her from Germany in little sacks, and that she liked to have sprinkled over her food, even her bread and butter not being spared. It seems that it was Lehzen who, provoked by Conroy in ways of which we have no details, one day alluded to him as a man "from the bogs of Ireland." She may have regretted it when it came to her ears that he had retorted with "the hogs from Low Germany." Inextricably bound together by the knot of necessity, these various characters moved on toward their individual destinies: destinies that all of them, unconsciously, were already themselves creating, and in which we shall before long see them most painfully involved. Certain people—for instance, King Leopold, the Duke of Wellington, Princess Lieven—realized what complicated human relationships were developing within the walls of Kensington Palace. But the casual observer would have seen a smooth surface only; the chief occupation a busy, incessant effort to train and trim a child's mind into the shape suitable for the mind of a queen.

So the days went on. At times one so alike another that they went by like the flicked-over pages of a book. And then something would happen. There was that day in the January of 1834 when Victoria received the Spanish Order of Maria Louisa; the first of the many that were to be showered on her during her life—enameled, jewel-studded fantasies that, inevitably drawn to her from all over the Continent, were to emphasize the luster around her. The same year she received the Spanish Order something still better arrived from Europe. Feodore—whom Victoria had not seen for six years—her husband, and two of their children, came to stay at the palace. But, alas, her arrival inevitably involved her departure, and once she had gone, the July days seemed to lag drearily.

"Sunday 27th July. . . . I missed dear Feodore here again terribly. . . . She used to be with me so much on Sundays always. . . . Last Sunday afternoon she painted in my room. At ½ past 3 we went with Lehzen to visit Aunt Gloucester, and then drove home through the park. How dull that drive appeared to me without dear Feodore. . . . We passed a sad dull evening." Occupation alone could counter this sense of loss. "I *love* to be *employed*, I *hate* to be *idle*," she exclaimed one day in her Journal the following year; for, even with her meticulously arranged days, she was discovering that in everyone's life there come bare spaces that have to be made fruitful by one's own energy.

On the day she wrote down this discovery they were "all in the bustle of packing" to get off to St. Leonards. It must indeed have been a fuss for those who actually did the packing, for not only Victoria's French bed, bedding, and chintz hangings always went with her, but the Kensington pets, waxbills and lapdogs, were of the traveling party, especially a King Charles spaniel, Dashy, who had become a much-cherished personality. But now, while the palace servants sorted and ran, strapped and buckled, "I have," wrote Victoria, "many occupations with Lehzen. And now, though we are all in the bustle of packing, I am constantly employed by myself in various ways; and I read French History to Lehzen, and one of Racine's tragedies with her in the afternoons which I delight in." Now that, gradually maturing, she was entering into a more sensitive awareness, Lehzen's single-minded devotion was making her realize how invaluable was that fund of love and service that was always there for her to draw on whenever she wished. *"Dear good Lehzen takes such care of me . . . that I shall never be able to repay her sufficiently for it but by my love and gratitude. . . . She is the most affectionate, devoted, attached and disinterested friend I have, and I love her most dearly."* As we have seen, this eager child's capacity for loving was as vital as everything else in her. Within this capacious affection Uncle Leopold held his place as firmly as ever. Letters went to and fro between the King of the Belgians and his "dear little soul." "Now comes the time," he wrote to her on her fourteenth birthday, "when the judgement must form itself, when the character requires attention. . . . To attain this object it is indispensable to give some little time to *reflection*." There follows the most practical mixture of casuistry and morality, the writer expatiating, as is the habit of most egoists, on the undesirability of selfishness. "Selfishness . . . ," he wrote, "makes the individual itself miserable . . . besides being the surest means of being disliked by everybody." Charming indeed when one considers some of Leopold's private activities.

Not many years back, sitting one night in the royal theater of the palace at Potsdam, Leopold had suddenly seen before him on the stage a young actress who, in appearance, was his adored Charlotte come to life again. The resemblance struck him as "literally astonishing." This charming and, incidentally, most respectable girl was Karoline Bauer, daughter of an officer in the Grand-ducal Baden Dragoons, and niece to Stockmar. Leopold, working on her emotions by representing himself as a heartbroken widower, and urging her to devote herself entirely to his happiness, raised in her kind young heart enough response to make her finally agree to throw over her career, to come to England with her mother, and to marry him morganatically.

All the subtleties of Leopold's ensuing heartless behavior to this sweet-dispositioned creature are recorded in the two volumes of her memoirs. Having completely broken up her life so as to acquire her for himself, he placed her and her mother in a pretty plaything villa in Regent's Park, where, himself enwrapped in melancholy and barely uttering a word, he would visit her with the then fashionable "drizzling box," demanding, however lovely a summer's

day might be afloat outside in the garden, that she should sit reading to him hour after hour while he ceaselessly "drizzled," that is,
by means of a little machine, turned the gold or silver in such things
as tassels or epaulettes back into their original powder. These
dreary séances were the Bauers' sole interest and amusement. A
morganatic marriage (whether genuine or mock is open to doubt)
took place in the cottage. Leopold, himself then going for a prolonged stay at Claremont, pushed the Bauers into a small, tree-
choked house close by, so dark, dismal, and cold that to the mother
and daughter, accustomed to the gay theatrical life of Berlin, it was
like being buried alive. Leopold made them live as economically
as possible, not even providing Karoline with so much as a pony
carriage to relieve the cloistered dreariness of her days. She implored to be allowed to return to Berlin, but each time she broached
the subject, her uncle, Stockmar, working on her feelings, persuaded her to stay. In 1830 Karoline's brother, a cavalry officer,
arriving on the scene, some money complications arose over which
Leopold behaved so offensively that the tie between him and his
morganatic wife was finally snapped, and the Bauers went back to
Germany.

But to Victoria her Uncle Leopold appeared as a compendium
of all the virtues, and his admonitory letters were received with the
same enthusiasm with which she greeted every facet that life turned
to her. Leopold's exhortations undoubtedly helped to develop her
intelligence. After considering one of his letters in particular, she
wrote back: "I am much obliged to you, dear Uncle, for the extract
about Queen Anne, but must beg you, as you have sent [it] to show
me what a Queen *ought not* to be, that you will send me what a
Queen *ought to be.*"

Leopold was slightly taken aback. "My dearest love, you have
written a very clever, sharp little letter. . . . Sure enough, when I
show you what a Queen ought to be, I also ought to tell you what
she should not be, and this task I will very conscientiously take upon
myself on the very first occasion which may offer itself for a confidential communication. Now I must conclude to go to town." Very
wisely, King Leopold had no intentions of entrusting, even to the

royal post bag, the secrets as to his management of his Belgian subjects.

With Victoria in her teens, Lehzen thought that now, the very breath of coming queenship on her treasure, she ought not always to be keeping herself so modestly in the background, but "ought to act more like the heir-presumptive to the Throne." But her pupil was shrewder. "No," she protested, "there is no saying what may happen; I may be what I am all my life," and, so she added, it was "better to make a mistake on that side than on the other. . . ."

12

Victoria's sixteenth birthday; and inevitably the swarm of engravings, earrings, scent bottles, portfolios, filigree ornaments, vases, japanned boxes, and albums passed from hand to hand. In the fashion of the time, the Duchess had had a snippet of her own hair framed within the brooch that was her present.* However, a week before her birthday the Duchess had given her daughter a quite different kind of present—a concert at the palace, when the Kensington guests, sitting on chairs "all across the room," listened to the entrancing risings and fallings, the trills and sostenutos of some of the loveliest voices of the day. At such moments Victoria's youthful spirit escaped completely from its cage of suppression, and was borne away on pinions of joy. Every note, every tone, as she sat there "in the first row with Aunt Sophia and the Duchess of Cambridge and quite close to the piano," was savored and evaluated by her eager mind. *The most delightful concert I ever heard.* Aunt Sophia, who had *never* heard any of these singers before, was delighted; but no one could be *more enchanted* than *I* was. I shall never forget it. It was Mamma's birthday present for me! . . . I stayed up till twenty minutes past one. I was *most exceedingly* delighted."

This year an American writer, Nathaniel Willis, went to the Ascot races. In one of the intervals, as he strolled beneath the King's

---

* This carrying about shreds of each other's hair was an obsession of the period. Lady Emmeline Stuart-Wortley, for instance, during her world travels invariably took with her "A lock of Byron's hair, given by Augusta Leigh and shrined in a silver lyre, together with a lock of the hair of Napoleon's mother, given by herself."

stand, his eye was suddenly caught by two elegant feminine figures leaning over the railing, both prinked out to give the fashionable big-bonneted, sloping-shoulder silhouette of the moment. The American realized he was face to face with Princess Victoria and her Aunt, Queen Adelaide. In the summery June air, Victoria's rosy face within the curving contour of her great pink bonnet was lit with young happiness at the varied, shifting scene before her— all the vociferous raggle-taggle of humanity that contrasted so sharply with the soft-voiced, summer-flounced ladies, and their attendant lounging males, hair curled and glossy above their high-collared coats. "The uniforms of the soldiery and the magnificent attire of the ladies of rank and fashion who attended in their thousands, combined with the glorious summer day, gave an *éclat* to a scene never to be forgotten." The American took his fill of this royal couple as they leaned there side by side listening to a ballad singer: Adelaide (whom he mentally dubbed "undoubtedly the plainest woman in her dominions") and the far more seductive little figure at her side dressed in "a rose-colored satin dress, *broché*, with a pelerine cape trimmed with black lace." "Much better-looking than any picture of her in the shops," decided Willis, "and for the heir to such a crown as that of England unnecessarily pretty and interesting." It may have been at this Ascot that Victoria won a bet from the King in the shape of a chestnut mare, which she named—if not already so named—Taglioni, after the dancer.

13

The next month, on a July morning breathless from heat, Victoria was dressed in a white lace dress, and a white crepe bonnet. Round this little bonnet was a wreath of roses, and they too were white. She was to be taken to St. James's Palace for her confirmation. That religious emotion, direct and sincere, that was to flow on, quiet and untroubled, through her whole life, is already apparent in her Journal entry for this day. "I felt deeply repentant for all that I had done which was wrong. . . . I went with the firm determination to become a true Christian, to try and comfort my dear Mamma in all her griefs, trials, and anxieties, and to become a dutiful and affectionate daughter to her. Also to be obedient to *dear* Lehzen who has done so much for me."

At half-past eleven they all came out into the courtyard, where, in the mingled sunlight and shadow, the carriages were waiting. The white-clad figure climbed into the "chariot," and sat down by her mother. The others from the palace who were going with them mounted into another carriage. Then they set off; the Kensington fields and gardens, as they drove along by them, the little cottages with their red-tiled roofs and vine-covered walls, all lying somnolent in the heat-burnished air. The two carriages arrived at the Chapel. "We went into the King's Closet with Lady Flora and Lehzen, where we were received by the King and Queen." Aunt Sophia was there too, the Duke of Cumberland, and many others. When the moment came for her to be confirmed, Victoria took off her little bonnet. On one side of her as she stood at the altar rail was the King, and on the other the befurbelowed Duchess. After the archbishop had confirmed her, he read out the address he had composed for the occasion. This exhortation proved to be of the most disintegrating nature. Was it an unconscious, masculine annoyance that this outstanding young feminine creature should before long be gliding into a position of immeasurable power that had goaded him, in the solitude of his study, to compose this treatise that represented her future so dark with responsibility; her inevitable coming struggles between the calls of this world and those of the next as so painfully acute? The white-clad figure continued to stand there at the altar rails confronting the two ecclesiastics, archbishop and bishop, who, towering above her in their sacerdotal robes, might have been two hierarchical figures stepped out of a stained-glass window to admonish and intimidate her. Victoria's realization that every eye in the Chapel was centered upon her, combined with the piteous straining of her extremely tender heart to be worthy of this spiritual initiation, was having a strong effect upon her emotions, and now, as this man of God, unaware of, or indifferent to, the vulnerability of the young thing before him, pursued his exhortation, those pellucid blue eyes riveted on his face became suffused, tears began to glisten, and finally, her head falling on the Duchess' stalwart shoulder, sobs shook her. Even the Duchess herself, that firmly rooted lady, was made so uncomfortable by the Archbishop's grim forebodings that she too was "very much affected."

A good deal shattered by this experience, mother and daughter finally came away from the altar rails. Then they went back into "the Closet," and here the inevitable present-giving burst forth, the King pressing into his shaken little niece's hands "a very handsome set of emeralds, and the Queen a head-piece of the same kind." Even when the Duchess and Victoria had driven home again, the horses trotting along through the torrid heat of early afternoon, still further presents passed to and fro, the Duchess giving Victoria a bracelet containing yet another snippet of her hair, also a set of turquoises. Lehzen, too, received a present from the Duchess.

But the archbishop had effected more havoc in his victim than perhaps even he had intended, and now, though she was at peace once more in the sun-drenched quiet of the palace rooms, her tears again began to flow. "I was very much affected indeed when we came home."

14

After all these anxious self-searchings within Victoria's young mind there came to her in the autumn an event that glowed for her with delight; a visit to England of King Leopold and his new wife, a daughter of Louis Philippe, whom Victoria had not yet seen.

To meet them on their arrival, the Duchess and Victoria went down to Ramsgate, and the Journal received the explanatory information, "The open, free, boundless (to the eye) ocean looked very refreshing." At four o'clock, she, her mother, Flora Hastings, and Lady Conroy went to the Albion Hotel, and all seated themselves at a window to watch the steamer bearing the precious couple as it drew in.

With beating heart [writes the little enthusiast], we sat at the window, anxiously watching the steamer's progress. There was an immense concourse of people on the pier to see them arrive. After about half an hour's time, the steamer entered the Harbour, amidst loud cheering and the salute of guns from the pier, with the Belgian flag on its mast. My *dearest* Uncle Leopold, King of the Belgians, and *dearest* Aunt Louisa were very warmly received. It was but the people's duty to do so, as dear Uncle has lived for so long in England and was so much beloved. After another ¼ of an hour of anxious suspense, the waiter told us that "Their Majesties were coming." We hastened downstairs to receive them. There was an immense crowd before the door. At length Uncle appeared, having Aunt Louisa at his arm. What a happiness it was for me to throw myself in the arms of that *dearest* of Uncles, who has always been to me like a father, and whom I love so *very dearly!* I had not seen him for 4 years and 2 months. I was also delighted to make the acquaintance of that dear Aunt who is such a perfection and who has been always so kind to me, without knowing me. We hastened upstairs, where Uncle Leopold and Aunt Louisa showed themselves at the window and were loudly cheered; as they ought to be. I do not find dear Uncle at all changed. On the contrary, I think he looks better than he did when I last saw him. Aunt Louisa is not quite so tall as Mamma, and has a very pretty slight figure. Her hair is of a lovely fair colour; her nose is aquiline, her eyes are quite lovely; they are light blue, and have such a charming expression. She has such a sweet mouth and smile too. She is delightful, and so affectionate to me directly.... She was very simply dressed in a light brown silk dress, with a sky-blue silk bonnet and white veil.

In the evening Aunt Louisa was, if anything, still more entrancing in white moire, "and her fine hair was so well done in a plait behind and curls in front with a row of pearls and three black velvet bows in it." "Aunt Louisa has the most *delightful sweet* expression I ever saw. . . . She is so gay and merry too."

On this exceptional September evening Victoria sat at dinner between her recaptured Uncle and the Duc de Nemours, "two *delightful* neighbours." But as Victoria wrote in her Journal describing how they were placed at dinner, it struck her she must add an explanation, for, ingenuous in some ways as she still was, the sense of her position was beginning to form round her a slight sheath of self-importance. Even her Journal must not commit *lèse-majesté,* must not for a moment imagine that when she wrote of herself as sitting "next" to anyone she was referring to precedence, and not merely to the placing of her body on its chair. "When I say *next* to a person, as for instance I said the other day. . . 'I sat next to the Duc de Nemours' etc. etc. I mean, as I did to-day, that I sat *between* or next to them at *dinner.*"

Meanwhile, without doubt, one of Victoria's joys in being with her uncle was that she could talk openly to him—as he sat close beside her with that melancholy but arresting face—of all the intricate difficulties of life at Kensington Palace, of the way she had to keep all natural feelings suppressed, and of the little confidence she could feel in her mother, influenced as the Duchess was by Conroy. That she did confide in him, and that he was well aware of the Kensington Palace entanglements, is evident from his saying to Victoria in one of his letters a year or two later, "the irksome position in which you have lived will have the merit to have given you habits of discretion and prudence."

In March the following year the Duchess of Kent's brother Prince Ferdinand came on a visit to England with his sons, Ferdinand and Augustus. This son, Ferdinand, had been married by proxy the month before to the Queen of Portugal, that former herbarium giver, already an extremely youthful widow. "Dear Uncle Leopold has managed a *great* deal of the business; he is ever ready and ever *most able* to assist his family." He was indeed. Some people, watching the gradual spread of the Coburgs across Europe, considered that Uncle Leopold was too able. These two young cousins greatly intrigued Victoria: their eyes, smiles, facial expressions, orderliness, and tidiness all being noted and duly registered by the Journalist; the general summing-up being, "They are both very handsome and *very dear*." It seems that never before had she had the chance of having delightful giggles with a young man over nothing. Augustus happening one day to come into her sitting room, they both started sealing some letters she had written, "and we both made a mess, and he burnt a cover in sealing it, dear boy, for me, which made us both laugh. . . . Oh! could I but have some more such days, with that dear Uncle and dear Augustus, whom I love so much! I shall feel very lonely and unhappy when they leave us. . . ."

CHAPTER VI
THE DUCHESS OF KENT SURPASSES HERSELF

F_{OR} the moment we leave the sixteen-year-old Victoria at Kensington Palace, and go back into the past, to Coburg in 1823. A children's royal ball, a fancy-dress one, is pursuing its way, the air filled with the chirping voices, the castanets of laughter from the excited guests. Partners for the little girls, perhaps for some quadrille, are being chosen by the grownups. Among these partners is one little boy in particular, a quite small boy with tossed yellow curls and great eyes, whom everyone in the room finds it a delight to look at, so dowered is he with charm and beauty, and perhaps especially at this moment when—presumably a mere suggestion of clothing about his tiny body, light wings springing from his shoulders—he skips about in the guise of Cupid. Now the children, arranged in pairs, are being told to go forward. All move on except Cupid, who merely covers his face with his hands and begins to scream. Every inducement brought to bear on him fails completely: this child of Venus merely screams, and screams. The din he creates, in fact, can only be equalled in volume by that which his little cousin of five across the Channel manages herself to create in her Kensington nursery. For this squealing Cupid is the Duchess of Kent's nephew Albert, son to her brother, the Duke of Saxe-Saalfeld-Coburg.*

This enchanting little creature had a horror of strangers. At the very sight of a visitor he would rush to the farthest end of the room, his face in his hands, and, if urged to come back, would merely give vent to a series of those accomplished shrieks. But, with those he knew well, his gentle affection, his enchanting little man-

---

* In 1826 he became Duke of Saxe-Coburg and Gotha.

nerisms were irresistible. It seems that even as his Coburg grandmother—a remarkably brisk-minded woman—had leaned over his
cradle, she had made up her mind that he and Victoria should marry
each other. He was, she wrote, "bewitching, forward, and quick as
a weasel." But all this quickness and bewitchingness were great
users-up of energy, and by early evening Albert's minute organism
was invariably overcome by an irresistible urge to go to sleep. The
tutor engaged to teach him and his elder brother, Ernest, was surprised at their supper on the first evening to see the five-year-old
Albert gradually dropping to sleep as he ate, and then, unconscious,
falling from his chair to the ground, where he continued his slum-
bers. As he grew older, this craving for sleep and yet more sleep
continued, and if for any reason prevented from going to bed at the
usual hour, he would creep behind the window curtains, and there
sink to oblivion. While still only five, he started a diary, and it is
evident from its pages that tears often stained that cherubic countenance.

23rd January. When I awoke this morning I was ill. My cough was
worse. I was so frightened that I cried.

26th January. We recited, and I cried because I could not say my
repetition, for I had not paid attention.... I was not allowed to play
after dinner because I had cried whilst repeating.

28th February. I cried at my lesson to-day, because I could not find
a verb: and the Rath pinched me, to show me what a verb was. And
I cried about it.

Tears, however, became scarcer as he discovered by degrees what
a multitude of absorbing things there are to do in life: to do, and,
above all, to learn. By the time he was thirteen he was absorbing
knowledge as a plant does water. Methodical schemes and schedules
for work were enthusiastically adopted by a mind that found positive enjoyment in mental effort. He had early discovered, as had
his little royal cousin in England, the blessings of occupation: "to
do something was with him a necessity."

When he was still only about five his father obtained a separation
order from his wife, and Albert never saw his mother again. This
sensitive little Princess Louise of Saxe-Gotha-Altenburg had been

married to the Duke at sixteen. After being divorced from him in
1826, she remarried.

A curious habit of Albert's father was always interfering with
the industry of the Coburg schoolroom. The Duke elected on fine
days, not only to have the family breakfast out of doors, but each
day to have it in a different place, this often necessitating a drive
for miles in search of the breakfast table. To the exasperation of
the boys' tutor, Councilor Florschütz, time earmarked for lessons
would be taken up with this continual rushing about the country
in pursuit of food: "the greater part of the forenoon," wrote the
irritated Florschütz, "was inevitably wasted. . . . The Duke, however, was indifferent to this." As Ernest and Albert grew older
and were promoted to dining with their father, still more lesson
time was wasted, as this meal, too, proved as much of a will-o'-the-
wisp as was breakfast. "We can only wonder," continues the tutor,
"that, notwithstanding, the Princes retained their love for study."
Albert was chiefly brought up at his father's country house, The
Rosenau. Insidiously the wooded hills around, the hushed solitude of this romantic sun-and-wind-enveloped little castle, the
stream sliding beneath the trees, crept into the boy Albert's heart,
and remained there for life. It seemed, indeed, as if all this shining
loveliness had itself woven the stuff of his being, so radiantly
charming was his disposition. Even when he was quite a small boy
those around him noticed his thoughtfulness for other people, and
how painfully any unhappiness of theirs would affect that already
compassionate spirit.

2

Early one May afternoon, a week before Victoria's seventeenth
birthday, she and the Duchess came side by side out of "the red
saloon." Then, stepping along the landing to reach one of the two
flights of lovely, iron-wrought staircases, passed by the little sphinx-
terminal busts of the balustrade—mute but appropriate creatures
to be witnesses of this moment—for the reason the Duchess and
Victoria were going down to the hall was that the Duke of Coburg
and his two sons, Ernest and Albert, were at this very moment
driving into the Kensington courtyard for a visit of several weeks.

This was the first time Victoria and Albert saw each other. After all the greetings were over, the group went talking together up the stairs, and then, writes Victoria, "after staying for a few minutes with them I went up to my room." Once there she sat herself down to play and to sing, to give vent, one may well believe, to the tremor of excitement that must inevitably have been running through her at having, only a few minutes since, first set eyes on, and talked to, this now sixteen-year-old cousin whom, as she knew, her mother and Uncle Leopold were eager for her to marry. For Leopold, having first taken the precaution of sending Stockmar to Coburg to find out everything about his young nephew, had decided that Albert was in every way the very husband for Victoria.

Serene as the arrival of Uncle Ernest and his sons appeared, they had, in reality, alighted on the very crest of a royal storm, for William IV, who, in the person of his Kent sister-in-law, had had quite enough experience of dealings with the Coburg blood, had become choleric when he discovered that in pursuance of the Duchess and Leopold's plans, Albert and his brother had actually been asked to stay at Kensington Palace. Determined to counter this project, he invited the Prince of Orange to bring his two sons over at the same time, with the intention that Victoria should marry the younger, Prince Alexander. In his annoyance at the whole situation, King William had protested "that no other marriage should ever take place, and that the Duke of Saxe-Coburg and his son should never put foot in the country: they should not be allowed to land, and must go back whence they came."

The noise of all this commotion had inevitably reached Leopold's ears.

I am really *astonished* [he wrote to Victoria], at the conduct of your old Uncle the King; this invitation of the Prince of Orange and his sons, this forcing him upon others, is very extraordinary.... Not later than yesterday I got a half-official communication from England, insinuating that it would be *highly* desirable that the visit of *your* relatives *should not take place this year—qu'en dites-vous?* The relations of the Queen and the King, therefore, to the God-knows-what degree, are to come in shoals and rule the land, when *your relations* are to be *forbidden* the country, and that when, as you know, the whole of your relations have ever been very dutiful and kind to the King. Really and truly I never heard or saw anything like it, and I hope it will a *little rouse your spirit;* now that slavery is even abolished in the British Colonies, I do not comprehend *why your lot alone should be to be kept, a white little slavey in England,* for the pleasure of the Court, who never bought you, as I am not aware of their having gone to any expense on that head, or the King's even having *spent a sixpence for your existence.* I expect that my visits in England will also be prohibited by an Order in Council. Oh consistency and political or *other honesty,* where must one look for you!

If Leopold thought the King of England's behavior "extraordinary" he might have been still more nonplussed if he had been aware of all the divagations of the King's mind on the question of a husband for his niece. Considerations on this subject were inevitably intermixed with yet another: the separation of Hanover and England that would ensue when Victoria succeeded to the throne. To avoid this separation the King had at times even contemplated the advisability of his niece marrying the Duke of Cumberland's son, a boy now completely blind from an accident. Meanwhile the King's younger brother, the Duke of Cambridge, had, as we have seen, his private thoughts on the subject, and looked on his own son, Queen Adelaide's special pet, as the suitable husband for Victoria. For some reason, however, Victoria took but little notice of this cousin, whereas, if the author of *Victoria, Queen and Ruler*— who possessed a great deal of handed-down information—is to be believed, Victoria "showed a tender interest in the Prince of Cumberland . . . after his sight began to fail. William IV, and still more the Duke of Wellington, had favoured the idea of preserving by a marriage the union between the Crowns of Great Britain and Hanover. The advantage in the Duke's mind was that it gave the Crown so much power to contend with the Liberal side of Parliament. George III displaced majorities in the House of Commons by the purchase for his friends, with Hanoverian funds, of pocket boroughs. As a High Tory, the Duke approved of this. . . ."

Certainly a tortuous and extraordinary consideration on which to base the marriage of England's future Queen.

"After the blindness of the Prince of Cumberland became utter and incurable," continues our authority, "the Duchess of Gloucester took upon herself to turn the thoughts of her young niece towards the Cambridge cousin." The author of *Victoria, Queen and Ruler*, from information that had been passed down to her from the Duke of Sussex's household, emphasizes "how hotly and anxiously the subject of the Hanoverian succession was discussed in the different Royal households in London. It agitated Clarence House . . . Buckingham Palace, Kensington, and even disturbed the even-tempered Duchess of Gloucester. The King wavered a good deal. He was one day for the union of the Crowns by a marriage between his niece and the blind Prince; another day he inclined to break through any survival of the Salic law": in which case, when Victoria became Queen, England and Hanover would have remained united.

However, the Duchess of Kent, instigated by Leopold, had, as we have seen, cut across all these cogitations by the simple gesture of inviting her brother Ernest to come to stay at the palace, bringing the prospective Coburg bridegroom with him. "I have not the least doubt," Leopold had written to Victoria, "that the King in his passion for the Oranges will be *excessively rude to your relations;* this, however, will not signify much; they are *your guests* and not *his*, and will therefore *not* mind it. . . ."

To return to Victoria in her sitting room on the afternoon of the arrival of the Coburgs. After she had calmed herself by playing and singing, she sat down to draw, but as her pencil twitched to and fro, the door opened, and Uncle Ernest and the two boys came in. Needless to say, Uncle Ernest instantly handed her a present: "a most delightful *Lory*, which is so tame that it remains on your hand. . . . It is larger than Mamma's grey parrot, and has a most beautiful plumage, it is scarlet, blue, brown, yellow, and purple." It seems almost shocking not to read of Ernest and Albert too immediately showering her with presents. But we do not hear of any. For the moment the lory was considered sufficient.

When the young men saw where Aunt Kent had lodged them in the palace, they considered their quarters rather cramped. "We have not a great deal of room in our apartment," Albert wrote home. It seems peculiar that the Duchess had not given them more space, as she had lately appropriated to herself seventeen extra rooms in the palace, which led on from those that had originally been allotted her. She had asked the King for these particular rooms a year before, but had been told she could not have them. With an effrontery that outran even her usual behavior, she had then, after a few months' pause, simply, and unknown to the King, taken possession of them. In the January of this year, returning to London after being at the seaside, Victoria, unaware of her mother's impudence, delightedly expatiates in her Journal on all their new acquisitions, though "to describe them minutely and accurately would be impossible. Our bedroom is very large and lofty, and is very nicely furnished, then comes a little room for the maid, and a dressing-room for Mamma; then comes the old gallery which is partitioned into three large, lofty, fine, and cheerful rooms. One only of these (the one near Mamma's dressing-room) is ready furnished; it is my sitting-room and is *very* prettily furnished indeed. My pictures are not yet in it. The next is my study, and the last is an anteroom; this last has no fireplace, but the two others have, and my sitting-room is very warm and comfortable. There is another room, belonging to me, on another side of the bedroom (Lehzen's former bedroom) which is not freshly furnished, but is a passage etc. Lehzen is now in our former bedroom. When I went down into my poor former sitting-room, I could not help looking at it with affection and pleasant recollections, having passed so many days of my life and many very pleasant ones there; but our new rooms are much more airy and roomy"; and, the next day, "Carried things from my old room, upstairs to my new room, and put them in the presses. Wrote my journal. My pictures are being hung up and my room is in a great confusion; the workmen in my study are making a great noise, so that I am *un peu confuse.*"

No doubt one of the reasons for this determined house expansion on the part of the Duchess was to impress her brother and nephews on their visit. She had certainly spread herself over a good piece of the Palace.

If she did not think it necessary to give Ernest and Albert larger breathing space, she showed them all that well-planned charm which made those who met her think her delightful. "Dear Aunt is very kind to us," wrote Albert, "and does everything to please us." Meanwhile, he must have been thankful to be anywhere where he had a floor beneath his feet that did not heave, so much had he detested crossing the Channel. "The journey to England has given me such a disgust for the sea that I do not like even to think of it."

This young man of sixteen no longer buried his face in his hands when confronted with a stranger, but, as much as ever, during those evening hours when everyone else seemed to become doubly awake, he, on the contrary, became drugged with sleepiness. Now, at all the dinners and concerts, at "the brilliant ball given here at Kensington Palace" by indefatigable, triumphant Aunt Kent, how cruel it was for this drowsy boy to have to stand about, to dance, to smile, to bow, to listen, to make intelligent replies in that difficult English language, when on every side, over every window, hung the most desirable curtains, festooned and tasseled, heavily drooping in their long, musty folds, behind which, as at The Rosenau, he would so gladly have crept to give way to that blurring sensation that was every moment pressing down his lids. "You can imagine I had many hard battles to fight against sleepiness during these later entertainments," ran one of his letters.

It was not only drowsiness that spoiled the modicum of pleasure that he might have drawn from these airless, crowded rooms filled with the chattering of fashionably toned voices, in addition he found it all most exhausting. "My first appearance was at a levée of the King's . . . long and fatiguing. . . . The same evening we dined at Court, and at night there was a beautiful concert, at which we had to stand till two o'clock." "The climate of this country, the different way of living, and the late hours, do not agree with me." All this emphasis on fatigue is in one letter alone. It may have been the invisible spiritual flame burning so strongly within that was consuming the nervous force in that fine-grown and otherwise physically energetic boy of sixteen. The proportions of his qualities differed from those of the normal. Behind his jokes, his spurts of whimsical gaiety, and, equally, behind his powers of application, and yawns of exhaustion, an exceptional being was in process of formation. Later, his body, steadily maturing, grew firmer, more close knit, and, except for this unusual craving for sleep, seemingly for many years all was well, but his mental and emotional alertness, his constant cerebral activity, and pursuit of ideals, created an obscure but perpetual strain that, finally, was to prove too great.

Now, during this two weeks' visit of the Coburgs to England, outside, in Kensington Gardens, the branches of the chestnuts and May trees were clotted with buds; and within the palace, Victoria, her silvery voice slipping now at any moment into delighted laughter, tripped about the great rooms, her mind tense with the exciting presences of her boy cousins. Her Journal received the overflow of her lightly happy emotions. Needless to say, Albert's physical characteristics were all carefully documented. "Albert, who is just as tall as Ernest but stouter, is extremely handsome; his hair is about the same colour as mine [a light brown], his eyes are large and blue, and he has a beautiful nose and a very sweet mouth with fine teeth; but the charm of his countenance is his expression, which is most delightful; *c'est à la fois* full of goodness and sweetness, and very clever and intelligent." Three days after their arrival, "I sat between my dear Cousins on the sofa and we looked at drawings. They both draw very well, particularly Albert; and are both exceedingly fond of music; they play very nicely on the piano. The more I see them the more I am delighted with them, and the more I love them. They are so natural, so kind, so *very* good and so well instructed and informed; they are so well-bred, so truly merry and quite like children, and yet very grown-up in their manners and conversation. It is delightful to be with them; they are so found of being occupied too; they are quite an example for any young person." The last remark obviously stolen *in toto* from her mother or Lehzen.

At this period we must envisage Victoria's immature body as entirely concealed within balloon outlines, for such was the accepted fashion of the moment. But though her smooth, immature face would have been, during this Coburg visit, lit with that animation that so enhanced it; though Albert played in his own charmingly droll fashion with her dog; though he was ready enough to sit close to her on the sofa while she showed him her drawings; though he was on all occasions most good-humoredly pleasant, his reactions to her were entirely devoid of that pulse of enthusiasm that marked hers to him. In fact the only comment he vouchsafed in his letters home was "our cousin also is very agreeable." But as for "our cousin," every day her tingling appreciation increased, until, cutting across all this springtime joy, there came that dreadful day, that heavy hour when good-bys had to be voiced. When, on that sad Friday morning, she came downstairs for the final leave-taking, she found the air full of music, for, "Dearest Albert was playing on the piano."

Then it was a case of the sphinx staircase again . . . but, alas, this time the whole party descending instead of ascending. "At eleven dear Uncle, my dearest beloved Cousins . . . left us. I embraced both my dearest Cousins most warmly, as also my dear Uncle. I cried bitterly, very bitterly. . . ." All that was left her now was the memory of these entrancing weeks, and a small ring Albert had given her. It was a simple little affair of enamel with a tiny diamond in the center—the kind of ring that a very shy young man presents to a very ingénue young girl.

After they had gone, the only thing left for her to do was to write down in her Journal all her emotions on the "beloved Cousins, whom I *do* love so VERY, VERY dearly. . . . Dearly as I love Ferdinand, and also good Augustus, I love Ernest and Albert *more* than them, oh yes, MUCH MORE." Augustus' deficiencies are next carefully dealt with, and then follows: "but dearest Ernest and dearest Albert are so grown-up in their manners, so gentle, so kind, so amiable, so agreeable, so very sensible and reasonable, and so *really* and truly kindhearted . . . they like very much talking about serious and instructive things and yet are so *very*, *very* merry and gay and happy, like young people ought to be; Albert used always to have some fun and some clever witty answer at breakfast and everywhere; he used to play and fondle Dash so funnily too. Both he and Ernest are extremely attentive to *whatever* they hear and see. . . . They were much interested with the sight of St. Paul's yesterday."

Though Albert's single comment on his cousin in his letter home showed but little ardor, he yet, as is evident later, was not only quietly satisfied with her, but pleased at the enthusiastic response he had awakened. For, to put it bluntly, Victoria was his career. His brother Ernest would in due course succeed their father as Duke of Coburg, while Albert had to find a niche for himself elsewhere, and he was in consequence—though he and Victoria were impelled toward each other by very different motives—as ready to have her as she him.

However, now, each having been shown off to the other as had been arranged by Leopold and Victoire, Albert returned to Germany. The next year he went to the University of Bonn to be further trained and equipped for the vocation that, so it was hoped, awaited him. Victoria was left to peruse through her tears such tomes as *Ikon Basilike, The Conquest of Granada, The Young Divine,* and so on, by means of which it was hoped she would attain the stature suitable for a queen. Some of Lehzen's efforts to this end sound peculiar, but perhaps, considering for what her pupil was destined, they were practical; for instance, setting her to copy out pages from the Peerage. In addition, Victoria, so that not a moment of her educational days should be left lying fallow, pushed her way every morning through these stiff volumes even "while my hair was doing."

Three days before Albert and his relations had left Kensington, Victoria had sat down and composed a letter to Leopold which she gave to her Uncle Ernest to hand to his brother when they met. This was, presumably, in Paris, as the Coburgs went there after leaving England, and Albert was entertained at an official dinner given by Lord Granville "which was taken to mean that good progress had been made with the scheme of the projected marriage."

When Leopold's eye ran down the letter from his seventeen-year-old niece, he must have realized that his carefully matured "scheme" had certainly made good progress.

7th June 1836

My dearest Uncle,—These few lines will be given to you by my dear Uncle Ernest when he sees you.

I must thank you, my beloved Uncle, for the prospect of *great* happiness you have contributed to give me, in the person of dear Albert. Allow me, then, my dearest Uncle, to tell you how delighted I am with him.... He possesses every quality that could be desired to render me perfectly happy. He is so sensible, so kind, and so good, and so amiable too. He has, besides, the most pleasing and delightful exterior and appearance you can possibly see.

I have only now to beg you, my dearest Uncle, to take care of the health of one, now *so dear* to me, and to take him under *your special* protection. I hope and trust that all will go on prosperously and well on this subject of so much importance to me.

Believe me always, my dearest Uncle, your most affectionate, devoted, and grateful Niece,

VICTORIA

Leopold's return letter was certainly a little flat, referring to Albert and his relations merely as "good, unsophisticated people," and urging Victoria to use "all your natural caution" when talking to Uncle William or Aunt Adelaide. "Never permit yourself to be induced to tell them any opinion or sentiment of yours which is *beyond the sphere of common conversation.*"

After her cousins' departure Victoria's mind, a mind that if left to itself would have liked always to be gay, was more and more taken up with oppressive thoughts of what was now clearly drawing close to her, for it was evident that the King's health was gradually going to pieces. The misunderstanding of the country over his attitude to the Reform Bill, and the consequent unpopularity this brought on him; his restless animosity against France ("whether at peace or at war with that country I shall always consider her as our natural enemy," he roared with his usual tactlessness at a regimental dinner); the truculence of his illegitimate sons and daughters, to whom, nevertheless, he was devoted; the exasperations caused by the behavior of the Duchess of Kent; and, as each spring came round, what looked very like the beginnings of mental derangement in his always excitable mind: all these combined had worn away his naturally enthusiastic temperament. "What can you expect," exclaimed an onlooker sarcastically, "from a man with a head like a pineapple?" That which when he first came to the throne had appeared as a flair for kingship, had now disappeared completely. The poor man had become, says Greville, "such an ass that nobody does anything but laugh at what he says."

3

It is noticeable that these groups of Victoria's visiting German cousins, the Württembergs, the Ferdinand Coburgs, and now Ernest and Albert, had had the same effect, if in different degrees, of making an indefinable something quiver about Victoria's easily aroused emotions like the flicker of summer lightning. Now that the last of them, Albert, who, to her mind, outtopped all the others, had departed, her singing master, the huge operatic maestro Lablache, was all that was left to supply, if only in a paternal manner, that masculine element in her life which, unconsciously to herself, was becoming a necessity. The portentous sounds that issued from Lablache were in keeping with his size. By the side of this barrel of a man the Duchess' solidity was reduced to nothing; and as for his little pupil, all quick breathings and parted lips and bemused, shining eyes as she listened to him, she became a mere wisp of sensibility wafted about like a feather on the harmonies that came booming out of him. At the first of these musical séances, faced with such size and such accomplishment combined, her nervousness, when she was asked to sing herself, had been so apparent that the giant had assured her that, *"Personne n'a jamais eu peur de moi,"* on which her tremulous tones had ventured forth. Sometimes the three voices, hers, the Duchess', and Lablache's, would be heard all gamboling away together; and it is to be hoped Victoria and the Duchess were more in tune than a year before when they had sung a duet on some country-house visit, and Lady Holland had heard afterward that "The singing of Mother and daughter was execrably inharmonious, but of course was highly lauded."

These singing lessons when Victoria was spirited away into the musical sphere by her leviathan teacher were for her gala hours. "I only wish I had one every *day* instead of one every *week*"; and again, after the last lesson on an August day before they were going off for a visit to Claremont, "I took leave of *il mio buon e caro Maestro* with *great* regret . . . I have had 26 lessons . . . and shall look forward with equal delight to next April. . . . It was such a pleasure to hear his fine voice and to sing with him. Everything that is pleasant, alas! passes so quickly. . . . I was exceedingly delighted with this my *last* lesson; the time seemed to fly even faster than usual, for it always appeared to me that these pleasant lessons were over in an instant . . . he was always ready to sing anything I like and to stay as long as I liked."

Psychologically, it is of great interest to glance for a moment at this enraptured girl at her singing lessons, and to listen to those three people warbling away in that quiet Kensington drawing room.

For to Victoria, Lablache, so fascinating in his solidly masculine, elderly way, was, in the musical sphere, an adumbration of Melbourne in the political: each a paternal dominie to his ardent, all but amorous young pupil.

Lehzen, her perceptions quickened by love, noted everything. For some time now she had been conscious how every fiber in this young apprentice of life was quickening, intensifying, and the governess was becoming nervous at these adolescent enthusiasms. Only too aware of Victoria's occasional fits of obstinate determination, she had constantly impressed caution on the Duchess, emphasized the danger of ever allowing Victoria opportunities of losing her heart in undesirable directions. We read that Conroy one day made the Duchess distraught by carelessly tossing off the idea that one of William IV's sons, that worldly, joking divine and bastard, Lord "Gus" Fitzclarence, was just the man one day to fling aside his surplice and scamper away to Gretna Green with an heiress: for at that time Gretna Green marriages were a very present reality, and a perpetual menace to parents and guardians. Some extravagant fear of this sort may have added to the Duchess' reluctance— to the increasing indignation of William IV—to allow Victoria to appear at Court, or to have much to do with William's family of undeniably attractive and amusing illegitimates. If the Duchess looked askance at the royal bastards, so did their father at the Duchess' advisers. "I have great distrust of the persons by whom she is surrounded," he remarked at a birthday dinner in 1835; and, about that time, Melbourne, meeting Greville one day in St. James's Park, told him as they walked along together that "the King was in a state of great excitement . . . that the thing which affected him most was the conduct of the Duchess of Kent—her popularity-hunting, her progresses, and above all the addresses which she received and replied to."

Victoria's life as a schoolgirl was not without its accompanying clowns. Chief of these was a middle-aged widower who possessed both property at Tunbridge Wells and a phaeton. Seated in this he would drive up as near as he could to the palace. If on foot, it seems that he was allowed quite close, so he would dismount and then walk up to watch for Victoria coming out into the courtyard for a ride or drive. The moment she appeared he would rush forward frantically bowing and blowing kisses. What made it still more ludicrous was that he was always accompanied by two attendants—a couple of Peel's new policemen, trussed up in glazed top hats and swallow-tailed coats, who were detailed to look after him. So as to keep as close an eye as possible on Kensington Palace this eccentric would at times set to work to weed the Round Pond. Constable Osborne, T. 174, and Constable Mount, T. 90, lolling near by in official attendance.

Bouquets and sheets of verses would arrive at the palace for Victoria from other admirers. It is even said that some young men, madly driven beneath the star of Venus, went so far as to shoot themselves for love of the Duke of Kent's daughter.

4

After these final cavortings over the piano with Lablache, in this summer of 1836, the Kensington group set off for their visit to Leopold at Claremont. If Creevey, with his shrewder mind, dubbed him "Humbug Leopold," to Victoria he was a compendium of wisdom ("To hear dear Uncle speak on any subject is like reading a highly instructive book") and he always gave her just that sense of support of which, particularly now, she felt in need. "I cannot expect to live very long," William IV had publicly announced the year before; and as the footsteps of Victoria's coming destiny sounded ever nearer, Leopold reassuringly held his niece's hand. "Went up to my room and copied out music," she wrote on one of these September days at Claremont. "At about a quarter to twelve dearest Uncle came and sat with me till quarter past twelve. He talked over many important things. He is *so* clever *so* mild and *so* prudent; *he* alone can give me good advice on *every* thing. . . . He is indeed 'il mio secondo padre'! or rather 'solo padre' for he is indeed like my real father, as I have none."

As for this "good advice on everything"—taking into consideration her uncle's reputation for chicanery—one cannot doubt but that now, as she fervently listened to his instructions, he had at the back of his mind a very lively sense of how useful it would be to him in the future to have an amenable niece seated on the English throne. Foiled of being Prince Consort to Charlotte, he might yet, though across the Channel, act Uncle Consort to Victoria. On this visit he not only gave good advice, in addition, so wrote his niece, he "always accompanied us upstairs when we went to bed," and further, even "came up and fetched us down to breakfast, as he has done already once before, and twice for dinner."

A certain Miss Jane Porter, who lived near Claremont, used on Sundays to go to Esher Church, and whenever the Claremont trio, the Duchess, Victoria, and Leopold, filed into the pew in their "colonnaded recess," it is evident that Miss Porter's attention was a good deal deflected from her Creator to those of high degree whom He had created. Especially had this been the case one hot Sunday when Miss Porter became entirely engrossed in watching the antics of a wasp that was whirling about in the most menacing manner "before the unveiled summer bonnet of the little Princess." As for Victoria, who, when she got back from church, always had to recount to Lehzen both the text and the headings of the sermon, she was far too occupied in acquiring this information to be even so much as aware of the wasp's existence. What, the enthralled Miss Porter asked herself, would be the outcome? Miss Porter's gaze became riveted, the wasp continued its gambols, then the hand of Uncle Leopold, who sat behind his niece, emerged. In the hand was a handkerchief, and adroitly, as the wasp frisked, the handkerchief whisked. And yet, noted Miss Porter, during all this silent scuffle between King and insect, Victoria remained "totally unobserving" of what was taking place. Those earnest eyes, pinned on the preacher, were not deflected for a moment. Miss Porter, astounded, went home and wrote it all down.

During this visit to Claremont there occurred an incident of greater import than the gyrations of a wasp. William IV's, Queen Adelaide's, and the Duchess of Kent's birthdays all fell in August; the Queen's on the 13th, the Duchess' on the 17th, and the King's on the 21st. This year, the King had asked her and Victoria to Windsor Castle, there visit to cover both his and his wife's birthdays, and the accompanying celebrations. However, that rancorous lady (who, it was observed, had "a really remarkable talent for giving offence whenever it is possible to do so") now discovered that it was necessary for her happiness that her own birthday should be passed at Claremont, and therefore wrote to her brother-in-law saying that she and Victoria would not arrive at Windsor until the twentieth, thus entirely ignoring poor Adelaide's birthday and its jubilations, which the Duchess in her letter did not so much as mention. Nothing rasped William IV more than a slight to his cherished Adelaide; and the Duchess' letter put him "in a fury."

On the day the Duchess and Victoria arrived at the castle for their visit, the King had to be in London to prorogue Parliament, and before returning to Windsor he decided he would look in at Kensington Palace for a general inspection of the Kents' apartments. Little did he think as he got down from his carriage into the courtyard of what awaited him within. Climbing the sphinx staircase, he walked into the Duchess' now deserted rooms, filled only with the drowsy silence of the August afternoon. To his stupefaction he discovered that in addition to the rooms originally allotted to his sister-in-law she had quietly appropriated seventeen more: the very ones she had the year before asked for, and had been definitely told by him she could not have. All her past aggressiveness, her slights and impertinences both to him and to his wife, were piled up unforgettably in the King's mind, and here was the culmination, the pinnacle of her insolence. He drove back to Windsor through the dwindling summer day, his mind seething. By the time his carriage drew up at the castle it was ten o'clock. He mounted the stairs. The Windsor party, which now included the Duchess of Kent and Victoria, were sprinkled about the drawing room when the door opened and in stumped that short, familiar figure. Ignoring the Duchess, the King went up to Victoria, took both her hands in his, and "expressed his pleasure at seeing her there and his regret at not seeing her oftener." Then, turning to the Duchess, he "made her a low bow," and "in a tone of serious displeasure," and so loud that everyone could hear what he said, he told her that "a most unwarrantable liberty had been taken with one of his palaces; that he had just come from Kensington, where he found apartments had been taken possession of not only without his consent, but contrary to his commands, and that he neither understood nor would endure conduct so disrespectful to him."

Wrought up as the King was, he had been careful, by speaking to Victoria so affectionately before he gave his jobation to her mother, to show his niece that he knew she was entirely innocent in the affair. But all the same, already precociously observant as she was of nuances in behavior, it must have been for her, standing there in the great room lit with its innumerable candles, surrounded on all sides with those only too interested, too observant faces, a moment of anguished humiliation. And also of complete surprise at hearing that all those spacious rooms into which they had so enjoyed spreading themselves had been deliberately stolen by her mother.

The King's sense of insult had only been momentarily assuaged by his slap at the Duchess. It was far from having spent itself, and Adolphus Fitzclarence, going into his father's room the next morning—the day being Sunday, the King's birthday—"found him in a state of great excitement." That evening at the castle there were a hundred people to dinner: members of the Court and various guests who had come from country houses around. The Duchess of Kent sat on one side of the King, and opposite him, across the table, sat Victoria. At the end of dinner, the King's health having been drunk, the monarch "in a loud voice," and "with an excited manner" made a speech, in the course of which, to the growing stupefaction of the faces around him, he burst out, "I trust in God that my life may be spared for nine months longer, after which period, in the event of my death, no Regency would take place. I should then have the satisfaction of leaving the royal authority to the personal exercise of that young lady (pointing to the Princess), the heiress presumptive of the Crown, and not in the hands of a person now near me, who is surrounded by evil advisers and who is herself incompetent to act with propriety in the station in which she would be placed. I have no hesitation in saying that I have been insulted—grossly and continually insulted—by that person, but I am determined to endure no longer a course of behaviour so disrespectful to me. Amongst many other things I have particularly to complain of the manner in which that young lady has been kept away from my Court; she has been repeatedly kept from my drawing rooms, at which she ought always to have been present, but I am fully re-solved that this shall not happen again. I would have her know that I am King, and I am determined to make my authority respected, and for the future I shall insist and command that the Princess do upon all occasions appear at my Court, as it is her duty to do." He ended his speech, says Greville, with "an allusion to the Princess and her future reign in a tone of paternal interest and affection, which was excellent in its way."

But this finale on a softer note could not allay the turmoil he had raised in the minds of those seated round the table. Victoria was sobbing. Adelaide's quickly responsive face was imprinted with "deep distress," and "the whole company were aghast." As for the Duchess herself she "said not a word." What an inconceivable scene it was for the Berkshire county neighbors to have been let into. . . . Everyone got up from their chairs, and the ladies left the room. Once outside "a terrible scene ensued; the Duchess announced her immediate departure and ordered her carriage, but a sort of re-conciliation was patched up, and she was prevailed upon to stay till the next day." It is not necessary to ask whose was the persuasive feminine voice that averted this dramatic exodus.

After a night's cooling off between his sheets the King, pleased with his performance of the evening before, was calmer, and eager to know the reactions of his dinner guests to his outburst; and when Lord Adolphus came into his room he asked him "what people said." His son told him that the general opinion was that the Duchess deserved to be scolded, but that it should have been done privately, "and not at table before a hundred people."

The King retorted "that he did not care where it was said or before whom," and that "by God he had been insulted by her in a measure that was past all endurance, and he would not stand it any longer."

The Kents were still at the Castle the following evening; and at dinnertime the Duchess, no doubt purposely, kept everyone wait-ing to go in; Adelaide herself politely not appearing before the company till their battered guest would admit she was ready. In the drawing room, the King, impatient at the delay, was demanding, "Where's the Queen?"

He was told she was waiting for the Duchess of Kent.

"That woman is a nuisance," he exploded.

His anger with the Duchess spread to her brother, and Leopold, arriving one day at the Castle found himself received "very coldly." When, at dinner, he asked for water, the King burst out, "What's that you are drinking, Sir?"

"Water, Sir."

"God damn it ... why don't you drink wine? I never allow anybody to drink water at my table."

Leopold, apparently annoyed at this interference with his diet, left the Castle. "All this," groaned Charles Greville, "is very miserable and disgraceful."

5

This Christmas of 1836 the Kents were back again at Claremont, arriving there on the morning of Christmas Eve. In the German fashion a table was allotted to each member of the party, ready to be piled with presents from the others, to be given in the evening. But even before this grand finale, Lehzen began her bestowals on her pupil. "Received from dearest best Lehzen as a Christmas box: two lovely little Dresden china figures, two pair of lovely little chased gold buttons, a small lovely button with an angel's head which she used to wear herself, and a pretty music-book; from good Louis (the housekeeper) a beautiful piece of Persian stuff for an album; and from Victoire and Emily Gardiner [two sisters] a small box worked by themselves. Wrote my Journal. Went down to arrange Mamma's table for her. At six we dined.... Very soon after her dinner Mamma sent for us to the Gallery." Here was displayed a regular bazaar of present-laden tables, and by the time they were all cleared the Claremont party must have been weary of perpetually thanking each other. "From my dear Mamma," goes on Victoria, "I received a beautiful massive gold buckle in the shape of two serpents; a lovely little delicate gold chain with a turquoise clasp; a lovely coloured sketch of dearest Aunt Louise [Leopold's wife] by Partridge, copied from the picture he brought, and so like her; 3 beautiful drawings by Munn, one lovely sea view by Purser, and one beautiful cattle-piece by Cooper (all coloured), 3 prints, a book called *Finden's Tableaux, Heath's Picturesque Annual for 1837, Ireland;* both these are very pretty; *Friendship's Offering,* and *The English Annual for 1837, The Holy Land* illustrated beautifully, two handkerchiefs, a very pretty black satin apron trimmed with red velvet, and two almanacks. I am very thankful to my dear Mamma for all these very pretty things. From dear

Uncle Leopold, a beautiful turquoise ring; from the Queen a fine piece of Indian gold tissue; and from Sir J. Conroy a print. I gave my dear Lehzen a green morocco jewel-case, and the *Picturesque Annual;* Mamma gave her a shawl, a dress, a pair of turquoise earrings, an annual, and handkerchiefs. I then took Mamma to the Library where my humble table was arranged. I gave her a bracelet made of my hair, the clasp of which contains Charles', Feodore's and my hair; and the *Keepsake* and *Oriental Annual.* Lehzen gave her two pair of little buttons just like mine. I danced a little with Victoire. Stayed up till 11."

If Victoria had by now known—and it is probable that she did—of her mother and Conroy's latest plot, the two twisting serpents on the buckle given her by the Duchess might have seemed peculiarly symbolic to her daughter.

Regarding this "plot": to the Duchess of Kent and her comptroller these few months were pregnant with both hopes and apprehensions, for, in the May of next year, Victoria would be eighteen, and then gone forever would be the Duchess' aching hope that she might be Regent. But an ingenious idea had entered the heads of the Kensington pair. They would, they decided, endeavor to get the Regency period extended. So that Conroy should still be the manipulator in every business, Victoria should be coerced into promising to take him on as her private secretary, and further, she should be made to give this promise in writing. So greedy was Conroy for this arrangement that, if Greville is to be believed, he actually tried to persuade the Duchess to lock Victoria up in a room "and keep her under duress till she had extracted this engagement from her." If this is true—but in fairness to Conroy one must admit the possibility that it was merely gossip—then it indeed opens one's eyes as to that egregious Irishman's real character. However, the pair had stiffer substance to deal with in Victoria than they had realized. She refused point blank to fall in with their arrangements. It would be extremely interesting to us if, perhaps at one of those little tête-à-tête dinners that Lehzen and her charge would sometimes have together upstairs, we could overhear Victoria and her governess' observations on the schemes of the Duchess and her comptroller.

The only possible excuse for the Duchess' attempting to coerce her daughter in this manner, and to keep her under her own and Conroy's supervision, is that, outwardly submissive as was this inscrutable girl of seventeen, the Duchess may sincerely have believed (and indeed, later, she herself said this was the case) that it was impossible that the child would be able to grapple all at once with her tremendous position, and would need her mother's assistance. If the Duchess had known the amazingly shrewd comments that that mouselike little person was already making on people whom she met, she would have been startled to realize how much development had been going on beneath that bland exterior. Before they went to Claremont this last Christmas, loquacious Mr. Croker of the Admiralty had come to dinner, and had sat next Victoria. "He told many anecdotes," she afterward wrote in her Journal, "and made many remarks upon the various nations.... Il aime trop à s'étaler, il n'a pas de tact; il prend trop le ton supérieur." Certainly, penetrating comments for a schoolgirl.

During this Christmas stay of the Kensington party at Claremont, there happened to be a gypsy encampment close by, and Victoria developed an almost abnormal interest in this group of, to her, refreshingly strange creatures with their hand-to-mouth, fetterless existence. It might have been thought that her mind, in which many matters of import, present and to come, were now jostling each other, would have been riveted on her own affairs; but, on the contrary, her chief excitement at Claremont was, when walking out with Lehzen, to meet one or another of this vagrant family. Not only the women in their voluminous cloaks down to their feet, and broad hats bound under the chin with curious swathings, but the whole raggle-taggle community intrigued her. A gypsy baby arrived, and broth and blankets (the inevitable panaceas at that time from rich to poor) were ordered for them by the Duchess, while Lehzen "sent them by our footman a little worsted knit jacket." The relieved Victoria wrote, "Their being assisted makes me quite merry and happy to-day, for yesterday night ... I felt quite unhappy and grieved to think that our poor gypsy friends should perish and shiver for want; and now to-day I shall go to bed happy." And then, when in January that dear, exciting encampment disappeared, "I am quite sorry when I pass the spot so long enlivened by their little camp, and behold it empty and deserted...."

To *my* feeling, the chief ornament of the Portsmouth Road is gone since their departure. But this is their life...the Gipsy family Cooper will never be obliterated from my memory."

In this vivid interest in a group of people leading this untrammeled existence—an existence the exact opposite to her own closely harnessed one—appears again the Peter-the-Wild-Boy note, that craving for a life of freedom which, intermixed with so many diverse, and often exactly opposite emotions, was to reappear at intervals all through her life, and, as part of it, a love of the simple, the rustic, almost of the rough. Here, we suddenly find ourselves confronted with a door through which, far off in time, John Brown is to enter. Certainly, as I have already shown, there were urgent reasons for the near approach that she permitted him. But his rugged sincerity, the way he trampled on all Court shibboleths and etiquette, pleased, and did not annoy her, seemed as if it supplied some hitherto unfulfilled need. She delightedly savored, too, the rusticity of drinking tea in a Highland cottage; and, yet another idiosyncrasy of the same genre, after she had been to Italy, she could never pass an Italian organ-grinder with a monkey without stopping to talk to him. Regarding organ-grinders, a charming incident when the Queen had become a very old lady indeed, was told by one of her young maids of honor, Sylvia Edwardes. When she first came into waiting she was warned that when driving about London the Queen was only too apt to go to sleep, and that the attendant maid of honor had at all costs to keep her awake. One day Sylvia Edwardes, seeing the approach of this fatal drowsiness, racked her brains to think of something to say...no idea came. At last, leaning forward, she exclaimed, "Ma'am, there was a barrel-organ outside the gates of the Palace this morning."

The somnolent features half stirred into life. "Was there indeed! How very interesting! *No-one tells me anything nowadays.*"

6

Victoria's path to the throne in Westminster Abbey had for some time appeared free from serious obstacles, but during the last year or two, before William IV's death in 1837, there arose, as it were, reverberations of earlier threats to her succession. In 1835 everyone was saying that Queen Adelaide was on the verge of another of her hitherto disastrous attempts to provide William with an heir.

"What do you think of the *grossesse* of the Queen?" wrote Princess Lieven to Lord Grey. And again, "The Queen's *grossesse* ... will lead to a most important event, and one entirely unexpected. I can well imagine the looks of all the people at the little Court of Kensington Palace. There never was anyone there who interested me much, except the little Princess, and I feel sorry for her, for she has already reached an age when such an immense change in her fortunes may produce distressing effects on her character ... what a come-down it will be for those who are about her!"

The rumor of this supposedly arriving infant got into the papers ("What damned stuff is this?" exclaimed the King), and Lord Munster (the King's eldest son) told Charles Greville that his stepmother was "between two and three months gone." Entirely innocent as were the Queen's relations with Lord Howe, there arose, now that she was believed to be *enceinte*, the inevitable titters. Lord Alvanley pointed out what an appropriate moment it would be for the psalm, "Lord, how wonderful are thy works." The repercussions at Kensington Palace to all these rumors and this chatter we do not know. But the report was false. The marble infant in her sitting room at the castle was the only child Adelaide was ever to possess.

This next year there was voiced in Parliament an uneasiness over the violently Tory Orange Lodges, whose behavior had lately been so suspiciously disloyal that it was suggested in a debate that when William IV died, this intensely powerful Tory organization intended to rise and declare for the Duke of Cumberland in opposition to his niece Victoria. A Committee of Enquiry was appointed in the House, and Cumberland, the Orange Lodge Grand Master, received a strong hint from the Government that he should sever his connection with the Orange association. If there was one thing that annoyed that Duke it was being asked to relinquish anything that he possessed, and the Government's hint was ignored. But the whole position was regarded as so serious that in the following spring the Government sent "an address to the King, praying that His Majesty would take such measures as should be effectual for the suppression of the Orange Lodges." The King was all agreement, and Cumberland had no course left him but to dissolve the various Orange societies; himself, as has already been stated, protesting that he was ready to shed his blood in the defense of his niece. But was he? It is doubtful. The whole problem of his actual intentions—always supposing he did have any clear intentions —is impossible to solve. Often of late years that gaunt figure with his mutilated but aristocratically wolfish countenance had sat at one of the Duchess of Kent's dinner parties, outwardly tamed and trimmed into an amenable guest, and it is impossible to believe in his harboring any definitely malign intentions toward his niece. On the other hand, he did not attempt to hide the fact that he was deeply and continuously indignant that Victoria should exist at all. Again and again he would confront the Duchess of Kent with his rude expostulation, "that the Duke of Kent had promised him not to marry and that he had no business to break it." In old age the Duchess would become "quite excited and stern" as she recounted to one of her ladies the disagreeable ways he had of showing his annoyance at her having brought Victoria into the world. On one occasion, meeting her, presumably, at some party, the Duchess said "he quite trod over her toes to show his contempt." Then there was that question in the royal family as to who in reality was the possessor of some particular jewels left by Queen Charlotte. Cumberland claimed them as his; and, one day, his eye lighting on his niece's adornments, out leaped the cry, "Victoria has got on my pearls."

In reality Cumberland was no monster. It is evident that in the recesses of his being he was a self-tortured, and even at times a rather pathetic, creature, and, taking into consideration all the evidence regarding his attitude to Victoria, one becomes convinced that he, personally, would never have organized an uprising against her. If, on the other hand, the influence of the Orange Lodges had finally so permeated the country that the general voice had been for him and not for his niece, then there is little doubt but that he would have ascended the throne with alacrity. If he had he would certainly have added a pungent page to Britain's history. Violent, unscrupulous, self-seeking as he was, he might yet be described as, according to his own lights, a kind of furious Christian; and murder was not on his agenda.

An odd, if trifling, incident seems to indicate that, privately, he could not at times resist caressing the thought that he might one day be King of England. He was dining with William IV, and, after proposing the King's health, he followed it up with the toast, "the King's heir and may God bless him." It may have been a slip: it may have been a gracious gesture implying that his brother might yet have an heir; but, nevertheless, it may have been a feeler. The King took it in the last sense, and was roused to indignation. "The King's heir, God bless *her*," he cried, and added, "My crown came with a lass, and my crown shall go to a lass."

As for the King, these last years of his reign were made wretched by the rough usage he received from some of his illegitimate off-spring, to whom he was so devoted: those "good-for-nothing bastards" as Greville dubbed them. Their father's financial generosity to them was limitless, he having, in addition to their allowances, given each of them nearly £30,000. Munster had a long-standing quarrel with William IV; the King constantly sending him friendly messages which Munster would fling aside, saying that "by holding out he shall make better terms"; ("Money," sneers Greville, "being his object.")

"What," exclaimed Munster, when talking to him one day of the King, "What do you think he did? When I had not seen him for fourteen months he sent to beg I would send down an Artist to Windsor to paint his picture for me." While Greville absorbed this information, Munster rattled on, "And what answer do you think I sent? That I saw no use in having his picture when it was very probable that in less than three years it would be in a pawnbroker's shop."

Then there was the third son, Lord Frederick, who was equerry to his father, and who having received and spent thousands "coolly sent the King in a bill for £12,000."

The King, in reply, told him to sell his house to liquidate his debts, and that he himself would make up any deficiency.

Frederick refused even to answer this suggestion, but "flounced off with 8 or 10 of the King's horses, half a dozen Servants and 3 carriages, without a word of notice."

Lord Erroll, who had married one of the King's daughters, Elizabeth, became infected with the bastards' insolence; his special line being, when he could, to torment the gentle Adelaide. When he was master of the horse, she had commissioned Lord Howe to inspect his official accounts. He refused to have them examined, and said he would resign. "The Queen went down to his room to make it up with him and persuade him to stay, when he abused her so violently and said such things to her *about Howe* that she threw herself on a couch in a flood of tears." Irrepressibly forgiving, she shortly afterward made him a present of four horses. He grabbed the horses, but continued to treat her with "brutal rudeness." When, one day at dinner, she placed "a bonbon" upon his plate, it was instantly "tossed back" on to hers. So it went on.

Heart disease, asthma, and bronchitis were now all dragging at William IV's strength but, notwithstanding, his thoughts were much with his niece, and he decided to offer her £10,000 a year which was to be at her own disposal: definitely beyond the clutch of her interfering mother. This side blow at the Duchess no doubt gave the King, considering her intolerable behavior to him, a good deal of satisfaction. Further, he gave Lord Conyngham instructions that the letter he had himself written making the offer was to be placed in Victoria's own hand, and in none other. When Conyngham arrived at Kensington Palace, he was received by Conroy, and "asked to be admitted to the Princess." It shows the tight surveillance that Conroy kept over Victoria that even when the King's Lord Chamberlain demanded to see her, the comptroller, instead of at once complying, asked "By what authority?" Told it was "By His Majesty's orders," Conroy walked off and left him, obviously to warn the Duchess that something was afoot. When Lord Conyngham was finally shown in, he found Victoria presided over as usual by her mother. After the mutual curtsyings and bowings, Lord Conyngham said that he "waited on her Royal Highness by the King's commands to present to her a letter with which he had been charged by His Majesty." He then produced the letter, and was just passing it to Victoria, when out came the Duchess' hand to intercept it. Lord Conyngham begged her Royal Highness' pardon, but observed that "He was expressly commanded by the King to deliver the letter into the Princess's own hands."

The Duchess, thus put in her place, drew back. Victoria received her letter. Lord Conyngham made his bow, and left the room.

That night Victoria wrote in her Journal with some triumph, "Received a letter from *the King*." But if there was triumph, it is only too evident that the Duchess had done her best to tarnish it directly the contents of her brother-in-law's letter were made known to her. She was not going to let ten thousand pounds a year slide into her daughter's pocket without making a strenuous effort to divert some of it to herself. It seems that the very day the letter was received she had begun to be disagreeable over it, as Victoria, after that evening's triumphant entry in her Journal, added, "Felt very miserable and agitated. Did not go down to dinner, but dined in my own room at 8 o'clock."

The Duchess lost no time before protesting to William IV over this monetary arrangement, insisting that out of the £10,000, £6000 ought to be allocated to her, the remaining £4000 being sufficient for her daughter. Confused sounds of warfare floated across the Channel to Leopold, and he became avid for details.

My dearest Child [he wrote to Victoria], You have had some battles and difficulties of which I am completely in the dark. The thing I am most curious to learn is what the King proposed to you.... The great thing is to act without precipitation and with caution.... I am very curious to know what he proposed.

The day after Lord Conyngham's visit, Victoria accepted the offer made her, and entered in her Journal, "wrote a letter to the King which Mamma had previously written for me."

CHAPTER VII
VICTORIA BECOMES QUEEN
OF ENGLAND

Five days after the arrival of the King's letter came Victoria's eighteenth birthday: her supreme birthday that made her of age, and qualified her to be, if and when the occasion arose, Queen of England. It was a day that inevitably scintillated in Kensington Palace—to some painfully, to all significantly. Again the May trees were frothed over with buds, while anyone passing by the palace that morning would have seen a great white flag languidly astir on the roof. The gold letters that glinted among its folds spelled "Victoria."

This May 24 had been made a public holiday, and along all the country roads leading to London mail coaches, post-chaises, and carriages were heading for Kensington Palace. A sylvan touch had been added to many of them, for holidaymakers from Dorsetshire and Devonshire had broken off sprays of lilac from the bushes and decorated the horses' heads. Those coming from the north had done the same with hawthorn buds. Around the palace, landlords of the little taverns—the Black Lion, the Hoop and Toy, the Feathers, the Adam and Eve, and all the rest of them—had nailed up bunting, both to show their loyalty and to attract the attention of the sauntering crowds that were early spreading everywhere, and especially around the palace, within whose walls the birthday heroine, intent for the moment on a personal matter, was pressing into the hand of "my beloved Lehzen a small brooch of my hair."

To the Duchess it must have been a day of mixed and chiefly rueful emotions, forced as she was not only to assist at, but to help enhance all the glamor of the day that was the death knell of her desperately held hope. And yet, perhaps, not even now absolutely and

entirely the death knell, for, incredible as it seems, though Victoria
had flatly refused to agree to that extension of the term fixed by the
Regency Act that her mother and Conroy had pressed on her, even
now, at the eleventh hour—with the King intermittently so piteously
ill that it was evident he had little longer to live—that graceless,
indefatigable couple at Kensington Palace had evolved a fresh
scheme for arrogating to themselves at least a few months of power.
The Duchess had, unknown to Victoria, written a letter to the
Prime Minister, Lord Melbourne, telling him her daughter herself
wished that a regency should be established "for a short time." As
fellow conspirator the Kensington plotters had Lord Duncannon,
who at this juncture was "eternally closeted" with Melbourne, endeavoring to manipulate his mind in accordance with the views of
the Duchess. Lord Melbourne, be it understood, naturally believed
that Victoria's views on the regency coincided with her mother's.
Whether, by Victoria's birthday, this deceptive letter had actually
been dispatched, or was, so far, only being composed and considered, is not clear; but the outcome will shortly be apparent.
Meanwhile this significant birthday, now in its early hours, had to
be attended to.

The first thing to impress her birthday importance on the just
awakened Victoria was a chorus of serenading voices rising from
the garden. The singers had brought musical instruments with them
as well as their capacity for singing, and there were thirty-seven
of them, all hard at it. In response, Victoria placed herself in view
of them at a window, and listening carefully, she caught in one of
the songs an allusion to her mother. Then, with her usual efforts
at appeasement in that quarter, she asked that that particular song
should be resung.

As for the Duchess, whatever, this morning, were her private
feelings, however bitter it was to her to realize what a merely
secondary part she herself would play in all the day's coming fanfare, she had to dress herself as effectively as possible, to be ready
to bestow her glancing smiles on everyone. Already she was putting
on the ball dress she had decided on for the occasion—for ball
dresses were then worn in the daytime for anything special—and
placing on her head "a magnificent plumed hat," one of those
huge, showy hats to which she was so devoted, whose massed,

nodding plumes were like her aggressive nature sprung into visible form above her piled-up curls. While dressing, she would have seen through her windows that looked onto the garden all those un- known holiday figures, loyally loitering and gazing at the palace. Victoria, too, was putting on her birthday ball dress and hat. Thus accoutered, mother and daughter descended to deal with the very doubtful pleasures of the day. From the other side of the palace came the perpetual grinding of carriage wheels in the courtyard as one important person after another was driven up to write down his name. "Numbers of people put down their names, and among them good old Lablache inscribed his."

Deputations, too, from many of the big towns were arriving, very intent and earnest over the business in hand. "All the great towns to which the Reform Bill gave seats in Parliament sent deputations, to which many outsiders hung on." The political backwash in fact of the Duke of Kent's activities. "In a general way it might be said that the Liberals and Radicals, the Evangelical Low Churchpeople, Nonconformists, and the Catholics crowded to London to press round the Princess on the 24th of May."

A certain Mr. Potter, founder of the Cobden Club, was one among the surrounding guests while the addresses to Victoria were being read, and his assiduous eye took in everything. "What most struck me was the hopefulness that pervaded the assembled well- wishers. The breath of Spring was in the air outside; the breath of a moral and political Spring, of renovation and resurrection, buoyed us up within ... we were all happy that day as the birds on the branches. The Duchess was an exception. She was, we thought, anxious and harassed, but was finely dressed, and had a fine neck to show, though rather a stout one. If there was anything the matter with her hair, a magnificent plumed hat hid it. The Princess stood beside her, also in an evening dress and a hat. She was pretty, but her face, somehow, was not quite satisfactory. I cannot tell at this distance of time what was the matter with it; but I was less taken with her than with her mother." (It is evident from this that Vic- toria was in her usual state of taut self-suppression when the Duchess was upset.) "The mother," goes on Mr. Potter, "did not strike us as a woman of race or breeding, only as an excellent, rather hand- some person, and a lady that would make a good mother-in-law. . . .

The Princess was as cool as she ever showed herself since ... she was quite grown up, but no height. The addresses were read to *her*, and were answered by her mother, who read with a German accent, but otherwise well."

Though the addresses were, as we see, definitely meant for Victoria, the Duchess, in answering them, took the opportunity to push the Princess' mother well to the fore, painting herself in the prettiest colors imaginable, pointedly drawing her audience's attention to the confidence shown in herself by Parliament passing the Regency Act, and her endeavor to justify such confidence by her devoted attention to the education and training of her daughter. Then, bringing in a touch of pathos, she emphasized how, by attending to these educational duties, she had been forced to remain in England, thus entailing "the neglect of important duties in Germany, severe losses, and separation from other beloved children."

For Victoria to have to listen to all this very personal rigmarole, while at the same time facing that crowd of strange faces, must have been embarrassing in the extreme; and it is not surprising that Mr. Potter, his questing eye searching that young bland countenance, should have decided that "her face, somehow, was not quite satisfactory."

At least some slight answer to the addresses was naturally expected from Victoria herself, and she, with her already extraordinarily developed sense of suitability, merely gave utterance to "A few words ... to signify that her beloved mother had fully expressed her sentiments"—probably the same phrase as she gave later to the Lord Mayor and aldermen when they too presented her with an address. "I am very thankful for your kindness, and my Mother has expressed all my feelings."

In the circumstances, a remarkably neat rounding off of an awkward situation. But what an unaccountable contrast the listeners must have felt lay between that cautious little sentence and the peculiarly sweet tones of the young voice that spoke it. Indeed, nothing could better convey her awareness of her mother's jealousy, and of how, for the sake of peace, the daughter had invariably to repress herself.

So this bespangled day went on, enthusiastic guests perpetually on the move within and without the palace. The whole atmosphere the very opposite to that of the usual repetitive routine of study and meals, when the languorous solitude of the old place was stirred only by the hourly strokes from the courtyard belfry.

At about three o'clock, Victoria and Lehzen climbed into a carriage to go for a drive, so that England's precious possession should be on view to as many as possible. A new figure, referred to in the Journal only as "Mary," went with them—probably the Miss Wynn who about this time became Victoria's maid of honor. "I like Mary very much...," Victoria wrote a few weeks later, "very susceptible of kindness shown to her; she is extremely discreet and retiring too." Only this moment eighteen, Victoria had already had plenty of opportunities of learning the value of discretion.

As the carriage bearing her and Lehzen drove along through the bright spring air, the streets and parks were teeming with the jumble of holidaymakers ("everything like a *Gala* day," thought Victoria), and whenever the people caught sight of that rosy face beneath its grand hat; of that politely, incessantly bowing little figure that was the center of all this commotion, their excited delight so flared that it awoke an equal delight in her.

Joining the crowd we will, now that she is just about to shine forth as the resplendent young Queen, take a critical glance at her. The plump young cheeks, sloping back like the sides of a vase, do not give enough support to the prominent, exceptionally intelligent blue eyes and the neat, but rather beaky, little nose, the small, one might almost say triangular, mouth, always slightly ajar owing to the upper lip being hitched up in the center—"peculiar and very difficult to render without being a caricature," wrote one of her maids of honor. Nevertheless, the whole is so redolent of soft-breathing youth and quick-flushing color, of young eagerness and health that at times she has a definite, and even, so we read, arresting air of prettiness. Her hair is light brown; her figure girlish, but the shoulders fashionably round and full.

The sick King and his saddened Adelaide, unwearied as ever in well doing, gave a ball for their niece on the night of her birthday. When in the evening she came downstairs to drive to St. James's Palace, she found the courtyard "crammed" with people agog to see her, the light from the great lamps on each side of the portico

glistening on the nearest of the peering faces. And again, all along
the only fitfully lit streets, as she drove by, there arose the same
affectionate screams as earlier that day; the same pressing forward
to see "poor stupid me," as she wrote in her Journal that night:
for if, in her later development, an occasional arrogance became a
characteristic that her detractors pounce on, there were yet always
to remain beneath genuine patches of humbleness.

It must be realized that at that time, unless the populace managed to snatch a glimpse of a living royal figure at a window, or
driving by in a carriage, they could have no conception of what
these, to them, mysterious beings looked like. There were then no
moving pictures upon which every eye in the kingdom could see
royalty benignly stepping along by the side of bishop or hospital
matron, no snapshots of them in a pictorial press. Even the *Illustrated London News* had not yet come into being. To the nation in
general the idea of the reigning monarch and his relations could
only be guessed at by rough prints, or from all but comic Staffordshire figures, garish with their splashings of blue, scarlet, and gold.
At the most, those who lived in or near the big towns could occasionally ponder over an engraving in a shop window that might
clear a little the obscurity that enveloped the occupants of Windsor
Castle and Buckingham Palace. Those with money in their pockets
could, of course, buy these engravings, and study the Hanoverian,
Mecklenburg-Strelitz, Brunswick, or Coburg features at their
leisure. Or sometimes, so it seems, large, richly dressed portrait
dolls of the royalties could be bought. One of these, purporting to
be the Duchess of Kent,* in a lemon-colored silk dress ornamented
with many bows, over a cream muslin underdress, might, a century
later, still be seen, sitting, staring into space, on a Victorian chair
in the drawing room of a house appropriately close to the one in
Belgrave Square where her prototype came to live.

2

The arrival in London, round about Victoria's coming-of-age
birthday, of Leopold's *alter ego*, Stockmar gave yet another twist
to the Kensington pattern. This German, now in middle life, was

* In Lord Holden's collection of Victoriana.

originally a doctor, whom circumstances had turned into a statesman. Like Henry Halford he was a forerunner of the modern
psychiatrist. Quite early Stockmar had realized that the science of
medicine is applicable to the divagations of the political mind, and
on this discovery he had built his successful career. "It was a clever
stroke," so this politician wrote, "to have originally studied medicine; without the knowledge thus acquired, without the psychological and physiological experiences which I thus obtained, my
savoir-faire would often have gone a-begging." "As a statesman,"
wrote his friend Carl Meyer, "he was fond of looking upon a
crisis in political or domestic affairs from his own medical point of
view." Years of practice in his rare gift of discernment had by now
constituted his mind a textbook into which kings could look to learn
their trade.

"I have never but once met a perfectly disinterested man of this
kind, and that is Stockmar," opined Lord Palmerston. As one's eyes
dwell on this doctor-statesman's portrait, integrity, intelligence, and
benevolence seem positively to leap forth from those abrupt, dug-
out features.

Leopold had sent over this tutor in sovereignty to instruct and
advise his niece during the coming critical weeks.* He loved to instruct royalty, not only in the art of clambering onto a throne, but,
once installed, of remaining there. So far his only pupil had been
Leopold, and him he had often found annoyingly restive under his
tutelage. In Karoline Bauer's memoirs she tells us how, when she
and her mother were living in the cottage Leopold had stuffed
them into near Claremont, her uncle Stockmar and her morganatic
husband Leopold would arrive alternately to pour out to the Bauers
all the exasperations each had endured at the hands of the other.
But in Victoria, Stockmar found the perfect neophyte, the ideal
pupil: eager and docile, not only ready but craving to receive all
he had to give. Each swiftly became delighted with the other:
"most exceedingly attached and devoted to me," Victoria informed

* King Leopold was so concerned about "the schemes and intrigues of those who would
exert all their power to entrap the almost isolated young Princess, hoping thus to rule the
future Sovereign," that he had this year, while Victoria was on a visit to Claremont, arranged with her that Stockmar should come over and "reside in England" as her "trusty
helper and adviser." (*Memoirs of Baron Stockmar*, i. 373-74.)

her Journal; and only a week after his arrival she had found him "of the greatest use to me." No doubt, in writing this, she was thinking, with relief and gratitude, of how he had discovered and dealt with her mother and Conroy's latest regency effort; for Stockmar, on finding that not only had Victoria no desire, when her uncle died, that her interfering mother should become Regent, but that she was emphatically opposed to it, went direct to the Prime Minister, Lord Melbourne, and told him that the Duchess' demand, which had been sent by letter, had been "made at the instigation of Conroy and without the consent or knowledge of the Princess." Melbourne, who up to now had been completely hoodwinked by the Duchess' letters, was "struck all of a heap," and at once gave an undertaking that he would not "have anything more to say to Conroy." An assurance which Stockmar passed on to Victoria.

Taking into account the pellucid honesty of her own nature, what must this young, vivid-minded creature have felt when she realized that her mother had been at work behind her back to filch her coming position from her? Wincing away from the knowledge now of what the Duchess was capable of, suffering from the bruise that trusting youth receives on first meeting with deception, it is not surprising that she wrote at this time of Lehzen as being "of course the *greatest* friend I have."

3

During these early summer days of 1837, while May slid into June, and at Windsor the King was now "desperately ill," then seemingly better, then again "alarmingly ill"; during these days the group at Kensington was enveloped with a sense of gathering speed, of approaching events about to pile one on another with almost terrifying haste and conclusiveness. Every hour that passed was an hour of suspense: as they moved as usual about the house, the garden, the courtyard, doing this, doing that, all the time their ears were pricked for news from Windsor. For now the very breath of the future was on their faces: that for which all these years of effort had been a preparation was imminent, was all but actually upon them, with its varied implications, its inevitable shifting and rearrangement that would affect every one of them. Life for each member of this closely knotted group might in the change-over prove to be better, or it might be worse, but infallibly it would be different from what it had been before.

This tension in the rooms at Kensington Palace stretched across the Channel, and reverberated in the mind of Leopold. As he sat at his writing table in his Belgian palace, one idea after another rose in his mind that he thought might be useful to the new Queen. There was, for instance, that almost overmodesty of hers . . . no, that would not be suitable now. "Avoid in future," he wrote, "to say much about your great *youth* and *inexperience*." And then again, relieved to think Stockmar was at her side, "*speak sometimes with him*," Leopold adjured her, "it is necessary to accustom you to the thing." Another day, a word of counsel in a different direction. "Avoid any breach with your mother," he cautioned, his mind on all the Kensington discords. "Be steady, my good child, and *not* put out by *anything*." "I have taken into consideration the advantage or disadvantage of my coming over to you *immediately*," he wrote on the seventeenth of June. "The result of my *examen* is that I think it better to visit you later. If however you wanted me at any time I should come in a moment. People mighty fancy I came to enslave you . . . as if I thought of ruling the realm for purposes of my *own*. . . . May Heaven bless you and keep up your spirits."

"Keep your mind *cool* and *easy*," he wrote another day, "be *not alarmed* at the prospect of becoming perhaps sooner than we expected Queen." But Victoria was not at all alarmed. It was characteristic of that exceptional young being that, intensely emotional, she yet possessed such clearness of head, such a sense of duty that must be performed, that she now faced unwaveringly what was upon her. Her mind stood sentinel waiting for what was to come. She had, too, the steadiness that arises from simplicity of outlook, and within her, like a small but steadily burning flame, was the belief that God who had laid this burden on "poor stupid me" would give her the strength to carry that burden. "I need not add much more, dearest Uncle," she wrote at the end of one of her letters, "but that I trust that the all-powerful Being who has so long watched over my destinies"—and for a moment her mother and Conroy's interchanging glances flicker across the page—"that the all-powerful Being who has so long watched over my destinies will guide and support me."

Leopold, however, was not so much concerned with her religious as with her cerebral reactions to queenship, and his letters continue to bristle with advice. "In high positions it is excessively difficult to *retrace* a false move ... and there exists very rarely, except in time of war and civil feuds, a necessity for an *immediate* decision." In his next letter he tries to encourage her by emphasizing how welcome a sovereign she will be to the present Whig ministry. "For them, as well as for the Liberals at large, you are the *only* Sovereign that offers them *des chances d'existence et de durée*. With the exception of the Duke of Sussex, there is no *one* in the family that offers them anything like what they can reasonably hope from you, and your immediate successor, with the mustaches, is enough to frighten them into the most violent attachment for you."

Meanwhile, the thoughts of the whole country were riveted upon that remote, hidden palace, that casket which contained the problematical, almost wholly unknown young girl who in such great measure held in her hands the destinies of the country. In the warm June air of that summer the politicians, strolling, restless with expectancy about Hyde Park, would see Charles Greville, center of social and political gossip, also on the stroll, and the beaver-hatted figures with their great black stocks, hunched collars, and peg-topped trousers would join each other, and, inevitably, would at once start talking of "this state of things, with the prospect of a new reign and dissolution," and of the "complete uncertainty of the direction which affairs would take under a new influence." "I met Melbourne in the Park," wrote Greville on June 11, "who told me he thought the King would not recover"; and, a few days later, "I met Sir Robert Peel in the Park, and talked with him about the new reign." He said that it was "very desirable that the young Queen should appear as much as possible emancipated from all restraint ... that the most probable as well as the most expedient course she could adopt, would be to rely entirely upon the advice of Melbourne." He concluded by saying, "King Leopold would be her great adviser," but that "If Leopold is prudent, however, he will not hurry over here at the very first moment, which would look like an impatience to establish his influence, and if he does, the first result will be every sort of jealousy and discord between him and the Duchess of Kent."

"The elements of intrigue do not seem wanting in this embryo Court," comments Greville a little blandly, not realizing what a ganglion of cross-purposes it actually was. "What renders speculation so easy and events so uncertain," he continues, "is the absolute ignorance of everybody, without exception, of the character, disposition, and capacity of the Princess. She has been kept in such jealous seclusion by her mother ... that no-one of her acquaintance, none of the attendants at Kensington, not even the Duchess of Northumberland, her governess, have any idea what she is, or what she promises to be."

There was one consideration that made the future still more doubtful. Was Queen Adelaide going to have a baby or was she not? Lord Lansdowne, who seems to have been either remarkably ignorant or remarkably forgetful of the Regency Act, fussily sent for Charles Greville, and said, "they were perplexed to know what steps, if any, they ought to take to ascertain whether the Queen is with child, and to beg me to search in our books whether any precedent could be found at the accession of James II."

"But," comments Greville, "they had forgotten that the case had been provided for in the Regency Bill, and that in the event of the King's dying without children, the Queen is to be proclaimed, but the oath of allegiance taken with a saving of the rights of any posthumous child to King William." "They ought to have known this," concludes the diarist.

4

On the seventeenth of June of this year, 1837, the King sent word that the annual Waterloo banquet was to take place as usual, in spite of his not being able to be there, and the next morning there was brought to his bedside the flag that Wellington sent to him each year on the Waterloo anniversary. His enfeebled fingers lovingly strayed about the folds of the flag. To his spirit, bellicose and romantic, an incident such as this was one of life's most luxurious moments.

His thoughts, we are told, often turned affectionately to his little niece waiting in the wings to come forward and take his place. "It will touch every sailor's heart," he exclaimed one day, "to have a girl Queen to fight for. They'll be tattooing her face on their arms, and I'll be bound they'll all think she was christened after Nelson's ship."

. . . . . .

On Monday, the nineteenth, Victoria wrote to Leopold, "I look forward to the event which it seems is likely to occur soon, with calmness and quietness; I am not alarmed at it, and yet I do not suppose myself quite equal to all."

That day ("while my hair was doing") she read *Les Veillées du château.* Later, she and Lehzen went for a drive beneath the thick-plumed summer trees and, coming back, she read again in *Les Veillées du château.* The hours of the June day passed one into another; and, as the evening drew in, she sat down and wrote up her Journal. Then, after some more reading ("in W. Scott's life while my hair was undoing"), she lay down, as usual, in her bed placed by the side of her mother's, with the Duke of Kent's tortoise-shell repeater close by ticktocking her to sleep in its industrious, familiar way. And hanging up in a cupboard or lying in a drawer nearby, a plain little dress of black bombazine that had been made for her was waiting.

5

In the very early hours of the next morning, along the still shadowy roads and through the streets of the little towns that lie between Windsor and London, a carriage with three men inside came racketing at full gallop. In the castle they were leaving behind them William IV lay dead; and within this carriage were the lord

THE DUKE OF WELLINGTON

From the painting by Count d'Orsay in the National Portrait Gallery

Baroness Lehzen
Drawn from nature

THE DUCHESS OF KENT AND
PRINCESS VICTORIA

From the painting by Hayter

chamberlain—Lord Conyngham—the Archbishop of Canterbury, and Sir Henry Halford,* on their way to Kensington Palace to tell Victoria that she was Queen of England.

Officially, was there any necessity for all this urgency? It seems not, for it is said that Lord Melbourne was annoyed at this precipitate awakening of Victoria. Himself, he had everything in readiness; summonses for the Privy Council were already prepared, and when at six o'clock he received the news of the King's death he thought it suitable that two or three hours should elapse before he attended at Kensington Palace. The only real urgency appears to have been within the minds of the three men now hurrying on their self-imposed mission, undertaken, apparently, merely to place themselves well in the foreground, and without a moment's loss of time, to make a favorable impression on the mind of England's new sovereign. Halford as well as Dr. Chambers had been at the King's bedside as he died. When all was over, Halford, according to the traditional account, "slipped out, and found the Archbishop and Lord Conyngham walking together in earnest conference up and down the corridor." Halford gave his report, and Lord Conyngham rapidly scribbled announcements for the *Court Circular* and *Gazette*. "All three then rushed down to the Lower Ward, where a carriage had been waiting for them." It was a long drive, and to the three men, their minds busied with anticipation, with the immense historic import of their undertaking, the ceaseless thudding of the "stout grey roadsters'" hoofs must have sounded on and on in the background of their thoughts as a relentless monotone.

Slowly the vacuous light that lay on the shifting scene around them whitened to a summer dawn. By the time the horses came hammering into Kensington village with the loose gallop of exhaustion all was touched with the soft glitter of a June morning. It was still not much past five o'clock. At the double iron gates of the palace drive the postilions jerked the horses to a standstill. In the two great iron lamps, clamped one to each of the gateposts, a ghost of a flame, now pallid in the early light, would still have been

---

* Sir Henry Halford had been Victoria's doctor, and, according to the outlook of the day, he may have thought that on hearing the news she might require medical assistance.

burning.* By the side of the gates, now closely locked, was the porter's lodge; but in this tranquil dawn no one was astir. They rang, and they rang. Nothing happened.... They rang again ... and again ... Silence. They thumped ... they banged.... But now a figure, hostile and suspicious, did at last emerge from the lodge. However, at first the porter refused to react to any idea but that of its not being the normal time for the daily mechanism of Kensington Palace to be set in motion. He saw it as his obvious duty to block the path of this urgent group arriving at such an incredible hour. Their demand to see Princess Victoria left him unmoved; but when they said "they must see the Queen on state business" the sense of a drama being on foot in which he had a part to play penetrated the porter's mind, and he shoved the key into the lock. The chaise swung in between the guardian lion and unicorn, and went headlong up the straight drive. Then, arriving at the shut wooden doors of the courtyard, the postilions again pulled on their reins, and the carriage came to a standstill. Now that the clatter of their arrival had abruptly stopped, they found themselves enveloped in stillness. Before them the great rose-brick mass of the palace stood shut and silent. They had again to ring and to thump before the wooden doors of the courtyard were swung back. This second porter, no less bemused than his colleague at the outer gates, "allowed them to go no farther than the Comptroller's parlour"; but by the time he had gone stumbling along the passages and staircases on his way to the attics to arouse the servants, he too had begun to respond to what was afoot, and, waking up one of the maids, "so hurried her that she had only time to slip on her petticoat and a mantle."

From within its cocoon of sleep Victoria's mind came floating up to awareness, and she realized that the Duchess of Kent was leaning over her and saying something. Then she understood. Her mother was telling her that "the Archbishop of Canterbury and Lord Conyngham were here and wished to see me." So it had come. That which for so long had been going to happen, had happened.

---

* These lamps, topped with the royal crown, still hang there, unnoticed by the scurrying Kensington High Street shoppers. There, too, to the left of the gates, is the old porter's lodge with its Georgian doorway, and beautifully weathered old roof of small tiles. But its walls, smothered in dark paint, now enclose an estate agent's office.

She at once got out of bed, pulled off her nightcap so that her straight lightish hair slid onto her shoulders, and then threw some sort of cotton wrap over her nightdress. Very clearly one can see her standing there by her bed, her hands moving quietly and swiftly, her rosy face grave and intent. At the same time someone was arousing Lehzen. The Duchess, too, had been getting ready to accompany Victoria down that treacherous staircase. Both, so we read, "hastily thrust their bare feet into slippers, threw on cotton *peignoirs* or toilet-table gowns."

It is noticeable that the Duchess did not, perhaps with her jealous nature she could not, bring herself definitely to tell Victoria she was now Queen of England, and so prepare her for the coming interview. And yet her mother did already know. The maid who had been hurried by the porter to the royal bedroom door had wakened the Duchess, and told her who was below, and that they had come to see Princess Victoria. But the Duchess, determined as usual to interpose herself between any direct communication from the Court and her daughter, had sent down to say that the Princess was asleep, and could not be disturbed. She must have wished she had not when she was brought a second message to the effect that Lord Conyngham had to speak with "the Queen" upon affairs of state.

By now the mother and the daughter's preparations were complete. Though outside lay the early radiance of the summer morning, presumably the big bedroom was still in close-curtained darkness, and they had done their scanty dressing by candlelight; for now one of them picked up a little silver candlestick * to light them on their way. Lehzen had joined them, and, prepared for any reaction of Victoria to such a stupendous moment, was clasping a bottle of *sal volatile*. The little company left the room, and opened a small door just outside that leads to the staircase. This door is still shown as being the one Victoria went through on her way down to play her part in one of the best-known tableaux in history: a very ordinary little bedroom-floor door, such as it would be natural to see a housemaid come jerking through with a slop pail.

---

* This actual candlestick was presented by Sir John Conroy's son (again a Sir John Conroy) to Balliol College, Oxford, where he was a don.

Having reached the foot of the stairs, the three women sound-lessly padded across the passage, and went on to the room where the Windsor messengers were waiting. Holding the little candle-stick, Victoria went in alone.

One cannot but think, as the three men saw her come gliding in— that insignificant child-figure with bare slippered feet, strands of hair catching on her dressing gown—that they must inevitably have been struck by the contrast between such nursery simplicity of ap-pearance, and the magnificence of the position they had come to an-nounce to her. It is tempting to symbolize this vision of her in the doorway, this good child of the Kensington schoolroom, whose early days had been so cramped and confined that she might be equipped for what she was destined; to trace an analogy between the light of her candle, now waveringly illuminating her face from below as she stood before the group of men, and the general im-pulsion there was to be during her reign away from the blatantly brutal toward the more humane. But these symbols must not be overstressed.

The two bowing figures of the Archbishop and Lord Conyng-ham came forward, and, as she wrote later in her matter-of-fact way, "acquainted me that my poor Uncle, the King, was no more, and had expired at 12 minutes p. 2. this morning, and consequently that I am *Queen*."

When she was told she was now Queen, she instantly held out her hand for Lord Conyngham to kiss. He appears to have been a shade startled at such unhesitating aplomb, as, later, he commented on it to his friends. Now, he at once knelt, and bestowed a kiss on the small hand; the Archbishop, too, knelt and kissed. Henry Hal-ford, presumably, did the same.

When Victoria rejoined the Duchess and Lehzen outside the door she threw her arms round her mother's neck and wept at not having been able to go the day before to see her uncle. One ques-tions whether it was her mother who had prevented her; judging from the Duchess' past behavior, it seems probable. "He was always so very, very kind to me," the tearful girl kept on murmuring, "he must have thought me so ungrateful and heartless. Then she climbed the stairs again and went back to her and her mother's bedroom, and put on the black dress that had been waiting for her.

It is evident from her Journal that, once her tears were over, and imbued though she was by a pervasive sense of responsibility, she did at the same time feel an inner elation, a sense that everything had at last come to a conclusion and solidified around her; and that she too, clothed in queenship, could now, after all these long years of repression, at last expand and be her genuine self.

CHAPTER VIII
LORD MELBOURNE FULFILLS
HIS DESTINY

Toward nine o'clock on the morning of this twentieth of June, yet another carriage, within which sat a man who was to be of paramount importance in Victoria's life, was hurrying along the road that led from London to Kensington. The occupant of this carriage, in build at once powerful and firmly knit, was Lord Melbourne. He was now fifty-eight, and time had ameliorated his once youthful countenance, that of stormy-browed handsomeness, into one that immediately charmed by its friendliness and sensitivity. Before his carriage reaches the palace, it is necessary, if we are to enter intelligently into the fine-spun relationship that was to be formed between him and Victoria, to glance back at some of the percussions he had suffered from life, and that had at times shaken his existence to its foundations.

By birth he was a cosseted son of the most fashionably gay and fashionably cultured English society. Two of the chief formative influences on his nature had been those of his mother and his wife: the first integrating his forces, and sharpening all his faculties toward worldly efficiency; the second disintegrating his emotional being, and laying him open to every torment of the spirit. Lady Melbourne, the mother of William Lamb—for this, till he inherited the title, was his name—was one of those society women whose type reappears in every generation: women whose minds are composed of some steely substance, and possess a driving power that rests not day or night. Her husband, the first Lord Melbourne, as much of a nonentity as she was a personality, had provided her with money, a title, and a great house in Piccadilly. Nature had already endowed this daughter of an old Yorkshire family with a most pleasing appearance, sound sense, unerring insight into the workings of the male mind, and a convenient lack of sensibility. Thus accoutered she had acquired all the prizes of the social world, prizes for which she felt an enduring enthusiasm without a hint of satiety. Each of her six children on their arrival in the world found existence laid open before them like a pleasure garden, their mother its tutelary genius, eager to initiate them into all its varied delights. Her husband would have been optimistic if he had prided himself on being the father of all the children who bore his name: one of the sons was generally supposed to have been fathered by the Prince of Wales; and William by Lord Egremont, Lady Melbourne's lover *en titre*. William Lamb himself, however, denied this parentage. The atmosphere of Melbourne House, that of William Lamb's youth, was one of ceaseless vivacity and vitality, of good-humored rending argument, of derision for sensitivity or an overscrupulous morality. But if, outwardly, all the goods of life had been heaped on William Lamb, his own exceptional personality—his manner at once negligent and suave counteracting something a shade too animal beneath—ensuring his welcome wherever he went, his inner life did not accord with his outer. Even as a quite young man, disillusionment, sadness, at times almost a sense of despair, had managed to penetrate his fortress of well-being, and one day he had tried to find easement by expressing in verse the inadequacy, when it was confronted with the realities of life, of that philosophy of hedonism which permeated his home.

> A year has pass'd—a year of grief and joy—
> Since first we threw aside the name of boy,
> That name which in some future hour of gloom
> We shall with sighs regret we can't resume.
> Unknown this life, unknown Fate's numerous snares,
> We launched into this world, and all its cares;
> Those cares whose pangs, before a year was past,
> I felt and feel, they will not be the last.
> But then we hailed fair freedom's brightening morn,
> And threw aside the yoke we long had borne;
> Exulted in the raptures thought can give,
> And said alone we then began to live;

With wanton fancy, painted pleasure's charms,
Wine's liberal powers, and beauty's folding arms,
Expected joys would spring beneath our feet,
And never thought of griefs we were to meet,
Ah! Soon, too soon is all the truth displayed,
Too soon appears this scene of light and shade!
We find that those who every transport know,
In full proportion taste of every woe;
That every moment new misfortune rears;
That, somewhere, every hour's an hour of tears.
The work of wretchedness is never done,
And misery's sigh extends with every sun.
Well is it if, when dawning manhood smiled
We did not quite forget the simple child;
If, when we lost that name, we did not part
From some more glowing virtue of the heart,
From kind benevolence, from faithful truth,
The generous candour of believing youth,
From that soft spirit which men weakness call
That lists to every tale, and trusts them all.
To the warm fire of these how poor and dead
Are all the cold endowments of the head.

This was no deliberate Byronic cynicism adopted to enhance a young man's personality by decking it with grief, but a hyper-sensitive nature's awareness of the reverse side of the Lady Melbourne aspect of life. For though more particularly in William than in her other sons she saw herself to a great extent satisfactorily mirrored—his robustness of mind, his ready appetite for all that society had to offer, his many-sided abilities, his detachment, the way his perspicacious mind drilled through humbug and false sentiment—yet, probably unrecognized by her, there was within him, as it were, a rare and delicate plant that stretched forth its leaves to the warmth of some sun other than that which lights the terrestial world. In his early life, denuded of the graciosities of idealism and romanticism, bereft of religion, his heart yet ached for what his cerebral faculties derided. His power lay in his refusal to be overimpressed by any personality, situation, convention, or shibboleth. Evasive, indifferent, with a laugh or a yawn, he eluded capture by any one of them. His dissatisfaction was that he could find no fundamental principle of life: study and ponder as he might, he could deduce no co-ordinated pattern of existence. In this fashionable worldly young man this dichotomy of his nature was to others only occasionally apparent when, dining with the Devonshires, or lounging among the yellow satin settees at Carlton House, a mood of abstraction would come over him, a fugitive air of melancholy stray across his face.

When he was twenty-one there skipped into his vision a little creature, half Ariel, half gamin, Lady Bessborough's fourteen-year-old daughter Caroline. Even at that age, with her intelligence, her surprising wit, her originality, she was already an embryo society figure, and as William Lamb watched that whimsical little face beneath its ruffle of short blonde curls, and listened to all the enchanting absurdities tossed off in that still childish voice, his spirit was beguiled. "Of all the Devonshire House girls that is the one for me," he exclaimed.

As niece to the Duchess of Devonshire, "Caro," as they called her, had been brought up for a time with the group of Cavendish children, legitimates and illegitimates, all mixed up in a gay hotchpotch in the Duke's somber brick house that Kent had built overlooking the trees of the Green Park. But if somber without, it was made bright within by the perpetual seething of the most exclusive bon-ton life of the day, led by that appreciated and applauded figure, Duchess Georgiana, whose seduction still radiates from a dozen canvases. The emotional disorder of life beneath the drawing-room chandeliers—the Duchess and her friends usually involved in, and, in fact, at heart constantly wretched from, either debts or complicated love affairs—was reflected in the disorder of the nursery floor above, where daily existence was a mixture of luxury and scrimmage: the children eating off silver plates, and then dashing down to the kitchen to collect more food, while at the same time in the dining room a magnificent dinner party might be filling the air with its clamor. The appearance of the head menservants being so resplendent with their ruffles, white gloves, and swords, that Lord

Broughton, after dining there, remarked that "the guests looked very shabby in comparison with the attendants."

Notwithstanding the disorder on the nursery floors, life for the children was obviously delightful. "Everyone paid me compliments shown to children about to die," wrote Caro of this period. "I wrote not, spelt not, but I made verses which they all thought beautiful." When she was about ten, "I was taken," she continues, "to my grand-mother, Lady Spencer's, where the house-keeper, in hoop and ruffles, reigned over servants, and attended the ladies in the drawing-room." Here she developed a taste for learning, and soon, languages, politics, and all kinds of desultory information were jostling each other in her eager brain. Or perched on a music stool she would be swaying over the pianoforte, or absorbedly dabbing at a sketch, for this last was in the forefront of *ton*. Sheet after sheet of drawing paper would be assaulted by the enthusiastic ladies of the day armed with brushes and polished wooden boxes filled with great slabs of water-color paint. If they were not satisfied with the result of any particular effort they might send it on to receive additions from another, and more competent artist. When Caro was married, and had a boy of five, a letter was written, purporting to be by him, to her father, Lord Bessborough. "By the cart to-morrow you will receive two drawings, now for what you are to do with them. Mama will be very much obliged to you if you will put the *sea* in for her, and the *sky*, not very rough, but just as you think best. The other favour she has to ask of you is to put a *mountain* and *convent* upon it for the background, and one of those *holy places* with a little *saint* or the *Virgin*, to which the girl is coming to confess. All this you will do so much better than Mama. . . . You are not to show them to anyone but Grandmama, who she hopes will like them."

However, Caro was not merely a snatcher at knowledge, a flippant votary of accomplishments. This volatile creature possessed within her something hard to define, something entirely individual that seemed to be of the essence of joy itself. Her early letters quiver with that bouyant lightness and grace, shot through with intelligence, that so enchanted those who met her. She was all froth, nonsense, and nothingness, and yet it was not entirely nothingness.

I am like the song of Rosa in love with everybody [she wrote to her cousin, Lord Hartington]. What a world it is, dear sweet boy, what a flimsy, patched, work face it has, all profession, little affection, no truth. That you love me I feel sure, dearly and deeply, though you now and then see my faults, but indeed it is but bad speculation to gaze on the black of every object. Mine are unfortunately all on the surface, I am pitted all over but it is but skin-deep.... How you prate, have you nothing better to say for yourself? ... God bless your highness, long life and happiness attend you. Pleasure strew her flowers for you. Health upon your steps attend.... Cozen dear, adieu, adieu ... if you wish to cause me merriment straight ways, send me more nonsense; there is a comfort in writing it to one who will take it down as a cockatoo swallows a spoonful of castor oil ... for in many respects you resemble that sagacious bird. How could you be false and deceitful to me?

> Oh Hartington thou base deceiver
> Still importunate in vain
> Giving to the rich deceiver
> What you steal from want and pain....

Why else did you abandon me and Mrs. Conyers, and go and offer yourself like an apostate to that Corisande O?

By the time Caro was seventeen she was a personality. To William Lamb, though five or six years older, disillusioned almost before he had had time to form illusions, the mere presence of this human bubble was an easement to his spirit; for, evading any possibility of definition, and thus outrunning criticism, she gave, by her individuality alone, the suggestion of some enheartening, though indecipherable, message from another order of being. As for herself, rooted in the patrician soil of her father and her mother's families, she never stopped to consider, in all her fantastic antics, what other people would think: her only concern was to give expression to all the whimsies that whirled about in her mind. Among the Gainsborough and Sir Joshua type of beauties around her with their fine-cut profiles, swan-breasts astir beneath muslin fichus, piled-up hair threaded with pearls or topped with ostrich plumes, silken, whispering skirts, and pervasive atmosphere of feminine allure, she struck an entirely new note: that of the short-haired, piquant boy-girl; debonair, reckless, and yet intensely provocative. Of this type, now ubiquitous, she might, in a degree, be said to be the forerunner. One of her caprices, for instance, was to dress as a boy, trussing herself up in the livery of her pages—pantaloons and silver-laced jacket.

William Lamb saw the compulsions of the whole world as more or less arbitrary, therefore the gyrations of this Pucklike creature would have seemed to him little more erratic than the activities of anyone else. She became for him the most desirable of all human beings, and when he was twenty-six, he married her. During the wedding service Caroline was in such a heightened state of nervosity that (if a letter writer of the day is to be believed), growing exasperated with the bishop who was officiating, she tore at her dress, and then, fainting, had to be lifted up and carried out.

At first all went well with the marriage. Caro loved her William: William loved his Caro. The Melbournes, having exchanged homes with the Duke of York, had moved into his great house in Whitehall, and William and his wife were given the first floor for themselves. This was the domestic background to their life of all that was most fashionable in the way of parties and amusements. Within two years, a son, whom they named Augustus, was born. Caro's Spencer grandmother gives a charming heat-wave picture of William, Caroline, and their baby one day when they were staying with her in the country. "Caroline and the child are very well, tho' both oppressed, as everybody must be with the heat. William is reading Swinburne's account of Spain to us—while she makes shoes [a favored occupation of the day], and I net to save my currants which the birds will devour."

At William's knee Caroline developed her literary and philosophical education, and *Newton on the Prophecies* would be sandwiched in between balls and dinners and amateur theatricals. For it was the habit of the feminine members of the Devonshire-Bessborough group to read books of a serious nature with as much gusto as they expended on the frivolous aspects of life; not perhaps so much from a direct intention of self-culture as from an instinctive desire to gather to their excited breasts everything within reach. But Caroline, unfortunately, learned more from William than was at first intended. Ignorant of any reliable valuations, muzzed with false sentiments, she was yet, at the time of her marriage, full of sincere and generous feeling, fine ideals and aspirations, and her mind—considering the society she lived in—was surprisingly undefiled. Her young husband, egged on by subconscious sadism, positively could not resist pricking her pretty bubbles of illusion; proving with masculine dialectics that her premises, surmises, and conclusions were all unsound; countering her girlish idealisms by revealing to her all the immorality that underlay the gracious silk and satin surface of their own social world. Later, Caroline protested at the way he had encouraged her to flout "all the forms and restraints" in which she had been brought up, and at his derision for what he called her "superstitious enthusiasms." William's actual phrase had obviously been "enthusiastic superstitions"; but however much she mixed up her husband's nouns and adjectives, it is evident that to quench her aspirations and to shock her sensibilities had proved to him irresistible. One can see him at it—that heavy-browed, toughly masculine young face, about which lurks a half-teasing, half-amused expression, as under his relentless logic he watches the sense of defeat gradually spreading over the mercurial little countenance that confronts him. Unconsciously he— in reality the most tender-hearted of men—was inflicting on his young wife a great injury. Instead of fortifying her frail nature, harmonizing its diversities, he was undermining the whole tippety structure. His own mind unsettled and sardonic, he took from her the little that she had, and gave her nothing to take its place. It is not surprising that her restless, excitable brain grew alarmingly explosive, that, subconsciously, she began to nurse hostile feelings toward the man who was gradually denuding her of all she had held dear. Disagreements turned to tiffs. She began to find him dull; he to suffer from her erratic behavior, her lack of sober intelligence about anything.

"Before marriage," he wrote in his commonplace book, "the figure, the complexion carry all before them; after marriage the mind and character unexpectedly claim their share, and that the largest, of importance." In this young ménage quarrels became rife. Exasperated by Caroline's unreasonableness, William would fly out at her, and then himself be completely wretched from remorse.

Caroline developed an infatuation for Sir George Webster (Lady Holland's son by her first marriage), and so openly advertised the emotions which she insisted that this extremely ordinary young man aroused in her that she even scandalized the usually unshockable Melbourne family.

Then, in 1812, Byron limped onto the scene. All the Gothic romanticism, the Wardour Street representation of life at that time fashionable, was floating about unco-ordinated in the mind of society, and now, in the author of *Childe Harold*, appeared its perfect human representative. What before had been nebulous ideas, vague concepts, became suddenly condensed, definitely visible in the person of a beautiful, moody young peer.

Actually, there was a peculiar lack of any penetrating conception of life in this young man who, alive or dead, was to hold the attention of the world. One day, when with Tom Moore, he remarked, "What do you think of Shakespeare, Moore? I think him a damned humbug." But the fact that Byron, if a brilliant versifier, was only rarely a poet, as secondary a writer—except in a few instances—as he was a secondary character, did not then, and does not now, weaken his immense drawing power. In what does this power consist? We are confronted with a pale and dramatic face: torrents of easy-flowing verse, a mysterious deformity, a peerage, incest, genius of personality, meteoric wit, a disastrous marriage, an aura of insolence and vice, publicized and constant amours, and, finally, a purging gesture of chivalry, and a romantic and early death. Certainly, in contemplating this program of fame, most of the cheaper of the human emotions receive a vivifying flick.

As with many of the socially first-rate, Caroline was emotionally second-rate. Glamour, trashy sentiments decked out in high-sounding phrases were her delight, and frantic attempts to attune her actions to this tinsel conception her constant effort.

"The cleverest, most agreeable, absurd, amiable, perplexing, dangerous, fascinating little being that lives," Byron wrote of her while her charm held. Later, exasperated, bored to satiety, he jeered at her "fermenting her weak head and cold heart into an ice cream." But this was not wholly accurate. It was not Caroline's heart that was cold.

Now, on their first meeting, nothing could have appealed to her more than the flamboyant atmosphere that quivered around the author of *Childe Harold*. Swiftly deflected in any direction, her whole being inevitably whirled toward this *phénix d'amour*. "That beautiful pale face will be my fate," she wrote in her diary; and no prelude could have been more apt for the theatrical fandango that was to follow, in which Byron, exquisitely flattered at the attentions of this adulated little creature, played his part with all the egoistical virtuosity of which he was past master. Whether they were actual lovers or not is a question that has no answer. One aspect of their relationship is, however, undeniable. Byron swamped Caroline's being entirely: her infatuation for him all but completely overthrew her already precarious mental balance. She would drive away from parties in his carriage seated by his side; or, thrusting herself into her page's pantaloons and jacket, make a sudden appearance in his rooms; she offered to sell her jewelry to provide him with money; they went through a mock marriage ceremony. "How very pale you are . . ." she wrote him, "a statue of white marble . . . and the dark brow and hair such a contrast. I never see you without wishing to cry." She would be found at Melbourne House lying on the floor shaken with sobs. After a scene one day with Lord Melbourne she threatened to go to Byron, rushed incontinently from the house, ran all the way up Pall Mall, sold a ring to pay for a hackney coach, borrowed money on another ring to set sail somehow for somewhere, and in the end was discovered by Byron in a surgeon's house in Kensington, and brought home by him. Their whole relationship was the most sensational seriocomedy that society had ever supplied *pour épater les bourgeois*. But within less than a year Byron, now wearied by this love that had become a persecution, turned his affections and attentions to Lady Oxford.

Finally, Caroline, meeting him at a ball at Lady Heathcote's, in desperation at his indifference, made a scene in which, either with a knife or a piece of broken glass, her hand got cut, the blood spurting over her dress. This was the end. Not only Caroline's own world, but the newspapers fizzed with gossip. Lady Bessborough hurried her over to Ireland. Byron sent Caroline a letter full of the kind of theatrical protestations that were their usual idiom of communication, but, on hearing that she was returning to England, followed it up with another that was a veritable viper of cruelty.

Since the scene at Lady Heathcote's ball the world had turned such a hostile face to Caroline that her husband's chivalry was aroused. All this time he had stood back and watched the conflagration with such philosophical detachment as he could muster, and now his understanding tenderness, his enduring patience and kindness so smote his wife, that, alternating with her cries for the vanished Byron, she would protest that in reality it was William who possessed her heart. And in a sense it was true. True, too, that she possessed his. She might, when she fell into one of her rages, fling every case, clock, and ornament within reach across the room amidst cries of abuse, but, beneath it all his devotion to her remained firm, and, himself possessing the feelings of a gentleman, he saw Byron for the cad that he was, and detested him, not so much for making love to his wife, as because he considered both the poet and the finger-pointing world had ill-used her. Her behavior, however, becoming more and more eccentric, at last the Melbournes, believing her to be mad, persuaded William to agree to a separation. The Melbourne family, noted for its outspokenness, now told Caroline their opinion of her in the plainest English. In the end she sat up night after night (dressed, for no known reason, in her page's livery) writing a novel, *Glenarvon*, in which, under assumed names, she set forth the story of herself, William, and Byron. In its pages the Melbourne family and several of their intimate friends also appeared, dealt with with no gentle hand. This time William was completely overcome. "I wish I was dead," he groaned, "I wish I was dead." However, even with this fresh stab added to those that had already been driven into his vulnerable spirit, he could not, when it came to the point, bring himself to sign the deed of separation. When the lawyers arrived with the papers for his signature they found themselves confronted with the spectacle of Caroline sitting on her husband's knee laughingly feeding him with slices of thin bread and butter. His sense of compassion would not allow him to desert her, for, not only were the most searing attacks being made on her on the score of *Glenarvon* by the newspapers (which at that time had constituted themselves moral duennas with a relentless eye on the behavior of society) but the whole world was hooting at her. He saw this unaccountable, whimsical creature, who had brought him at once such enchantment and such torment, standing isolated and forlorn, and he could not endure it. To her ear came the assurance, "Caroline, we will stand or fall together."

From then on, for the next fourteen or fifteen years till her death, Caroline's life was one of social and moral declension. Shut out from the world of *ton* that was her natural habitat, she tried to fill the vacuum of her days by writing further novels, taking up with the intelligentsia, staging tawdrily romantic episodes with any man whom she could persuade to act the part.

Through the most crowded of London's streets would at times be seen a small, reckless figure perched on a black horse going at a canter. Caroline, on her way to somewhere; perhaps, at that moment, to visit her dear friend Mr. John Murray, the publisher. In this friendship, John Murray had to be prepared for all emergencies. "I wish to leave my trunks with you," she wrote to him on one occasion, preparatory to leaving for Italy, "and my cockatoos and two Blenheim puppies and three pages. If you do not write instantly counter-orders they will be left at your door with a French lady and child lately escaped stark mad from Bordeaux."

"I am like the wreck of a little boat, she wrote to a friend, "for I never came up to the sublime and beautiful—merely a little gay, merry boat which perhaps stranded itself at Vauxhall or London Bridge."

William continued in his endeavors to act as rudder to this impetuous craft, and though her behavior became so outrageous that he did finally procure a legal separation, he still allowed her to live at his country home, Brocket, where he constantly paid her visits, gladly fostering any scheme for her happiness. By the time she was forty-two she was a dying woman. Surprisingly to those around her, she bore her intense suffering without a murmur, her only anxiety the thought of the distress she had brought on others. "I consider," she wrote to her sister-in-law, Lady Duncannon, "my painful illness as a great blessing—I feel returned to my God and duty and my dearest husband: and my heart which was so proud and insensible is quite overcome with the great kindness I receive. . . . I see how good and kind others are, and I am quite resigned to die"; and to Lady Morgan, "remember the only noble fellow I ever met with is William Lamb."

Abnormal, bizarre sprite, her mind a pandemonium of contradictions, and yet full of such generous impulses, so vital, so gaily humble ("ugly, thin, mad and despised as I am"), that to William Lamb she was always to remain a being enveloped within a nimbus of light. "In spite of all," he protested, "she was more to me than anyone ever was or ever will be." The years passed, but if he heard her name so much as mentioned, those near would catch the sad-voiced murmur, "Shall we meet in another world?"—would note that his eyes had become suffused with tears.

Their son, Augustus, was the only one of their three children to survive infancy; but the pomp of his name sat with sad inappropriateness on this boy who, though not entirely imbecile, failed to mature in the normal way. Though year succeeded year and he had reached the age of twenty-nine with no improvement, his father still deluded himself that one day the longed-for change would be apparent. It did come, but only the moment before his death, in 1836. "Augustus was lying on a sofa near me," wrote Melbourne* afterward, "he had been reading, but I thought had dropped asleep. Suddenly he said to me in a quiet and reflective tone, 'I wish you would give me some franks, that I may write and thank people who have been kind in their enquiries'. The pen dropped from my hand as if I had been struck, for the words and the manner were as clear and thoughtful as if no cloud had ever hung heavily over him. I cannot give any notion of what I felt; for I believed it to be, as it proved, the summons they call the lightening before death. In a few hours he was gone."

Concurrently with all the distresses of his private life William Lamb had pursued a public career. Starting with law, he had turned to politics: had sat in Parliament; been Chief Secretary to the Lord Lieutenant of Ireland; then, in 1834, Prime Minister for four months, when he resigned, waving aside William IV's offer of the Garter and an earldom. Within a few months, in April, 1835, he was back again as Premier, and was to remain so for six years.

He had since his wife's death been cited as corespondent by Lady Brandon's husband; and, a year before we see him driving along on this June morning, he had, quite unjustly, become involved in a divorce case. Always fond of women's society, he had become an

---

* He had now succeeded his father as second Baron Melbourne.

intimate friend of one of Sheridan's granddaughters, Caroline
Norton, a young woman as intelligent as she was dramatically
beautiful. Her husband, a most repulsive character, becoming
anxious to get rid of her, searched for a corespondent—a difficult
undertaking as none existed. Finally, he cast Lord Melbourne for
the role, and started divorce proceedings. "I am sorry you cannot
hold a brief for me," Melbourne remarked to Serjeant Wilde, "for
I give you my honour as a gentleman that this charge is false."
Norton lost his case.

Such had been some of the experiences and stresses that Melbourne had undergone in his course through life. And he had
triumphantly surmounted them. About him lay a kind of ample
splendor, the outcome of his garnered years. His griefs and dis-
illusionments, all now distilled into wisdom and charity, had given
him a peculiar penetration into the processes of life and into the
minds of others.

A settled urbanity, something at once calm and reassuring, lay
across that once tempestuous countenance, his general conclusion
being that since no entirely certain decision on any subject is possible, it was better to leave things as they were for fear worse
should supervene. This leaning to the *status quo* was perhaps
tempting to a nature one of whose chief characteristics was indolence. Possibly this very indolence gave added charm to a voice which
was said to be so harmonious that to hear him let fall the most
ordinary observation was a delight. Meanwhile, on the surface he
was the most companionable and cheerful of hedonists, inclined to
be too appreciative of all those luxurious meals so succulently outspread before him in the great houses in London and the country;
lounging about in the armchairs of those tranquil libraries and
drawing rooms, and then, suddenly splitting the air with his "loud,
abrupt, breaker of a laugh," while from sheer enjoyment he would
violently rub his hands together. "One of the most straight-for-
ward, sagacious, disinterested men I ever knew," wrote Lord
Broughton. "Really an excellent creature, very honest and single-
minded," comments Princess Lieven. But he was far from being as
simple as the patronizing Princess imagined, though his "Can't
you leave it alone?" which was "supposed to express his frame of
mind whenever a trouble presented itself" deceived a good many

people as to the force of character that lay behind. Even Talleyrand was taken in by his mental slouch. *"Trop camarade* for a Prime Minister," he had opined. But the more perspicacious considered it was as much his rare personality as his capacities that had floated him into the premiership. "He had risen to be Prime Minister apparently because he did not care to fill the place," remarks Lord Lorne.

No man had more thirst for close family affection than Melbourne. In contrast to the general confusion of life, to the conflicts engendered in his own mind by his literary researches, it might be said that to him family affection was the one anchorage. Now, with his mother, Caroline, and Augustus all gone, the family hearth within him was desolate indeed. "A man with a capacity for loving without having anything in the world to love," so Greville, who knew him well, wrote of him.

Now, on this June morning of 1837, his horses, bearing him to Kensington Palace, trotted steadily onward; and like the earlier-arrived post chaise, his carriage turned in between the stone lion and unicorn, and breasted the drive.

2

We are back now at the palace at the moment when Victoria is returning to her room filled with the realization that she has become Queen. As soon as she had put on her very plainly made black bombazine dress—the fashion then being voluminous sleeves, tightly compressed body and waist, and long skirt, stiffening out at the feet—she went to breakfast. While she was having it, Stockmar came in to talk over the situation with her. He stood with his shrewd glance on the small, black-garbed figure seated there busily eating. She always enjoyed her food. ("I may say she gobbles," remarked one of her more outspoken subjects.) While Stockmar looked on, he gave her final hints and advice, and, as she listened to him, we know that at the back of her mind was the thought that Uncle Leopold and Feodore must at once be written to; for, breakfast once over, she sat down and revealed to them the happenings of the last few hours. "Dearest Feodore," ran her letter to her sister, "two words only to tell you that the poor King died this morning at 12 minutes past 2, that I am well, and that I remain for life your devoted attached sister V.R."

One can hardly imagine a more succinct, tactful expression of affection, announcement of her just acquired sovereignty, and assurance that it would not change their relationship.

Then Lord Melbourne arrived. Everyone appears to have been up very early on this irregular day, for even now it was only nine o'clock. She interviewed Lord Melbourne alone. There were no onlookers when that fine, upstanding male figure—a figure, we are told, massive without corpulence—bowed before the curtsying sylph, whose unrelieved black bombazine must have seemed strangely at variance with the light summer air afloat in the room.

Melbourne kissed her hand, and then that exceptionally pretty girl-voice trilled out the phrase, no doubt learned from Stockmar at breakfast, that "it had been my intention to retain him and the rest of the present Ministry at the head of affairs, and that it could not be in better hands than his."

Melbourne again kissed her hand. Then in his mellifluous voice (Victoria was already charmed by his voice: this and all details of their interview she gives in her Journal) he read her the declaration which in a few hours she would have to read to the Council. After this they had further talk.

Very curious it must have seemed to this sophisticated son of the Regency, with his liking among men to talk broad, and with women accustomed to gayest interchange of ideas with those who were virtuosos in the art, now to be dealing out stiff state phrases to that intent, earnest little person in her dismal frock. As they went on quietly talking we do not know what was in Melbourne's mind, but we cannot but think that he, as an absorbed reader of history, must have been exquisitely relishing the uniqueness of the occasion, consumed with interest in this problematical child who had been awakened that morning to be told she was the most important person in England. His thoughts are not known to us, but of Victoria we do not know that as she watched him bowing himself backward to the door, a warm feeling of satisfaction invaded her. "I like him very much and feel confidence in him," she wrote that night in her Journal.

Also, this morning, she had another reason for pleasure, something that she found perfectly delightful. She had seen her Prime Minister, "of *course quite alone* as I shall *always* do all my Ministers." For the first time in her life she was savoring the freedom of letting her own personality function without supervision of any sort. Without, above all, having to consider how every word she uttered might affect the jealous ear of her mother.

In the great red saloon at the palace there must now have been an incessant coming and going, a shoving and arranging of furniture around the room's twelve massive pillars, for everything was being got ready for the Council that was to be held in two hours' time. Charles Greville, that ubiquitous social figure and indefatigable diarist, arrived with the official papers relating to the ceremony. His mind, as Clerk of the Council, was naturally occupied with wondering how this child-Queen would get through her ordeal. "The first thing," he wrote afterward, "was to teach her her lesson." He explained the papers to Melbourne, and Melbourne in turn went off and explained them to Victoria. He asked her if she would like the great officers of state to walk by her side when she entered the red saloon; but no. Filled as she now was with elation at the way she was managing things entirely by herself, she said she preferred "to come in alone."

It is of interest to note that when, under Lord Melbourne's direction, the Privy Council "drew up their declaration to the Kingdom," the young Queen was referred to as "Alexandrina Victoria," and that on this her day of accession all the peers who subscribed the roll in the House of Lords swore allegiance to her under those names. It was not till the next day that her designation was altered to "Victoria" only; this necessitating no end of trouble in the issuing of a new declaration, and a re-signing of the peers' roll.

The red saloon had by now become a shifting mass of male figures, all filled with anticipation of what they were going to witness. Among these were Victoria's uncles of Cumberland and Sussex, the Duke of Wellington, Brougham, and Peel. The time for the ceremony arrived. Victoria was waiting in the next room, as she had been warned that in a moment the double doors would open, and that her uncles, the two Archbishops, Melbourne, and the Chancellor, would come in to her, and officially announce the death of William IV. She felt peculiarly calm. ("I was not at all nervous.") Her clear, accurate mind was, like some mechanical indicator, quietly doing everything for her in the most satisfactory way. An elder figure—one supposes that of her mother—hovered around her while she waited, but, as the double doors were slowly pushed back from the other side, the arriving deputation saw this figure quickly vanish through another door. The announcement made, the group departed.

Then again the doors were opened wide, and, like an actress taking the stage, Victoria, with that graceful walk she had learned from Taglioni, glided toward the crowd of gazing men to perform her first public function as Queen. Her noticeable lack of embarrassment arose perhaps partly from her unself-consciousness as to her own appearance, though certainly she would have liked to be taller. "Everybody grows but me," she sighed later to Melbourne. But she was so imbued with the sense that it was the Almighty's wish that she should be Queen of England that to her pellucid mind any idea that she was not a fit instrument would have seemed almost impious.

Now, as she entered the saloon, the monumental figures of her two uncles advanced to meet her. She bowed to the Lords, and took her seat at the head of the long table, her every movement noted by the scrutinizing eyes of the men near enough to see her. All about her in the big room such a hubbub and commotion was going on that a young man who was there said afterward that it was like being at an auction. Then she "read her speech in a clear, distinct and audible voice." (A few days later, Lady Granville wrote from Paris, "Mme de Lieven gasps for breath and cries over the young speech.") Now, as Charles Greville listened to her, his eyes took in every detail. "Though small in stature, and without much pretension to beauty, the gracefulness of her manner and the good expression of her countenance gave her on the whole a very agreeable appearance." All the onlookers were astounded at her self-assurance. Peel said he was "amazed at her manner . . . her modesty, and at the same time, her firmness." The Duke of Wellington, as he too watched and listened, was thinking that "if she had been his own daughter he could not have desired to see her perform her part better." "Never," protests Greville, "was anything like the first impression which she produced." A curious comment came afterward from Lord Duncannon, who had noticed how remarkably closely her eyelids fitted her slightly prominent eyes.

Every few moments during this now far-famed Council there would be a scuffle at the doors as further members of the hastily summoned two hundred and twenty Privy Councilors pushed their way in. The noise and fidgeting made by these constant arrivals was increased by the behavior of the Lord Mayor and the Attorney General who, rightly present for the reading of the Proclamation, had then been officially asked to have "the goodness to retire." But this form of goodness was beyond the Lord Mayor and his companion. Absolutely determined not to be parted from the royal child at this unique moment, they managed, in the general "bustle and confusion," to reinsert themselves into the room. Greville, however, spied the furs and scarlet of the Lord Mayor and had him and his friend chivied out. Not only did they smuggle themselves in yet again, but when Greville went later to sit for his portrait in Wilkie's picture of the Queen holding her first Council, there, confronting him on the canvas, were the indomitable pair; Wilkie explaining that they had come hurrying along to him and implored to be put in, each asserting that he had actually been present on the occasion.

The wearying confusion of the Council was still progressing. The room being vast enough for conversations to be risked in the background, comments on the speech were being murmured from mouth to mouth. Most of these were appreciative; but the politician, Brougham, invariably striking an individual note, and now, for some reason, in that wrought-up condition when the tip of his long nose would twitch from excitement, began to take exception to the wording of the peroration.

"Amelioration," he burst out to Peel, "that is not English. You might perhaps say melioration, but improvement is the proper word."

"Oh," protested Peel, "I see no harm in the word."

"You object to the sentiment," retorted Brougham, "I object to the grammar."

Now Victoria was signing the oath for the security of the Church of Scotland. Then the Privy Councilors, and the Dukes of Cumberland and Sussex were sworn; and when this few-hours-monarch saw those familiar figures of her uncles actually on their knees before her—that well-known skullcap of Uncle Sussex, that wildly whiskered face of Uncle Cumberland bent low as they gave voice to their protestations of allegiance—then the submissive training of her youth welled within her, and, says Greville, "I saw her blush up to the eyes."

"She seemed rather bewildered," he wrote, "at the multitude of men who were sworn, and who came one after another to kiss her hand . . . occasionally looking at Melbourne for instruction when she had any doubt what to do, which hardly ever occurred, and with perfect calmness and self-possession, but at the same time with a graceful modesty and propriety particularly interesting and ingratiating."

At last, the business over, she rose, and the Council this time had a moment's view of a demure nape of neck beneath smoothly brushed-up hair as she glided away through the double doors; and Greville, interestedly peering, notes, "I could see that nobody was in the adjoining room."

Evidently the Duchess did not wish to risk being seen by the Council, but she was hovering somewhere near, and as Victoria passed through the rooms the inevitable figure was upon her. "I need not ask you how you acquitted yourself," she exclaimed as she bent to bestow a kiss, "for you are quite composed"; and then, trying to push her little daughter back into the state of dependence that was so convenient to herself, she added, "Were you startled at finding yourself in a room alone with so many gentlemen?"

"No," came the annoying answer, "it was my duty to face them, and God gave me all the strength I needed."

On her side Victoria now had something to ask, really something very simple indeed, but she had spent every moment of her eighteen years in such subjection that before saying what it was she felt she must first, so as to countenance such an audacity, draw her mother's attention to her own new status, and therefore whimsically remarked, "I suppose, Mamma, it must be true I am Queen of England?"

"Yes, love, you see that you are."

"Well, then, I have a request to make." This following on such an opening, what must not the Duchess have hoped and expected?

Here at last, no doubt, was to be some flattering recognition, some most gratifying reward for all her years of care. Even perhaps, child that Victoria still was, she was now going to suggest that her capable mother, though not Regent *en titre*, should yet act as such. And then the request came.

"I want to be alone and undisturbed for an hour."

So that was the mother's recompense. Her daughter's first thought on this momentous day was not to share her emotions with her, but to lock herself and her feelings away from her. Unpleasant character in many ways though the Duchess was, one cannot withhold from her a momentary pity. But worse was on its way. When Victoria rejoined her after her hour of solitude, she asked "that a small bedroom next to that of the Duchess should be made ready for her, so that she could sleep in it alone."

Her demand to be left to herself had been painful, but this must have been lacerating. Ever since six o'clock that morning the Duchess had been receiving rebuffs, and bewildered apprehension was beginning to invade that hitherto compact mind. We are told that her full-blooded face had gone quite pale "from agitation," and it is not surprising. For Victoria, that mere child, to be going on in this absolutely unforeseen manner, sweeping from room to room in her black bombazine frock with such perfect composure; so calmly announcing to her mother that all the help she required was being supplied direct from the Almighty; and making no mention whatever of any need for assistance from her mother. Certainly her education had been directed to encourage her to rely on Divine Providence, but the Duchess had never foreseen that she would carry it to these lengths. This day-in, day-out familiar little figure, with her curtsies, her subservience, her schoolroom occupations, to turn in one moment into this self-possessed, self-motivated young person, doing everything as competently for the first time as if after years of practice—it seemed incredible. All the psychological scaffolding behind which she had been forced since childhood to hide herself was down indeed, and the vigorous entity behind become startlingly visible. The Duchess' stupefaction arose from her never having dreamed that Victoria's former attitude had been merely a blind. For her mother it must have been the most calamitous morning of her life, for, so she later told Princess Lieven, she clearly realized there was "no longer any future for her, that she had become a nobody." Painful in the extreme, too, must it have been for the poor lady on that June morning to have Melbourne in and out of the rooms, as he was at all hours; for her not only to have to be civil to, but, probably, to have to entertain at mealtimes the continually appearing Premier, knowing as she did that at the back of his mind must be the recollection of that shameful letter she had lately sent him insisting that it was Victoria's wish that her mother should be Regent. While the Duchess dealt with all the various incidents that would have arisen during the day; while, with her charming air, she welcomed one important personage, or speeded the departure of another, all the time there lay the wounds beneath her, in a sense so slight, and yet so penetrating, that Victoria had inflicted. And yet, through these confusing hours that from top to bottom had turned the whole palace upside down, there was no single moment the Duchess could lay her finger on, and say that at that moment Victoria had behaved badly to her. On the contrary, on the surface she was as dutifully polite and deferential to her mother as ever, whenever, be it understood, there was an opportunity for any contact at all between the Duchess and this just born Queen, who was incessantly occupied receiving people, giving audiences, settling who should be her physicians, composing letters. . . . There she was at this moment, writing to the dowager Queen Adelaide in the kindest possible manner, urging her to stay on at Windsor as long as she wished. Then it was the turn of her Journal, to which, even on this phenomenal day, she punctiliously applied herself, noting down every detail of what had happened: this daily duty presumably having been originally imposed on her, as were all her habits, by the Duchess herself. If her mother could have looked over her shoulder at the particular page above which Victoria's quill was twitching, she would have seen appearing in that dashingly elongated writing—"I shall do my utmost to fulfil my duty towards my country; I am very young and perhaps in many ways though not in all things, inexperienced, but I am sure that very few have more real good will and more real desire to do what is fit and right than I have."

Yes, Victoria's behavior was without flaw, and yet, from the Duchess' point of view. . . . However, perhaps at dinner she and her child would have an intimate half-hour to themselves. But no. "Took my dinner upstairs alone" runs the entry.

As for Conroy, that once busy schemer, what of him? Hurrying circumstance had drawn his every claw. Completely passed over and ignored by Victoria, where he stands is a stunned silence. It is as if this new revelation of herself that she had sprung on them all had removed from him the very power of speech.

Turning to Lehzen, we may be certain that Victoria had flown to her between each audience, each incident. Lehzen, who must have exulted at seeing her treasure lit with such an aura, dowered with such ascendancy. We know that Victoria, her hands now full of gifts for whomever she pleased, had found time among the day's urgencies to lay before her devotee suggestions for self-aggrandizement, for that night she wrote in her Journal, "My *dear* Lehzen will always remain with me as my friend, but will take no situation about me, and I think she is right." That sentence alone cancels any supposition that she was eager for power. Her sole wish was to continue to be the close companion of this child of her spirit.

After her dinner Victoria had another talk with Stockmar, then another with Melbourne. And each time it was an easeful consulting in private. "I had a very *comfortable* conversation with him," she wrote that night after her final interview with Melbourne. "Each time I see him I feel more confidence in him; I find him very kind in his manner too." When he left her, her vigilant eye glanced at the time. Not very late yet, "near 10," but the day, successful as it was to look back on, had been a strain, and she decided to go to bed. So, while the sound of Melbourne's carriage wheels dwindled into the summer night, she "went down and said good-night to Mamma etc." Into that limbo of "etc." we may presume were flung Conroy and the closely linked Flora Hastings.

Now at last this extraordinary day was over and done with. As the night went on, one by one, each performer in the drama climbed into bed and lay down, each with his or her burning thoughts of apprehension or triumph, while Victoria, alone in her small room, lay in the feather darkness, savoring the longed-for felicity of being at last an entirely separate entity.

3

There followed three weeks of preparation for the move from
Kensington to Buckingham Palace. If the packings up at different
times to go to Ramsgate, Tunbridge Wells, or Claremont had been
strenuous, this time they must have been overwhelming, for it
appears that not only were intimate possessions to be transferred
(these including trunkfuls of every doll, frock, pelisse, parasol,
muff, or mitten that Victoria had ever played with or worn since
she was a child, trunks which were reopened after her death), but
the very rooms themselves were to be stripped bare.

Meanwhile, the pages of the Journal had begun to vibrate with
satisfaction. "The *very frequent* communications I have with Lord
Melbourne, Lord John Russell etc. etc. as also the other official
matters I have to write and receive." The charm of interviewing
all these outstanding statesmen "alone" was to Victoria as if she
were walking through shafts of sunlight, such a sense of importance, of deliverance of spirit did it give her after these years of
compression. "I really have immense to do; I receive so many
communications from my Ministers but I like it very much. . . ."
And again, a week later, "I repeat what I said before, that I have
so many communications from the Ministers, and from me to them,
and I get so many papers to sign *every* day that I have always a
very great deal to do; but for want of time and space I do not write
these things down. I *delight* in this work." Every page of the
Journal now is vocal with conversations between her and Melbourne. "At 10 minutes to 9 came Lord Melbourne and stayed
with me till 10. I had an agreeable and important and satisfactory
conversation with him." Another day, "At about 10 minutes to 4
came Lord Melbourne. . . . I talked with him as usual on Political
affairs, about my Household, and various other *Confidential* affairs." One may take it that one of these confidential affairs was
the payment of her father's debts, which she insisted should at
last be settled. A silent comment on the fact that her mother had
left them unpaid. It was probably in the course of these snug, continuous talks with Melbourne that she decided on Conroy's fate.
For, whether guessed by him or not, Nemesis was at the Irishman's
elbow. No place whatever at Court was to be offered to this man

who had so crassly misunderstood her feelings for him that he had, only a few months earlier, conceived the idea that she would, when she came to power, accept him as her secretary. She did, however, as far as we know, without demur, face the fact of his now becoming secretary to her mother: the conspirators were not yet to be wrenched apart. Invariably doing the correct thing, Victoria had an interview with Conroy, asking that he would "name the reward he expected from his services to her parents." He had his demands ready: the Red Riband, an Irish peerage, and a pension of £3000. It must have seemed grotesque to Conroy, considering what his and Victoria's attitudes had been to each other all these years, to stand in front of her as a supplicant, and to hear her familiar voice, those carefully enunciated, girlish tones, informing him that she would grant the pension he asked, but that the bestowal of his other two requests rested with her ministers.

Any and every occasion now seemed to contain within itself something for the eager Victoria to enjoy. She proudly announces that the day the addresses from the House of Commons were read to her, "I wore the Blue Ribbon and Star of the Garter." Even the fact that, when she had to confer the Grand Cross of the Bath on Lord Durham she found the Sword of State so heavy she could not lift it, this embarrassment was turned into a pleasure by Lord Melbourne holding it for her, so that "I only inclined it." Some of her explanatory asides to her Journal are charmingly naïve. "Seated myself on the Throne," runs an entry for July; "I then conferred the order of the Bath (*not sitting* of course) upon Prince Esterhazy." However, amidst all these absorbing satisfactions one depressing duty could not be avoided—a visit to Queen Adelaide at Windsor, a step for Victoria into the shadows from which her own happiness had sprung. Her peculiarly competent mind, always casting astute glances around and ahead of her, foresaw that when she went to Windsor for this visit the royal standard, now at half-mast for William IV, would be run up for her arrival. This, so her affectionate heart realized, might be painful for her aunt, and therefore must not be; and she asked Melbourne to attend to it. "*He* had never thought of the flag," comments the astounded Greville, "or knew anything about it." Another considerate thought this "sceptred child" had for Adelaide was in connection with her royal saddle horses. Victoria, knowing they would all automatically become her own, said that she would like her aunt to choose out several that she was especially fond of to keep for herself. Now, on this day of the Windsor visit, "At quarter to nine went with Mamma to Windsor.... We went instantly to the poor Queen's apartments. She received me *most kindly* but was much affected." Here was the reverse of Victoria's gay obverse of the medal of queenship. "Altogether the whole rather upset me." However, no sooner had she and her mother driven back to Kensington that June afternoon, and she again set foot in the palace, than her life's new tune restarted as merrily as ever, for she heard that the Duchess of Sutherland had accepted her offer to be her Mistress of the Robes. To have acquired that luminary, the Duchess of Sutherland, was a triumph; an outstandingly beautiful woman, genuflected to by all, showered with the world's prizes, some won by exertion, some gratuitously bestowed; immensely rich; as moral as she was popular; and as successful in espousing the cause of paupers, miners, bullied Poles, or American slaves as she was in entertaining royalties and ambassadors. Her London setting was Stafford House. One thorn alone marred her great crimson rose of satisfaction: the fact that Stafford House was not freehold. The Duke of York had started building it—the lease being one granted by the Crown—but not having the money to complete it, had sold it to the Duke of Sutherland. Later, the Duchess tried to induce Melbourne to advise "the Crown" to sell it her, but Melbourne's genial easiness could at times stiffen surprisingly, and he told her he "thought it his duty to advise the Crown to keep what it possessed."

It was well that this very young Queen should have at her elbow someone who dealt so efficiently with life as did Harriet Sutherland, and who yet, when at Court, kept her own luster hidden away— even too much tucked away, some people thought. ("What sort of impression does the Duchess of Sutherland make at Court?" wrote Princess Lieven from abroad to Melbourne's sister, Lady Palmerston. "I hear that she is a little too humble, a little too much like a head housemaid.") Another woman than Victoria might have thought it bad policy to have that Venus face constantly seen by the side of her own, but such considerations had no place in Victoria's mind. Envy or spite were unknown to her. To put it on a lower level, it would have been unwise for her to compete where she could not but have failed; and in the final issue she had no fear of comparison with any feminine rival, so much did her integrity of personality gain her the ascendancy over any woman who came near her. This instinctive art of imposing herself was, of course, reinforced by her position, but all the same, from the first instant she magnificently met her position. She rose to it. The only portrait perhaps that reveals this inner force in her, even at a very early age, is Winterhalter's painting of her seated by the side of one of her Coburg cousins, the Duchesse de Nemours. The look at once of fine breeding, self-assurance, and sagacity in those young eyes is arresting.

To return to her in all her youthful excitement over choosing her various ladies. Besides the satisfaction of having acquired the Duchess of Sutherland, "I forgot to say that Lord Melbourne wrote me word yesterday evening that Lady Mulgrave was very desirous to become one of my Ladies of the Bedchamber": and then, in a few days, "Lady Lansdowne brought Miss Pitt and Miss Spring-Rice (the two Maids of Honour) to kiss my hands."

4

Inevitably there arrived the July day when Kensington Palace, home of nearly all Victoria's memories, had to be parted from forever. For a moment she withdrew her eyes from the luminous landscape that lay outspread before her with all its varied delights, its promise of yet fairer to be revealed, and with a tightening of heart walked through those well-known rooms, all of them of a sudden become so touchingly dear, but which now, denuded of furniture, ornaments, bird cages, and every familiar object, already looked bare and melancholy. "Though I rejoice to go into Buckingham Palace for many reasons, it is not without feelings of regret that I shall bid adieu *for ever* to this my birth-place, where I have been born and lived. . . . I have seen my dear sister married here, I have seen many of my dear relations here, I have had pleasant balls and *delicious* concerts here, my present rooms upstairs are really very pleasant, comfortable and pretty, and *enfin* I like this poor Palace. I have held my first Council here, too! I have gone

VISCOUNT MELBOURNE IN
HIS YOUTH

From the portrait by
Sir Thomas Lawrence, P.R.A.

VISCOUNT MELBOURNE
WHEN OLDER

From the portrait by Sir Edwin
Landseer, R.A.

QUEEN VICTORIA AND HER FIRST COUSIN THE DUCHESSE DE NEMOURS
(PRINCESS VICTOIRE OF SAXE-COBURG)

From the painting by F. Winterhalter

By gracious permission of H.M. The King

through painful and disagreeable scenes here, 'tis true, but still I am fond of the poor old Palace.... The poor rooms look so sad and deserted, everything being taken away."

Two o'clock arrived, and a little after came the sound, which to the ears of the Duchess and Victoria must have been so familiar, the grinding and clatter of carriage and horses on the courtyard flagstones. Then mother and daughter appeared beneath the portico; and, as they climbed into the foremost of the carriages, the cord that had bound them to Kensington Palace was cut conclusively, never to be rejoined.

As their carriage turned into the short avenue to the gates a curious figure that had been keeping watch in the courtyard tore along in front of them: Victoria's admirer, who used to weed the Round Pond in the hope of catching sight of her. Now, having reached the gates, he scrambled into his waiting phaeton, and adroitly managed to head the cortege to the palace, thus giving himself the delightful illusion of being the one to conduct the young Queen to her new home.

5

The decoration of the interior of Buckingham Palace, the last brushfuls of paint, the final festooning of the curtains, had only been achieved shortly before Victoria's arrival. The old Buckingham House had been practically rebuilt—at immense cost to the nation—by George IV, in the Palladian style, from designs by Nash; but though the outside was completed before the King died, the interior was left unfinished. This rebuilding by Nash had not been accomplished without some sharp scuffles between architect and monarch. George IV's first idea had been to add "a few more rooms to the old house." Nash, thinking this a mistake, "continually urged his Majesty to build in some other situation." George IV refused. Nash's wish was to rebuild "higher up in the garden, *i.e.* in a line with Pall Mall," and to have a road across the Green Park as an approach.

George IV again refused. "I must have a *pied-à-terre*," he said. "I do not like Carlton House standing in a street and ... I will have it at Buckingham House . . . in the same place. *There are early associations that endear me to the spot.*"

Having originally pretended that he only wanted the addition of "a few rooms to the old house," and telling Nash ("good-humouredly") that it was "at his peril ever to advise me to build a palace" there, as the work proceeded, the King changed his mind completely, and, sending for Nash, announced to his stupefaction, "Nash, the State Rooms you have made me are so handsome that I think I shall hold my Courts there."

Nash burst into protests, pointing out "how unfair such a determination was to him as an architect—the original intention having been merely to make the new building a 'residence,'" that it "was not suited to a State Palace; that no provision was made for a Queen, nor for the Lord Chamberlain's and Lord Steward's offices."

"You know nothing about the matter," retorted the King in his usual rude way when annoyed, "it will make an excellent palace."

One day when George IV was discussing the plans with William Sequier, "'There,' said His Majesty, marking the spot, 'is the entrance and road for people who come in hackney coaches. Here is the entrance for Ministers and Ambassadors. This is the one for the Royal Family, and this,' he continued [says Sequier] with some hesitation, 'is for Us—on great occasions.'"

The homely William and Adelaide had viewed that great stone façade with distaste and dread. "The King," wrote Creevey, "never ceased to impress upon Duncannon that all he and the Queen wish for is *to be comfortable*. He says that both he and the Queen find it inconvenient to be obliged to move all their books, papers, etc. out of their own sitting-rooms, upon every Levee and Drawing room, because their rooms are wanted on such occasions; but as for removing to Buckingham House, he will do so if the Government wish it, tho' he thinks it a most ill-contrived house; and if he goes there, he hopes it may be *plain*, no gilding, for he dislikes it extremely. But what he would prefer to everything, would be living in Marlborough House. . . . Billy says if he might have a passage made to unite this house with St. James's, he thinks he and the Queen could live there very comfortably indeed." ("Now," concludes Creevey, "was there ever so innocent a Sovereign since the world was made?")

When, about three years before William IV's death, the House of Lords and the House of Commons were burned down, he had seen in this disaster a blessed opportunity for getting rid of even the idea of having to move into the hated Buckingham Palace. "Went to St. James's," wrote Lord Broughton after the fire, "and saw His Majesty. I cannot say he was much affected by the calamity, rather the reverse, and seemed delighted at having an opportunity of getting rid of Buckingham Palace; he said he meant it as a permanent gift for Parliament Houses, that it would be the finest thing in Europe." Later that day, the King and Queen had driven down to see the ruins. "The King," wrote Broughton, "looked gratified as if at a show.... Just before getting into his carriage he called the Speaker and me to him and said, 'Mind, I mean Buckingham Palace as a permanent gift. Mind that.' " In the end he did manage to evade ever having to move there.

Once the work on the palace was finished, Creevey, needless to say, was soon inside it, peering and commentating. "Well ... as for our Buckingham Palace ... never was there such a specimen of wicked, vulgar profusion. It has cost a million of money, and there is not a fault that has not been committed in it. You may be sure there are rooms enough, and large enough for the money; but for staircases, passages etc., I observed that instead of being called Buckingham Palace it should be called the 'Brunswick Hotel.' The costly ornaments of the State Rooms exceed all belief in their bad taste and every species of infirmity. Raspberry-coloured pillars without end, that quite turn you sick to look at.... The marble single arch * in the front of the Palace cost £100,000 and the gateway in Piccadilly cost £40,000."

Even now, when Victoria and her mother arrived at the Palace, the inside must have presented a very unfinished look, for Lord Broughton, going there for an interview a few days later, found "the apartments in great disorder; housemaids were on their knees scrubbing the floors, and servants laying down carpets." Victoria, neither at eighteen nor at eighty, had any aesthetic discrimination as to decorations or furnishing, and was quite impervious to the raspberry pillars that quite turned Mr. Creevey sick. Her only

---

* Now the Marble Arch. Later, the other arch too was moved, and now forms the entrance to Constitution Hill.

comment on her new home was to inform her Journal, "I am much pleased with my rooms. They are high, pleasant and cheerful. Arranged things." Then, as the day wore on, she and the Duchess of Kent, probably going through the great, low-ceilinged room opening on to shallow steps that lead to the garden, went out together into the green solitude, and anyone happening to look out of one of the palace windows would have seen the two strolling figures, with a King Charles scurrying around them, as they wandered along, now here now there, gazing at the lake that lay glistening within its fringe of rushes, pursuing their way along the shelving grass lawns. "Large and very pretty," commented Victoria that night.

Though Kensington Palace now lay behind her, her tenderness for it remained. Indeed, it is owing to her steady affection for it that the rambling old place is still in existence, as part of it was at one time condemned by the Office of Works to be pulled down. The Queen refused to allow this, and during the last year of her life arranged with Lord Salisbury and Sir Michael Hicks-Beach that in return for her giving up the use of Bushey House and the Ranger's House at Greenwich, the Government should buy Schomberg House, place it at her disposal, and restore Kensington Palace. Parliament voted £36,000 for the purpose, with the stipulation that the State Rooms should be open to the public.

6

All this time King Leopold, seated in his Belgian palace, was listening with taut ears for the slightest sounds that came from Buckingham Palace, agog to learn how his niece, filled with his admonishments, was grappling with her position. Certainly the tone of her letters was so remarkably self-assured ("I have very pleasant large dinners every day. I invite my Premier generally once a week to dinner as I think it right to show that I esteem him") that Leopold must have realized that his injunction of a few weeks back, "be not alarmed at becoming Queen," was entirely uncalled for; and soon he was writing to her, "Your spirit in all these new and trying proceedings makes me happy beyond expression." Nevertheless, more and more ideas kept cropping up in his fertile brain, and some that he felt convinced would be useful to his niece. "I should advise you to say as often as possible that you are *born* in England," he wrote with delightful disregard of the English tense. "George III *gloried* in this, and as *none* of your cousins are born in England, it is in your interest *de faire reporter cela fortement.*"

"My beloved uncle," came the rather lofty reply, "Though I have an immense deal of business to do, I shall write you a few lines to thank you for your kind and useful letters."

All the same, her shrewdness warned her to pay the most careful attention to what he handed out to her of his collected wisdom ("Your advice is always of the greatest importance to me"), and she would carefully carry out his injunctions, often to the bewilderment of those she had to do with officially, who did not realize that while with one ear she listened to what they had to say, with the other she was listening to certain precautionary whispers from across the Channel. Melbourne, for instance, could not understand her refusal ever to give him an answer to a question on the same day that he asked it. He found this a special enigma, as in the end she practically always followed his advice. Her Premier was unaware that somewhere in her private sitting room there lay a letter that ran, "I make it a rule not to let any question be forced upon my *immediate* decision; it is really not doing oneself justice *de décider les questions sur le pouce.*"

Princess Lieven, too, was nonplussed at that young person's "extreme reserve" on one occasion when they talked together, and afterward told Greville that she found the new Queen "timid and embarrassed," and that she "talked of nothing but commonplaces," whereas, if the Lieven had but known it, behind that "pretty smile" turned so sweetly upon her was the remembrance of a certain warning from Belgium: "Princess Lieven and another individual recently imported from her country seem to be very active in what concerns them not, beware of them."

The same day that the Russian Ambassadress had this, to her, unsatisfactory talk with Victoria, she had a very snug chat indeed with the Duchess of Kent, who was now in a state of lacerated emotion that ached for an understanding ear. Princess Lieven found her burst of confidences extremely revealing. "It is plain to see," she remarked afterward of the Duchess, that she is "overwhelmed with vexation and disappointment, and painfully feels her own insignificance." It is now that the Duchess complained to her *"qu'il n'y avait plus d'avenir pour elle, qu'elle n'était plus rien,"* sighing out that "for eighteen years this child had been the sole object of her life . . . and now she was taken from her."

On this Princess Lieven, striking a conventional and rather tiresome note, pointed out that the Duchess ought now "to be the happiest of women to see the elevation of this child, her prodigious success, and the praise and admiration of which she was universally the object." But the Duchess, sitting there with her once hearty face now bereft of all its former self-satisfaction, had in mind aspects of this "prodigious success" of which Princess Lieven was ignorant. Not only was there that corrosive memory of her regency *manqué*, but also the fact that Baroness Lehzen had a sitting room at Buckingham Palace next to Victoria's, and was forever in and out in the cosiest way possible, while she, Victoria's mother, if she wished to see her daughter, had to send a note asking permission, which, as likely as not, would be refused.

So now, in reply to Princess Lieven's encouraging arguments, the defeated woman "only shook her head with a melancholy smile." So spiritless had the poor lady become that when, on her birthday, Lord Broughton said something complimentary, she merely breathed out, "Ah, I am too old for many happy returns." It was understood that she craved for the rank and precedence of a Queen mother, but Victoria tossed any such idea aside. "It would," she remarked, "do my mother no good and would offend my aunts." As for the Duchess' accumulated debts, her formerly crushed daughter, on being told that "there were differences in the Cabinet as to the mode of paying these," exclaimed tartly enough, "I hope there is no difference of opinion as to whether I am to pay them."

Victoria could be not only tart. Was it she who originated what we now look on as a modern slang expression? In her second year on the throne Mr. Hook, preaching before her one warm July Sunday in the Chapel Royal, cried out "that the Church would endure let what would happen to the throne." Lord Normanby asked her afterword, "Did not your Majesty find it very hot?" "Yes, and the sermon was very hot too."

Ignored by the now paramount Victoria, Conroy's reaction was to become more aggressive than ever, that is to say, in such parts of the palace in which he was allowed to show himself at all: to wit, the quarters of the Duchess of Kent. There he made fullest use of his post as her secretary, being determined to keep up, with her and Lady Flora Hastings at least, the old intimacy. When the Duchess' Coburg relations came from time to time to stay with her, they complained of the way he was "always haunting the Palace." What especially exasperated them was his habit of pushing into the particular room where the Duchess and her relations liked to congregate; and they protested to the Duke of Wellington—who might well have been called Receiver of Court Complaints—of the way Conroy "used insolently to come and sit there."

The two Kensington factions had in fact moved *en bloc* to Buckingham Palace: the environment had changed, but the antipathies had not. On the one side was the now diminished Duchess, and the inseparables, Conroy and Flora Hastings; on the other the great little person with her stalwart bodyguard of Lehzen, Melbourne, and Stockmar, all of them with a concealed scowl for Conroy. It might have been thought that Victoria's position in regard to that small group in a corner of the palace was now impregnable; but as events will show, a weapon was before long to be put into Conroy's hands with which he was to do her untold harm.

It is evident that Victoria had confided in Melbourne all the former Kensington Palace stratagems. The Duchess doubtless guessed this, and it must have increased her aversion for that genial man who had thwarted her regency tricks. Leopold, casting his eye back to the Kensington Palace days, wrote warningly to Victoria, "Your life amongst intriguers, and tormented with intrigues, has given you an experience ... which you will do well not to lose sight of, as it will unfortunately often *reproduce itself* though the names and manner of carrying on the thing may not be the same." Hence Victoria would often conceal her now exultant spirits beneath a deliberate reticence; display obvious circumspection in her choice of words. "Melbourne thinks highly of her sense, discretion and good feeling," wrote Greville, "but what seems to distinguish her above everything are caution and prudence, the former to a degree which is almost unnatural in one so young." "She conducts herself,"

wrote an onlooker, "with surprising dignity; the dignity which pro-
ceeds from self-possession and deliberation. The smallness of her
person is quite forgotten in the majesty and gracefulness of her
demeanour." In this subtle poise, this power of quietly imposing
herself, no royalty ever surpassed her. "Those who were much with
her were never allowed to forget that she was the most important
person in the room," writes one who knew her intimately. Her
astuteness was undefeatable. In her acumen in the reading of character, in her subtle expansions or contractions according to the merits
or demerits of anyone she was talking to, she was, psychologically,
equipped to the finger tips. "I chose to have a headache last night,"
she would, as an older woman, remark when a too great easiness
had been shown by some diner. These powers of self-protection
were already within her in embryo; and, as she grew older, were
to increase to that point when "her cryptic phrases, short and vague,
with the drawn lips and the investigating eyes, fairly baffled her
ministers."

But to return to her in her very early years. No one had more
opportunity of studying her complex character than had Melbourne, for every day it became more of a delight to her to have
"my Premier" at her elbow. Besides being Prime Minister, he
acted, not only as the Queen's unofficial secretary (Lehzen filling
the post of the most private one),* but as adviser and confidant. He
was her companion out riding, at dinner (for she always had him
sitting next to her), and in the drawing room after dinner. It was
the first time in her life that, apart from her tutorial Canon of
Chester, she had had daily intimacy with any man, and what a contrast was her whimsical, unaccountable Premier to the tepid Canon
of Kensington days! "No man," observed Greville, "is more formed
to ingratiate himself with her than Melbourne. He treats her with
unbounded consideration and respect, he consults her taste and her
wishes, and he puts her at her ease by his frank and natural manners,
while he amuses her by the quaint, queer, epigrammatic turn of his
mind, and his varied knowledge upon all subjects."

Victoria was always charmed with originality of mind; anyone
who managed to get across the threshold of her discrimination was

---

* Stockmar, too, practically played the part of a third secretary. He stayed on in England
for over a year.

received, and, if he merited it, received enthusiastically, as a valuable human being. Her appreciations were as generous as her condemnations were severe. Before a month was over Melbourne was outshining everyone—except perhaps Lehzen. Her Premier's mind was as preoccupied with this most unusual girl in her unique position as was hers with him. He had the satisfaction not only of knowing her need at this juncture of her life to have such a man as himself by her side but of finding in their relationship balm for his loneliness. A few days after settling in at Buckingham Palace she had to prorogue Parliament, and though her small body was hardly able to support "the Robe, which is enormously heavy," she yet found the whole ceremony delightful because of "Lord Melbourne bearing the Sword of State walking just before me. He stood quite close to me on the left hand of the Throne, and I feel always a satisfaction to have him near me on such occasions, as he is such an honest, good, kind-hearted man, and is my friend, I know it."

He was indeed her friend. His position called at once for so many and such varied qualifications, for such scrupulosity of feeling, outlook, and conduct, that the world might have been combed through without finding the man who was equal to it. But Melbourne was equal to it; and throughout history there is no counterpart to the relationship, at once so close and so flawless, that gradually established itself between these two.

More and more the Journal became impregnated with the Prime Minister. "I sat on the sofa ... and Lord Melbourne sat near me." "Lord Melbourne rode near me the whole time. The more I see of him ... the more I like and appreciate his fine and honest character." "He is *so* kind to me; I have the GREATEST confidence in him. He is so truly excellent." "I generally *hear from* him and *write to him* every day, and very often two or three times a day." And, finally, after being at Windsor in the summer, "I have seen a great deal of him, every day these last five weeks. ... I have seen him in my closet for Political Affairs, I have ridden out with him (every day), I have sat near him constantly at and after dinner, and talked about all sorts of things," and so on and so on. Soon he, and he alone of the ministers, was ensconced within the intimacy of her own special sitting room, Victoria "in her white silk *robe de chambre*," "I being seated on a sofa, and he in an armchair near or close opposite, the other ministers and visitors I saw in another little room."

The disruption in the atmosphere of Kensington brought about in former days by Conroy had been lamentable, and yet, such totally unexpected patterns may evolve from the weavings of life that, in reality, it was this man's unsavory character that had been one of the most formative influences in the turning of Victoria into the circumspect, shrewd young monarch that she had become. It was in protecting herself from his intrigues that she had matured so early, and had learned to keep her own counsel. Melbourne, his heart tender for her happiness, noticed that the usual openness of youth, careless of light confidences, was no longer hers; even with her maids of honor she would not let it appear whether she had any special likings. "It is strange," Melbourne one day remarked to her, "for so young a person not to show any preference."

"I said I dared not."

Apprentice to life that she still was, she was already a virtuoso in her sense of aptness, of what was suitable in any situation or relationship. Melbourne might, and did, fill her days with a heady sweetness—an emotion which she was too inexperienced to analyse—but no onlooker, watching them after dinner, drawn up to the round mahogany table that spread its glossy surface before them, Victoria on the sofa, Melbourne on a chair at her side, no onlooker could discover anything the least flirtatious in her manner toward this man who made a central glow in her life. It was noticed, however, that when he left the room her blue, thoughtful eyes would follow him to the door.

Those who before had known Melbourne intimately would watch with suppressed amusement that once carelessly lounging figure now sitting, evening after evening, scrupulously upright in his chair with an attitude of respectful attention to the small figure chattering away at his side. Very differently indeed used he to behave at, for instance, the renowned gatherings at Holland House. Tom Moore tells us of one of these when Brougham and Melbourne were both there; Brougham "in his black frock coat, black cravat; while upon the sofa lay stretched the Prime Minister ... also in frock and boots, and with his legs cocked up on one of Lady Holland's fine chairs. Beside him sat Lord Holland, and at some distance from this group was my Lady herself, seated at a table with Talleyrand, and occupying him in conversation to divert his attention from the Ministerial confab at the sofa." Melbourne's conversation, too, had been noted for its masculine pungency, but no one was quicker to sense the exact tone of any society he found himself in, and he had realized at once that his approach to certain subjects ("Damn it—another bishop dead!") would have to be sedulously concealed from this earnest little novice. Their conversations were almost entirely an imparting on his side of every kind of information—talks on the past, on former courts and royalties, on society, on laws and procedure, or scraps of enlightenment on any subject that came into his head. "Spoke of Aunt Louise," wrote Victoria one evening, recapitulating their after-dinner talk, "of the Queen of Portugal; of Clementine, Augustus etc. of Feodore, her happiness, her not being rich . . . mentioned Goethe's *Wilhelm Meister* . . . he knew Madame de Staël, spoke of her . . . spoke of actresses . . . of marriages *in general* and most cleverly and sensibly; of their often being broken off—the reasons why." "I should not *wish* to be on the same confidential footing with any of my other ministers," she explains to her Journal.

She doted, and indeed most wisely on receiving all the information that Melbourne could give her. She would go chirping on, asking about this, about that; pecking at his mature mind like a small bird digging into a ripe fruit. Once before in Melbourne's life a young and ardent being had been confided to his care, and it is impossible but that that self-communicating, generous spirit must at times have questioned whether he had not himself originally been partly to blame for the catastrophe of Caroline's life. It is probable that that consideration in his mind was one of the explanations of his undefeatable chivalry toward that tragic figure. Now, once again, he had the molding of a young girl's mind put into his hands, and this time he would not fail. In all his dealings with Victoria is evident his acute sense of responsibility, his determination, as far as in him lay, to strengthen and equip her for what lay ahead; for that future which, whether it held good or ill, must inevitably be momentous.

Did he, one wonders, muse at times on the comparison between those two most opposite characters? The one all self-abandonment, the other all self-discipline; so girlish in instinct, so mature in intention. If he did so muse, he must too, at times, have inwardly smiled at the contrast between that figure—which still so entrancingly, so sadly, disturbed his memory—and the tiny, composed person before him; her only allurements her sweet livery of youth, her quick mind, her graceful dignity, her very individual voice that, we are told, was like the ringing of a little bell. Caroline, in careless self-condemnation, did not hesitate to dub herself an "untamed tiger" or, in more modest mood, merely as "a fly"; but never would Queen Victoria, even in her occasional moments of humility, have thought of aligning herself with either an animal in the jungle or an insect. One characteristic she and Caroline did have in common. Both vital in the extreme, they were both highly sexed; apart from the physical aspect, the close companionship of one man or another, daily contact with the male mind, was a necessity. As for Melbourne, though to him the final confirmation of the value of a life of continuous endeavor and self-discipline was not apparent, his experiences by the side of Caroline had at least convinced him that, once the first splash and spray of youth are over, an existence conducted in violent opposition to these principles ends in chaos, and in incalculable suffering both to the doer and to others. "He has," Victoria wrote in her Journal, "the greatest horror of any woman who is eccentric."

At times when, from his height, he looked down at that doll-like figure, at those intelligent but guileless eyes gazing up at him so confidently, at the curiously birdlike little mouth half-parted with eagerness, Victoria would notice how moved he appeared. For at these moments—his mind filled with the realization of the world's maelstrom into which she was entering, of the forces that surrounded this child, of the immense power with which she was invested, of her tender reliance on his guidance and affection—the tidal waves of sensibility would invade his heart, and the small image before him become blurred.

The attention of society was steadily focussed on these two shining figures, and no one was more occupied with them than Princess Lieven. "I have seen the Queen twice," she wrote to Lord Aberdeen. "I have seen her alone, and in the evening in Society with her Prime Minister. She has an aplomb, an air of command and dignity that, with her childlike face, her tiny figure and pretty smile create one of the most extraordinary impressions it is possible to imagine. In conversation she is most reserved.... When near her, Lord Melbourne has an air of affection, of contentment, one might say of self-complacency, mingled with the greatest respect, which, with his easy manners ... his dreaminess, his gaiety, make up such a picture as you can imagine." *"He alone,"* Victoria wrote of Melbourne in her Journal, "inspires me with that feeling of great confidence.... I feel *so safe* when he speaks to me and is with me."

Every day now for this Queen was a gala day, every hour a festooned hour. All the business of her position was merely so much pleasurable occupation, glistening with novelty. "I ... do regular hard but to *me delightful* work.... It is to me the *greatest pleasure* to do my duty for my country." After her eighteen years of subjugation, the sense of mental freedom outspread each day before her young eagerness was an intoxication. Having formerly been so supervised in her reading, now even the perusal of *The Bride of Lammermoor* was an excitement that had to be passed on to Melbourne. To be able to give orders instead of receiving them, to choose what she would do, whom she would see, and whom she would not see, was a felicity. In later life, her mind sobered by the Prince Consort, and harnessed, though most willingly, by the mind of another, she looked back scandalized at the spontaneous gaiety of those early days of her reign; and, in actual shame, tore up the pages of her Journal that too pungently recorded them. But to the onlooker, those days, quivering as they were with the Melbourne idyll, that young gay interlude interposed between her cramped childhood and her maturer, more prosaic days, are an enchantment over which one lingers. She herself, in later years, referred to it as "the dream"—one that had vanished. "The dream," so she wrote them, "is past."

The great sun-scorched space around the palace—its bareness not then mitigated as now by municipal geraniums and the painful fantasy of Queen Victoria and the mermaids—all this open space was then haunted by loitering nursemaids and their charges. On one side of them were the railings and walls of the great palace, behind which this Perrault fairy-tale Queen led her hidden life; on the other side stretched four or five parallel tree-shaded avenues along which, not so many years back, might at times have been seen a small procession of jolting sedan chairs—royal sedan chairs in which Queen Charlotte and her daughters were being borne along to the garden door of Carlton House to dine with the Regent. When Victoria came to the throne, there lay around the palace itself "a grey waste of sand which led into dirty roads and squalid alleys.... No sooner, however, did ... the Queen take up her abode ... than Pimlico, the most desolate suburb in Middlesex, started out of its caterpillar condition ... barbers burst forth into fashionable perfumers, and tobacconists repainted their wooden Highlanders." This grouping of nursemaids and children in front of the palace must have made a delightful picture—the little boys in white duck trousers and colored jackets, shouting over their hoops, then immensely popular, even at schools; the little girls in bonnet and mittens, balloon skirts, and white drawers below. While idling about for a glimpse of the Queen, they would often see, careening up to the palace, the ornate and emblazoned carriages of ministers or ambassadors, the heavy iron-rimmed wheels churning up the sand; twin lackeys with long, silver-headed sticks and cocked hats, standing clinging on at the back on their precarious little shelf: the whole confection in its rococo beauty tricked out to enchant the eye. Now, without any consideration as to whether the exchange is worth while, this beauty (and at that time every vehicle, even the poorest, had a charm) has been bartered for speed. Speed before everything.

As one looks back at the nineteenth century and compares it with our own, one is struck by a peculiarly gruesome parallel. The inhumanity with which the factory children of that day were treated is not only equaled but surpassed by our yearly victimization of children, maimed and killed, in this road racket. Before, we had the factory profiteers: now we have our speed-profiteers, owing to whom nearly one thousand children are murdered every year.* As with the brutality to factory children (till some determined champions arose), nations in general view this yearly slaughter with perfect complacency.

---

* During the two years 1948 and 1949, one thousand eight hundred and thirty-three children were killed in Britain.

7

In the summer the scene changed to Windsor Castle, and Victoria experienced the new pleasure of being hostess to Leopold, his wife, and baby. "Now, dearest Uncle, I must invite you *en forme.* I should be most delighted if you, dearest Aunt Louise, and Leopold (*J'insiste*) could come ... you could bring as many gentlemen and ladies, bonnies, etc. etc. as you pleased, and I should be *too* happy and proud to have you under *my own* roof." The infant that Victoria so insisted should be of the party to cross the Channel was to grow up into that devil of cruelty, Leopold of the Congo atrocities.

Perhaps the greatest of Victoria's Windsor pleasures were her afternoon riding parties, equestrian follow-my-leaders of which she was the head. Sometimes the Duchess of Kent would be of the party; and sometimes dearest Lehzen would follow, seated in one of those little pony carriages that were such a feature of country life at the time. Inevitably Lord Melbourne would be at Victoria's elbow, astride a powerful mount. ("Lord Melbourne rode his own horse, a very fine black mare which came down from London this day," runs one Windsor entry.) The cavalcade behind Victoria and her Premier would be composed of other ministers, various members of the royal household, and guests staying at the castle. On these rides, the ermine of her position tossed aside, Victoria would allow her ebullient youthfulness to gush forth. An entrancing little figure in her sweeping but tight-fitting green habit, with romantic lace collar, veil wildly blowing back from her coquettishly low top hat, she would put her horse to the gallop with all her troupe tearing after her. These moments, when the pounding of her horse's galloping hoofs were like the joyous beating of her own heart, and the reverberating thud of Melbourne's sweat-stained mount a reminder of his protective presence; when her ears were filled with the oncoming rush of her Court plunging breathlessly in her wake; when she could fling every inhibition of mind and body to the wind which she created by her own reckless speed—these moments of physical energy were a symbol of the liberation of spirit of her new life. Even if, as on some occasions, she would be in a "pony phaeton," even then, away would go the whole company, pony carriage and all, at a "furious rate," Lord Melbourne and the other horsemen scampering along, a devoted bodyguard, around her small carriage, some at the side, some behind; Victoria, so we read, laughing with delight to see how young Lord Alfred Paget dominated his "fiery black steed."

One September day during her stay at Windsor this year of her accession, she emerged from the castle door to mount her horse looking most unusual. She had dressed herself up in a riding habit that approximated as nearly as possible to the Windsor uniform worn by her gentlemen of the household. It was navy blue with scarlet collar and cuffs; while, perched above her pleased young face, was a military cap with a golden strap beneath her chin. Across her chest gleamed the broad ribbon of the Garter. She was about to review her troops, and was so delighted with her thought-out martial appearance that she described it in detail to her Journal. The insistent blue of the Garter must have bitten cruelly against the scarlet of her lapels, but considerations of that sort never disturbed her. This day her whim was to immerse herself in the male element, to associate herself as closely as possible with the masculine; and she noted with some satisfaction that, except for Alfred Paget (who looked, she noticed, "remarkably handsome in his uniform of the Blues"), nearly all "my other gentlemen wore the Windsor uniform." It was generally believed that she had a tenderness for Alfred Paget—that "handsome Calmuck-looking young fellow" as an onlooker described him; and certainly she often glanced in the direction of this particularly attractive member of the Paget family.*

Once on the throne, this new Queen instinctively regarded the Army as her personal property; and now, as she expertly sat her horse on the review ground, as she saw her Grenadiers, Life Guards, and Lancers maneuvering before her in their emphatic-colored uniforms that glowed in the strong September light, as the clipped words of command, the light jingle of bit and chain were borne along on the autumn air, and the assertive martial music swung and curvetted in her ears; as she saw surrounding her on all

---

* Count d'Orsay had encouraged his nephew, the Duc de Guiche, an attaché at the French Embassy in London, to make a bid for Victoria's affections; but he discovered that all her attention was fixed on "old Lord Melbourne or Lord Alfred Paget."

sides those upstanding male figures, a stirring of her blood, an exaltation of spirit swept through her unlike anything she had before experienced. "I felt for the first time like a man, as if I could fight myself at the head of my troops."

This Boadicea attitude on that September day had been a fortuitous aspect of her vigorous nature, and was in reality most alien to her spirit, which called upon every man in her entourage for protection. *"How* I *shall* miss you my dearest, dear Uncle! *every, every where"* she wrote to Leopold after this visit of his to Windsor. *"How* I shall miss your conversation! *How* I shall miss your *protection* out riding!"* Though, one might rather think it was those who rode with that recklessly galloping, very accomplished young horsewoman who were more in need of protection from her, than she from them. But this conviction of a need for male support was embedded deep in her consciousness; and it was never absent. Arising from the sense of heavy responsibility that had been laid upon her, and the determination not to fall short in any particular, there infallibly followed the desire that with both brain and muscle all the men about her should sustain her to their utmost. This feeling, naturally, persisted throughout her life. Inevitably, as the years went on, as problems multiplied and difficulties increased, and, most especially when she was bereft of the Prince Consort, this attitude was intensified, and it became difficult for her to keep the personal aspect of Victoria the woman separate from the impersonal one of Victoria the Queen. The question how far monarchs are justified in demanding the entire absorption of another human being's life and personality in their service is one that calls for the finest evaluations. But as regards Queen Victoria this question is one for the future. At present the protection motif ornamented her youthfulness most charmingly; chivalry at that date was a fashionable emotion, and to the elderly men about her, her instinct seemed as proper as it was appealing.

We are given charming vignettes of the Windsor party in the drawing room during these summer evenings. "After dinner," she wrote while Leopold and his wife were there, "I sat part of the evening on the sofa with Lady Tavistock, dearest Uncle and Lord Melbourne sitting near me. . . . The rest of the evening I sat on the sofa with dearest Aunt Louise, who played a game of chess with me, to *teach* me." The chessboard was placed on the ever-present round table, about which sat others of the company to watch the game. "Lord Melbourne, Lord Palmerston, Sir J. Hobhouse, and later, too, Lord Conyngham, all gave me advice, and *all different* advice about my playing at chess, and *all* got so *eager* that it was very amusing; in particular Lord Palmerston and Sir J. Hobhouse, who differed totally, and got quite excited and serious about it. Between them all I got quite beat, and Aunt Louise triumphed over my Council of Ministers!" During these evenings the Duchess of Kent would be seated somewhere in the room at a card table, and deadly indeed it must have been for those sharing her rubbers of whist ("a horrible player she is," groaned Creevey), for the chief object of the game was not pleasure, but to keep the Duchess from falling asleep. The victims chosen for this boring occupation would be brightly picked out by Victoria, herself extremely wide awake, and, further to bolster up the Duchess, on occasion some man would be detailed to play her hand for her. "Sir Frederick Stovin played the hand of the Duchess," wrote Lord Broughton after one of these evenings, "but she seemed confused. We won the rubber, and then we changed partners.... The Duchess was taken ill; but after one of her ladies had given her some salts to smell she continued her game, and won this rubber. Russell had to pay her eight shillings, and put down a sovereign. She gave him nine shillings, saying 'I believe that is right.' He smiled and took his change; but did not seem pleased with this specimen of royal arithmetic."

What Victoria herself obviously preferred to any other occupation that the evenings offered were long rambling talks with Lord Melbourne as they sat side by side, while all around them in the great room the wax candles in chandelier and luster slowly dwindled in their sockets...on and on their conversation would meander, the fluting girlish voice posing question after question; the deep male tones informing or explaining. But sometimes the heat from that multitude of burning candles around them, the soothing effect of other conversing voices that here and there across the far-stretching carpet would be heard murmuring, and the, it must be admitted, not very interesting questions issuing from the inquirer at Melbourne's side—all this, intermingling, would have such a soporific effect that the handsome head of "my Premier" would be seen to droop, then to droop still more, and at last, as no answering voice at all came from the oracle, Victoria would realize that, most unmistakably, her dear Lord Melbourne was asleep. It was evident that the time had come for everyone to go to bed; but she, the Queen, could not rise and leave the room while her Prime Minister, now nothing but an inert mass slumped in his chair, was not in a condition to rise too and make his good-night bow. Seizing a newspaper, she would crackle it frantically, hoping that that might stir him. "It was so embarrassing," she would exclaim amusedly when, as an old woman, the remembrance of those evenings arose in her mind. "It was so embarrassing!"

8

Victoria's youthful mind was so balanced that, in spite of the newness and glory of her position, she neglected nothing which that new position demanded. Not only was all business punctiliously attended to, but her alert brain was always eager to acquire every scrap of necessary information about what was demanded of her. "M[elbourne]," writes the informative Creevey, "speaks of the young one with the same enthusiasm as ever, and has the highest opinion possible of her understanding." Meanwhile Leopold, eyeing the situation from across the Channel, and fearful lest his niece should get beyond his controlling counsels, would make efforts to prevent her becoming too self-satisfied. "You are too clever," he wrote to her, "not to know that it is *not* the being *called* Queen or King which can be of the *least consequence* when to the title there is also not annexed the power indispensable for the exercise of those functions. All trades must be learned, and nowadays the trade of a *constitutional Sovereign, to do it well, is a very* difficult one."

But Victoria was not finding it so at all: her duties were pleasures; her days halcyon.

Her brisk mind was everywhere at once. "She always remembered the day fixed for the coming and departure of every guest," wrote Lord Lorne, "and for everyone of those of the household who came on duty or whose waiting was ended." "I never saw," chimes in Sir Charles Murray, after taking part in one of those breathless rides at Windsor, "a more quick or observant eye. In the course of the ride it glanced occasionally over every individual of the party, and I am sure that neither absence nor impropriety of any kind could escape detection."

In all her intimate relations the warmth of her young affections remained unabated. Her faith in her mother's private loyalty to herself completely gone, she could not, with Conroy still in the Duchess' confidence, do otherwise than keep up a mental barrier between herself and her parent; but outwardly she treated her with such scrupulous kindness and deference that even Creevey's quick eye was deceived as to the relationship beneath. "I never saw a more pretty and natural devotion than she shows to her mother in everything," he exclaimed.

Queen Adelaide and the Duke of Sussex found their niece full of just the same affection that she had shown them as a child at Kensington Palace. When Mrs. Louis died, the old housekeeper at Claremont who had loved her from her childhood, Victoria was overcome with grief. "I felt very unhappy at dinner, in spite of my being gay when I spoke, and I could have cried almost at every moment . . . when I got into bed . . . more than half an hour elapsed, in tears, before I fell asleep. And before I was asleep I saw her, in imagination, before me, dressed in her neat white morning gown, sitting at her breakfast in her room at Claremont; again, standing in my room of an evening, dressed in her best, holding herself so erect and making the low dignified curtsey so peculiar to herself."

Over the matter of pensions, Victoria was all for generosity. "*A propos* to our little Vic," comes Creevey's voice again, "we are all enchanted with her for her munificence to the Fitzclarences. Besides their pensions out of the public pension list, they had nearly £10,000 a year given them by their father out of his privy purse, every farthing of which the Queen continues out of *her* privy purse, with quantities of other such things." When Lord Adolphus Fitzclarence heard of Victoria's generosity he "burst into tears and said it was unexpected, for they did not dare to hope for anything." Then there was Sir John Lade, an old reprobate who had companioned George IV in the noisy passage of his youth. George IV and William IV had allowed him £300 a year from the Privy Purse, and when Victoria was asked whether this pension should be reduced or discontinued altogether, she asked if Sir John were not over eighty? Told that he was, she "would neither have the pension enquired into nor reduced, but continued on her own privy purse."

In the autumn of this first year of Victoria's new existence, Creevey throws open a door through which we can watch the progress of an evening at Brighton Pavilion, to which Arabian Nights' palace Victoria had for the time transplanted herself and her Court.

Yesterday [writes Creevey on October 13] Lady Sefton and her two eldest daughters, and myself, sailed forth in the yellow coach to dine with the Queen at our own old Pavilion. Lord Headfort, a chattering, capering, spindle-shanked gaby, was in waiting, and handed Lady Sefton into the drawing-room. . . . Presently Headfort was summoned, and on his return he came up to me with his antics and said: "Mr. Creevey, you are to sit on the Duchess of Kent's right hand at dinner—" Oh, the fright I was in about my right [left?] ear! . . . Here comes in the Queen, the Duchess of Kent the least bit in the world behind her, all her ladies in a row still more behind; Lord Conyngham and Cavendish on each flank of the Queen . . . she was told by Lord Conyngham that I had not been presented, upon which a scene took place that to me was truly distressing. The poor little thing could not get her glove off. I never was so annoyed in my life; yet what could I do? But she blushed and laughed and pulled till the thing was done, and I kissed her hand. Then to dinner. . . . The Duchess of Kent was agreeable and chatty, and she said:—"Shall we drink some wine?" My eyes, however, were all the time fixed upon Vic. . . . A more homely little being you never beheld *when she is at her ease*, and she is evidently dying to be always more so. She laughs in real earnest, opening her mouth as wide as it can go, showing not very pretty gums. . . . She eats quite as heartily as she laughs, I think I may say she gobbles. . . . She blushes and laughs every instant in so natural a way as to disarm anybody. Her voice is perfect, and so is the expression of her face when she means to say or do a pretty thing. . . . At night I played two rubbers of whist, one against the Duchess of Kent, and one as her partner. . . . The Queen, in leaving the room at night, came across quite up to me, and said:—"How long do you stay at Brighton, Mr. Creevey?" Which I presume could mean nothing but another rubber for her mother. So it's all mighty well.

Once on the throne, Victoria was concerned as to whether her pronunciation of English was in all cases correct. Hearing the

Duchess of Kent speak of inhaling the London "fogues," the daughter must have realized that she could not altogether rely on her German mother for the inflections of the English tongue. Then there was this fidgeting question over certain words that, pronounced one way at Queen Charlotte's Court, were now, by some people, pronounced quite differently. The adherents of the old Court would, for instance, say *yaller* for yellow; *goold* for gold; *Room* for Rome; *Proosia* for Prussia. Over this Proosia–Prussia business Victoria became so agitated that she applied to her ministers for clarification. The Duke of Wellington, that paramount arbitrator of the day, gave the final decision: Pr*u*ssia. A conclusive little chat with Lord Melbourne as to when one should plump for "who," and when for "whom," "which I said puzzled me," and whether "it was right to spell Despatches with an i or an e," and the young Queen felt that her grammatical path lay clear. One questions indeed whether there was any situation, large or small, that she might have to deal with that this unusual girl did not envisage beforehand. When, this December, Hayter was painting her, she suddenly exclaimed, "I am very curious to know how you mean to place my hands. Just take them and place them as you intend in the picture." ("A very delicate commission to execute," observed Hayter afterward.) When he had posed them, "The Queen turned to Lady Mulgrave. 'I have often thought,' she said, 'if I had to paint a Queen how I would place her hands, and curiously enough, this is the very position I would hit on.' "

Inevitably, there was the reverse side of this meticulous mindedness in all matters large or small. Was she at times a shade too conscious of her Queenship, a shade too self-opinionated? So far, no one was quite sure, though occasionally even the devotedly admiring Melbourne grew a trifle anxious at what he considered signs of a "peremptory disposition." Occasionally, too, one of her ladies would secretly feel a little irritated at something that lay behind those full-orbed blue eyes, that peculiarly comprehensive gaze, when, without being able to show her annoyance, she had to bend her own inclinations to those of her child mistress. Lady Tavistock, for instance, one day went whimpering to Creevey relating how this vaunted little Queen had been the means of getting her, Lady Tavistock's, feet wet. "She told me," writes Creevey, "she was in the second carriage after Victoria on Sunday at Windsor; and that the Queen, according to her custom, being cold in the carriage, had got out to walk, and of course all her ladies had to do the same ... and the ground being very wet, their feet soon got into the same state. Poor dear Lady Tavistock, when she got back to the castle, could get at no dry stockings, her maid being out, and her clothes all locked up." But surely the disaster was due to poor dear Lady Tavistock's bad arrangement of allowing her maid to go gallivanting off with the wardrobe keys in her pocket. Lady Tavistock, however, thought otherwise; and, giggles Creevey, "I am sure ... she thinks the Queen a resolute little chit."

Obviously, it needed the shrewdest and most sensitive adaptation for this girl of eighteen so suddenly to wear her crown with absolute correctitude; instantly to adopt the exact nuance in relation to everyone; to keep the perfect balance between being extremely kind—as she invariably was—and yet maintaining just that ascendancy that was demanded by (in the words of the old Duchess of Coburg) the "dangerous grandeur of royalty." An opposing picture to that given by the irate Lady Tavistock rises before us. It is a year or two later. Lady Lyttelton comes in at the door. "I went down to the Queen last evening for something," she writes, "and she told me this bad news [about Lady Exeter, who was ill] and seeing I was a good deal shocked, she was so kind, and said directly,

" 'Oh, but perhaps I am overstating what is in the letter. You must see the letter, where is it? Oh ... I'll go for it.'

"And tho', of course, I deprecated, think of her actually taking her little feet out of a *bain de pieds* she was taking, and putting on any shoes she found, no stockings, and all wet, she ran all along her private corridor to fetch me the letter! Wasn't it nice of her?"

9

Beneath the daily life of all these brightly lit palace beings, supporting them and making their luminous existence possible, revolved a vast domestic organization; if such a wasteful muddle as the life that then went on in the royal kitchens and pantries could be called an organization. In the various memoirs and paintings of the day we get fugitive glimpses of the more decorative members of this belowstairs population. The whiskered face and scarlet coat of one of the innumerable liveried menservants come into the line of our vision for an instant as he crosses a room or disappears down a staircase. Out of doors, too, this heartening vermilion, flaming against the varied greens of garden or park, enhanced every scene. So thought Lady Lyttelton on an August day at Windsor when she was one of Victoria's driving party. "The Queen and Princess Victoria [of Coburg] and the Duchess of Kent and one of the Princes went first," she writes, "and their beautiful carriage and four white ponies, attended by grooms in scarlet, and many gentlemen riding, were a great ornament to the foreground." Guests at the castle would occasionally be taken belowstairs to gaze at "a perfect load of ornaments for the table (four among these ... cost £11,000 each) of richly gilt silver, besides the shield of Achilles in gold, and a heap of candlesticks. ... All in this room," goes on Lady Lyttelton, after being taken to inspect this glittering mass, "was silver-gilt etc. being like pure gold. 'Silver was nothing accounted in the days of King Solomon' was in my head the whole time. Then the next room contained most curious splendours; cups of crystal mounted in diamonds and rubies; chased vases of Benvenuto Cellini's work. A huge tyger's head, *entirely* of pure gold, as large as life ... and a peacock of good size (not natural size ... but not small) *entirely* of diamonds, rubies, emeralds, and sapphires, upraised train and all! which last belonged to Tippoo Saib and was taken at Seringapatam."

This secret Aladdin's cave, with its wealth of jewels that gleamed unseen in the dark beneath the royal feet moving about in the rooms above, was guarded behind massive and triple doors; but in general the domestic arrangements were so happy-go-lucky that a boy called Jones managed one day with the greatest ease to insert himself into Buckingham Palace, and to remain there a week before he was discovered. Ornate cinemas, restaurants, and people's palaces were unknown to the populace of that day, neither were there then as now, occasions when the doors of some of the big houses are open to all who choose to pay to enter. Therefore, to this boy-explorer, his surroundings once he was within the great royal bower were astounding. Tiptoeing from room to room, feasting his eyes on those, to him, incredible indoor landscapes—the Marble Hall, the

Throne Room, the Great Drawing-room, the Grand Staircase, the Sculpture Gallery, the Picture Gallery—this bemused boy had no wish to do anything but to gaze and to observe: those endless curtains, draped, festooned, fringed, and tasseled; that grandiose furniture; that awe-inspiring throne; those lofty pillars and gilded moldings. To him it must all have seemed hectic as a dream. Cautiously treading the vast carpets, creeping under a settee at any sound of footsteps, peering from the shelter of pillar or curtain, to and fro went the furtive figure. Late at night a shadow might have been, but was not, seen gliding to and fro in the kitchens: the boy Jones taking a midnight meal. One wonders whether, at night, he ever saw, padding through the silence of those huge rooms, another flitting figure, as solitary and improbable as himself—Baroness Lehzen clothed in her bedroom attire, now opening, now shutting a door, as she went on her self-imposed nightly tour to make certain all was well in the vicinity of her treasure. But Jones's week came to an end. He was discovered and turned out. Such fascination, however, did the palace exercise over him, so simple in execution had he found his adventure, that he got in a second time. Again he was caught and sent packing. Yet a third time he embarked on his now familiar occupation. By then Victoria was married, and Jones declared that, while hidden under a settee, he had listened to a conversation between her and Prince Albert who were seated on top. This was Jones's last acquaintance with the glories of palaces, for, willy-nilly, he found himself a member of the Royal Navy. It is said that he made an excellent sailor.

10

A daughter of the Dean of Chester—that gentle tutor (then Mr. Davys) of Victoria's early days—was just four years older than the Queen, and when she came to the throne she gave Mary Davys a little appointment at her Court. Mary's grand title of Extra Woman of the Bedchamber covered duties that were almost nil, and in her letters home the girl-courtier bemoaned—for Mary was of an earnest nature—that her new life, one of hitherto untasted delights, was nevertheless at most one of "busy idleness." She experienced at first a great fluttering of heart at thus suddenly finding herself flung, amid a blaze of candelabra, cheek by jowl with all "the rank and fashion of London." This new existence was so different from the quiet day-in-day-out tempo and ecclesiastical atmosphere of her home life in their house in The Terrace—then part of Kensington High Road—that for the first few weeks Mary's royal surroundings had the strangest effect on her. "I sometimes muse upon it in astonishment . . . it seems like a dream of grandeur." But gradually she got her bearings, and soon she is recording, not Lord Melbourne's polite, conventional bow on her first evening, but how most of the household had fallen into the habit of calling her "Humphry" *tout court*, a nickname turning on a new safety lamp. From the moment of Mary's advent, Lehzen, now a powerful Court personage and always referred to as "the Baroness," was her encouraging friend, putting forth all those little fronds of kindness that she invariably did to any timid arrival at the palace, and making, as one of the maids of honor wrote, all their days "pass away so happily." This maid of honor was Harriet Lister, in person so charming to the eye that, as she entered a room one day, she drew from the deaf Duke of Cambridge one of his irrepressible shouts, "She's a damned pretty girl." As for the Queen herself she was, wrote Harriet, "the dearest, gayest, and most engaging little thing I ever saw." "They seemed," she went on, describing one of the royal evenings, "to have a great many jokes at dinner," and she noticed that the Queen appeared "very fond of Lord Melbourne, and very very fond of Prince Leopold." "That darling Queen!" she exclaimed another day. On the particular evening that called forth this exclamation Victoria had been presenting most of the female members of her Household with what is referred to as "their Order." "The Ladies' is a miniature of the Queen; the Women (of the Bedchamber) a gold massive bracelet with the initials V.R. in turquoise and the Queen's hair inside." Harriet Lister's Order had not yet come from the jeweler. "Poor Baby, it is very hard on you," cried the Queen.

On these evenings, before sitting down to whist, or to chess—both being then much to the fore at Buckingham Palace—there would be a moving to and fro of the figures in the great drawing room, and Mary found herself on these occasions often singled out by the Duchess of Kent, who would make herself particularly pleasant to this quiet new arrival with her dark hair and hazel eyes. The Duchess would start a discussion on Walter Scott's novels, naming those she had read, and asking which had Mary read? No doubt she hoped, poor lady, to use her daughter's household as a liaison to keep in touch as much as she could with the enigmatic Victoria—on the surface all affectionate consideration: at heart so evasive. Mary obviously soon became aware of the peculiar relationship between mother and daughter, and watched the Duchess with much the same interest as a doctor his patient, reporting in a letter home that the Duchess "looks very tolerably happy, but I think her life must be a dull one."

Mary, like all the ladies of the Queen's and also of the Duchess of Kent's Households, had her own sitting room, also a room for her lady's maid close by. A maid of honor, Elizabeth Bulteel, who came into the Queen's service some years later, tells us of the furnishing of a sitting room she shared with a girl colleague at Osborne, and this was probably very much a replica, in double, of what Mary found in her own sitting room at Buckingham Palace. "Two little red morocco writing-tables, with blotting-book, paper and ink stand ... two arm-chairs—a round table—two footstools —two pair of silver candlesticks—a sofa—two pieces of furniture, with red silk cabinets for books and work-boxes—a pianoforte . . . there," wrote Elizabeth Bulteel, "is the picture of the sitting-room." When not on duty in the State Rooms below, Mary and the rest of the Queen's ladies would be perpetually paying each other visits in their sitting rooms, Mary's being a high-up one overlooking the Green Park. She and whichever two young things were in waiting would read Shakespeare, history, or Italian together; sit side by side striking duets off the pianoforte; sing songs; or one would read aloud while the other worked at the chair backs and arm pieces of a set of chairs that they would all attack at intervals. Possibly a present for the Queen. At other times their heads would be bent over a German grammar, hoping by this means in time to be able to decipher the unusual syllables that so often flew through the air in the royal drawing room; or the visiting friend might merely look at her hostess' drawings kept in a portfolio, this being a much-favored occupation of the day, the forerunner of our own idle turning over of illustrated magazines.

Perfect little collector's pieces of the past rise from Mary's letters. "After this [viz. luncheon] I went to Lady Mulgrave's room, looked over her drawings and talked with her for some little time. Then the Baroness came into one of our rooms to show us all (Lady Mulgrave included) that old trick about the sixpence vibrating in a wine-glass, and striking the hours." But occasionally a hated footstep, a hated voice would be heard approaching along the passages leading to those friendly little upstairs sitting rooms—Conroy. Perhaps on some small business matter of the Duchess' Household that had to be discussed with Lady Mary Stopford, one of the Duchess' ladies. Then, like a flock of gentle birds scared at the arrival of a bird of prey, there would be a swift scattering. "Did I tell you," writes Mary, "of a rencontre with Sir John the other day. I was with Lady Mary when he was announced and I, not feeling disposed for an interview, made my escape into her adjoining bedroom and there remained. Lady Mary cannot bear him, but he came to speak to her upon some business." "Saw the Conroys at a distance and avoided them," Mary wrote another day after a great party at Lansdowne House.

Visiting guests at Windsor Castle would also have their private rooms. When, during the winter days of 1838, Lord John Russell and his wife stayed there, "I was delighted with little Lord John. . . ," Mary wrote to her family. "Both he and Lady John were particularly good-natured to me; Miss Lister and I sat with them a good deal in their room, and were quite cosy and comfortable. You would have been amused at seeing us all having some tea and bread and butter together one day before dressing for dinner; this is a very usual practice I find amongst the *haut ton.*"

On these winter evenings we glimpse through the half-open doors of these snug sitting rooms the curtsying flames of luxuriously banked-up fires: feminine figures circumspectly glide in and out of the rooms in their full skirts of poplin or "satinet," a thin gold chain, or a brooch containing a minute plait of hair glints on the tight bodice; their hair falls "in rather long and low curls," or frames her face "in a large puff at each side." As the dinner hour draws near the ladies' maids quietly emerge from their rooms close by and begin taking out of the cupboards the light-hued evening dresses of moire, or of figured or plain net over satin; and lay on the dressing tables those knots or wreaths of artificial flowers that, says Mary Davys, were "the most usual headdress with everybody." We see her face, lit by the wax candles, reflected in her looking glass one evening, her flatly brushed hair banded with "red velvet, and red artificial flowers on each side." The constant effort was to achieve enough different effects. Mary, with "the white beads, the Queen's combs (a Christmas present), gold combs etcetera," would in this way "make out a tolerable variety." Then all these carefully decked heads, all these moires and figured nets, soft colored as clouds would appear one after another till they formed a cluster in "the beautiful corridor and wait there for the Queen and the Duchess (of Kent)." But among these clustering ladies of the Household we see one who is singled out, not only in our own minds, knowing her a doomed figure, already—unguessed by herself—entangled in the threads of adverse destiny, but also singled out by all the Queen's ladies as one with whom it was impossible for them to fraternize. Lady Flora Hastings, still only a little over thirty, was accustomed to general admiration for her vivacity and accomplished manner; and her technique of living had, from her own point of view, so far succeeded. A slim figure, a small, angular but pretty enough head set on her long neck, she moved about among the other palace ladies, more sophisticated than most of them, securely rooted in her own personality and her position in the Duchess' Court: a little aloof, a trifle feared, and in consequence not entirely liked. The very opposite in this respect to Lady Mary Stopford, a red-haired "nice, ugly lively little body," an especial ally of Mary Davys, and adored by the whole household for her irrepressible, joking good-humor. But when she was not in waiting, and "Scotty," as Flora Hastings was secretly called, took her place, it was a very different matter. "Lady Flora is civil to us all," explains Mary Davys, "but restrained and uncommunicative; there will be no *friendship* with her." And again, "very civil to me especially; but we never think of going to her room; she does not wish it, and I should be afraid of meeting *Sir John* who is there a good deal." For it was chiefly the thought of Conroy that darkened the atmosphere round Flora Hastings: though excluded in person entirely from Victoria's Court, he was yet, when anyone was talking to Lady Flora, only too visible in spirit, peering over her shoulder.

For their close friendship was known to everyone. How indubitably, how bitterly different for Conroy everything was now compared to those former amusing days when he and Flora used to bait the little Kensington girl according to their humor. It must have been a ceaseless exasperation to such an astute man to realize the mistake he had made all these years in bestowing his attentions on the mother instead of on the daughter; and it was now whispered, rightly or wrongly, that he was even beginning to bully the defeated Duchess herself. Flora found herself still able to carry on the Kensington warfare by annoying the Queen and Lehzen in many subtle ways. We see Mary Davys driving one day with Lady Mary Stopford through the Park at Windsor. "Scotty," it seems, would shortly be coming into waiting and, as the two Marys bowled along side by side in the royal carriage, the elder woman "gave me," writes Mary Davys, "some hints about my conduct to Lady Flora Hastings, and said now was the time that I might by a little *tact* be useful to the Baroness and Queen whom she will try to annoy." "She [Mary Stopford] says I must often write to her when she is away, and tell her how things go on when *Scotty* . . . is here. I do not look forward with much pleasure to that time. The poor Baroness will be much plagued, I fear!" And again, "I do not know what will go on then; I fear there may be some awkwardnesses but we will hope for the best."

The kindhearted Mary Davys would not like to see her dear Lehzen plagued, but all the same this secretly carried-on scuffle at the very core of the palace life certainly added a yet further lilt of excitement to her new existence that already, daughter of the Church that she was, she began to fear she was finding "too attractive, too fascinating." Would the very charm of it all, she often asked herself, prove dangerous to the health of her soul? "I am constantly afraid of being too well satisfied . . . and growing careless about subjects of higher importance." For it is a mistake to think that the pietist movement in the upper classes of the last century was given its original impulse by Queen Victoria's Court. On the contrary, when she first came to the throne, the daughters of the quieter side of society were already immersed in evangelicalism, and not only youthful Mary would read Jeremy Taylor's *Holy Living and Holy Dying*, but this one or that one of the maids of honor would do so too; would eagerly arrange to meet each other for morning prayers in one of their sitting rooms. "I am pleased to find she [Miss Dillon] is quite religiously disposed," Mary writes of one of the maids of honor; and further, "Lady Barham is so nice good kind and delightful! I had a long talk with her in her bedroom just now; she says we may come to her before breakfast every morning and have prayers for she meant to read them and a chapter with her maid. Will not this be nice? I am sure Lady B. is a most valuable friend." So each morning Lady Barham's lady's maid came punctiliously trotting from her room, and she and her mistress and the attentive girls composed themselves for Scripture and prayers. Composed themselves that is to say if the room was not so thick with smoke that they could do nothing but gasp and splutter; for the smoke in those upstairs sitting rooms was appalling, and with smarting eyes the occupants would have to rush from one room to another, take refuge even in a fireless bedroom— "utterly impossible to remain in my sitting-room. . . . Really that smoke is the greatest annoyance possible; it spoils everything, and as to keeping oneself and one's clothes *clean*, it is out of the question." But this new arrival at the palace doubted if the smoke was a sufficient chastener of her spirit, so increasingly seductive did she find royal life. Again and again in her letters arises the fear that in this world of luxury and glitter her character will go to pieces. "Oh, in what a different sphere I am living now to what my natural one is! . . . I hope it will not do me harm." Was it, for instance, perhaps quite nice of her to have written home that Lord Tavistock "does certainly resemble a chimpanzee"? . . . Was this sort of not very kind observation proof that the world's slow stain was already beginning to contaminate her? Was it possibly Lord Melbourne's presence that induced this kind of flippancy? "You see we have a good deal of fun even in a court. I cannot tell you all the little jokes, in which even the Queen joins; it would be too trifling." How puzzling it was though that what was too trifling to record should yet be so charming to experience. Her anxiety as to the condition of her soul increased. This constant association with the palace's "grand company"; this surround of peers, all, after the first shock of meeting such a swarm of them at once, so agreeable in their various ways—Lord Glenelg (soon to become her close friend);

Lord Melbourne with his sudden hoots of laughter and gobbling up his food with such shameless appreciation (Melbourne was always to remain to her an unsolved problem. "They say he is a most thoughtless man, and quite regardless of *time*"), and then Lord Palmerston—his very nickname "Cupid" only too embarrassingly suggestive. Where would it all end, or, rather, where would Mary's soul end? And yet again comes that fidgeting anxiety as to whether "this Court life is not doing me harm." It was all "so very dazzling," would it make her "unfitted for *common life*"? Certainly, for her, life at Buckingham Palace was remarkably uncommon: all those footmen, for instance, here, there, and everywhere in their crimson livery. And they were not only for the State Rooms. The Queen's ladies in their upstairs life could if they so desired pull the bell rope of their sitting room, and along the corridor would come hurrying one of these flamelike figures ready to take messages or to conduct anyone to whatever part of the palace they wished to be taken. These "red footmen" formed a muted background to all the "grand company" lit by the reckless blaze of hundreds of wax candles. Even when Mary slipped downstairs from her loftily perched rooms on her way to dinner, it was through "brilliantly lighted marble halls and staircases," and at dinner itself ("A sumptuous dinner, with forty red footmen and pages, champagne etcetera," wrote a later arrival at the palace), even then, as the Dean's daughter pursued her way through those beguiling menus, her spirit was at the same time lulled by the cajoleries of the royal band. Then would come the general gathering in the great drawing room. Mary, playing chess there one evening with Harriet Lister, happened to glance up from the board, and her eye took in the landscape of that far-spreading room with the ladies of the household grouped about in their variously hued dresses giving the effect of human flower beds; an intent party of four all vis-à-vis at a card table—the Duchess of Kent, Lord John, Lord Uxbridge, and Mr. Murray—on the card table high silver candlesticks; some of the visitor ladies "round the Queen's table,*

* The drawing, facing page 304, by Eugène Lami, depicting a scene two or three years after Queen Victoria's marriage, shows how the round table of the day was used in the vast rooms of the royal palaces as a kind of inner intimate chamber around which the royalties and their special guests could cluster, behaving in as desultory a manner as they pleased.

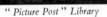

" Picture Post " Library

EOPOLD THE FIRST, KING OF
HE BELGIANS, WHEN OLDER

Marquis of Conyngham   Marchioness of Tavistock   Earl of Albemarle
      Duchess of Sutherland   Her Royal Highness the Duchess of Kent

HER MAJESTY AS SHE APPEARED ON HER FIRST VISIT TO
COVENT GARDEN THEATRE, NOVEMBER 17TH, 1837

the rest scattered about." As Mary gazed she was struck by the charm, romantic as a painting by Winterhalter, of the whole thing, "that beautiful drawing room full of company in the evening is a very pretty scene." Another day there was a royal concert, and how amusing it was, once the concert itself was over, for Mary, standing about "in pink trimmed with blonde," to have a subdued titter with her friends at the sight of Melbourne collapsed sound asleep in a chair "in the middle of the crowd" who walked, quite regardlessly, around him. And here now is the Duke of Cambridge bearing down on these young girls of the Household, enveloping them as usual in the torrent of his conversational shouts, "we had difficulty to restrain our laughter at his extraordinary ways"; at times it "made one quite hot to answer his incessant questions, and laugh at his droll jokes." As for Victoria when confronted by this overwhelming uncle, "He almost frightens the poor little Queen."

If all this evening hilarity and general bedazzlement began to prove rather too overpowering, Mary knew that upstairs was awaiting her a bed that was "quite the essence of comfort, sheets like floss silk and heaps of hot water and tubs." Amid all this material comfort and pretty surface scene of life at the palace it was a relief to her gradually to discover that those who played their part in this mellifluous existence were not always so serene at heart as their appearance might lead one to suppose. She found Lady Lansdowne very reassuring on this point. "There is no one among the ladies so interesting as Lady Lansdowne . . . her manner is rather cold, but it conceals, as is often the case with these great people, very deep feeling. . . . I do not think she really cares for company and gaiety. The other night, on leaving the ball, I am told that she was quite overcome, covered her face with her hands, and leant against one of the marble pillars of the hall." Mary herself had no inclination to lean against the marble pillars of the palace in protest against the worldly merry-go-round in which she had become involved, but she did earnestly try to offset it by solemn reading in her sitting room and patient threading with her needle at those eternal chair backs. "Talents well employed," she reassured her family at Kensington. But how bored she and her young colleagues were beginning to get with those chair backs, in spite of having got "a beautiful pattern of the Crown, garter etcetera drawn out at Wilk's." The whole thing was becoming a nuisance, "some of the young ladies detest it." How much more amusing Mary found it to plot a new dress with her maid, that treasured Podevin, who was so clever at making them. "My winter morning gowns are the satinet, a purple figured poplin, and a black satin with very nice collars, cuffs, scarf etc; for walking I have a black velvet bonnet with blonde and red flowers inside; a handsome chocolate coloured merino cloak trimmed with velvet; it cost a great deal of money but looks very well. . . . I have also my black shawl." Fortunately with her £400 a year from the Queen, she could settle the bill for that expensive merino cloak, and for the evening she was helped out with presents from Victoria. In Mary's wardrobe hung "a white figured net, and a yellow one, these were reckoned the least smart." "Then I have the pale pink poplin, the Queen's watered silk, the new muslin and satin one, and Her Majesty is going to give me a *blue* watered silk."

But as the first spring of her stay at the palace began to brighten the air, her clothes and her appearance became a concern rather than a pleasure. "Dress is a great plague," she wrote this April, "and now that daylight is coming on it is necessary more than ever to be *clean and nice*." During the winter months she had been confined more or less within the walls of Buckingham Palace, surrounded by all "the dirt, noise, smoke and bustle of London," into which, nevertheless, she would at times penetrate, seated in one of the royal carriages, companioned by one or other of the maids of honor, on their way "to Bedmayne [Redmayne?] and the Western Exchange for some purchases." But this Easter of 1838 the whole palace contingent set off for Windsor Castle. These departures for Windsor were not accomplished without bewildering upheaval. "At three o'clock," wrote Mary of a similar departure the December before, "after a morning of greater confusion than I can describe, we all set off." Presumably this Easter expedition necessitated the same ferment. However, at last Mary found herself ensconced in one of the string of royal carriages with "the dear Baroness, Miss Cavendish and her dog, a very pleasant party." It was a day of warm sunshine, their carriage was open, and around them cantered an escort of Lancers.

Mary, all these winter months immersed in her palace world, had almost forgotten what had meanwhile been going on in the country, and now, as the procession gradually drew off from the London atmosphere, she received the exquisite blow of finding herself surrounded on every side with all the sweetness of spring. The nearer they drew to the castle the deeper they penetrated into this lushness and freshness. "You cannot think how pretty the last part of the way was, coming across the grass in the Little Park towards the Castle." Her eye was caught by the charm of the Lancers' particolored tunics as their spruce, jiggeting forms flicked from sunlight into shadow, from shadow into sunlight—"they looked so bright . . . amongst the trees and the sunshine. The bells rang and everything was merry."

The sheen of springtime lay over all that Easter visit to "Dear delightful Windsor." Now Mary is on the Windsor Slopes with Lady Mary Stopford, both of them plucking away at the pallid primroses and their crumpled leaves. Now she is seated in a carriage companioned by one or two of the Household. "To-day . . . Lady Gardiner, Miss Lister and I shall drive out probably. We did so on Thursday, and only think how grand we were in an open carriage and four with postillions, an outrider before and footmen sitting behind. I was ashamed of it, particularly as people bowed, thinking it was the Queen." Indeed the whole thing so agitated Mary that on getting back to the castle she "asked the Baroness whether it was not wrong to go out in that grand way." But the more dashing Lehzen tossed any idea of wrongness aside: "no harm," she told Mary, "providing we did not have the Queen's grey horses."

After luncheon on Good Friday "we were all summoned to walk with the Queen down to Adelaide Cottage." About a dozen of them set off, and, arriving at those closely packed flower beds, the cries and the exclamations and the picking began; "all the gentlemen and the ladies too on their knees before the flower-beds. I was glad to see that the Queen enjoyed anything so much." We, too, see them there scattered around the beds; the feminine cloaks flung back as the wearers bend to their work, wearing the then fashionable little bonnets of white or stone color put on in response to the spring sunshine. "There was," says Mary in conclusion, "a great gathering of violets, and presenting them to each other and wearing them afterwards at dinner, and all that sort of thing."

And there, amid the scent of their violets, smilingly pressing on each other those dank fragrant little bunches, we reluctantly leave them.

CHAPTER IX
FORESHADOWINGS

W$_{HILE}$ Victoria was accustoming herself to the profession of queenship, over in Germany, in the town of Bonn, a young man of beguiling beauty would often have been seen striding along the streets, two greyhounds at their undulating trot at his heels. This was Leopold's nephew Albert, who, since we saw him leaving Kensington Palace after his visit to his relations in the spring of 1836, had been, with his brother Ernest, strenuously at work on self-education.

If the other young men at Bonn University thought the position of this student prince enviable, to himself it was both invidious and embarrassing, for he was being intensively trained to fit him for the post of Consort to that astoundingly successful young Queen, but without any certainty that she did intend, finally, to summon him to her side.

Under the instruction of Monsieur Quetelet, a brilliant statistician and mathematician, the Prince had probed into "the application of the law of probabilities to social and natural phenomena," but the probabilities concerning the final conclusions of Victoria's mind were beyond Monsieur Quetelet's calculations. Certainly, during the Kensington Palace visit, there had been engendered between the cousins that ephemeral condition known as "an understanding," and Victoria, overcome at having had her cousin taken away from her after their playmate fortnight together, had written to Leopold: "I have only now to beg you, my dearest Uncle, to take care of the health of one, *now so dear* to me." But at the present date, when compared with the reports that had drifted to Germany of Victoria's "astonishing self-possession," and of the admiration with which she was surrounded, compared with all this, those few weeks' companionship at Kensington Palace, that unspoken understanding between the very youthful cousins, must have seemed to Albert remarkably little to rely on.

When he had heard of the death of William IV, he knew that, indubitably, he must write to Victoria, but the composition of that letter must have required thought. How, at such a moment of remodeling of her life, intrude himself; how do it just sufficiently, with not one word too many. . . . It must have been a problem. "My dearest cousin," ran his letter, "I must write you a few lines to present you my sincerest felicitations on that great change which has taken place in your life." Then followed several platitudes about assistance from Heaven, difficult tasks, glory and happiness, and then came the crucial paragraph. "May I pray you to think likewise sometimes of your cousins in Bonn, and to continue to them that kindness you favoured them with till now." And then, fearful of just that shade too much, he hurried away from the subject with, "I will not be indiscreet and abuse your time," and so concluded.

Now that Victoria was actually on the throne, rumors inevitably thickened round that young, masculine head bent so assiduously over the crammed notebooks; and Leopold, who acted as *compère* of the situation, considering it tactful to remove his nephew for a time from the world's too inquisitive eye, suggested that Albert and Ernest should go with a tutor on a tour to the south of Germany, to Switzerland, and to Italy. The three set off. Albert acquired an album into which he stuck views, presumably little engravings, of the places they visited. A dead rose was pushed in too; and the young man having managed to obtain a scrap of Voltaire's handwriting from his servant, in went that as well, the idea behind this modest little collection being that it should finally be sent to Victoria. It was; and probably, at the moment, the offering seemed paltry enough; but later, in her widowed years, wherever she went, the album went with her.

After the tour, then Bonn University again; Albert lightening his studies on Roman law, political economy, history, anthropology, and philosophy, with extraordinarily effective mimicries of his professors. His pencil, too, would flick off the most spirited caricatures. It is understandable how this ridiculing of those around him helped counteract the sense of his own position being at the moment slightly ridiculous: kept dangling as he was with no definite information as to his ultimate fate.

By the end of 1837 Leopold considered that it was time some "decisive arrangement" should be made, an agreement that should take effect in 1839. Victoria demurred. When Albert had stayed at Kensington Palace a year and a half ago, she had not then experienced the charm of intimacy with ripened men of the world. Now, in her daily, altogether delightful association with Melbourne, with other men in various high positions treating her with such deference, and Alfred Paget with his attractive Calmuck face constantly about her, Albert appeared in a very different light. Compared with the richness of her present life, what a very jejune episode the Kensington Palace one seemed—that bashful little ring Albert had given her, those spurts of schoolgirl and schoolboy laughter, that final dance they had swayed through together while the dawn whitened around the trees in Kensington Garden. What, now, did it all amount to? In her mind lay the memory of a good-natured but quite unsophisticated boy, too pulpy, too soft-looking altogether, with a tiresome inclination to go to sleep at moments when he ought to have been particularly wide awake. This recollection of Albert received merely from the presence of the socially finished men around her an unspoken rebuff. Compared with them, her cousin appeared an inept, all but boring boy. Marry him ultimately as a tiresome necessity she supposed she must, but it was a thought that she preferred to keep pushed away in her mind like some unwanted object at the back of a drawer. Certainly there was no one else whom she thought of marrying . . . but should she decide not to marry at all? That was an alternative which she murmured to her Journal, and one that at times glowed quite pleasantly in her mind. For her abundant nature believed itself, but erroneously, to be completely fulfilled by her present mode of existence; her new life that was like a great nosegay pressed to her bosom, the morning dew on every petal. As to the "decisive arrangement" over which Uncle Leopold was fidgeting, he received from his niece a whole list of excuses. She was, she insisted, too young; and so was Albert. Then, too, his English was far from what it ought to be, that must be attended to. Further, he ought to have a "wider experience, more practical habits of observation, and more self-reliance." How the shadow of Melbourne, himself so outstandingly in possession of these very qualities, blotted out Albert!

The realization that it was demanded of her to make a definite decision, combined with her reluctance to make it, induced a conflict in her mind, and she began to feel exasperated at the whole situation. Her annoyance began even to tincture her letters to Uncle Leopold. "My dearest child, you were *somewhat irritable* when you wrote to me," came the reproving voice from Belgium. Victoria, with her now heightened enthusiasm for soldiers, had apparently considered that it would smarten Albert up if he were turned into one, and had made the suggestion to Leopold, as he, in return, protests that "to make him *enter the Service* would not do at all."

Finally, Victoria hit on the idea that Stockmar would be the best person to put that polish on her cousin which was required if she were really going to marry him; and it was decided that that mentor of royalty should go to Belgium and do what he could. This was followed up by Leopold having a long talk in Brussels with the young man himself, Leopold putting "the whole case honestly and kindly before him." If Leopold put the case as honestly as he said he did, it must certainly have needed a great deal of kindness to blunt the sharp edges. In return his nephew had, dampingly enough, observed that "if one must be subject to plagues and annoyances, it is better to be so for some real and worthy object than for trivial and paltry ends." This would-be husband of Victoria was aware that the affair as it stood held the possibility of final humiliation for himself of the most painful nature. "I am ready," he told his uncle, "to submit to this delay if I have only some certain assurance to go upon. But if after waiting, perhaps for three years, I should find that the Queen no longer desired the marriage, it would place me in a ridiculous position, and would, to a certain extent, ruin all my prospects for the future."

This was undeniably true. As has been said, Victoria represented to him not only wife but career. In an endeavor to keep him from becoming too restive his uncle certainly went a shade further than he was justified in doing by assuring him that, "The Queen had in no way altered her mind, but did not wish to marry for some time yet."

Meanwhile, Victoria had evidently told Stockmar exactly in what ways she considered Albert needed improving. "There is another *sujet*," she wrote to Leopold, "which I wish to mention to you, *et que j'ai bien à cœur*, which is, if you would consult Stockmar with respect to the finishing of Albert's education; he knows best my feelings and wishes on that subject."

Leopold was enchanted. "Concerning the education of our friend Albert; it has been the best plan you could have fixed upon, to name Stockmar your commissary-general; it will give *unité d'action et de l'ensemble* which otherwise we should not have had."

So the young man was sent off with Stockmar for an Italian tour in the final endeavor to remold him nearer to Victoria's wishes. "Stockmar will make a regular report to you on this subject," wrote Leopold.

It was certainly fortunate that Albert could not overlook his uncle and his cousin's correspondence.

2

A May evening in 1838. Within the walls of Buckingham Palace, clouds of music are afloat, billowing, dissolving. It is the elder Strauss himself, who, baton in hand before his massed orchestra, is conjuring this music into being.

England's new Queen was giving her first ball, and she was in a state of exaltation. "I had not danced for *so* long," she almost apologized to her Journal. To begin with, as, just before ten o'clock, "the doors were opened and I went through the Saloon into the other Ball-room next the dining-room in which was Strauss's band," at that moment an unusual nervousness suddenly assailed her, "I felt a little shy in going in." But with her spirit borne on those uplifting cadences, self-consciousness vanished: she soon "got over it and went and talked to the people."

What a glittering, bespangled evening that was—an evening that seemed a climax of all the expansions and delights of her new life. Now, in this tumult of Strauss's harmony, the air was reft as if with flashing streamers. Now there came floating beguilements and whisperings of infinite tenderness. Now it was as if the room were being sprinkled with flowers, incorporeal flowers that seemed as if about to quiver into being, only again to be ravished into vapor. . . . "I never in my life heard anything so *beautiful* as Strauss's band."

As with gay precision she glided through the figures of the square dances, as the music wove its siren strains in the air, her eye took in without envy all the animated charms of the women around her. "There was a great deal of beauty there," she noted afterward, "amongst which were Lady Ashley, Lady Fanny Cowper, Lady Wilhelmina Stanhope, Lady Seymour, Lady Clanricarde. . . ." This was only the beginning of the long list of generous appreciation. She did not, and, in one sense, knew she need not, envy any one of them. At this, her first ball, whatever face smiled opposite hers in a quadrille, however much the nothingness of her own general appearance contrasted with the human swans and humming birds that surrounded her, she alone was enfolded with queenship. Subconsciously she was always aware of the pinnacle on which she was placed. She was the new phenomenon, the hidden child in Kensington Palace who had suddenly emerged and drawn to herself the absorbed interest of the whole country. And, too, in spite of her insignificant figure, her indecisive prettiness, she had a delicate poise, a little air of dignity and command that was unique and wholly delightful. To and fro through the shifting ballroom scene the Queen came and went surrounded on all sides by this kaleidoscopic clustering of uniformed men and meticulously arrayed women in their bell-shaped shimmering skirts sticking out like pincushions, all satin and lace: the central royal figure in "very light and high spirits." "It was a lovely ball, so gay, so nice and I felt so happy and so merry."

Waltzing she did not allow herself. "I did not think it would do," she confided to Melbourne next day.

"I think you are quite right; that's quite right," exclaimed her mentor "eagerly."

So when at the Court balls her guests, clasped two and two, went revolving over the floor, she would place herself "on a sofa somewhat elevated in the drawing-room," where she would sit, heavily surrounded by the too expansive figures, the too ripe faces, of her mother and aunts: this clump of femininity given a dramatic touch by the gentlemen of the Household, with their upheld wands, standing protectively around them. When supper was announced, the tiny but self-assured figure, looking like a doll-Queen freshly unwrapped from an expensive toyshop, would rise, and gracefully glide ahead, the rest of the Royal ladies galumphing along after her. "Her exceeding youth," remarked an onlooker, "strikingly contrasted with their mature ages."

Beneath all the froth of joy of this her first ball there did how-ever lie a small but insistent disappointment. "One *only* regret I had—and that was that my excellent, kind, good friend, Lord Melbourne, was not there."

She was young enough to be excited at finding she had not left the ballroom "till 10 m. to *four!!*" and noticed, with a delightful sense of dissipation, that when she got into bed at a quarter-past, the early morning sunshine was making long pencils of light down the edges of her curtains.

The next day she received a note from Lord Melbourne explain-ing the reason why he had not come to her ball. He had been, he said, "Unwell and so disturbed." The reason for this disturbance was that a political crisis was imminent. It was a question of rescind-ing the resolution of 1835 regarding the Irish Church; and when on this day Melbourne came to the palace, all the reassurance he could give Victoria was to concur with the opinion of Lord John Russell that "a majority of ministers, though a small one, is toler-ably certain."

To Victoria, the merest suggestion that she might lose her Premier was intolerable. This political threat came like a wing of darkness across all the gayness and sweetness still afloat in her mind from last night's ball. "All this distresses me much; would to God none of these Motions, which are so *useless*, were brought on." The next day Melbourne's opinion of the situation was more dubious, and though he opined that if they did have a majority, "why then all is well," he added that, "from the nature of the House it made it 'ticklish.'" In consequence, when he and Victoria parted, she nearly broke down. "I cannot say . . . HOW LOW, HOW SAD I feel when I think of the POSSIBILITY of this excellent and truly kind man . . . not *remaining* my Minister! I should have liked to have expressed to Lord Melbourne my anxiety, but the tears were nearer than words. . . . I felt I should have choked."

However, four days later comes the entry, "Got up at 10 and heard from Lord John that on a division *we* had a majority of 19, which he said was more than he expected. How thankful I am and feel!"

CHAPTER X
VICTORIA'S "DEAR CORONATION"

J UNE, 1838, had arrived; and the turmoil caused by the coming coronation filled the air.

The Duchess of Richmond was much occupied settling what the dresses for Victoria's trainbearers should be; her great determination, as she remarked later, being "that I would have no discussion with their Mamas about it." It would have been better if she had, as she was getting into a wretched muddle over the whole thing, tricking out the chosen girls with trains of their own, which, at the actual coronation, were miserably in their way. As for the trainbearers' headdresses, here the Duchess' lack of any sense of design was only too apparent. Instead of leaving the charming wreaths of silver corn that she had given them, isolated, she insisted that tiny flowered ones, like minute birds' nests, should be clapped on top of their heads where their plaits terminated. For plaits, festooned over the ears, were the fashion of the moment, and it is said that in imitation of that then up-to-date figure, the ethereal Gothic heroine, the young women of the day would have their blood drawn off from behind the ears to give them the desired pallid and "interesting" appearance; the plaits coming in useful to hide the scars made by the leeches. Victoria, who certainly would not have tampered with her naturally rose-bloom cheeks, had nevertheless adopted these plaits, and then asked Lord Melbourne how he liked them. "He said, looking at me, and making one of his funny faces, 'It's pretty; isn't it rather curious—something new?'"

In the embrace of a burning summer, an excited, sweating London prepared for the great event. "There was never anything seen like the state of this town," exclaimed Charles Greville, "it is as if the population had been on a sudden quintupled; the uproar, the confusion, the crowds, the noise, are indescribable. Horsemen, footmen, carriages, squeezed, jammed, intermingled, the pavement blocked up with timbers; hammering and knocking, and falling fragments stunning the ears and threatening the head; not a mob here and there, but the town all mob, thronging, bustling, gaping, and gazing at everything; at anything; at nothing; the park one vast encampment, with banners floating on the tops of the tents, and still the roads are covered, the railroads loaded with arriving multitudes."

There was to be a gigantic fair in Hyde Park, preparations for which of course added to the general confusion. "Stoppages in every street . . ." runs a letter of the day. "The Queen herself was stuck for three quarters of an hour in Piccadilly the day before yesterday. She had been warned not to attempt Hyde Park, because from the carts carrying the fair goods, and the barriers only admitting one at a time, nobody could move there." All was fuss, flags, gaiety, and heat. The parks were merrily sprinkled with small white tents for the artillery, "banners" afloat on top; interspersed with little booths and stalls, and various contrivances to do with the coming balloon ascents. Victoria, braving the scrimmage and the sun-scorched streets, would glance into the cool green of the parks as her carriage went trotting by, and thought the whole confetti-like effect "very pretty."

The excitement in England reverberated across the Channel; and Continental monarchs were considering which were the most suitable young men to be attached to the staff of the envoys who were to attend the coronation. "The identical . . . idea of the Continental sovereigns was to send their greatest and most wealthy subjects . . . with staffs of the most brilliant young men they could find." Louis Philippe intended that his choice of Marshal Soult as French envoy should be accepted as a graceful gesture consigning the Peninsular War and Waterloo to oblivion. It being known abroad how devoted England's Queen was to riding and dancing, young society Frenchmen, outstanding as "accomplished equestrians and dancers," were chosen for Soult's staff. "They belonged to the brilliant set of the Duke of Orleans, and were selected either from the old aristocracy or from the Bonapartist nobility." The Russian envoy, Count Strogoff, "had with him Prince Anatole Demidoff, the Russian Crœsus, who lived at the Palace of San Donato, and came prepared to spend at the Coronation in proportion to his boundless fortune. They had in their following a number of Asiatic Princes. . . . In Prince Putbus, the King of Prussia was represented by his wealthiest and noblest subject; Prince Schwarzenberg was accompanied by his beauteous wife, and had as attachés the pick of the Magyar nobility. They were adapted to shine as dancers, or on horseback at reviews, or in the Windsor cavalcade. The jewellery the Hungarians had on their national suits was so valuable as to make insurance against the risks of the road to England and back most difficult." In a word, an additional influx of all that luxury and show which were then an intrinsic part of the life of the favored few was flowing into the country: the French and English quays must have been scenes of scrimmage, the one with departing, the other with arriving, guests, surrounded with all their redundant appurtenances, and voluble servants. Beautifully varnished carriages, painted with armorial bearings, adorned with fringed hammer cloths and every finely executed detail that the coachbuilder's art could devise, were being transferred from ship to quay; startled horses led by grooms trod gingerly; harassed ladies' maids, uttering birdlike cries, ran hither and thither in the confusion, grappling with the transit of their mistresses' band boxes and vast trunks filled to the brim with all the latest caprices of the Parisian and Viennese milliners and *couturiers*.

The choice of the day on which Victoria decided to give a ball at Buckingham Palace in honor of all the distinguished foreigners who had come over for the coronation was unfortunate. Quite incredibly, the day fixed on was that of the anniversary of Waterloo, June 18. The tongues of Paris were at once at work, bitingly referring to *Le bal de Waterloo*, and at a supper party given by Dumas père, "a young poet, Emile de Labedollière, improvised a comic song on *Les Trois Estropiés de la reine*"—the three alluded to being Lord Anglesey, who had lost a leg; Lord Fitzroy Somerset, who had parted with an arm; and the Duke of Wellington, who, in spite of Monsieur Emile de Labedollière's wit, still possessed all his limbs.

Meanwhile, the owners of some of London's great houses had

taken the opportunity of letting them to the foreigners at fantastic prices: Count Strogoff being said to have rented one belonging to a member of the Ponsonby family at £3000 for a few days' tenancy.

2

June 28. All the intricate preparations for Victoria's "dear Coronation," as Uncle Leopold called it, had been completed; and now the ceremony was taking place.

Within the Abbey's stone setting, splashed now with Turkey red calico and crimson velvet, were pressed together "above ten thousand of the greatest and most famous," all tricked out with every telling effect that they had been able to achieve. Coronets, those fabulous little crowns, with their inescapable fairy-tale atmosphere, were everywhere: some carried by their owners, some borne along on cushions upheld by pages. One side of the aisle was banked with peeresses. Opposite there was a similar bank of peers. Among the beplumed heads, the variegated blaze of dresses and uniforms glinted the pin flash of thousands of jewels. Prince Esterházy, the Austrian Minister, "was literally covered with jewels down to the heels of his boots." An onlooker said the effect was as if he had been "caught out in a rain of diamonds and come in dripping." Harriet Martineau, who had taken her seat at the Abbey at a very early hour, writes that "about nine, the first gleams of the sun slanted into the Abbey. . . . I had never before seen the full effect of diamonds. As the light travelled, each peeress shone like a rainbow. The brightness, vastness, and dreamy magnificence of the scene produced a strange effect. . . . Prince Esterházy, crossing a bar of sunshine, was the most prodigious rainbow of all. He was covered with diamonds and pearls; and as he dangled his hat, it cast a dancing radiance all round." The uniform of another foreigner, Prince Eugène Zichy, was encrusted with turquoises.

Young Arthur Stanley (later, the Dean of Victorian renown) was among the waiting mass in the Abey. "At nine," he writes, "the guns announced that the Queen had left the Palace; an electric shock ran visibly through the whole Abbey." "The Queen," he continues, "with her vast crimson train . . . when she came within the full view of the gorgeous Abbey, paused, as if for breath, and clasped her hands. The orchestra broke out into the most tremendous crash of music I ever heard. . . . Everyone literally gasped for breath from the intense interest, and the rails of the gallery trembled in one's hands from the . . . trembling of the spectators. I never saw anything like it. Tears would have been a relief."

All the enchantments for the eye had now become merely the setting for the small figure slowly moving the whole length of the Abbey toward the throne; the group of trainbearers dutifully clinging, four a side, to her train—that heavy encumbrance of ermine and velvet that stretched out far behind her; Lord Conyngham having wisely been placed as a solid masculine supporter at the farther end of it. The Duchess of Richmond must have realized, as the procession of Queen, Bishops, and Household drew slowly along before her eyes, what a mistake she had made over the trainbearers' dresses, for there were her victims in the most embarrassing difficulties, forever trying to scrabble their own trains away from under their feet while with both hands they clung to the Queen's. "Impossible to avoid treading on them. We ought never to have had these," exclaimed the exasperated Lady Wilhelmina Stanhope. In their endeavors not to fall, "we carried the Queen's train very jerkily and badly," goes on this trainbearer, "and it must have been very difficult for her to walk, as she did, evenly and steadily, and with much grace and dignity, the whole length of the Abbey."

It must be realized, as every man and woman in that huge throng turned to take their fill of their new Queen as she quietly processed by them, what an absolute novelty she was. For years the nation had witnessed the undignified, if benevolent, capers of William IV, already, when he came to the throne, in appearance a white-haired old gentleman. Behind him there still lived in their minds the memory of a bloated, lecherous face beneath a brown wig; behind him again a piteous lunatic peering from behind his Castle windows across the flats of Eton; farther back still, successively, two disreputable old men, as odious in their persons as they were unsanctified in their minds. Now, as that great concourse of onlookers remembered the past and looked on this all but child, this spring flower who represented the present, a surge of sentiment, an emotion of delight, of chivalry, of love, swept the Abbey. "Thunders of applause" burst simultaneously from every side; in a moment the air was a swaying confusion of gesticulating hands, of fluttering scarves and handkerchiefs. The center of all this vehemence, in her gold tissue beneath an overdress of red velvet, continually bowing her neatly brushed head with its dazzle of diamond circlet, composedly pursued her way; but one of the trainbearers noted that at this discharge of emotions around her "The colour mounted to her cheeks, brow and even neck, and her breath came quickly." As she stepped along with her own peculiarly individual grace, behind her the two rows of trainbearers—their rose-sprinkled, white and silver tissue dresses making a soft billowing around her—all those young faces, unsoiled by time, must have given the impression of a masque of youth that was being enacted; and yet, to all those who gazed, more than a masque; a very living and historically significant reality.

The procession reached the throne, and the emblematic, intricate ceremony commenced, with all its ritual of oaths, crown, scepter, orb, dalmatic, robe, supertunic of cloth of gold, spurs, purple velvet kirtle, and mantle.

Lehzen, needless to say, was there, drinking it all in with one can imagine what sense of triumph, what tenderness of feeling, in a box immediately above the velvet-trimmed royal box: this exclusive casket containing, among others, the Duchess of Kent dressed in purple. And another of the Kensington Palace figures familiar to us was with her, old Späth, who had no doubt been wafted across the Channel in Feodore's entourage. In spite of the complications of the ceremony (made more so by the Bishop of Durham, who, though standing close to the Queen so as to help her, was, so she said afterward, "remarkably maladroit, and never could tell me what was to take place"), in spite of having to keep her mind on everything she was called on to say, do, take hold of, put on, or take off, she did not forget "another most dear Being present at this ceremony ... and who witnessed it all; it was my dearly-beloved, angelic Lehzen whose eyes I caught when on the Throne, and we exchanged smiles." Incidentally, Leopold and his wife were not present. His niece had invited them, but King Leopold's reply had been, "More mature reflection has made me think that a King and Queen at your dear Coronation might perhaps be a Hors-d'œuvre."

There arrived the crucial moment when the heavy crown was pressed downward on the Queen's plaits; and, on the instant, as if this symbolic action had released some hidden nervous force within and without the Abbey, there burst forth a cataclysm of shouts, trumpetings, reverberation of drums, and shock of cannon, while the organ flung into the confused din the full volume of Handel's *The Queen Shall Rejoice.* Concurrently with this frenzy of sound there arose a forest of uplifted arms, as peers and peeresses placed their coronets on their heads, shouting, "God save the Queen," "which was, I must own," writes Victoria, "a most beautiful impressive moment. . . . My excellent Lord Melbourne, who stood very close to me throughout the whole ceremony, was *completely* overcome . . . he gave me *such* a kind and I may say *fatherly* look."

The Duchess of Kent, enclosed within her purple velvet sheath, was, poor diminished lady, shaken with sobs; as she well might be, such a culmination of feeling must all this ecstatic fanfare have induced in her, so bitterly did it emphasize the gulf that now lay between her and her child. She was in such a fuddle with her emotions, her tears, and her handkerchief, that her lady in waiting had herself to try to balance the coronet on her mistress' head.

Arthur Stanley, his eyes riveted on the Queen, and absorbedly taking everything in, wrote afterward, "All the movements were beautiful. She was always accompanied by her eight ladies, floating about her like a silver cloud. . . . It was all more like a dream than a reality—more beautiful than I could have conceived possible." The moment came for the peers to do homage, that is, to touch the Queen's crown, and to kiss her hands. Knowing what was before her, she had purposely had her crown made to fit her head as firmly as possible, and it was fortunate she had, as not only was it cuffed and jerked by her loyal subjects, but one particularly clumsy member of the peerage actually clutched hold of it, apparently in an effort to steady himself. Among the stream of peers, the decrepit Lord Rolle tottered up to pay his homage. Harriet Martineau, her eyes fixed on this "large, infirm old man," tells us what happened. He was, she says, "held up by two peers, and had nearly reached the royal footstool when he slipped through the hands of his supporters, and rolled over and over down the steps, lying at the bottom coiled up in his robes. He was instantly lifted up; and he tried

again and again amidst shouts of admiration of his valour." Then,
the Queen, rising, came forward and sympathetically held out her
hand to him, at which the now almost hysterical congregation burst
into further applause. In addition, any especially popular character,
as he knelt before the Queen, was enheartened by loud cheers. The
Duke of Wellington received a special roar of approval, so did
Melbourne. "When my good Lord Melbourne knelt down and
kissed my hand, he pressed my hand, and I grasped his with all my
heart, at which he looked up with eyes filled with tears."

These volleys of appreciation were only part of the general
clamor that was going on. Lord Surrey, for instance, had chosen
this juncture for a particularly exciting scramble among the choirboys and pages for the coronation medals. The struggling and confusion became "desperate," and "some of the ladies of the Court
were pushed about close to the Queen"; while one of the ambassadors was startled by a handful of the medals suddenly hurtling into
his box. Lord Surrey himself was, says Wilhelmina Stanhope,
"nearly torn to pieces in the universal excitement. The pages were
particularly active, and some of them collected ten or twelve medals
apiece. The trainbearers wrung out one each from Lord Surrey,
whose temper was entirely gone, and who looked as red and voluble
as a turkey cock. I had another given to me by one of the pages."

When the last peer had paid homage "the House of Commons
gave more hearty cheers, accompanied with frequent cries of 'God
save Queen Victoria,'" any member of the congregation who so
chose joining in.

Wilhelmina Stanhope tells us what was to her the most moving
moment in the whole arduous ceremony, when the Queen knelt
before the altar: "As she knelt . . . with clasped hands and bowed
head, with her loose robe of gold brocade hanging from her shoulders, she looked exactly like the representation, in some old picture,
of a fair young devotee in the costume of the Middle Ages." As,
kneeling there, she heard *Come, Holy Ghost, Our Souls Inspire*
winging around her on the choirboys' voices, her thoughts were her
own; but one may be assured that no monarch ever more ardently,
more humbly, asked for Divine guidance than did she at that
moment.

Finally, she went with her ladies, trainbearers, and all the chief personages about her into St. Edward's Chapel, which, with a sofa, and, remarks Victoria, with "what was *called* an *Altar* . . . covered with sandwiches, bottles of wine etc.," struck a comfortable note. At once everyone flung aside whatever ritualistic role the ceremony had imposed on them, and on the instant became his or her everyday self. "The Queen complained of a headache from having her crown very unceremoniously *knocked* by most of the peers"; also the Archbishop had insisted on putting the ring on the wrong finger, relentlessly cramming it down, so that, later, only with great pain, and iced water, was she able to get it off. Now, once in the Chapel, she lifted off her crown, unclasped her mantle, and, says one of her trainbearers, "having got rid of all her royalty, sat down on the sofa and amused herself." She noticed that Lord Melbourne "took a glass of wine, for he seemed completely tired." As they were all munching and talking very cosily, the Archbishop (who appears to have been in a sad state of bewilderment over details that he should have known) came wandering in, and, says the Queen, "*ought* to have delivered the Orb to me, but I had already got it." This information came as a great surprise to the prelate, and made him "*so* confused and puzzled," and in a few moments he had drifted away again. The last event of all was the procession in reverse, wending its way from throne to door. The Queen had again decked herself with those weighty objects, crown, orb, and scepter, and, as she says, "thus *loaded*" arrived at the Abbey porch and climbed into her awaiting state coach.

This golden coach with its many glass windows and tiny looped and tasseled curtains behind them, had originally been built for the coronation of George III. Such an exquisite extravaganza is the whole affair, it gives more the impression of having taken form in the world of reverie. From thick, molded swags on its gilded exterior spring heads of lions and large allegorical figures, the whole design culminating in the royal crown on the roof. Each of the panels, pictorially executed by Cipriani, further intrigues the imagination. In the past, as now at Queen Victoria's coronation, eight deep-cream-colored, long-tailed horses from Hanover would draw along this swaying object of beauty at a foot's pace; the heavily knotted cords of crimson and purple that formed part of their trappings contrasting, in triumphant aesthetic achievement, with the matt ivory of the slow-stepping splendid beasts. At the head of each walked a watchful groom, his frock-coat livery an encrustation of gold braid. The Queen gradually developed a warm affection for her "cream ponies," as these powerful animals were fondly nicknamed by the nation, and in later years would have among the multitudinous objects that crowded her tables an inkpot made from the hoof of one of these horses that had been an outstanding character in the royal stables.

In the procession that preceded and followed the Queen's coach were carriages that, though built on more normal lines than the royal coach, were yet models of perfection; the two that outshone all the others in glory being those of the Duke of Devonshire and Marshal Soult. The Duke's was "a gorgeous vehicle which had been built when he went as Envoy Extraordinary to St. Petersburg." Soult's was of cobalt blue relieved with gold; the lining of nankeen picked out with scarlet, "more elaborately decorated than any other carriage... and vociferously applauded."

All London was in the streets to view, through the windows of her fantastical coach, the great little person borne along, crown on head, scepter in one hand, orb in the other. "The enthusiasm, affection and loyalty was really touching.... I shall ever remember this day as the proudest of my life. I came home at a little after 6—really *not* feeling tired." So little, in fact, that, once out of the cramping grandeur of her robes, she worked off all the emotions of the last few hours by seizing her dogs and giving them a wash.

Dinner at the palace that evening was at eight o'clock. When the diners were assembled ready to go in, Lord Melbourne came up to Victoria, and lit her with happiness by saying, "I must congratulate you on this most brilliant day." Then the royal party, enlarged by relations from Germany, went in and placed themselves around the table; in the air a delightful sense of easement, of satisfaction that the huge event was safely behind them. Now each could expatiate to the other on his or her experiences and endurances during the day. Victoria was seated between "my Premier" and Uncle Ernest of Coburg, with dear Feodore—a living souvenir of Kensington days—the other side of Lord Melbourne. He and Victoria confided to each other what kind of a night they had had before this terrific day; and she learned with absorbed interest that "he had slept very deeply till he was woke at 6."

"I said I did not sleep well."

Naturally, all round the dinner table there was but the one topic, cut across only by Uncle Ernest's firmly expressed determination that, so far as he was concerned, he was going after dinner to drive out to see the illuminations. Meanwhile, between Victoria and Melbourne, the usual interchange rambled on. "I felt a little tired on my feet," she told him.

" 'You must be very tired...' " emphasized Melbourne, "and he turned round to me and said *so* kindly, 'And you did it beautifully,—every part of it, with so much taste; it's a thing you can't give a person advice upon; it must be left to a person.' "

"To hear this from this kind impartial friend gave me great and real pleasure." No doubt she had accomplished it all as charmingly as Lord Melbourne said, but one questions whether "impartial" was here precisely the right adjective.

Lord Melbourne disclosed to her that there had been "a large breakfast in the Jerusalem Chamber, where they met before all began," adding that "whenever the Clergy, or a Dean and Chapter had anything to do with anything, there's sure to be plenty to eat."

There came the removal of the diners to the drawing room, and then, after a time, at last the new-crowned Queen began to talk of going to bed.

"You may depend upon it," Lord Melbourne urged her, "you are more tired than you think you are."

Himself, he thought he might possibly look in at the Duke of Wellington's, where a great ball was in progress; but had not quite made up his mind.

However, the day's heroine, filled with the sense both of relief and success, was restless, and instead of going to her bedroom, wandered on to the Duchess of Kent's balcony that faced the Green Park, and stayed there to look at the fireworks, at those long pencils of colored light, that one after another, speeding up into the soft darkness, gently exploded and then showered languidly downward in great bouquets of stars. Away on the farther side of the Park, over at Apsley House, the Duke of Wellington's ball was pursuing its course: beguilingly the music poured itself into the warm night, and to its sweet monitions the dancing figures twirled and whirled. As for the fair in Hyde Park that stretched from the Serpentine to Grosvenor Gate, it had become with its flares of light a magical place of shifting glimmer and shadow about the long lanes of booths, tents, and cafés. A man from Hackney had put up a tent "the interior of which, decorated with fluted pillars of glazed calico, had a really beautiful appearance." Beneath the trees came bursts of music from various bands vying with "the melodious beating of gongs." What a scene, if of vulgar and noisy hilarity, yet, to the eye, of lovely enchantment. The usual obscurity of the streets was dispersed with blazing illuminations, pictures made of light that perpetually trembled and fluctuated; while within and around all the theaters the general excitement of the evening must have reached seething point for, on this summer night of summer nights, all the theater doors were flung wide for any man or woman who felt so inclined to enter freely at their pleasure.

While all this furore was taking place, ensconced in some, to us unknown, house in London, Miss Harriet Martineau, returned from the Abbey, "satisfied my thirst, and went to sleep; and woke up to tea and to keep house with my mother while everybody else went out to see the illuminations." Recovered from her exhaustion, she found too that she had recovered from the bedazzlement of Prince Esterházy's diamond hat and from the general glamor of the day, and began to take up a very sharp attitude toward coronations in general, and Victoria's in particular. She had already impressed on her mother the "impiety" of all coronations, and now she exclaimed that today's affair "had turned out even worse than I expected." In imagination we see the two sipping at their cups of tea while the scolding voice harps on, as in her diary, over the "highly barbaric" ceremony she had just witnessed "worthy only of the old Pharaonic times in Egfipt . . . such a mixture of the Queen and the God, such homage to both . . . it made one's blood run cold." Further, "the Jewish or heathen ascription to him [God] of military and aristocratic rank and legal prerogative, side by side with the same ascription to the Queen, was the most coarse and irreverent celebration that I was ever a witness to." Further, the whole thing was "offensive" to Miss Martineau . . . and further . . .

and further ... But the upbraiding voice and the chink of teaspoons become merged ... confused ... and fade away into nothingness.

.   .   .   .   .   .

On the dim balcony the little figure still stood drinking in the warm night air and the transformation scene before her, of which she was the cause—she to acclaim whom every illumination quivered, each note of music rose in the air, each beaten gong reverberated.

Then, at last, she turned, and passing back through the window, disappeared into the heart of the palace.

CHAPTER XI
BRIGHTNESS FALLS FROM THE AIR

Wℋᴇɴ Lord Melbourne told Victoria that she had gone through the whole coronation ceremony "beautifully—every part of it, with so much taste," he was giving voice to what others in close proximity to her were to remark on all through her life, that innate theatrical sense which was curiously at variance with other sides of her nature. One who knew her well spoke of her "strongly-defined dramatic instinct"; saying that she "possessed to a degree shared with her by certain distinguished actors only, the genius of movement." Her actions as well as her movements were on occasions enhanced by this dramatic instinct. When she and Prince Albert visited Napoleon III and the Empress Eugénie in 1855, the Parisians at first hesitated as to their opinion of England's Queen. They were shocked at her clothes, her lack of chic, the smallness of her figure; *"La reine Mab"* flew with sardonic intonation from lip to lip. Then came the gala performance at the Opéra. "Everybody was watching for the sovereigns, and the moment was highly critical. The Empress was looking magnificent, a dream of silken splendour; the Queen . . . had made no effort to shine. But when the party arrived at the box of the Opera, her innate genius for movement inspired her. The Empress of the French . . . loitered at the door of the box: the Queen of England walked straight to the front, waiting for no help. . . . She stood there alone for a moment, surveying the vast concourse of society and then she slowly bowed on every side, with a smile which the most consummate actress might envy." That smile of the Queen's! "No smile was the least like it . . . no shadow of it is preserved for posterity in any one of her published likenesses." Now, as the crowded Opera House received that exquisite royal acknowledgment of their presence, an emotion ran through the audience. It was "a great moment ... the way it struck the French was extraordinary. 'La reine Mab' became from that day forth the idol of Parisian Society, and 'the way she did it,' the consummate skill of the thing, was celebrated everywhere by the amateurs of deportment."

To return to the coronation. While the excitement over it was in the air, many were the prospective husbands for the Queen that society suggested, championed, or protested against. The Tories, suspicious of the overwhelming influence Melbourne had acquired at the palace, imagined at one moment that he was intriguing to unite her with his nephew and secretary, William Cowper, at another that he was going to appropriate the national treasure for himself: while Mrs. Norton—if we are to believe the Paris correspondent of *Truth*—romantically sighed for Lord Eglinton, exclaiming, "What a pity it is that Lord Eglinton has not an opportunity of seeing the Queen often. If he had, she would surely fall in love with him. He is the most chivalrous among her subjects, and is just the right age, twenty-six. What life such a husband would throw into the Court." According to Thiers, Louis Philippe was full of plots and plans to acquire Victoria as a daughter-in-law; while England in general kept its eye on Lord Alfred Paget and the undoubted prestige given to him and his relations at Court.

At the moment Victoria's inclinations were turning more away from than toward marriage. That earnest schoolgirl who a year ago had ascended the throne was temporarily overlaid by a new personality which had been formed by a sense of continuous success, by being perpetually deferred to, applauded, admired. When she was an aging and saddened woman she remarked one day, "I can never be sufficiently thankful that I passed safely through those two years to my marriage." What was it in those early days that with youth at the prow and Lord Melbourne at the helm so menacingly drew near? This unnamed danger, preservation from which the older woman looked back on with such fervent gratitude? Certainly, cautious as Lord Melbourne was in what he imparted to her, daily intimacy with that sophisticated being, that accomplished hedonist, could not but ameliorate the child's early imposed primness of outlook, reveal to her attitudes of mind remarkably different from those that had been popular in the Kensington schoolroom. It was not in front of her that Lord Melbourne one day exclaimed, "Things have come to a pretty pass when religion is allowed to invade the sphere of private life." All the same, chance remarks he made must often have seemed to her like the twitching aside of a hitherto accepted curtain; such as, for instance, when the two had been discussing Macaulay's "immense learning."

"I observed," writes Victoria, "he was odd-looking."

"Uncouth, and not a man of the world," replied Lord Melbourne, "his father was a great Saint, and that restrained him a good deal."

Harriet Martineau noticed that about this time "The expression of her face was totally altered from what it had been at her accession." "It has become bold and disconcerted." Fundamentally her whole nature, as we have seen, was passionate, the Hanoverian blood was athud in her veins, and even Melbourne would at times have to tussle with her to turn her from an undesirable path. "For God's sake don't do that," he was one day overheard to cry out in alarm. There is no doubt that these first formative years of power before her marriage, filled as she was with all the dawn-energy and vivid emotions of youth, were for her a precarious period. It is possible her nature might have solidified and finally deteriorated into something very different from what, when she first took up her royal obligations, she had intended. Emphatic as her character was, she yet, like her mother, was curiously malleable in the hands of whoever at the moment held her deepest affection.

Her coronation had been the culminating point of this her first year of triumph and of self-realization, but, unknown to her, unguessed by Melbourne, without any premonitory whisper, a sinister happening was on its way that was to darken everything, and for the time entirely strip her of her popularity.

However, before she reached the entrance of that lamentable passage, there yet stretched before her several months on which the sunshine lingered.

2

A summer evening in the coronation year. There is a continuous murmur in the air, and as we listen we realize it comes from the drawing room of Buckingham Palace, from two voices that are conversing ... conversing; a mellifluous male voice that, now and again, explodes into shattering laughter, a young voice, tuneful as a little bell, asking for information, for enlightenment ... forever asking ... now one question, now another.

There was nothing Lord Melbourne was not ready to expatiate upon, and nothing that his listener was not eager to hear. Topic trod on the heels of topic—the new railroads; the vulgar shape of Lady Holland's mouth; the fashion, in Melbourne's young days, for well-bred, intelligent men to argue so furiously that they "got into a passion and swore at each other." Thunderstorms ("I told Lord Melbourne I never could forgive him for having stood under a tree in that violent thunderstorm at Windsor." "A sublime death," remarked Melbourne). Carnivals came under discussion, the singing of birds; Byron ("a pretty smile but treacherous beyond conception"), Victoria's clothes ("I assured him I had quantities of English things, but must sometimes have French"). And then, Eton! How delightful it was for Lord Melbourne to luxuriate on his days there to such an absorbed listener, those pristine days before the long-drawn pain of living had revealed itself to him. Who but England's Queen would not have thought him a plaguy bore when he related how on one occasion there he ate so many tarts that his face had burst into spots? But Victoria was engrossed, and down into her Journal went her Premier's "irruptions," jostling with Parliamentary procedure, magnetism, Richard III's deformity, and Heaven knows what else.

If Melbourne saw any signs of his pupil's self-assurance beginning to flag, he would set to work to reinstate her in her own good opinion. "Very nice party... everybody much pleased," he remarked one day about the concert she had given.

I smiled and said I feared I have done it very ill ... was not civil enough.

He said most kindly, "Oh no, quite the contrary, for I should have told you if it had been otherwise."

I had felt so nervous and shy.

That wasn't at all observed.

I said that I often stood before a person not knowing what to say.

The longer one stood thinking the worse it was . . . the best thing was to say anything commonplace and foolish better than to say nothing.

But if he endeavored to increase her self-assurance he did not hesitate to condemn anything he did not like.

I couldn't [she writes on one occasion], get my gloves on.
"It's those consumed rings," burst out Melbourne, "I never could bear them."
I said I was fond of them and that it improved my ugly hand.
"Makes it worse," retorted Melbourne.
I said I didn't wear them of a morning.
"Much better . . . and if you didn't wear them, nobody else would."

Regarding her difficulty on occasion of thinking of suitable observations to make to the numbers of people she had to be civil to, Charles Greville was far from letting her off so lightly as did Lord Melbourne. "As the words of Kings and Queens are precious," he writes sardonically, "and as a fair sample of a royal after-dinner colloquy, I shall record my dialogue with accurate fidelity."

The Queen: "Have you been riding to-day, Mr. Greville?"
"No, Madam, I have not."
"It was a fine day."
"Yes, Ma'am, a very fine day."
"It was rather cold though."
"It *was* rather cold, Madame."
(A pause when I took the lead through adhering to the same topic.)
"Has your Majesty been riding to-day?"
The Queen (with animation): "Oh yes, a very long ride."
"Has your Majesty got a nice horse?"
"Oh yes, a very nice horse."
Gracious smile and inclination of head on part of Queen, profound bow on mine, and then she turned again to Lord Grey.

The reader, to say the truth, is most struck by Greville's paucity of invention in himself clinging to the riding motif. One suspects him of plotting a piquant paragraph for his Diary.

3

During the Victoria-Melbourne duets, the Prime Minister, in his casual way, would occasionally pull out of his pocket a Bill that was to be read in the House, explaining it "in the *most clear and agreeable* manner possible." Inevitably, as his ascendancy over her grew, that of King Leopold began to suffer a slight decrease. That once paramount uncle was becoming increasingly aware of the fact, and instead of, as formerly, manipulating the movements of his niece's mind from his desk at Laeken, found himself impelled on one occasion to write her an almost whimpering, if at the same time ironic, letter craving her to lend an ear to his concern, this summer of 1838, regarding France's attitude toward Belgian policy.

"All I want from your kind Majesty is that you will *occasionally* express to your Ministers, and particularly to good Lord Melbourne, that, as far as it is *compatible* with the interests *of your own* dominions, you do *not* wish that your Government should take the *lead* in such measures as might in a short time bring on the *destruction* of this Country as well as that of your uncle and his family." This letter was duly shown to Lord Melbourne, who read it with "great attention," and then explained its political implications to Victoria, who in her turn confided in him that she thought it "rather hard to Uncle appealing to my feelings of affection for him." Finally, Lord Melbourne pocketed the letter to show to Lord Palmerston, who, as Foreign Minister, no doubt found the perusal of it infinitely amusing.

So, in discursive chat, evening after evening slipped by; some of the members of the royal household always decorously placed about the round table at the head of which sat the important pair. "By common consent the Royal evenings are the dullest possible, and no one *presumes* to make them less so," groaned Creevey who, at times, inwardly yawned his way through them. His ears, and those of others scattered about the big room, continuously filled with the murmur of that colloquy *à deux*, may well have been wearied to extinction, but Victoria was not. To her they were the most vivaciously interesting evenings she had ever spent. The art of conversing had most unwisely not been included in the Kensington curriculum, but with Melbourne she found herself involved, and with delightful ease, in the most perfect conversational web; and for the moment she asked nothing more.

Society, all eyes, all ears, ceaselessly watching and conjecturing, became ever more intrigued as to what would be the outcome of this intimacy. "She really has nothing to do with anybody but Melbourne, and with him she passes ... more hours than any two people, in any relation of life, perhaps, ever do pass together.... He is at her side for at least six hours every day—an hour in the morning, two on horseback, one at dinner, and two in the evening. This monopoly is certainly not judicious," wrote Greville. "I hope you were amused at the report of Lord Melbourne being likely to marry the Queen," observed Creevey. "I for myself," remarked Princess Lieven to Lord Grey, "cannot help imagining that she must be going to marry him."

Were the two actually in love? A trite question to which there can be no clear answer. To both, the idea of marrying each other was so outside the bounds of probability or feasibility that one cannot imagine it so much as crossed the mind of either. But one thing can be said with certainty. Each, at this time, was the delight of the other's life. Both capable of intensely loving; both instinctively desirous of that state: each was to the other, in a spiritual sense, the substitute for a lover.

4

While the warm rays of success and popularity still envelop the new Queen, we will draw close and watch her during the course of one of her ordinary days; for, thanks chiefly to the Duchess de Praslin (daughter of the French Ambassador), who was constantly treading the royal carpets, and noticing everything with an eye perhaps more shrewd than charitable, we are well informed on the subject.

"Queen Victoria," writes our French observer in a letter to a friend, "is an early riser.... She dresses quickly, and takes a turn in the Palace gardens with her dog, Dash, spends two hours signing papers, and shows a naïve belief in the necessity of this quill-driving work.... At a quarter to ten she breakfasts." Breakfast with Lehzen was an easygoing meal in Victoria's private room, and it is extremely doubtful whether the Duchess of Kent was invited to share this

CONCERT AT THE
CHATEAU D'EU DURING
QUEEN VICTORIA AND
PRINCE ALBERT'S VISIT
TO KING LOUIS-PHILIPPE
AND QUEEN ADELAIDE
IN 1843

The two Queens and the
King are seated at the
table, Prince Albert standing behind them

From the water-colour by
Eugène Lami

*By gracious permission of
H.M. The King*

QUEEN VICTORIA AT THE OPERA

From the portrait by E. T. Parris

intimacy. She did, however, always appear at dinner; a show occasion when everything was tightened up to the most ceremonious. To return to Victoria's breakfast. "She has a good appetite," goes on the Duchesse de Praslin, "enjoys having a French *chef*, or at any rate the dainty dishes he sends to her table. Baroness Lehzen is always with her in the morning. . . .

"The Duchess of Kent is without influence, greatly neglected, and feels it bitterly. . . . Mother and daughter only meet at table and in the drawing-rooms. Their conversation is generally in the forenoon on the letters the Duchess receives from abroad,—from Brussels, Paris, Stuttgart, Frankfort, Leiningen, Thün, and Coburg, and on the new books she reads. The Duchess mother is a great devourer of books, and gives verbal summaries of her readings. Lord Melbourne is often kept waiting as these chats go on." (No doubt purposely by the Duchess, who, as we have seen, detested Melbourne.) "When the Queen breaks them off she kisses her mother, and goes into another room to receive the Prime Minister. . . . She is capable of great self-control; yet her countenance is often the index to her mind and feelings, though it can hardly be called expressive. But she cannot hide anger or annoyance, which does not embellish her. The Melbourne Cabinet is now dependent on her favour. Ministers tremble when this young being shows discontent at anything. . . . She is not pleased at the inability of the Woods and Forests to turn the King of Hanover out of Clarence House, which she wants for the Duchess of Kent. He sticks to it 'as a British Prince,' and when she marries—whenever that may be—the Queen will have to hire a residence for the Duchess." For the Duke of Cumberland, now marooned in his own small kingdom of Hanover, kept a sharp and, with his character, inevitably jealous, eye on his far more important niece, and anything that he considered belonged to him in the country of his birth he was determined to keep a tight clutch on. "Careless about etiquette at the time of her accession," goes on the Duchesse de Praslin, "the Queen has undergone a marked change in this respect. She has a strong sense of ownership, of her personal rights, of her regal supremacy, and is exacting of respect, as shown in the small rules and regulations that make her closet a sanctuary. The smallest infringement of etiquette is met with a sharp, not to say irate, glance. The household ceremonial bristles with etiquette. Methinks the Baroness [Lehzen] has persuaded her that the rigid observance of etiquette will prevent the party she keeps out from slandering her."

But it seems that here—taking etiquette in the sense of decorous behavior in general—the Duchesse de Praslin thought wrong. Unexpectedly, it appears to have been Melbourne who had cast this strict aegis of propriety over the royal household. Himself shrugging his shoulders in contempt of "this damned morality," when it was a question of the Queen's personal Household, he was one of the first, with his strict rules of propriety, to promulgate what now, in the moral sense, is known as Victorianism. He must have been well aware that the Tories had a handle against him regarding his tutorial situation in the palace, for had he not been cited as corespondent in the Norton suit, and involved in that scandal over Lady Brandon? "It was inevitable," wrote Emily Crawford, the recipient of much passed-on Victorian talk, "that the Carlton Club should redden with virtuous indignation, and the more dunderheaded members of the country clergy denounce the Queen, and speak of her palace as the resort of roués and wantons." No doubt news had reached these clerics' ears—and the news was true—that the Queen's Lord Chamberlain, Lord Conyngham (whose wife, incidentally, was a Paget), had inserted his mistress as housekeeper at Buckingham Palace; also that Lord Uxbridge (the head of the Paget Palace group) had found a place for his chosen amorata among the royal domestic staff. The gutter press edged as near the truth as it dared by dubbing Windsor Castle "The Paget Club House." The Queen would have been as ignorant of these facts as Lord Melbourne must have been cognizant of them. The reason that he, so zealous for his charge's reputation, made no move is in all probability because he considered that to try to effect a palace purge would, by drawing the world's attention, create a worse scandal than if he left things alone.

Having had his own skin scorched had made him doubly alive to the circumspection necessary in the ordering of this very young unmarried Queen's female entourage if she was to live unscathed by criticism. It was he who regulated the very steps of the youthful maids of honor when they begged to be allowed to escape for an hour or so from the chilliness and the tedium of their individual sitting rooms at Windsor. It certainly seems curious that it should have been left to the Premier to arrange in what meshes of propriety the young maids of honor should be confined. "Lord Melbourne seems amazingly at his ease," writes Lady Lyttelton; and it is obvious it was his to give *the* final word in any matter in which he chose to arbitrate. "I should think," Lady Lyttelton continues, "it would be hard to displace Lord Melbourne by any intrigue, constitutional or otherwise, while her present Majesty lives, unless he contrives to displace himself by dint of consommés, truffles, pears, ices and anchovies, which he does his best to revolutionize his stomach with every day." "His situation," wrote Croker, "is certainly the most despotic that the world has ever seen. Wolsey and Walpole were in strait waistcoats compared with him ... as between himself and the Sovereign he is a perfect Maire du Palais."

"The maids of honour (Miss Lister and Miss Paget) are very coaxy and wheedly with me," writes Lady Lyttelton at the time when she was in authority over their comings and goings.

"Lady Lyttelton," would come the cry, "*Mayn't* I walk *just for once* by myself on the slopes? I know it's against the rules, but what harm *can* it do? We *used* to be allowed, but now Lord Melbourne won't let us. I'm sure we *never* have met anybody there, except once only Mr. Van de Weyer, and what could that signify?"

But the shadow of Lord Melbourne lay across Lady Lyttelton's mind.

"No, no," she would protest. Another day there would be "a gentle knock: 'Lady Lyttelton, *may* I go out? My feet are *so* cold, poking up in my room all the morning! I will only go on the Terrace, and keep quite in sight. *Pray* let me.'"

Here was something Melbourne permitted. "Yes, yes," would be the answer.

But the Duchesse de Praslin is continuing to act as cicerone....

"Her [the Queen's] facility in speaking foreign languages is remarkable. She controls her shyness, sets diplomats at their ease by her composure, and speaks to them in French, German and Italian.... Her favourite recreation at Brighton is riding on the Downs. She rides with Lord Melbourne there as at Windsor, a cavalcade of visitors and equerries sweeping after her. On Council days the rides follow the Councils. She changes her dress for a habit in a few minutes, and is off. . . . Those about Court miss the friendly unceremonious ways of William IV, who always asked people to whom he gave audiences to sit down, and waived every kind of ceremony at Brighton. . . . In giving audiences he sat with his face to the light. Had his tongue been as discreet as it was the contrary, his face, full lighted by the window, would have betrayed him. He sometimes sat for a few hours with the sun on him, talking to the same person. Queen Adelaide, or Lady Mary Fox or some other Fitzclarence daughter, was free to listen to the King's conversation with his Ministers. His successor is reticent from education, and has got *finesse*. . . . Not a soul but herself and Melbourne knows what goes on when she gives him audiences. Perhaps he tells his colleagues; she tells nobody.

"The Queen has adopted the French fashion of making the middle of the dinner-table the head. . . . When she was quite fresh to the throne, the highest gentlemen present sat to her right and left; but since Melbourne has become a favourite, he always sits beside her. The Queen is fast losing her girlish prettiness; one can almost see it vanishing. I should now call her plain, unless when she listens to music, which has an extraordinary effect in beautifying her. She sings prettily. Hers is a sweet but rather small voice (*un petit filet de voix*). She chats prettily too, but it is noticed that she never says anything worth repeating. The whist-tables are spread every evening, and the Duchess [of Kent] after a little doze in a corner has her rubber. Attention has now been called by the Tories to the good lady receiving Paris *modes* through British and Belgian diplomats. Everyone is in bed at the Court before midnight! but when there is a ball, the Queen dances until four or five in the morning. She has a passion for dancing."

"One lovely summer morning," writes one of the girl guests, who often went to the small dances at Buckingham Palace, "One lovely summer morning we had danced till dawn, and the quadrangle being then open to the east, Her Majesty went out on the roof of the portico to see the sun rise." A sprinkling of her guests, the young girls soft-looking as doves in their light-hued dresses, were about her. All the youthful faces were turned to where, across the trees, the sky behind St. Paul's began to glow and intensify.

The dawn hush that enveloped this scene of leafy tree tops hid, in reality, beneath its outspread tranquillity, sordid miseries and horrors of which, enclosed within her gentle Utopia behind the Palace walls, the Queen had no conception. Now, bemused with happiness and the dance rhythms still vibrating through their veins, the little group were caught up in that expanding splendor before them. "One of the most beautiful sights I ever remember," wrote one of that cluster years later; "it rose behind St. Paul's which we saw quite distinctly; Westminster Abbey and the trees in the Green Park stood out against the sky ... the scene remains to this day ... fixed on my memory."

5

In the general way dinner at Buckingham Palace and at Windsor was nominally at half-past seven, at which time the guests would mass themselves to wait for that small royal procession of, first the gentlemen of the Household, then the diminutive person of the Queen, then the Duchess of Kent, and the Queen's ladies. Except for herself and Melbourne, endlessly gossiping and amusing each other as they eat up all the succulent offerings of the royal chefs, it does not seem that anyone else much enjoyed this grandiose meal. "Barely endurable from stiffness," groaned Lady Lyttelton soon after her arrival as a lady of the bedchamber; her one wish at these palace collations being to be within talking distance of Lehzen, whose conversation apparently contained more substance than did that of most of the Court. "Baroness Lehzen sits further off from my exalted rank every day," sighed Lady Lyttelton, "and I am sadly by myself and pinnacled up with only one tight little hand over my head."

The owner of the tight little hand did not realize what a perspicacious gaze this shrewd member of her Household often turned on her, and that Lady Lyttelton already had surmised "a vein of iron that runs through her most extraordinary character"—a vein of iron passed on from her father.

Lady Lyttelton emphasizes Lehzen's goodness to her when, at Windsor Castle, she first took up her post at Court. "Arrived," she writes, "and found Mme Lehzen very kind and helpful. . . . The

Queen is perfectly kind and civil and good natured.... There is such heartiness and seemingly good temper about all the Royal Family to judge from manner and look, it is nice to see them.... On our drive home she [Victoria] read a *lesson book,* Sir Robert Walpole's life by Coxe, very attentive and good.... Duchess of Kent struggling with sleep." Later Lady Lyttelton talks of going to the play in attendance on her youthful mistress. "Going to the play in this private way is very pleasant, sitting, and in shawls all the time. If her Majesty would wear less than *four* different wraps (all to be taken care of and to be put on) and go there without a bouquet, *and* a bag, *and* an opera-glass, there would be no difficulty at all. But she continues quite patient and kind."

To return to Lehzen. She had become well known for the spiritual cordial she administered to all bewildered newcomers. "Madame de Lehzen is the lady to whom I would refer you whenever you have anything to ask for," wrote Lady Ravensworth to her youthful daughter when she was about to become a maid of honor. "She is (I have heard from Minnie) a kind and motherly person to the young ladies."

How serene now, compared with past days, was the life of this closest companion of Victoria's childhood and girlhood. She was still the *alter ego.* Hers was the day-in, day-out familiar figure that Victoria loved to see moving about her own personal rooms that looked out on the palace gardens. Or the faithful creature would be bent over her writing desk as she industriously wrote out copies of all Victoria's private correspondence. Lehzen, swept into this new and exalted atmosphere, had preened her feathers—those feathers often so sadly ruffled at Kensington—and, as we read of her, her personality seems as if it had become enlarged. An intelligent woman, and an extremely voluble one, she savored living at the core of the palace life, enjoyed this constant arrival of outstanding people to talk to. We hear her one evening at Windsor keeping up "a lively fire upon Lord Glenelg, accusing him, half in fun, of being too lazy." Charles Greville, who for conversation demanded a worth-while companion, wrote in his diary after a royal evening, "Sat next Baroness Lehzen at dinner, a clever, agreeable woman." "I had," chimes in Lord Broughton after being at the castle, "a pleasant talk with Madame Lehzen."

Lehzen, Melbourne, and Stockmar formed the palace trium-virate. All three being exceptional characters, fundamentally wise and appreciative of each other's qualities, they functioned, each in their own sphere, without jar. Certainly the Duchesse de Praslin considered that Lehzen "is not pleased at the extraordinary favour Melbourne enjoys," but if this was so, she did not allow her private feelings to poison the palace harmony. We catch in one of Lady Lyttelton's paragraphs a revealing glimpse of Lehzen at Windsor —a paragraph so charming that it must be quoted all but in full.

Sunday Evening October 1838.
Twice to church, and after the last having walked as fast as was at all convenient just an hour on the Terrace and round the great *parterre* with the Queen. A most beautiful sight and sound it was. The crowds of people!—among whom the Queen walked, hardly able to get along at first, they press up to her so. *Il faut la voir* tripping up towards a thick-set row of men, women, and Eton boys, as smiling and spirited as if *they* would do her no harm, till at last they fall back and make way for her. Her courtiers just tap them back as she gets close. Then the scene! The castle on one side, with the great standard over it; the view on the other; and around us the garden, the *jet d'eau*, and all under the influence of the *very* finest military music; and not least pleasing to me, Mme de Lehzen's pale face (the only face I ever see that seems to feel what is going on *at all*), with her usual half-anxious, smiling, fixed look following the Queen from one of the castle windows.

That all should be well with this child of her spirit was her one consuming desire. Yes, at present all was harmony for the German pastor's daughter. Conroy's bodily position, safely removed to the Duchess of Kent's apartments and never allowed in Victoria's, was symbolic of his lapse from any power of reaching her with his gibes and his intrigues. To all appearance Lehzen's warfare was accom-plished. Certainly the Tory newspapers were beginning to fidget over the influence that the three foreigners, Lehzen, Stockmar, and Leopold, had over England's Queen, suggesting that it was they who, for reasons of their own, were alienating her from her mother. But Lehzen, surrounded by the living hedge of her former pupil's affection, knew herself secure from the comments of any newspaper.

"My *precious* Lehzen," Victoria had written the year before she came to the throne, "My *precious* Lehzen... my 'best and truest' friend I have had for nearly 17 years, and I trust I shall have for 30 or 40 and many more!" and though at seventeen emotions are more in bud than in flower, Victoria's years of maiden queenhood were not to deflect her in the slightest from her devotion.

Now, as Lehzen looked ahead, never could the least suspicion have crossed her mind that the warning, "*Put not your trust in Princes,*" could have any application to herself.

CHAPTER XII

DISASTER AT BUCKINGHAM PALACE

THE year of 1839 had reached no further than January before the first indications arose of the disaster that, for months to come, was to disturb the tranquillity of the Palace, for the time being to turn England's "baby of a queen" from a figure of love into a target for censure, to convulse the whole country with argumentation and partisanship, and to reverberate in all the capitals of Europe. No incident so clearly reveals the social tone and valuations of the day as does the Flora Hastings scandal: it is an education in the understanding of the temperament of the upper classes especially, both men and women. And yet, from inadvertence, or from exaggerated prudery, this, to the onlooker, valuable and absorbing human document, with all its intricacy of action, its mental interplay between some of the most conspicuous characters of the time, has, in any life of Queen Victoria, been merely glanced at in a few hasty paragraphs. This affair was the culminating point, the final ugly fruit, of all the personal hostilities, the atmosphere of malice that we saw engendered in Kensington Palace, chiefly by the presence of Conroy, and continuing only too thrivingly within the walls of Buckingham Palace. There became closely involved in this "grand scampiglio" not only the Queen herself, but her doctor, Sir James Clark; the Duke of Wellington, Melbourne, Brougham, the Duchess of Kent, Lord Hastings and his mother, Lord Portman and Lord Tavistock and their wives, and Flora Hastings' uncle, Mr. Hamilton Fitzgerald. These are the most outstanding of the actors, backed by a confused jargon of disputing voices, English, French, Belgian, Italian. The tragic aspect of the affair was the victimization of a blameless young woman who was already within a few months of her death.

In the Duchess of Kent's drawing room at the palace the tittering little jokes between Conroy and Lady Flora still flicked to and fro between them as they used to in former days at Kensington. This January they had a special cause for merriment—one that lent itself to many a giggling innuendo; for Lady Flora, just returned from a visit to Scotland, had on the way there traveled in the same post chaise as Conroy. This splendid joke was unfortunately not kept caged within the Duchess of Kent's drawing room; it began to flutter about in other parts of the palace. And, still more unfortunately, it began, in the minds of the occupants of the palace, to ally itself with their knowledge of "the familiar habits in the Duchess' apartments": those easy flippancies that were an everyday feature in the life of the Duchess of Kent's group.

On the day of Lady Flora's return from Scotland, which was on January 10, she went into waiting. Also, the same day, having a pain in her side, and her figure being unusually distended, she consulted Sir James Clark, who was physician to both the Duchess of Kent and the Queen. From now on Lady Flora began to see Sir James about twice a week concerning her health. Though she was such a close friend of Conroy, the Queen included her in the general armistice that she maintained—but to outward appearance only —between her own Household and her mother's.

Lady Lyttelton, writing one day of the Queen's accurate memory, remarks, "So much for her memory, which, as well as Her Majesty's eyes, nose and ears, nothing escapes ever," and now, when on her return from Scotland, Lady Flora in her attendance on the Duchess was constantly seen moving about here and there in the Queen's drawing room, Victoria's prominent blue eyes would at times thoughtfully, if surreptitiously, dwell on the outline of her figure. There was no doubt about it: it had changed. Unmistakably, she had every appearance of a woman who was pregnant. Lady Portman, one of the Queen's ladies, had also been observing and pondering. She one day voiced her suspicions to the Queen, and when she "found it was her Majesty's own idea," she, so she admitted later, "talked a great deal to the Queen on the subject." Lady Tavistock, another of Victoria's ladies in waiting, made a third in these intimate talks. All three became convinced, either that Flora Hastings was secretly married, or that she was an immoral woman, and they decided that some step must be taken. The natural thing, as Lady Flora was in the Duchess' service, would have been for Victoria to go straight to her mother and leave the matter for her to deal with. But it seems that relations between the two Households had now reached that point of prickly hostility when such a course was out of the question. The next best thing was to approach Flora Hastings directly, and Lady Tavistock now took on herself the role of investigator.

"I felt much desire," she said later, "to speak to her at once upon the subject, but circumstances occurred which prevented my carrying the wish into effect." What circumstances? These are never revealed; and it was just her allowing these unnamed circumstances to trip her up that was, if circuitously, yet actually, to bring the whole rumpus into being. Lady Tavistock had made a muddle over that affair of her wet stockings, and, by letting herself be deflected from carrying out a sensible decision, another muddle was to start now. Ignoring her original intention, she asked Lord Melbourne to come to see her, and in what she calls "the most delicate and cautious manner," told him of the suspicions afloat. That urbane man remarked that he did not believe in these rumors, and, further, that he "desired the ladies of the Court to be quiet." Afterward, however, he sent for Sir James Clark and questioned him on the subject. Sir James told him that "without more ample means of observation I could not venture to give an opinion." On hearing this Melbourne decided that "no steps should be taken."

As Lady Tavistock had placed the responsibility for action, or no action, on Lord Melbourne, she and her colleague, Lady Portman, had no need to torment themselves further about, as they phrased it, "the honour of the Queen's household." The whole thing was now out of their hands. But they did not think so, or, one cannot help suspecting, they did not wish to think so. It is evident that they hoped to bring about a moral disruption in the Duchess of Kent's Household: a consummation which in the circumstances they no doubt thought was justified. But why this eagerness? Someone must have had a desire to pay off old scores. From various indications, one gets the impression that it was not Flora Hastings herself against whom Lady Portman and Lady Tavistock had any particular animus, but another behind her. Proved culpability on her part would practically be proved culpability on the part of Conroy, so appositely would that fatally-shared post chaise and all the jokes that clustered round it fit into the undoing of these two close friends. If we are right in believing that it was Conroy whom Lady Portman and Lady Tavistock wished to get ousted from the palace, this was a desire shared by many. By Melbourne himself for instance. Only a few months before, he had met Lady Harriet Baring at dinner—at one of those London summer dinners when all the ladies, by placing their bouquets in their tumblers, turned the table into a bed of flowers—and had expatiated to her on the nuisance that Conroy was making himself to everyone, how he was always in and out of the palace, and how regrettable it was that they "had not made it part of the bargain when they gave him his pension that he should go abroad." The Duke of Wellington, too, his grandfatherly eye forever benignly bent on Buckingham Palace and its youthful Queen, longed to see the mischievous fellow pushed out of the country.

Flora Hastings was an intelligent, levelheaded young woman, and had a sense of humor; therefore it is worth consideration that she speaks later of the "diabolical conspiracy from which it has pleased God to preserve the Duchess of Kent and myself: for that it was intended to ruin the whole concern [viz. the reputation of the Duchess' Household] though I was to be the first victim." She also, rightly or wrongly, believed that Lehzen ("whose hatred to the Duchess is no secret") was working away in the background.

To return to the watchful ladies Portman and Tavistock. Finding that Melbourne made no more, they decided themselves to take drastic action. On February 16, which was a Saturday, Lady Portman had a talk with Sir James Clark, during which he "found it had been determined upon that he should acquaint Lady Flora with the suspicions which existed in the Palace." Not only this, but it was clearly impressed on him that nothing less than a medical examination could put to rest the suspicions of "the ladies of the palace," so certain were they that their surmises were well founded.

As Clark listened to what it was that she required of him, he must have clearly realized that if he allowed himself to be used as an instrument by "the ladies of the palace" to insult Lady Flora by these suspicions, and demands for a medical examination, he would be cutting himself off from any possibility of continuing physician to the Duchess of Kent and her Household. What the impulsion was that made him decide to break with the Duchess' group, and to throw his weight entirely on the side of the young Queen's, is not known. But it is clear from his subsequent behavior that he did so decide, and that the successful proving of Flora Hastings' guilt was the rich offering that he hoped to be able to present to the Queen's ladies. And, incidentally, not only to present to the Queen's ladies, but to the Queen herself, for the condemnation of Lady Flora would, as we have seen, involve the complete undoing of Victoria's lifelong detestation, Conroy. It is evident that her two ladies would not have embarked on the course they were so enthusiastically pursuing without her consent, but, considering her youthful inexperience, and the reliance she would naturally have placed on these married women, one cannot feel that any serious blame should be attached to her.

Now, at the end of his talk with Lady Portman, James Clark, inevitably foreseeing the applause he would gain for himself in the Queen's Household if all went according to plan, did not hesitate a moment. "Immediately after this interview with Lady Portman," so he wrote later, "I went to Lady Flora." He found her alone; and her stupefaction can be imagined when he asked her point blank whether she was "privately married."

She gave him an "emphatic denial." This denial, however, instead of quieting the doctor, stirred him in the most surprising manner. "He became excited," so she wrote later, "urged me to 'confess' as the only thing to save me—stated his own conviction to agree with that of the 'ladies,' that it had occurred to him at first that 'no-one could look at me and doubt it,' and remarks even yet more coarse."

"I observed to him that the swelling from which I had been suffering was very much reduced." As proof of this she offered to show him the dresses she had worn when her shape was distended, so that he could compare them with those she was wearing at present. But Clark waved aside any idea that her figure had become normal.

"Well, I don't think so," he shot back at her. "You seem to me to grow larger every day, and so the ladies think."

The wrought-up man went on to say that pregnancy was "the only supposition" which could explain at once "her appearance and state of health." "Or else," he added, "you must have some very bad illness." As he himself admitted this alternative, why, when during this interview Lady Flora emphatically assured him that "his supposition was untrue and perfectly groundless," did he not accept the possibility of this alternative? Instead, he only flung at her "nothing but a medical examination could satisfy the ladies of the palace, so deeply were their suspicions rooted." It must be noted that one of the most disgraceful aspects of this palace racket was that the Duchess of Kent, who, as royal mistress of Flora Hastings, should have been the first person to be consulted when suspicions arose about her lady of the bedchamber, had not so far been approached by anyone.

To return to the strange colloquy that is taking place in one of the rooms at Buckingham Palace. Sir James now informed his—to use her own adjective—"shattered" victim that it was Lady Portman who had whispered the supposition in his ear, and that therefore he must now hurry off to her with Lady Flora's denial. And leaving the room, away he went on this mission.

Before long he was back; but all he had to bring her was Lady Portman's still fixed belief that she was *enciente*. He then reiterated his demand for a medical examination and, so it appears, added that "it was the more imperative as the rumour had reached her Majesty." Ill as Lady Flora already was in body, and now harrowed in mind, she kept her head admirably, and told him that "I should not shrink from any examination however rigorous, but that I considered it a most delicate and disagreeable procedure, and that I would not be hurried into it." Realizing now what hostility was ranged against her, she also most sensibly insisted that at this examination another doctor, Sir Charles Mansfield Clarke, who had known her from childhood, should be present. To this Sir James agreed, but he now burst into "earnest entreaties" that the examination should take place that very day, and, when she refused, so excitedly eager was he for her condemnation, and so warped in consequence had become his outlook, that, so he later admitted, this refusal on Flora Hastings' part for an instant examination "lessened very considerably on my mind the effect of her Ladyship's denial."

The interview at last came to an end, and Flora Hastings was left with the realization that in the eyes of Buckingham Palace she was now under suspicion of conduct that, if true, would have branded her as a moral outcast to the day of her death. Position, reputation, respect, social acceptance, possibility of marriage, all sunk for ever. As first proof of this, and conclusive thrust on this dreadful Saturday, a message was given her that "it was her Majesty's pleasure that I should not appear until my character was cleared by the means suggested." This message was curiously unjust. Why should she be considered more of a criminal this Saturday than she had been for these last weeks, when she had been allowed to take her place at the Queen's dinner table? The explanation must be that Victoria and her overzealous ladies had accepted Clark's view that the victim's wish to put off the examination till the next day indicated the probability of her guilt.

As for Lady Flora herself, her knowledge of her innocence can only have partly lessened to her the overwhelming nature of such an accusation, for at that date even the suspicion of scandal was enough to smirch the reputation of any woman, and most especially of an unmarried woman, for life. One might say that at that time the pattern of society, as far as sex was concerned, was arranged differently from what it is at present. Across it lay a band of semi-obscurity, a terrain at once murky and perturbing, the world of the great demimondaines, a race of women whose type is now all but extinct; for this race is to be distinguished from the thousands who ply their trade along the night streets, though in some cases it was from that class that they originated. The demimonde was composed of the most exclusive and *recherché* courtesans who, expensive mistresses of the well-born and fashionable young men of their day, lived in visible and triumphant sin. The names of these women, if seldom known in the drawing rooms of Mayfair or in the big country houses, were common knowledge in the billiard- and gun-rooms of these houses. These baleful flowers of humanity, leading their peculiar lives at once of glamour and mortification, of luxury and insecurity, were often women of marked personality, of intelli-

gence, and sometimes of unusual wit. Such a one was Mary Anne
Clarke, the famous mistress of Victoria's uncle of York; such, equal
in fame if not in wit, was Harriet Wilson, who has left behind her
a very doubtfully accurate autobiography. Another was that outstanding mid-Victorian figure "Skittles," who, starting as a pros-
titude in the glaring, gas-lit "flash-crib" world of the Haymarket,
became mistress to a future Duke, and a habituée of Hyde Park,
driving along the Ladies' Mile to an accompaniment of lifted top
hats from the young guardsmen and other loungers who had been
leaning on the railings waiting to see her drive by. Landseer exhibited a portrait of her (under another name than her own) at the
Academy. Wilfrid Scawen Blunt wrote poems in her laudation,
and referred, a little surprisingly, to "those childish eyes." As the
years went on, though she stayed chiefly at Brown's Hotel, she
rented houses in Mayfair where she entertained royalties, diplomats—English as well as foreign—sportsmen, the Shah, and on
one occasion, even Mr. Gladstone. She lived on and on, and, when
an old woman, Lord Kitchener would be seen bending over her
bath chair as it was slowly drawn along the paths of Hyde Park.
The gaiety and the laxer morals of the Marlborough House set
under Edward VII, reverberating through the more pliable and
imitative section of English society, had no doubt much to do with
the gradual disappearance of the world of the great courtesan; but
on the Continent it was to last longer.

    To compete with these beautiful women, and women as astute as
they were beautiful, who, body and soul, lived but to please men,
the young girls in society, if eager for marriage, had to treasure
any attribute they possessed that their formidable rivals did not;
hence the supreme value of an unblemished reputation. Even the
dullest or dowdiest debutante could lay claim to this shining
treasure: the one virtue that those seductive creatures, ensconced in
their little houses in St. John's Wood and Kensington with their
flower-decked balconies, definitely could not lay claim to. Bearing
all this in mind, the completely disruptive nature of the accusation
leveled at Flora Hastings can be understood. Charles Greville,
writing of the affair, says that "though such things sometimes
happen in the servants' hall, or housekeepers charge still-room or
kitchen-maids with frailty and pregnancy, they are unprecedented

and unheard of in good society, and among people in high, or even respectable, circles."

It is said that in medieval times unicorns were preoccupied with the virginity of maidens to an exceptional degree. They had indeed developed second sight in the matter, and as they galloped about Europe would kneel in homage before any immaculate maiden they encountered, thus bestowing on her as it were an accolade for virtuous behavior. But, alas for Flora Hastings, the only outstanding one of these discerning animals in England was occupied in guarding the royal coat of arms, and showed no interest in the justification of virgins. Therefore it behooved every young woman to behave with the utmost circumspection and regard for her good name if she wished to remain in the ranks of those among whom eligible men would consider choosing a wife. People in general had then fewer matters of public interest to occupy their minds, so that any scandal in what was then called "high life" reverberated with a din and a continuity, was canvassed in the press and discussed in every class of society with a heat and excitement that to us seems surprising.

Here then on that Saturday evening was the once flippant-tongued but now stunned Flora Hastings, realizing the unwisdom of all those sprightly little post-chaise jokes tossed to and fro in the Duchess of Kent's drawing-room, foreseeing the gossip that would inevitably percolate through the palace walls to the world outside, and, whatever the result of the examination, the lasting harm that would accrue to herself.

After Sir James's ultimatum to her, he had gone to the Duchess of Kent and announced to her his determined "conviction" that her young lady of the bedchamber was pregnant. He was followed by Lady Portman emphasizing to the Duchess the extraordinary situation that had arisen by bringing her the Queen's message forbidding Flora Hastings to appear at her dinner table "till the examination had decided matters." Lady Portman also took this opportunity of "distinctly pressing" her own opinion of the young woman's guilt. The Duchess' response to all this surprising information was at once to dismiss Sir James Clark from her service, to refuse to see Lady Portman again, and to announce that if Lady Flora was not to appear at the Queen's table, neither would she.

On Sunday, the next day, the medical examination took place. In the room, besides the two doctors, James Clark and Charles Mansfield Clarke, were Lady Portman, and Flora Hastings' maid. The examination proceeded. At its conclusion James Clark found himself signing, in conjunction with Charles Clarke, a certificate stating that "there are no grounds for believing that pregnancy does exist, or ever has existed." The cause of Flora Hastings' enlarged figure was a growth on the liver.

That evening Lady Portman did what she inevitably had to do. She came to Lady Flora "to express her regret for having been the most violent" in her accusations. Her victim seems to have shown little resentment, merely voicing her surprise "that knowing my family as she did, she could have entertained these suspicions."

That evening, and, so it appears, for weeks afterward, the Duchess would not allow the injured girl to attend the Queen's dinner, nor would she take her place at it herself. Victoria, however, sincerely kindhearted as in reality she was, was most distressed at the whole affair, and as she made her apologies to Lady Flora, the tears came to her eyes.

2

In one of the rooms of his Leicestershire home, Donington Park, Lord Hastings was undergoing all the discomforts of an attack of influenza.

He was just over thirty, two years younger than his sister Flora, and a chivalrous, warm-blooded, and extremely determined young man; especially ready for prompt action in any direction in which he considered the honor of himself or his family was involved.

One day this February he opened a letter from his sister at Buckingham Palace, and read—to use his own phrase—that "her honour had been most basely assailed." She gave him no particulars; but for her impetuous brother, that was not necessary. The walls of Buckingham Palace gleamed before him as a goal for his wrath, and the same day, within the shortest possible time, he was seated within a post chaise that night and day without pause, stopping only for relays of horses, was bearing him along the road to London.

On arriving, he went straight to his sister, and, so he says, was "horror-struck" at "the disgusting truths" which he now heard in detail. He at once fixed on Melbourne as the instigator of the whole business. Nothing, he decided, would meet the case but a duel, and he hurried off to Lord Winchelsea to ask him to act as his second. Lord Winchelsea sensibly advised him, first, to see Melbourne himself. He did, only to discover that Melbourne's sole part in the affair had been to beg everyone to keep quiet. At this, Hastings changed his plans, and announced that he was now determined on an interview with the Queen, so as to discover from her "who were the originators of the plot." The harassed Melbourne, horrified at this threat of a further stirring-up of the situation, entreated him to be "as quiet as possible for the sake of . . . the youth of the Queen, and the delicacy of the affair."

Then an idea came to the Prime Minister. He would pass on this hotheaded champion to the Duke of Wellington. He would know how to make him see reason. And, too, the Duke would thoroughly enjoy the process. Deprived now of a Napoleon to circumvent, he found in any dispute at Buckingham Palace just such a field for advice and arbitration as he most delighted in. He loved, wrote an intimate, "being consulted and mixed up in *messes*," and most especially, so it seems, did he enjoy the excitement of any royal mess. Therefore, to Wellington Lord Hastings was sent.

That experienced old man advised "for the sake of avoiding the painfulnesses of publicity, that the matter should rest where it now is."

But to leave the matter *in statu quo* was exactly what Hastings was determined not to do. He now wrote to Lord Melbourne, demanding an interview with Victoria herself. Then, within the solid sobriety of the Burlington Hotel, in the vicinity of Bond Street, he awaited a reply.

Two days passed, and none came. Exasperated to a degree, he sat down, and drew toward him a sheet of writing paper.

My Lord,

Having in vain waited for two days, in the hope of having an audience with Her Majesty, which I requested (if not as a matter of right as a Peer, at least as one of feeling), my patience being exhausted, and being anxious to return to the bosom of my afflicted and insulted family I am forced to resort to the only means now left in my power, of recording my abhorrence and detestation of the treatment which my sister has lately sustained, by addressing myself to you as the *organ* through whom all things are *now* carried on at Court...though by your assertion on your word of honour as a gentleman, that the whole thing rests with the ladies of the Court, yet I cannot bring myself to think that it has been the deliberate act of *Her Majesty*, judging more particularly from the conduct of the Queen since she had discovered the foulness and the falseness of the accusation; but I ascribe it to the *baneful influence* [viz. Lehzen] which surrounds the throne, and poisons and deadens all the best feelings and dictates of human nature....

The Queen has expressed her *sorrow*, and here, I suppose is to end as cruel a case as ever disgraced the Court of a British Sovereign: but the matter will not rest in my breast; and should it appear that I have not now learnt all particulars, or that more have taken part in this infamous transaction than I am at present aware of, I am ready at any moment to take it up again, and, as far as lies in my power, will punish all concerned in it....I now close this painful and disgusting business, and retire from the *polluted* atmosphere of a Court in which I hope my poor sister will no longer remain.

Melbourne had apparently been out of London the last day or two, as, on coming into his house in South Street on the evening of the same day on which Hastings wrote his letter, he, in his turn, sat down and composed a few explanatory sentences.

My Lord,
    I found your Lordship's letter here on my return home this evening, and I am much concerned to learn from it that you have been waiting for a communication from me. I can assure your Lordship that I had no idea that this was the case. I conceived myself to have explained to your Lordship that if, after your conversation with the Duke of Well: you still persevered in asking an audience, I would submit your request to her Majesty...[and so on].

Hastings did persevere, and two days later, at one o'clock, in a room at Buckingham Palace, he and the Queen confronted each other. If he had thought he was going to probe further into the affair than that resolute young person intended he should, he soon discovered his mistake.

"It might be improper for me," he wrote later of this interview, "more particularly to state what occurred on that occasion, beyond the assurance of her Majesty that my sister should be treated with honour and kindness. All information, or satisfaction on the subject of my inquiries as to who had been the *originators* of the plot having been denied me at the palace, further than the exculpation of Lord Melbourne."

The Queen, Lord Melbourne, and the Duke of Wellington, having all three presented him with an impenetrable front, Hastings realized it was no use hoping to get anything out of them, and therefore returned to Donington. But, though he had left the scene of action, his determination to get justice done still burned within him. Before he left London, Lady Portman had offered to see him at Buckingham Palace—at the curious hour of seven o'clock in the morning—but knowing now that she had been one of the chief attackers of his sister, he had refused this invitation.

It is evident that he was now aware, at any rate in part, of the growing excitement all over England regarding this Buckingham Palace scandal, and he knew that though his sister had been proved innocent, her reputation so bandied about would be injured for life unless the accurate facts of the case were published for the public to read. Also, it seems, his intention was, if he could once put his finger on the original accuser, to demand, in fairness to his sister and in order to reinstate her in the eyes of the world, that the delinquent should be dismissed from the Court. According to our elastic modern views the young man may seem overpertinacious, but actually, as was soon to appear, Lady Flora was even more urgently in need of a defender than he realized.

Hastings would, he decided, endeavor, through Lady Tavistock's husband, to find out the particular fact that he was so intent on bringing to light.

Donington Park, March 1, 1839

Dear Lord Tavistock,

From the length of time I have known you, from the respect and regard which I have ever entertained towards you as a man of the highest honour and integrity, I have determined to write to you on the most painful subject that it has ever been my lot to be called to act upon.... I need tell you no more than that I allude to the gross lie which has been circulated about my unfortunate sister Flora.

He goes on to say that Melbourne had mentioned that Lady Tavistock "sent to him," and, therefore, he continues,

it is to know from *her* with *whom* this accusation first originated that I write to you.... I know that my poor sister will have the painful ordeal to go through of every version which the public may give of this story, and that I myself must submit to the same, and *am* at this moment submitting to the same *unfair* judgment, *till I publish* everything connected with the business.... May I then ask, *was not* Baroness Lehzen the first person who originated this foul slander, and mentioned it to Lady Tavistock; and if she *be not* the individual, *who was?*

Lord Tavistock wrote back.

Oakley, March 6th, 1839

My dear Hastings,

Your letter has annoyed me very much, but I feel thankful to you for the frank and friendly spirit which dictated it.... I am unwilling even now to name the subject of your letter to Lady Tavistock, as I am sure it would distress her greatly; nor do I like to write upon it except to say that she was influenced by the best motives in communicating the information she had received to Lord Melbourne.

I am persuaded you would feel this as strongly as I do, if you could have an opportunity of conversing with her ... but how this is to be brought about, at the distance we are from each other, I know not. I much wish, however, that you would contrive to see her.

The next day Lord Tavistock wrote a further letter to Hastings saying that he had "had some conversation with Lady Tavistock on this unfortunate subject, without saying that I had heard from you," but that, "I did not ask Lady Tavistock, nor did she tell me (for she is one of the most discreet of ladies) from whom she had received her information, nor do I think she would feel justified in doing so under any circumstances."

"Not justified," because not only she and Lady Portman, but

Victoria were all inculpated. The eyes of all three had been misled by appearances, but the Queen's name could not and must not be mentioned. At one moment, now or later, Lord Hastings considered bringing the matter before the House of Lords, but was told that if he did it would be "immediately silenced as an attack on the Throne."

To Lord Tavistock's letter Hastings replied on March 11.

Your two letters I have duly received but they are so unsatisfactory I hardly know how to answer them.... Put yourself for one minute in the painful position in which every member of my family now stands, and ask yourself if you should like to be first insulted, infamy cast upon your name for ever, and then, when you seek redress, by asking who is the originator of the base and false calumny raised against you, you were to be told—It is well known who that person is—but you must sit down quietly, bear all this, ask no more questions, and be subject to the false judgment and lies of every scoundrel in England?

. . . . . .

The questions I wish answered are simply these.

By whom was Lady Tavistock requested to name the business to Lord Melbourne?

By whom was Lady Tavistock informed of the opinion entertained with respect to my sister's health?

"I repeat," replied Lord Tavistock, "that I am unable to answer this question you have put to me, and I do not think I should be justified in requiring Lady Tavistock to do so. If you do not consider this *'frank'* I am sorry for it."

In a letter the following day he entirely exculpated Lehzen from being the original informer.

Turning aside from this fencing match between Lord Hastings and Lord Tavistock, we hear sounds of the hubbub that had arisen, not only all over England, but all over the Continent, about the scandal. "The affair of Lady Flora Hastings at the Palace," wrote Greville, "excites greater interest than any matter of a public and political character"; and he adds that the "Duke of Wellington wrote a capital letter to the Duchess of Kent advising conciliation and quiet."

But however much the Duke advised quiet, that was the one thing that was now impossible to obtain. Every day the whole distraught Hastings family—Lady Flora herself, her brother, mother, and sisters—were confronted with "the garbled statements and the lies which daily fill the papers." An uncle of Flora Hastings, Mr. Hamilton Fitzgerald, was living in Brussels, and so that he should hear the rights of the case, she wrote to him to explain exactly what had occurred. His response was a letter to the *Examiner* in which he set out "a narrative of the principal facts," and he followed this up by coming to London to see if there was anything he could do to set matters right. And certainly, from a statement he made later, one realizes how necessary it was that the true facts should be generally known, to such fantastic heights had "the grand scampiglio," as Greville calls it, now risen.

Letters poured in on me from all quarters [wrote Flora Hastings' uncle] containing the same injurious reports. I found that Lord Hastings' proceedings were unknown except in his own circle and at the palace; that he was abused in the London clubs for not having acted with sufficient spirit, and that infamous stories were circulated about his sister ... everyone except his own family were acquainted with them. ... It was said that the present was, at least, her second error, as when she left the palace last year she was certainly pregnant. Numerous bets were laid on the time when her situation would force her to "bolt" from the palace. At Vienna it was believed ... that she had remained on her knees an hour begging mercy of the Queen, and that Lord Hastings, having as a Peer forced his way into the Royal presence, had upbraided her Majesty; who made him no answer, but curtsied and retired when the tirade was over. I immediately went to England. When I arrived in London, I found all these reports in full circulation. Lady Flora's family were not in town, and were ignorant of them; the generality of indifferent people were inclined to believe them. The known fact that no one of the Queen's household had been punished for the insult Lady Flora had received, seemed to say that the Government did not think her assailants deserved punishment, or in other words, that she had not been ill-treated by them. The inference from which was, that she was guilty, but had been favoured and spared from motives of humanity. Nothing seemed to check the complete establishment of this opinion but the prompt punishment which the Duchess of Kent had inflicted on Sir James Clark by dismissing him from her Royal Highness' household.

I landed in the city, and remained there many days, to ascertain what judgment the respectable and unprejudiced citizens had passed on the case. I consulted with many friends, and by their assistance was present at many discussions, held by people who did not know me. At those respectable houses, where men of business pass their evenings, and discuss the news and speculations of the day, I found public opinion was universally against Lady Flora. The general idea was that she had been treated with unnecessary harshness: that she should have been got quietly out of the way: that such things occur every day in palaces; that people who place their daughters in them must take the consequence of doing so. It was often said that her brother would not have been so quiet if he had not known "that more than he liked would have come out if the thing had not been hushed up." I concluded that the opinion of the people at large was the same as that of the people of London, as both were acted on by the same fallacious evidence—anonymous statements in newspapers; and I was confirmed in my original opinion that it was the duty of some individual of Lady Flora's friends to extinguish all false reports by publishing a full statement of the case, and openly challenging contradiction. I felt that Lord Hastings could not do himself justice in publishing his own acts, and that delicacy, brotherly love, and family pride, might prevent him from being sufficiently accurate and minute in stating his sister's wrongs. I, therefore, determined to publish it myself.

Meanwhile, Hastings, having failed to get what he wanted from the Tavistocks, now turned elsewhere; and one day Lord Portman, on opening a letter from Donington, found himself confronted with the embarrassing question, "whether Lady Portman's suspicions were suggested to her, or occurred to herself."

Lord Portman evaded this crucial inquiry by telling Lord Hastings that as he had "declined" to see Lady Portman at Buckingham Palace when she had suggested it, he, Lord Portman, must now "decline" to answer, what he called, "isolated questions." He added that Lady Portman was still ready to give him an interview, either in the country or at their house in Belgrave Square, where she would be returning in April.

Back came Lord Hastings' answer.

Donington Park, March 14th, 1839

My Lord,

I have the honour to acknowledge the receipt of your letter of the 12th March and I think you cannot wonder at my not being over anxious to speak to Lady Portman after the line of conduct she had pursued. At least she must herself have been conscious of having in some measure acted unfairly to my sister, or she would not have sought the forgiveness of one whose character had been stamped with infamy and disgrace by one of the basest calumnies that ever disgraced a British Court. What particular part Lady Portman took in the business still remains to me a mystery. If her sorrow for what has passed be sincere, she has now the only opportunity she ever will have of making atonement for the deepest injury which could be inflicted on a guiltless woman, by giving up the name of the originators of this monstrous and villainous transaction. Put yourself for one moment in the painful position of one of my family, and I only ask you to look at the garbled statements and the lies which daily fill the papers, and answer me as a man of honour and a gentleman (and, though a stranger to you, I have every right to think I am addressing both the one and the other) whether I have not a perfect right to inquire into Lady Portman's conduct on this occasion; or am I to remain suffering the taunts and false statements of the world till April.... The same feeling which prevented me from meeting Lady Portman in London acts still more strongly now in forbidding me to put foot under your roof; and Lady Portman must remember that I stated to Sir James Clark at the time my reason for not meeting her Ladyship at seven o'clock in the morning at Buckingham palace. I did not ask the interview, but her Ladyship was pressingly anxious to explain her conduct... and I demand it as an act of common justice to my sister... I ask for the whole truth and nothing else... and if I do not get it in this shape, I must resort to the only means then left in my power....

One point is clear. Hastings was set on getting Lady Tavistock or Lady Portman, the one or the other, to make a written, as opposed to a verbal, statement of "the whole truth and nothing else." Once he had this in writing he could publish it for all England to read. The husbands of these two agitated ladies were obviously fully alive to this fact, and were both of them equally determined not to let their wives commit themselves. Therefore all Hastings got in answer to his letter of March 14 to Lord Portman was a protest against the writer having "chosen to express yourself in so unfair a manner towards Lady Portman." At the same time Lord Portman did enclose a kind of statement from his wife; though it revealed nothing that would help Flora Hastings' brother in his investigations, except that it cleared the situation up to the extent of exculpating Lehzen, as Lord Tavistock had already done, from having been the originator of the slander.

While Hastings skirmished with the Portmans, his mother had not been idle. Determined to force Victoria to make what reparation was possible to her daughter, Lady Hastings had exerted herself to write a letter of some length to the child-queen, a letter that, though bewilderingly involved, had obviously been composed with the greatest care.

Loudoun Castle, March 7, 1839

Madam,

It is hardly to be imagined that your Majesty should feel any surprise in receiving the present letter. The anguish of a mother's heart, under circumstances such as mine, can only be understood by a mother. But no one can be at a loss to know that loyalty to your Majesty and justice to my innocent child, demand from me an explicit reference to your Majesty on the atrocious calumnies and unblushing falsehoods against my daughter's reputation, which the perpetrators have dared to circulate, even in the palace of the Sovereign. I have had the honour of remembering your Majesty in childhood—I am deeply and gratefully attached to your admirable mother—and I have cherished in distance, absence, bad health, and many sorrows, a deep interest in the real honour and glory of your reign. My husband served his country honourably and with devoted zeal, and was particularly known to your Royal race; and my own family, during a long line, have been distinguished as faithful servants of their Kings. My grandfather lost his life in the service of his Sovereign. With so many claims on my feelings of old—although now unfashionable—aristocracy, it is impossible to suppose me capable of disrespect or want of loyalty towards your Majesty—a feeling, Madam, not less unbecoming towards you than repugnant to what I feel suitable in myself. But I trust a sense of morality is not yet so callous a thing as [not] to be held in some due respect even in the sight of a thoughtless world, and to justify my appealing directly to your Majesty to refute, by some act, calculated to mark your indignant sense of the slanders which some person or persons have ventured to cast in your Majesty's presence upon my daughter: and betrayed your Majesty to follow up by a course of proceeding such as was no doubt done on their part with a wish to try to degrade the victim of their persecution. It is my duty, respectfully to call your Majesty's attention to its being not more important for my daughter than essentially consonant to your Majesty's honour and justice, not to suffer the criminal invention of such falsehoods to remain without discovery. To a female sovereign especially, women of all ranks in Britain look with confidence for protection and (notwithstanding the difference of their rank) for sympathy. To such honest feelings of respect (for they take their origin in that) I ought not to suppose your Majesty indifferent, far less can I imagine that, as your Majesty increases in years, you will not feel, Madam, more and more the value of that estimate of your high place, which would make no one doubt your commanding reparation (as far as reparation can be made) for an infamous calumny, as not less incumbent as an act of necessary morality in the case of the public, as it assuredly is to the individual who so severely suffers from such defamation. This is not a matter that can or will be hushed up, and it is all-important that no time shall be lost in calling the culpable to account. With this appeal to your Majesty's upright feelings, I have the honour to be, Madam, your Majesty's dutiful subject and servant.

F. HASTINGS and (MURE) LOUDOUN *

Lady Hastings sent this to Melbourne, in order, so she said in a covering note, "to ensure its *immediate* and SAFE delivery."

Four days later, she received Melbourne's answer, written from Downing Street. He told her he had given her letter to the Queen, and then proceeded:

The allowance which her Majesty is anxious to make for the natural feelings of a mother upon such an occasion tended to diminish that surprise which could not be otherwise than excited by the tone and substance of yr Ladyship's letter.

Her Majesty commands me to convey to yr Ladyship the expression

* Flora Mure-Campbell, Countess of Loudoun in her own right, married the first Marquis of Hastings.

of her deep concern at the unfortunate circumstances which have recently taken place. Her Majesty hastened to seize the first opportunity to testify to Lady Flora Hastings her conviction of the error of the impression which had prevailed, and her Majesty is still most desirous to do everything in her power to soothe the feelings of Lady Hastings and her family which must have been painfully affected by the events which have occurred. I have the honour to remain, Madam, your ladyship's obedient and humble servant.

Lady Hastings, feeling she must justify herself for what Melbourne called "the tone and substance" of her letter, which had excited "surprise" in Victoria, now penned a further letter to the Premier.

My Lord,

Any expression of Her Majesty's sorrow for late occurrences is consolatory to me.

If the Queen wishes explanation of any part of my letter, which, from a dubious expression in your lordship's, I am uncertain of, I am quite ready to give it.

If her Majesty had been thoroughly aware of all the circumstances of the case "the tone and substance" of my letter could not have excited any surprise. Although a *woman*, the oath of allegiance which I have taken to her Majesty is as dear to me as to any man; and to that, and the true circumstances of the late transactions I refer your lordship.

I am, my lord, your lordship's most humble servant,

F. HASTINGS and (MURE) LOUDOUN

Melbourne replied:

Madam,

I have the honour of acknowledging your Ladyship's letter of the 15th inst which I received yesterday morning.

I neither had, nor have, it in command to express a wish for any explanation of your ladyship's letter addressed to her Majesty nor any part of it.

I have the honour to remain, madam, with high respect, your ladyship's humble and obedient servant

MELBOURNE

Before Lady Hastings had received Melbourne's answer to her first letter, it had struck her that it would perhaps be better to be more explicit as to what she actually meant by "reparation"; and that, knowing as she did Melbourne's all-powerful influence over everything connected with the Court, it would be as well to write to him direct. He, so Lady Hastings now decided, must point out clearly to this youthful Queen what she must do. Here is Lady Hastings' second, and explanatory, letter.

My Lord,

When I observe that no steps are taken to repair the indignity offered, three weeks ago, to my daughter, within the precincts of her Majesty's Palace, your lordship cannot be surprised at receiving this letter from me.

She then adds, with a touch of sarcasm:

I am told that as the responsible adviser of the Sovereign your lordship considers it as your constitutional right to appoint and dismiss her Majesty's household.... The nature and the manner of the course pursued in this atrocious conspiracy (for it admits of no other name) were unexampled, and yet Sir James Clark remains her Majesty's physician. I claim at your hands, my lord, as a mark of public justice, the removal of Sir James Clark.

This idea of the Hastings family that Melbourne, this *"maire du Palais,"* would turn anyone out of the Palace according to their dictates is harrowing, for reparation of some sort to Lady Flora was certainly due. On the other hand, how could the Queen dismiss her doctor when, it is fairly evident, she herself must have given permission for him to act as he did? One cannot believe that her ladies would have dared to instigate Clark to harry their victim without her permission. Therefore, according to strict logic, Victoria, to make just reparation, would have had to dismiss herself. Unrealized by the Hastings family, the situation was one of complete deadlock.

This explanatory note of Lady Hastings, written three days after her letter to the Queen, got delayed on its way, and Melbourne only received it after the above correspondence had passed between them. In reply, he first explains his dilatoriness so as "to acquit myself of any delay or neglect in replying to your ladyship's communication," and then continues:

The demand which your ladyship's letter makes upon me is so un-precedented and objectionable that even the respect due to your lady-ship's sex, rank, family, and character would not justify me in more, if indeed, it authorises so much, than acknowledging the letter for the sole purpose of acquainting your ladyship that I have received it.

I have the honour to remain madam, with the highest respect, your ladyship's obedient and humble servant,

MELBOURNE

Here, once for all, was the door slammed conclusively on any hopes the poor lady had hitherto entertained of some dramatic reparation. Her son, however, on reading this final letter from Melbourne to his mother, seized on the word "unprecedented," and himself wrote a further letter to the Prime Minister, demand-ing that "that harmful influence which now surrounds the Throne" should be removed. Then he added, "My Lord, you have stated that the removal of these persons would be unprecedented. Need I say that their conduct has been unprecedented...? I once more urge upon you, my Lord, *that* course which you say is without precedent."

Lord Hastings' belief that mere legerdemain with a word would have any power of forcing Lord Melbourne into action only under-lines the harassed young man's ignorance of the insoluble situation with which he was confronted.

One fact now starkly confronted the Hastings family. Repara-tion to the injured Flora was not within their power. But publica-tion was; and Lady Hastings forthwith published in the *Morning Post* her letter to the Queen, of March 7, for every man and woman in England to ponder over. She also made public her cor-respondence with Melbourne. "The Hastings affair..." wrote Greville, "has been rendered much worse and more mischievous by the publication of the correspondence.... The letters are very bad productions on both sides; the Lady's ill-written, intemperate, and rhapsodical, the Minister's rude and unbecoming. The whole affair has done incredible harm, and has played the devil with the Queen's popularity and cast dreadful odium and discredit on the Court."

Melbourne was only too well aware, one might say without exaggeration, only too agonizingly aware, of this odium and discredit. He who had exerted the utmost circumspection to keep the Queen and her Court free from the slightest tarnish, had now to stand by powerless while on every hand he heard her and her Court decried. The effect on him was such that it is said he never entirely recovered from it. Those who knew him formally found him not the same man that he had been.

(Meanwile over in Paris Lady Ravensworth was occupied in "making the Flora case quite clear" to Princess Lieven. "Ith all talking that doth the mithchief: why will people talk, my dear Printhethe de Lieven?")

The publication of the Lady Hastings and Melbourne correspondence coming on top of the letter from Flora Hastings' uncle that had appeared earlier in the *Examiner*, naturally increased the general hubbub. Apart from, and, as it were, going on beneath these letters now made public property, there were endless runnings to and fro, harassed interviews, and crucial talks taking place both in and around Buckingham Palace. The Duke of Wellington was in constant request, "consulted and appealed to by all parties"; for he had now become psychologically to the Royal Family much what Sir Henry Halford had been to the generation before—general arbitrator and consoler. That national figure in blue coat and white trousers would constantly be seen passing into Buckingham Palace for further and yet further discussions. Whichever of the "Palatians" he happened to be calling on would hopefully greet their adviser as he stepped into the room with that indefinable something in his poise which, sticking out his coattails, gave him the air of a spruce, if elderly, swallow. Besides trying to quiet down Hastings, the Duke would, at one moment in that *"aquiline"* voice of his, be having things out with the Queen; at another, in confabulation with the Ministers; at another, grappling with Conroy. Then, having sorted out such threads of the entanglement as could be straightened, away across the carpet would slowly glide that neat figure.

What part Conroy was quietly playing in the background is impossible to say, but Wellington's belief was that it was he who—once the scandal was under way—had been "the grand mover" in

LADY FLORA HASTINGS
From the portrait by K. McLeay, R.S.A.

THE DUKE OF WELLINGTON AND SIR ROBERT PEEL

From the painting by F. Winterhalter

By gracious permission of H.M. The King

the embroilment still going on within the Palace itself. "He it was," so the Duke considered, "who incited the Duchess and Lady Flora to jeter feu et flamme." When, at the outset of the scandal, the Duchess of Kent, swelling with indignation, had sent for the Duke, his advice to her had been "to hush the matter up."

"It is now," he exclaimed, "between these four walls; if they were to tumble down it would be for ever buried in the ruins—so let it be." But why the walls of Buckingham Palace should disintegrate, and why the thought of this projected disaster should bring comfort to that already distraught lady, is not clear.

Meanwhile, as the days went on, the commotion, forever whipped up by the papers, and the inevitably increasing gossip, made the wretched young woman who was the center of it suffer "dreadfully in mind and body." In body because, so as to allay suspicion, she felt her wisest course was to remain in full view of the world, and would therefore force herself to appear at "the palace, in the parks, at the royal chapel, at the opera," when actually she was suffering so much from the disease from which she was slowly dying that she only longed to remain quiet. Mentally, too, she was tormented "from being such an object of attention and curiosity, and still more because every sort of excitement was kept up, in and around her, by the faction who made an instrument of her." By now the whole thing had developed into a political racket; the Tories enchanted at getting hold of such a scandal with which to belabor the Queen and her Whig Minister. Flora Hastings' supporters would cheer her in the street as she drove by. The Buckingham Palace victim had become England's virtuous maiden *par excellence*.

Though spring was now turning to early summer, "the excitement of the tracasserie" did not abate. "The public," wrote Greville, "takes it up (as it took Q[ueen] Caroline) on the principle of favouring an injured person, and one who appears to have obtained no reparation for the injuries inflicted on her." From house to house engaging in one perturbed talk after another, went the male relations of the ladies principally concerned; each hoping to smooth things down. "Since Lord Harewood came to town he has taken it up on account of his daughter Lady Portman." Off went this distressed Peer to the Duke of Wellington, hoping that from his "wisdom and integrity" he might collect a few helpful ideas. Lord Portman, too, visited the Duke, "and entreated him to interpose to set matters straight, and he at once said that he would do anything; he would see Melbourne or the Queen, or the Duchess of Kent." Lord Tavistock on his part was "worried to death by the attacks on his wife in the *Morning Post.*" As for Lady Hastings, concealed within the depths of Loudoun Castle, she was trying as best she might to recover from the battering Victoria's Prime Minister had given her. "She had," comments Greville, "never got over the letter Melbourne wrote her." Her son now carried about with him not only his burden of indignation on account of his sister, but a further one on account of his mother. Before long Brougham, that most mischievous of politicians, inserted himself into the general melee, for, wrote a contemporary, he "hates the Queen cordially and would gladly increase the prejudice against her." Now he "struck up a mighty friendship" with the tormented Hastings, becoming "wonderfully zealous and active in the business." Brougham was determined to force an apology out of Melbourne to Lady Hastings, and in turn off he went to Apsley House to persuade Wellington to agitate in the matter. The Duke agreed that Melbourne "might and ought to do this," and said that he would speak to him about it. But Lord Melbourne was not the man to withdraw anything that he had once said. And though by appointment he too passed in beneath the pillared façade of Apsley House, crossed the hall, and went in to talk things over with the Duke, by the time he re-emerged into the hall he had convinced Wellington that it would be better that he should not himself write either apology or explanation, "though what his arguments were" no one but himself and the Duke knew.

While all this jangle was going on outside the palace, within, the whole Court continued "to be plunged in shame and mortification at the exposure." All serenity had fled those spacious rooms: "the Palace is full of bickerings and heart-burnings." The Duchess, showing every tender kindness to Flora Hastings, emphasized her own resentment at the way in which her Lady of the Bedchamber had been treated, by absenting herself from Victoria's "Court circle"; while the Queen, on her side, says Greville, had "neither a particle of affection nor respect for her Mother, and is either so thoughtless or so careless of consequences that She desires no better than that the Duchess should quit the Palace, and take up her abode elsewhere."

It must be noted that Greville was at the moment annoyed with Victoria for what he considered a lack of realization on her part of the magnitude of the Duke of Wellington. It must, however, also be noted, and this time regretfully, that Victoria was so exasperated at Mr. Fitzgerald's letter being published that, from that moment, in spite of her former tearful apology to Lady Flora, she thereafter entirely ignored her, until June 9 when she sent "to ask how she was."

CHAPTER XIII
THE QUEEN CONFRONTS
SIR ROBERT PEEL

WHILE the air was still thick with the fumes of the Flora Hastings affair, a further drama, but one of an entirely different nature, supervened in the palace.

Once Victoria's daily intimacy with Melbourne was firmly established, she feared nothing in life so much as that their relationship should be disturbed: her dread being that on some issue the Government should be defeated, and her Prime Minister be Prime Minister no more.

One day, early in May, this year of 1839, she made the entry in her Journal: "I awoke at ½ past 8—and heard from Lord Surrey that we had only had a majority of 5! [on the Jamaica Constitution Bill]. This struck to my heart and I felt dreadfully anxious."

She must, she decided, write a letter to Lord Melbourne immediately. Hardly was her messenger dispatched with it than a letter for her arrived from Melbourne himself. "He feared," runs her Journal, "they had no other alternative—can *I write it*— but to resign...." So what, as yet, had been but a hideously envisaged possibility was upon her. For the next hour or two Lehzen was the recipient of her grief: faithfully endeavoring to bestow comfort when there was none to give.

Just after twelve o'clock Victoria heard that Melbourne had arrived in the palace. "It was some minutes before I could muster up courage to go in." But at last she did bring herself to enter the room and, as her small hand slipped into his, he heard her distressed murmur, "You will not forsake me."

"I held his hand for a little while, unable to let go; and he gave me such a look of kindness, pity and affection, and could hardly utter for tears 'Oh no,' and in such a touching voice."

Then they "sat down as usual, and I strove to calm myself."

"I was afraid this would happen," said Lord Melbourne.

At three o'clock the Queen had to have another distressing interview, this time with the Whig leader, Lord John Russell—a man so minute in figure that when he stood at the table of the House to make a speech his face could scarcely be seen above the brass-bound boxes. But if his person was diminutive, his self-assurance was immense. Now, after telling Victoria the Cabinet would resign, he "thanked me," she writes, "for my kindness—which quite set me off crying, and I said it was a terrible thing for me."

Later in the day she received a further letter from Lord Melbourne advising her to send for the Duke of Wellington, and telling her that if the Duke should be unwilling to form a Government and should suggest Peel, then, so wrote Melbourne, he counseled her to agree.

She saw clearly what must be done, and schooled herself for the undertaking. But, most unwilling cog that she had been forced to become in the political machinery, there lay in her mind all the time the realization of that which was lacerating to realize.

In the afternoon Melbourne was at the palace again. They discussed this and that. "Lord Melbourne then said, pulling a paper out of his pocket, 'I have written down what I think you should do.'" Then he read it out. He concluded, "Your Majesty had better express your hope that none of Your Majesty's Household, except those who are engaged in Politics, may be removed." "I think," added Lord Melbourne, "you might ask him for that."

Finally, telling him that she was not going out that night, she begged him to come back in the evening.

"Yes, Ma'am, I will," he said. There was a pause, and then he remarked, "I don't think it would be right...it would be observed."

"I pressed him, and said it would not be," adding that he could "come after dinner."

He demurred again. "It wouldn't do," he said, and remarked, "I'm going to dine at Lady Holland's."

"I said he must come and see me."

"Oh! yes ... only not while these negotiations are going on."

" 'I shall feel quite forsaken,' at which he gave me such a look of grief and feeling."

"God bless you, Ma'am," said Lord Melbourne, and kissed her hand. "I'll come to see you to-morrow morning before the Duke comes."

All through this talk between them Victoria, so she writes, was "in a dreadful state of grief." During the following hours of this miserable day a further letter from Melbourne was brought in to her, and then, later, yet another. In these he put any little consolatory reflections that he could; saying in one of them that he "felt his attendance upon your Majesty to be at once the greatest honour and pleasure of his life," and that when he had had to refuse coming to see her that evening "nothing ever gave him more pain," but that "it was absolutely necessary not to give occasion to any jealousy or suspicion."

Needless to say, a letter from Buckingham Palace at once came flying back to him. Then, so runs the Journal, "wrote one line to the Duke of Wellington to request him to come."

That evening there was no royal cortege in and out of the palace dining room, for the central figure of these processions felt she could not face the great lighted rooms, the Household spaced out round the table, and, above all, no Lord Melbourne sitting at her side. Instead she had her dinner sent up to her private room. Doubtless Lehzen had it with her, as in the old days at Kensington when the atmosphere downstairs had become too taut, and governess and pupil would take refuge on the floor above. However, on this evening England's Queen felt so wretched that when her dinner was before her she could not eat it.

Though she and Melbourne were to meet at eleven o'clock the next morning, directly she awoke she scribbled him a note. "The Queen thinks Lord Melbourne may possibly wish to know how she is this morning; the Queen is somewhat calmer; she was in a wretched state till nine o'clock last night ... couldn't touch a morsel of food ... nor can she this morning."

Punctually at eleven she and Melbourne were again interlocked in talk, Melbourne trying to strengthen her for her interviews with the Duke and Peel. They talked of Wellington's deafness. "Mind the Duke understands what you say," warned Melbourne. As for Peel: "You must try and get over your dislike for Peel, he's a close stiff man." Finally, Lord Melbourne went off and left her.

Just before one o'clock the saddened girl "went over to the Yellow Closet," and going in, found herself confronted by the waiting figure of the Duke, by that bronze eagle face that contrasted so arrestingly with the completely white hair. He made a pretense— for it surely could not but have been a pretense—of having "no idea" why he had been sent for; was deaf, kind, and understanding; and did not flinch even when his sovereign gave vent to the contradictory statement that she was going "to prove her great *fairness* to her new Government" by warning them from the start that she intended to contrive seeing a great deal of Melbourne. The Duke told her he did not feel equal to forming a Government and advised her to send for Peel. Before he left he suggested that, regarding any projected changes in her Household, she should not herself "begin with conditions of this sort," but should "wait tell the matter was proposed."

The situation for Victoria was becoming ever more bitter. To exchange Melbourne for Wellington would not have been nearly so hateful to her as to exchange him for Peel, for whom she had already acquired "a lively aversion." "The Duke I like by far better than Peel" was her cry, and now she had actually herself to request Peel to take the place in her life of the entrancing companion who at present dominated her every sense.

The reasons for her aversion to Peel were various. He would do small but gauche things that annoyed her. She had not, for instance, forgotten a little incident at a party given by her Aunt Mary, the Duchess of Gloucester. "Peel never came up to me at Gloucester House," Victoria complained later to Melbourne.

"Stupid man," exclaimed Lord Melbourne. "When I came to the Duchess of Gloucester's... I met Lord Fitzgerald whom I know very well, and I took him by the arm and said to him, 'Now mind Peel goes up to the Queen,' and he nodded his head as if to say, 'I know what you mean.'"

And, apart from his behavior and his politics, as a man the Tory statesman made no appeal to her. His face was far from possessing that direct masculine beauty with a touch of a noble Landseer animal about it that Melbourne's had achieved. Peel's physiognomy was composed of indecisive contours; the general effect slightly effeminate and spongy. The thick hair, hanging limply down on either side, lacked virility. It would have required an older and a subtler-minded woman to appreciate the balanced intelligence, the confluence of manifold reflections that informed that mild but incalculated gaze. He had, moreover, a trick of mincing about on his feet as he talked that Victoria found irritating.

Now, before the prospect of having to ask this unpleasing man to form a cabinet, all her carefully built-up constitutional personality seemed on the point of dissolving entirely, revealing beneath nothing but a grief-torn girl. Nevertheless her stringent sense of duty steadied her sufficiently to do what was demanded. She wrote to Peel, and he came. The Queen, looking up at that tall figure, realized that he was "embarrassed and put out." It is not surprising; for he was perfectly aware that she neither wanted him nor liked him. Continuously jigging about in front of her, he reluctantly agreed to form a ministry, at the same time throwing out that he felt "unequal to the task," and assuring her that he was "far from exulting in what had happened, as he knew what pain it must give."

The question arose as to the Queen keeping on her present ladies of the Household who, chosen by Melbourne, were all Whigs. Peel, so Victoria wrote afterward, remarked that "he would require me to demonstrate... confidence in the Government and that my [change of] Household would be one of the marks of that."

Instantly Victoria shot back, "Then Sir Robert, I am to understand that you look to the ladies for support in the House of Commons."

This unexpected attack visibly shook Peel. (Later, Victoria exultantly re-enacted the whole interview to Lehzen who remarked afterward that "the Queen's description of Peel's face was perfect.")

Now, all that he could think of to answer was "that the country would require a proof that he enjoyed the entire confidence of Her Majesty."

But the astute girl caught him out again. "To suppose that I would allow my ladies any intervention in political affairs is to suppose that I would intrigue against my government. That is an

insult to me, and I don't believe the country can require that . . ."
and so on.

The restless, shifting figure, scarcely recovered from this on-
slaught, was then informed by his monarch "of her great friendship
for, and gratitude to, Lord Melbourne"—after which confidence
it struck her, as she gazed at Peel, that he was "such a cold, odd
man" it was really impossible to "make out what he means"; but
posterity, having listened to this unique conversation, is not at all
surprised to read that "My impression is he is not *happy* and
sanguine."

If Victoria had disliked Peel before the interview, she liked him
still less after it. "The Queen," she wrote of herself to Melbourne,
"don't like his manner after—oh! how different, how dreadfully
so, to that frank, open, natural and most kind warm manner of
Lord Melbourne." In this letter she assures Melbourne that she
was "very much collected, civil and high, and betrayed no agitation
during these two trying Audiences."

But afterward, the tension once relaxed, Peel's erstwhile crafty
antagonist admits that "again *all* gave way," for "what is worst of
all is the being deprived of seeing Lord Melbourne." And she
feared, too, that she might even be asked to part with Lehzen
herself. But "in her opinion," so Lehzen told Lord Clarendon, "the
crisis had been very useful, as Peel and the Duke evidently had not
the slightest notion of what stuff the Queen was made; that they
thought to impose upon her every condition they liked, and to con-
vert her into an instrument for themselves; but they now had far
different notions."

One can indeed believe it.

Meanwhile, every few hours Melbourne and Victoria tried to
keep up their spirits by dispatching letters to each other. He begged
her "not to mind Sir Robert's manner," but at the same time urged
her not to give way over having her Ladies taken from her; and
assured her it was his belief that if she told Peel that he "pressed
me harder than any sovereign ever had been pressed before," Peel
would feel he could not refuse.

It was during the morning of Thursday, May 9, that the
messengers were scurrying to and fro between the Queen and
Melbourne with these letters, but early that afternoon "the Yellow

Closet" at the Palace witnessed a most unlooked-for development. Those two figures, the lanky, uneasy Tory politician, and the diminutive, tightly set Queen, were again confronting each other. Peel first began about the formation of his ministry: Victoria, on her side, assuring him that she "would suppress every personal feeling and would be quite fair." In this forecasted cabinet, Peel was to take the Treasury and the Exchequer as well as the Premiership; the Duke of Wellington the Foreign Office. This part of the proceedings passed off calmly enough, but, shortly after Peel threw off, "Now about the Ladies."

"I said I could *not* give up *any* of my Ladies."

"He asked if I meant to retain *all*."

"*All*."

"The Mistress of the Robes and the Ladies of the Bedchamber?"

"*All*."

Peel protested that "they were the Wives of the Opponents of the Government."

"I said that would not interfere, I never talked politics with them."

Peel explained that "he didn't mean *all* the Bedchamber Women and *all* the Maids of Honour, he meant the Mistress of the Robes and the Ladies of the Bedchamber."

"I replied they were of more consequence than the others, and I could *not* consent."

As this conversation gathered momentum Victoria had noted with delight that her adversary was becoming "quite perturbed," and at this emphatic and final refusal, "I never," so she gleefully wrote afterward, "saw a man so frightened; he said he must go to the Duke of Wellington and consult with him, when both would return." In addition, Peel, thus brought up short, declared that "this must suspend all further proceedings," and asked her if she "would be ready to receive a decision." She said she would.

He then went off, and she, hurrying to her writing table, dashed off an excited and triumphant note to Melbourne. "The Queen writes one line to prepare Lord Melbourne for what *may* happen in a very few hours. . . . Keep yourself in readiness for you may soon be wanted."

Peel's perturbation had suddenly revealed to her acute mind a hitherto undreamed possibility. Perhaps Peel, realizing that she absolutely insisted on keeping her ladies, would in his turn feel that he definitely could not form a ministry. And then—ah! what sweet fanfares of hope were beginning to blow about her ears. In this letter to Melbourne she assures her sympathetic friend that during the interview she was "calm but very decided and I think you would have been pleased to see my composure and great firmness."

Melbourne, on receiving this communication warning him of some unnamed event that *"may* happen" was, as indeed he well might be, "greatly astonished."

About an hour after the Queen's interview with Peel the Duke of Wellington arrived at the palace to discuss the situation with her.

He already knew of the scuffle she and Peel were having over her ladies, and so now, as he entered the room, he exclaimed, "Well I am very sorry to find there is a difficulty."

"O *He* began it not me," she exclaimed.

The Duke, who it will be noticed, took the opposite view regarding the affair to Melbourne's, "argued the point with her, and tried to persuade her that nothing had been proposed to her but what the circumstances of the case rendered necessary."

"But," she protested, "I thought you said that my situation demanded peculiar consideration. . . ."

"So I did say, Madam . . . but I warned you against any contest upon principles . . . however you might make any objections you pleased upon details. . . ."

"It is offensive to me," cried Victoria (who was beginning to show "some marks of irritation"), "It is offensive to me to suppose that I talk to any of my Ladies upon public affairs."

"I am quite certain you do not . . . but the public does not know this, and it is on account of the impression necessarily to be produced on the public mind . . . that the proposal is made to you."

But though Melbourne was not in the room Victoria was aware of his approval in the background, and decided that firmness was again her strong suit. Firmness touched with sarcasm. So now she threw out, "Was Sir Robert so weak that *even* the Ladies must be of his opinion?"

Finally, the Duke left her; and Peel, who had been waiting in the next room, came in, but only "stopped a few minutes," telling her he would return in two or three hours.

The wrought-up girl filled this stretch of time by—needless to say—yet another letter to Melbourne. Then she attacked her Journal. The palace clocks ticked on till their hands pointed to ten minutes past five, and then Peel reappeared. He came bringing a gift that matched her most extravagant hopes. He informed her that he and his colleagues had come to the conclusion "that unless there was *some* . . . demonstration of my confidence, and if I retained all my Ladies, 'they agreed unanimously they could not go on!' "

("This," she wrote that night in her Journal, "was *quite* wonderful! The Ladies his only support!! What an admission of weakness!")

At once another letter was written, and within a few moments the messenger to whom it was entrusted was hastening through the spring evening to Lord Melbourne's house. Opening the note Melbourne found that his Queen "begged him to come as soon as possible."

She filled in the moments while she waited for him by again picking up her quill, and entering in her Journal all such details as she had time for about what is commonly, but erroneously, known as the Bedchamber Plot: erroneously because on either side was there any intentional "plot." It was merely that fortuitous twists to the situation played into the Queen's and Melbourne's hands.

The result of her hurriedly dispatched note to him was that, "At ½ past 6 came my dear and excellent Lord Melbourne." They met in an atmosphere tingling with expectancy. "It was a true and real . . . happiness to see him again." Now everything that had occurred during the last few hours was poured out on her ex-Premier's head in a torrent: what she had said; what Peel had said; what the Duke had said. Lord Melbourne listened absorbedly. Occasionally he interjected a comment. "You did say that . . ." or "There you had the better of him, and what did he say?"

In sum, "Lord Melbourne approved all." But the crucial nature of the situation cut sharply into his mind. At the end of their colloquy, "I must," he exclaimed, "summon the Cabinet at once; it may have very serious consequences; if we can't go on with this House of Commons we may have to dissolve Parliament."

The position at the moment was strangely entangled; Charles Greville amused himself by adjudicating on the principal actors. He first dealt with Victoria. *"She,"* he wrote in his diary, "might be excused for her ignorance of the exact limits of constitutional propriety and for her too precipitous recurrence to the Counsels to which She has been accustomed; but *they* ought to have explained to her that until Sir Robert Peel had formally and finally resigned his commission into her hands, they could tender no advice. . . . As it was the Queen was in communication with R[obert] Peel on one side and Ld Melbourne on the other, at the same time; and through them with both their Cabinets."

But now, as just after seven o'clock, Melbourne hurried away from the palace to collect his cabinet around him, considerations of this nature troubled him not the slightest. No one ever rested more firmly and complacently on his own basis than did that easygoing man. The opportunity had suddenly been put into his hand to manipulate the situation according to his desire, and whether his behavior was constitutional or not was all one to him.

By this time it was London's dinner hour; and his Whigs, dispersed in every direction, had *nolens volens* to be fetched away, this one from the house where he was dining; that one from the opera; a third from somewhere else. Finally, Melbourne had them collected around him. There was a great deal of discussion, and in the outcome it was decided that the Queen should be advised to write to Peel saying, "The Queen having considered the proposal made to her yesterday by Sir Robert Peel to remove the Ladies of her Bedchamber, cannot consent to adopt a course which she conceives to be contrary to usage and repugnant to her feelings."

Receiving this communication at the Palace, Victoria "immediately wrote a few lines in answer to Lord Melbourne, and copied the letter to Sir R. Peel."

Obviously only one course was now open to Peel. He wrote to the Queen resigning his commission.

Melbourne and the Queen had won. They had won, but inevitably their victory was followed in certain quarters by an aftermath of indignation. Charles Greville concluded his scoldings on the impropriety of the whole proceeding. "The Cabinet of Lord Melbourne discussed the proposals of Sir Robert Peel, and they dictated to the Queen the reply in which she refused to consent to the advice tendered to her by the man who was *at that moment* her Minister, and it was this reply which compelled him to resign that office with which she had entrusted him."

Politically, the whole proceeding was, indeed, as improper as it could be. Greville continued with a few comments of a more personal nature. "The simple truth . . . is that the Queen could not endure the thought of parting with Melbourne. Her feelings which are *sexual* though She does not know it . . . are of a strength sufficient to bear down all prudential considerations." He added some ruminations on how shocking it was that "this mere baby of a Queen" should in this matter run counter to the advice of Wellington—"this great man, the decus and tutamen of her kingdom."

But, apart from Melbourne's physical attraction for her, Greville, in his upbraidings, overlooked the fact that running counter to one great man she was following the advice of another whom she believed equally great, and whose counsels she considered to be in all things right. It was only natural she should feel triumphant in having downed the Tory faction, that Hydra-headed animal which she had been brought up from her cradle to regard as impious.

The Duke, though he advised Victoria to concede to Peel's wishes, looked on chivalry to women as a component of good breeding, a *sine qua non* in the composition of a gentleman, and had exclaimed to Greville's brother that "they must do what they could to help that poor little thing out of the difficulty in which she was placed." Less chivalrous, his Tory colleagues flew into a pet at this attitude, and at the clubs men began to exclaim that he was "in his dotage."

As for Peel himself, both as man and politician he had been placed in the most invidious and embarrassing position possible, and it is not surprising that now he could no longer "conceal the indignation" with which he was "boiling over" at the way Victoria had spoken to him, and at "her peremptory and haughty demeanour." To his credit, in spite of the hostility he had during their interviews felt issuing from that bristling little figure, the abashed man had himself behaved in the most temperate and generous manner, and when during one of their talks she had shot out, "You must not expect me to give up the society of Lord Melbourne," he had replied that "Nothing could be further from his thoughts than to interfere with Her Majesty's society in any way, or to object to her receiving Lord Melbourne as she pleased." All through this political drama there had been in the background the disapproving, gesticulating figure of Brougham. Now, when the late situation came under discussion in the House of Commons, Peel made an excellent speech, managing "to justify himself without saying a word offensive to the Queen." Not so Brougham. Up rose that spare, tense figure, his features darting acrimony, and then, wrote Greville, a "torrent of rage, disdain, and hatred ... broke forth with resistless and overwhelming force. He spoke for three hours, and delivered such an oration as no other man in existence is capable of—devilish in spirit and design, but of super-human eloquence, and masterly in execution. He assailed the Ministers with a storm of invective and ridicule; and while he enveloped his periods in a studied phraseology of pretended loyalty and devotion, he lashed the Queen herself with unsparing severity ... it was the peculiar merit of the speech that it abounded in truths, and in great constitutional principles."

But in this cataract of brilliance, the application was too personal; a consideration very present in the minds of both Wellington and Greville. "The wilful, obstinate child of 20 deserves the severest reprehension," continued Greville, "but the castigation She merits cannot be administered without impairing the authority, the dignity, the sanctity of the Crown She wears, and it is necessary to spare the individual for the sake of the institution. This it is which the Duke of Wellington feels." But all this splutter of indignation from the Tories that beat like an angry sea around the walls of Buckingham Palace not one whit disturbed the serenity of the two sitting cosily chatting within, now so enchantingly restored to each other's company. The evenings of this May were chilly, and on the Sunday that finished this convulsive week, while the two talked, "we sat down," writes Victoria, "near the chimney," Lord Melbourne "very much excited the whole evening, talking to himself and pulling his hair about, which always makes him look so much handsomer."

How delightfully, shamelessly frank they could now be with

each other as they discussed the ardors of the campaign they had just emerged from! Lord Melbourne confided in Victoria that Palmerston had said, "I think it a great bore to go out; I like power, I think power is very pleasant." Victoria's newly returned Premier could not but feel secretly smug at the knowledge of Peel's failure to please in the quarter where he himself shone with such luster. "You must remember," he said, apropos of that unhorsed, disconsolate figure, "that he is a man who is not accustomed to talk to Kings: a man of quite a different calibre: it's not like me; I've been brought up with Kings and Princes. I know the whole Family, and know exactly what to say to them."

An observation not, perhaps, entirely complimentary to the royal family of that day. However, this aspect of it did not strike his listener.

As they talked away, "I caught his eye," writes Victoria, "when he was frowning very much, and he smiled and rubbed his forehead and said, 'Never mind, I was only knitting my brows; I know it looks tremendous . . . one shouldn't judge from expression.' "

Now more than ever each basked in the appreciation of the other. Victoria's exultant mood led her the next day to put on for dinner a particularly successful effort of her dressmaker, and as she and Lord Melbourne again sat warming themselves over the fire, "I asked him if he liked my dress."

"Beautiful," cried Melbourne.

At the end of the month the Queen held a levee; but among the successively bowing figures who passed through the Throne Room those of Peel and Wellington did not appear.

"Very rude," Victoria considered, and told Lord Melbourne so.

"I don't think they mean that," he protested.

"So foolish of Peel to act in this way, as by so doing he has made me dislike him."

"Very ill-judged of him," agreed Lord Melbourne.

Before we finally draw the curtain over the Bedchamber Affair, two considerations regarding the part the Queen played must not be overlooked. First: there was no definite precedent to go on for the changing of a regnant Queen's ladies. (Melbourne assured her that Peel was pressing on her "a measure which no Minister before ever pressed upon a Sovereign.") Secondly: that Melbourne had written to her that he "advises your Majesty to urge this question of the Household strongly as a matter due to yourself and your own wishes"; then adding the slightly ambiguous rider, "but if Sir Robert is unable to concede it, it will not do to refuse and to put off the negotiation upon it."

In the upshot he approved of the line the Queen had taken, telling her, "I think you were quite right to reserve your ladies."

However, sixty years later the Queen—no longer a marionette at the end of Melbourne's string—while talking one day at Osborne to Sir Arthur Bigge, remarked, apropos of the affair, "I was very young then, and perhaps I should act differently if it was all to be done again."

2

This same year of 1839, Victoria wrote in her Journal:

Friday, 24th May. This day I *go out of my* TEENS and become 20! It sounds so strange to me! I have much to be thankful for; and I feel I owe more to *two* people than I can ever repay! My dear Lehzen and my dear excellent Lord Melbourne! I pray Heaven to preserve them in health and strength for *many, many* years to come!

It is noticeable, and not without import, that Lord Melbourne has now acquired two adjectives to Lehzen's one.

Three days after she had written this, Victoria was settling in at Windsor. The spring day was light and lovely as a madrigal, but, all the same, she says that as she looked about her at all the greenness and brightness that flashed from the trees, a feeling of sadness invaded her and she felt puzzled that her first impression on arriving at this beautiful Windsor was "always a triste one." In the early evening as she glanced out of one of the castle windows she saw, as if an embodiment of the spring evening itself, a Russian youth, one of her guests, arriving with his suite. This was the Grand Duke Alexander.* Himself looking up, the young man saw the little porcelain face gazing down at him, and he "bowed up to my window." He had already been received by her on this visit of his

---

* The future Emperor Alexander II.

to England, and had partnered her in a quadrille at a Buckingham Palace ball. "I think we are great friends already and get on very well; I like him exceedingly," she had scribbled to Melbourne after this ball. Then, too, only a few days after the bedchamber campaign, the young Grand Duke had pleased her by coming to her box at the theater one night and staying with her—as she notes with satisfaction—"at least half an hour"; and while they sat there, shut off from the world within the looped draperies of her box, she had confided to him all the details of her passages with Peel; and the adroitly tactful young man, "his fine blue eyes" fixed on her eager face, had been properly *"shocked."*

Greville's opinion was that this Grand Duke was "by no means remarkable in appearance one way or the other," but now, this evening at dinner at Windsor, seated next Victoria, he was certainly remarkable in the way he flung his golden net around her. "I really am quite in love with the Grand Duke," she that night informed her Journal. "He is a dear delightful young man." They had had dancing after dinner in the red drawing room, and the dear delightful young man had asked if she would dance the Mazurka with him, "which I did (never having done it before) and which is very pleasant; the Grand Duke is so very strong, that in running round, you must follow quickly, and after that you are whisked round like in a Valse, which is very pleasant." And later in the evening they had a dance called the Grossvater "which is excessively amusing; I danced with the Grand Duke, and we had such fun and laughter; Patkul and the Countess Potoska led the way. It begins with a solemn walk round the room ... one figure, in which the lady and gentleman run down holding their pocket-handkerchief by each end, and letting the ladies on one side go under it, and the gentlemen jump over it, is too funny. This concluded our little Ball at near 2 o'clock. I never enjoyed myself more. We were all so merry." And when at last she lay down in bed, the gay oscillation of life, and especially the sweet seductions of the Grossvater when danced with a young Russian, were so pulsating within her that it was two hours before she could compose herself for sleep.

The next day the Grand Duke brought himself still further into favor by talking to his royal hostess "of his very fine reception here, and said he would never forget it. 'Ce ne sont pas seulement des paroles, je vous assure, Madame.' "

Meanwhile, the young man (in spite of the fact that he "scattered diamond boxes and rings in all directions," and—to the surprise of the members—bestowed three hundred pounds on the Jockey Club) was not moving the Englishmen around him to the same degree as he did England's Queen. "Does not appear to have made any great impression," wrote Greville. "Looks rather livid," sourly commented Melbourne. But Victoria was bemused by his personality. The presence of this vivacious young man and his gentlemen ("Patkul and Adlerberg are 2 such merry young creatures") had pressed the diurnal tune of Windsor Castle into a faster lilt. . . . A sweet and heady fragrance impregnated the air.

"All this excitement," exclaimed Victoria enthusiastically to Lord Melbourne, "did me good."

"But you may suffer afterwards," opined Lord Melbourne, "you must take care of your health . . . you complain of that languor increasing, and dislike of exertion; now it would be a dreadful thing for you if you were to take a dislike for business."

"I assured him I never should."

"You lead rather an unnatural life for a young person," went on her mentor. "It's the life of a man."

" 'I did feel it sometimes,' I said."

That evening there was more dancing; and Victoria and the Grand Duke discovered that *Le Gay Loisir* (as Victoria wrote it) was the favorite quadrille tune of both. But afterward Victoria "went to the little blue room next my Dressing-room," and there her entrancing partner of a few minutes ago was ceremoniously brought in by Lord Palmerston to make his official adieu. Notwithstanding, the young man did not allow this Court ceremoniousness to deprive him of his role of romantic charmer. "He looked pale and his voice faltered as he said, 'Les paroles me manquent pour exprimer tout ce que je sens.' "

Lord Palmerston stood by witnessing the farewell flutterings of these human lovebirds, these final kissings on royal hands and royal cheeks. "He . . . pressed and kissed my hand, and I kissed his cheek; upon which he kissed mine (cheek) in a very warm affectionate manner. . . . I felt so sad to take leave of this dear amiable young man, whom I really think (talking jokingly) I was a little in love with."

When, the next evening, an evening so noticeably bereft of the Russians, the band suddenly broke into *Le Gai Loisir,* it "made me quite melancholy," wrote Victoria, "as it put me in mind of all, and I felt sadly the change."

In her depression she turned to the elderly, ever-faithful figure at her elbow. "Talked to Lord M. of my feeling the change, and of its being so seldom that I had young people of my own rank with me, of my having so disliked the idea of the Grand Duke's coming and that now I was so *very, very* sorry at his going."

"Very often the case," commented the more experienced Melbourne. Now that he was no longer irritated by the Grand Duke's presence, ready to be generous, he admitted that he was "a very good-natured young man." Thus encouraged, Victoria confided in him "the strange feeling" she was experiencing now that "all the excitement was over," and they discussed the difficulty in London of having "these sorts of dances"—intimate dances, *soit entendu,* in which delightful young foreigners could leap to and fro over outstretched handkerchiefs without adverse comment. To indulge in this sort of thing Victoria observed "there must be many young people."

"And you had a great posse of them," exclaimed Lord Melbourne, his thoughts on last night's youthful bacchanal.

"A young person like me," went on Victoria, "must *sometimes* have young people to laugh with."

"Nothing so natural," agreed Lord Melbourne; and, smitten by the realization of how heavily harnessed were her youthful inclinations, tears of kindness came to his eyes... and then their two voices go murmuring on beyond our hearing.

3

Beyond a doubt the "heir to all the Russias" had left the atmosphere behind him peculiarly tense, and the effect on Victoria was one of alternate lassitude and irritability. The sparkle, the quivering excitement of her first year on the throne, that *annus mirabilis,* had vanished. When, this year of 1839, the second anniversary of her accession came around, it was recorded with bleak terseness.

Thursday 20th June. Got up at 10 and breakfasted at ½ p. This day 2 years I came to the Throne. It seems much longer and shorter, both.

Not one exclamation mark; not a single underlining. As one reads of her during these summer months it is as if a blight had fallen on that once glowing little being. Those formerly voluminous conversations between her and Melbourne, her mind bustling around his for information, now sometimes petered to a standstill. The truth is that during these two years she had received a good deal of information at first hand from life itself, and some of it of a pungent, not to say, extremely painful nature. No longer could she flatter herself that she was the royal treasure whom the country, eyes moist with sensibility, had at first regarded with such adulation and tenderness. "The Hastings business," commented Greville this spring, "has played the devil with the Queen's popularity, and cast dreadful odium and discredit on the Court."

Victoria herself was aware of an alteration in some of her characteristics. "I asked Lord M. if he didn't think me very much changed, and much more silent than I used to be." "You are more silent to-night," he admitted.

Now she would be tactless, even a shade cruel with that beloved companion, telling him one night of "my liking to live with young people, for that then I felt that *I was young,* which I really often forgot; living so much if not entirely, with people much older than myself." She then passed on to Uncle Leopold having tiresomely asked "if I intended to travel this year." Why should she when she did not wish to, and she and Lord Melbourne discussed the matter, "I stating very strongly my great dislike of doing so."

"You must do it one day; there's no need of doing it now," and he threw in a word for the claims of Scotland and Ireland to have sight of her. But she only envisaged "the dreadful trouble and fatigue it would be." Scotland and Ireland were incontinently pushed out of the room.

Leopold had been proving tiresome in other ways besides this idea of her traveling about. He did not consider that the interests of Belgium were being sufficiently taken into consideration by the four Powers—England, France, Austria, and Russia—and in consequence his letters to his niece had had at times a decided under-crackle of sarcasm. "You know from experience," he had written to her the autumn before, "that I *never ask anything of you*. I prefer remaining in the position of having rendered services without wanting any return for it but your affection."

Needless to say he did definitely want a return, and a substantial one. He wished her to implement her affection for him by directing her ministers' policy in his favor. When he found this was not forthcoming, the underlinings in his letters rivaled those of his niece.

"I am glad I extracted some spark of politics from your dear Majesty, very *kindly* and *nicely* expressed ...," so he had written to her this April. "We have not been listened to, and arrangements *are forced* on us ... when by consulting the *real interests* of Holland and Belgium, both countries might have been placed on a footing of *sincere peace*.... This country now feels humbled and désenchanté with it's *soi-disant* political independence," and so on and so on. He was also unwise enough in one of his letters to whimper to his niece about the humidity of his new kingdom. All he got in return being, "I don't like your *croaking* so about damp climates."

This April he so annoyed Victoria that she complained to Melbourne "that my Uncle had written me a cross letter." She was, so she told Melbourne, "very angry but didn't know if I ought to answer him sharply."

"Lord Melbourne leant close towards me and said in his kindest manner, 'You mustn't get into any controversy; you must waive it, and speak of something else.'"

Her Prime Minister confided in her one day that, whenever he himself felt "annoyed or worried," he always, even on a hot day, ordered the fire to be lit in his room; "it's astonishing," he exclaimed, "how it dissipates that," and, again, "Always should have a fire if it rains."

But Victoria's present mood of discontent, this summer of 1839, was not to be dissipated by such a simple expedient. For in the background there were good reasons for her general sense of lassitude and spleen. Not only was the uproar over Lady Flora Hastings still going on, but a fresh aspect of the affair was now drawing attention. "They," wrote Greville this June, referring to the Queen's supporters in general, "are in a great fright lest Lady Flora should die. She is very ill, and if she should die the public will certainly hold an inquest on her body, and bring in a verdict of wilful murder against Buckingham Palace."

If Victoria picked up the *Morning Post* her eye might any moment light on "the violent and libellous articles" that continued to appear about this wretched affair. Further, when she went to Ascot this summer an extraordinary and most unpleasant incident occurred. The Duchess of Montrose and Lady Sarah Ingestre were perched on "Erroll's stand" watching the Queen bowing from her carriage as it came bowling along in all its royal *éclat* up the center of the racecourse; and as these two ladies gazed, standing there in all their summery, Ascot froufrou, from out their throats suddenly issued unmistakable hissings. Hoots, too, directed at Melbourne, arose from the crowd; and, still more embarrassing, as "the Queen stepped out on the balcony" a cry of "Mrs. Melbourne" came from some men in the enclosure, "gentlemen in respect of rank."

An evening after this, when Victoria was in one of her new silent moods, Lord Melbourne, guessing what she was brooding over, alluded to these hissing ladies. "You shouldn't give way too much to personal dislikes," he adjured her. "Now, are you sure they did it?"

"Quite sure."

"They did it at me," protested Melbourne, trying to draw the odium to himself.

"That was just the same. . . . I knew they did it at me also."

"I heard it," Melbourne had to admit. Then her exasperated mind slid to Peel. "I said I had every reason to be angry with Peel."

"You both say just the same . . . he says 'I feel I can never be the Queen's Minister' and you say he never can be your Minister."

"I said that was so."

"It's very odd," went on Melbourne, "that two such interviews should have produced so much irritation. . . ."

"I said I couldn't conceal my feelings . . . that it might get me into a good many scrapes, but that I couldn't help speaking up my feelings."

"Well I should appreciate that," threw out Melbourne, "but everybody does not."

This summer even the flowers in the Buckingham Palace gardens received a scolding from their disgruntled owner. They had, she said, lost their scent, "neither the lime blossoms or the flowers smelt hardly at all." In fact she found the whole garden "very dull."

"All gardens are dull," agreed Lord Melbourne, "a garden is a dull thing." He even said he disliked trees, especially in London, and on the whole would prefer the park to be turned into a plain.

By the end of July, Windsor Castle, to which she used to set out so eagerly, now rose before her merely as a boring residence. "Talked of my fearing to go to Windsor this year; of my getting tired of the place." But the next day she was complaining "of my being kept so long in London, which, when the Opera was over I should dislike, as I hated *not* going out, and staying at home every day."

"Lord M. said 'in the country I must stay at home.'"

"'Then I submitted,' I said."

"He said I might go out more next year."

"I said I felt tired."

"Lord Melbourne asked why."

"I didn't know, but that I certainly was tired."

Dear, affectionate Lord Melbourne. During this difficult time his attitude to life, at once quizzical and serene, held a steadying quality. It amused Victoria to go to visit him while Grant was painting his portrait in one of the rooms at the palace. "At 5," she writes one day this July, "I went downstairs with Lehzen...to the Equerries' room, where Lord Melbourne was sitting to Grant... on that wooden horse without head or tail, looking so funny, his white hat on, an umbrella in lieu of a stick in one hand, and holding the reins which were fastened to the steps in the other; he sat there so patiently and so kindly, doing just what he was told; but as Grant said, he is not easy to paint, for he either looks grave and absorbed, or laughs and goes into the other extreme...I was *so* amused. Grant kept telling him, 'Now, Lord Melbourne hold your head in the right position'—for he kept looking at Islay [her dog] and trying to touch him with his umbrella; and then, 'Now sit up, Lord Melbourne.' Grant has got him so like; it is such a happiness for me to have that dear kind friend's face, which I do like and admire so, so like; his face, his expression, his air, his white hat, and his cravat, waistcoat and coat, all just as he wears it . . . I remained 20 minutes in the room."

But when on these summer evenings the royal band would mellifluously glide into the quadrilles (oh, that poignant *Le Gai Loisir* and the memories that clung), it would bring all her diverse discontents to a climax. She would be invaded by an unaccountable feeling. Especially while one evening at dinner she sat listening to that treacherous music, the emotions it raised in her became unbearable, and, turning to Melbourne, she exclaimed that the quadrilles made her feel "quite frantic."

Melbourne was startled. "Those Quadrilles," he warned, "are dangerous if they produce that effect on you."

If the memory of the Grand Duke was, in a nostalgic sense, one irritant, another was a matter that could be ignored no longer, that positively now had to be faced: the question of her marrying Albert. It could be said without exaggeration that to her the thought of it loomed horribly. Would it, she asked herself again, be preferable not to marry at all? "For myself," she exclaimed one day this spring to Melbourne, "For myself . . . at present *my* feeling was quite against ever marrying."

"It's a great change . . ." said Lord Melbourne, feeling his way gingerly, "a very serious thing, both as it concerns the Political effect and your own happiness." And a few moments later he added, "if one was to *make* a man for it, one would hardly know what to make; he mustn't be stupid—nor cunning."

As the summer went on, the thought of having to take Albert to share the throne that, except for the last few months, she had so delightedly occupied by herself, annoyed her more and more, and one evening, when the subject of Albert and his brother coming over on a visit this year was under discussion, she protested that she had "no great wish to see Albert," that the whole subject was "odious," and further, one which she "hated to decide about."

"It's very disagreeable," agreed Lord Melbourne.

"I said I wished if possible never to marry."

"I don't know about that," remarked Melbourne.

The Queen's friendship with her Premier had reached that comfortable stage when she knew she could give him a buffet without fear of leaving a bruise. "The Queen anxiously hopes Lord Melbourne has slept well . . ." she wrote to him one morning this summer, the day after a small dance at the palace. "It was very wrong of him not to wish the Queen goodnight, as she expected he would in so small a party, for she *saw* that he did *not* go away immediately after supper. When did he get home?"

And this August he received a quite sharp jobation. His indolent drifting habits that could be so laughably endearing could also, she discovered, at times be definitely provoking, and this month her dear mentor received a letter from her in which real anger was stirring between the carefully chosen words.

"The Queen," she wrote him, "has received both Lord Melbourne's notes; she was a good deal vexed at his not coming, as she had begged him herself to do so, and as he wrote to say he would and also as she thinks it right and of importance that Lord Melbourne should be here at large dinners; the Queen *insists* upon his coming to dinner to-morrow." And not only this but, further down the page, "The Queen has been a good deal annoyed this evening at Normanby's telling her that John Russell was coming to town next Monday in order to *change* with *him*. Lord Melbourne *never* told the Queen that this was definitely settled . . . considering the great confidence the Queen has in Lord Melbourne, she thinks and feels he ought to have told her that this was *settled*, and not let the Queen be the last person to hear what is settled and done in her own name; Lord Melbourne will excuse the Queen's being a little eager about this, but it has happened once before that she learnt from other people what had been decided on."

She was quite right to complain. Either she was Queen of England or she was not. Having been accepted by Government and country her youthfulness had to be ignored. She was England's figurehead, and her shrewdness—already mature—made her aware she must be treated as such. However, later in the same letter she softens the severity of the rap she had bestowed. "The Queen has such unlimited confidence in Lord Melbourne that she knows all that he does is right, but she cannot help being a little vexed at not being told things."

She also tried to brisk him up over his somnolent habits, telling him one day that "he mustn't go to sleep before so many people, for that he generally snored."

"That proclaims it too much," remarked her genial Premier.

"I *quite* agreed."

4

In the background Miss Harriet Martineau's uncompromising gaze was often upon her young sovereign: "the Queen went abroad abundantly," so she writes, "and I saw her very often." As a child Miss Martineau had thoroughly approved of the little Princess, for one day when the authoress had been at a concert at the Hanover Square Rooms Conroy had come over to speak to her, sent by the Duchess of Kent "with a message of acknowledgement of the usefulness of my books to the Princess." This was very proper, and most satisfactory to Harriet Martineau's feelings; and still more so was the news given her by a friend who had happened to be at Kensington Palace "when my Political Economy series was coming to an end," and this friend told her "how the Princess came running and skipping to show her mother the advertisement of the 'Illustration of Taxation' and to get leave to order them." All this running and skipping in response to Miss Martineau's pipings placed the heir to the throne within an ambient glow, but, once she had become Queen, Harriet began to give her some sharp digs. There was, for instance, that evening at the theater when Macready was acting Lear, and Miss Martineau kept glancing up at the royal box so as to ascertain whether her Queen was reacting to Lear's griefs in the manner in which Miss Martineau considered she should. She was not. To the authoress' indignation there, in her ornate box, sat the little person, her eye not even on the actors, but "chattering to the Lord Chamberlain and laughing, with her shoulder [that young shoulder whose plumpness was at once so fashionable and so charming] turned to the stage." How shockingly different was her behavior from that of another occupant of the box, Lord Albemarle, who, Harriet Martineau approvingly noted, "by degrees leaned forward between the Queen and the stage and wept till his limp handkerchief would hold no more tears."

Tears! Tears! Where are the sobs of yesterday? How ubiquitous they were at that time; how sought for, how welcomed: on the stage, in private life, between the covers of a novel. To weep oneself or to induce another to weep was an accomplishment of which either man or woman was proud, the sob being regarded as proof of a fine disposition. What deep-seated alteration has taken place in the nation's mind that has placed tears at such a discount? That the general demand now should be, not to be made to sob, but to be amused.

5

On July 5 this summer, that which the Whigs had feared would happen, took place; Flora Hastings died. Now arose more than ever a melodramatic note; a note intensified by the hapless young woman having requested that there should be an autopsy on her body so as to emphasize still more conclusively the falseness of the charge against her. When Victoria heard of her death she "wept bitterly" and "ordered the Palace to be closed," but the royal carriage that she sent to represent her at the funeral had stones flung against its varnished panels.

Here were indeed matters for discussion round the Mayfair and Belgravia drawing-room tea tables "with the lace curtains blowing in from the windows on a warm summer Sunday afternoon"; for Sunday was then *par excellence* the day for intimate clusterings of friends.

The *Morning Post,* far from letting the business drop, was increasing the agitation over Lady Flora Hastings "*ad nauseam*" and daily inveighing against the Queen "with the most revolting virulence and indecency." Meanwhile, Brougham was at his usual firebrand tricks. He would, wrote a contemporary, "gladly increase the prejudice" against Victoria, and at the moment was urging upon Lord Tavistock "the duty of defending the character of his wife without any regard to the consequences as they might affect the Queen." The doorbells of all the little bookshops were tinkling as one customer after another hurried in to lay down his or her shilling on the counter for one of those vituperative but revealing leaflets that had sprung into being, setting out the entire scandal in all its details: leaflets in which the "Sceptred Child" (as one scolder dubbed her) and her entourage were condemned, and Flora Hastings and her relations exalted. These productions had been given titles of the most lurid nature: *The Court Doctor Dissected. The Victim of Scandal. The Lady Flora Hastings Her Life and Death: With Questions for the Queen and Criticisms of her Court. The Dangers of Evil Council.* Another struck a macabre note. *A Voice from the Grave of Lady Flora Hastings to her most gracious Majesty the Queen.* And, finally, came a rhyming satire, *The Palace Martyr! A Satire by the Honourable* * * *

One questions, when one reads his effort, where The Honourable Three Asterisks had been educated; one questions, indeed, whether he had a corporeal existence at all.

> But we are told that Majesty at length
> To show its kindness and its sorrow's strength,
> When round the Palace Martyr's dying bed
> The friends were gathered, and all hope was fled—
> Ev'n in that hour of misery and gloom,
> Ordered *'refreshments'* in the dining-room!

Within the palace the Duchess of Kent's attitude, not only to Lehzen, but to Lord Melbourne, had become by now so hostile that the Duke of Wellington, in one of his talks with her, tried his utmost to break it down. It seems that ever since the Flora Hastings business had started she had contrived all through the summer to absent herself from "her place in the Court circle," and Wellington now begged her "to adopt a good-humoured and conciliatory tone generally."

"But what am I to do if Lord Melbourne comes up to me?"

"Do? Why, receive him with civility and cordiality ... besides, why should you not? ..."

"Oh, I don't approve of the way in which he comes here."

"Nonsense—all stuff and nonsense.... He is quite right to come as he does.... I tell you that if I had been in his place I should not only have done the same, but have done more...."

"Well... I must say you are a just man—but what must I do if She asks me to shake hands with Lehzen?"

"Do? Why, take her in your arms and kiss her."

The Duchess began to laugh.

"I don't mean you are to take Lehzen in your arms and kiss *her*, but the Queen," cried the Duke, himself starting to laugh. "She is your daughter, and this is the way you must treat her, and be civil to Lord Melbourne, and Lehzen and all the persons in attendance upon her."

About a month before Lady Flora died a significant alteration had taken place in the usual Buckingham Palace pattern. With infinite subtlety the Duke of Wellington had persuaded Conroy to resign and to leave the country. "It was the Duke and He alone" who did it; and the way he brought it about was "by cajoling and flattering Conroy himself and representing to him that his conduct in retiring would not only be gratifying to the Duchess's family but be honourable to himself... and by honied words like these he prevailed on him at last to go."

Ultimately, now rendered harmless by time and circumstance, Conroy returned to England and settled into a house not far from Reading. We see him sitting there, that once truculent character, gradually fading out of the Victorian scene, becoming ever dimmer to our eyes within a setting of royal figures watching him from out their frames: Kensington Palace still present, but now only in two dimensions as a print; and gazing from one of the walls of his library the silent face of Flora Hastings.

CHAPTER XIV

REAPPEARANCE OF THE COBURG PRINCES

This August and September there was a rush of Coburgs to visit England's Queen—King Leopold and his wife: Leopold's brother Ferdinand, his daughter Victoire, and two sons.

After all the tormenting experiences Victoria had passed through this spring and summer we see her gratefully sinking back into the easy, the familiar atmosphere of her Coburg relations, and most especially savoring that of King Leopold, surrounded as he always was for her with memories of those early and, if compared with the late lacerating incidents, most peaceful days at Kensington. However, on this occasion his brother and his family came over first; and a little vignette of this advance family party amusing themselves one evening after dinner is given to us. Lord Melbourne is attempting and succeeding in the manipulation of "the Cup and Ball." Pleased with his own adroitness he informs the company that "the only way to do it" is "perfect tranquillity,—which is the only way to do anything." No one seems to have been particularly interested in this piece of advice, and he fell back on talking of the pictures that hung on the walls. Other amusements besides the Cup and Ball were sprinkled about on the great round table, at the head of which, on a sofa, sat Victoria with Prince Ferdinand; "some of the young people being seated round the table, playing at games; at draughts, and at a game of tee-totums in a bowl," at which Victoria "also joined occasionally." With her relations she always spoke in German, and as those rigorous syllables split the air in chorus, it struck her what a tedious evening it must be for Melbourne who did not know the language. "I said to Lord M. it must be so tiresome to hear German always spoken before him, which he didn't understand."

"Oh! not at all," he exclaimed, probably considering that as regards Uncle Ferdinand's observations and the squeals of the young over tee-totums he was not missing anything of much value.

But the great arrival for Victoria was that of Uncle Leopold. She sat waiting for him one September evening in her habit, having just come in from a ride, and believing he would arrive within the hour. She found the thought of seeing him again so delightful that it is clear that any spiky observations in their letters to each other had vanished from her mind. Certainly some of her remarks in her letters had at one time almost scared Leopold. He had begun to suspect that not only was she losing her affection for him, but that, equally, he was losing his ascendancy over her. Besides a tenderness of heart for his niece that was real, he had through all these years enjoyed equipping her for her position: in doing so he had savored a certain amount of the power that would have been his if Charlotte had lived. But the question was, had he equipped her too efficiently, made this glorious young Queen too capable of getting on without him? The dreadful idea even crossed his mind that she was beginning to look on him as of no more importance than a discarded old table or chair. "I thought I had been put aside as one does with a piece of furniture which is no longer wanted." This was terrible, but the little royal hand with the quill bestowed comfort, and the horrid fear subsided. And now Victoria, awaiting him in the Castle, was undergoing all those quickening heartbeats of affection that he used to arouse in her. "I waited till ¼ p. 8 in my habit, and no one arrived.... I read Despatches. I then took off my habit and was only half dressed when I heard they were coming; I rushed down ... and received my dear Uncle and dear Louise at the door.... I took Uncle and Aunt to their rooms, and soon left them; none of their things being come, they did not wish to come to dinner."

The only drawback to the joys of this reunion was that it was the prelude for a visit to England of King Leopold's nephew, that menacing Albert; for, during these days the final arrangements for the young man's arrival at the Castle were made.

Meanwhile, Leopold sat about in the great Windsor drawing

PRINCE ALBERT OF SAXE-COBURG AND GOTHA

From the portrait by John Partridge

By gracious permission of H.M. The King

QUEEN VICTORIA AND THE PRINCE CONSORT

room effectively spreading around him his particular self-chosen atmosphere, "imposing, melancholy and dignified." He certainly did it very well. With his ivory face, "his half-closed eyes and his peculiar smile," it was a sure thing that he would intimidate anyone who was open to intimidation. "I am rayther afraid of him," Lady Lyttelton admitted to herself, for even that observantly critical lady had her fluttery moments.

Only too soon came the days of heartrending farewells; and most bitter they were, not only to Victoria but to her mother; for that once obstreperous Duchess, now deprived of Flora Hastings by death, of Conroy by departure, and still kept in a kind of moral purdah by Victoria, was indeed isolated. The sight of her daughter, Lehzen and Melbourne, all progressing interlaced in their triumphal car, daily emphasized to her how she herself had got left behind, so it seemed, forever. So now, when she and Victoria went down to Woolwich to see the first departure, those of Prince Ferdinand and his family, we are not surprised to hear that the Duchess was "hardly able to let go the hand of 'my bruder.' " Meanwhile, "the two young and pretty girls," Victoria and her cousin Victoire, were "sobbing over each other." Victoria went below to see Victoire's cabin, and there "I made dearest Victoire take off her little handkerchief and give it to me; and I gave her mine." Lady Lyttelton, witnessing all these Coburg wrenchings apart, found it "quite throat-lumpy."

And then, three days later, it was still more distressing for Victoria, for she had to say good-by to her Belgian Uncle and Aunt. "I got up," runs the Journal on September 20, "at ½ p. 4, put on a dressing-gown and bonnet, and went to Louise's sitting-room ["with your dear honest face looking so dear in your morning attire," so Uncle Leopold wrote her the next day] where I found her and Uncle at breakfast by candlelight; they were much pleased to see me. I took some bread and butter and an egg.... I went with them to Mamma's room, and then took leave of them at the top of the staircase.... I watched them from my window; day was dawning and it looked grey and melancholy."

Most dreary too seemed the prospect of what had begun to appear to her as not much more than a State marriage. The one thing from her point of view was to keep the project vague, to push it well into the future. "I couldn't *think* of marrying for *three or four years*," she had exclaimed one day this spring. So now her great concern was that no one should make the mistake of thinking Albert's arrival was "to *settle matters*." That would never do. Some of her ministers were coming to stay at the castle for a few days, and if Albert came while they were there people might jump to ridiculous conclusions. Therefore, so she decided, he and his brother must be restrained from putting foot on English soil till October 3, and Leopold received instructions to that effect. "All I want," she wrote him, "is that *you* should detain them one or two days longer." "I think indeed a day or two at Brussels will do these young gentlemen good," wrote the Windsor monarch patronizingly, "and they can be properly fitted out there for their visit."

However, on the last day of September, she received a letter from Albert himself in which he had the presumption to say "they could not set off, he thought, before the 6th." She was a little scandalized. "The *retard* of these young people," she wrote to her uncle, "puts me rather out. . . . I don't think they exhibit much *empressement* to come here, which rather shocks me."

Meanwhile, along the roads of Germany an extended line of carriages was galloping toward Brussels. On the floor of one of these Albert and his brother Ernest were squeezed together consumed with laughter, for, seeing ahead of them all the townspeople of some little place come out to applaud them as they drove by, it had struck the two young men as extremely droll to crouch down out of sight while they held up in the window, as a substitute for themselves, Albert's pet greyhound, Eös.

    ·   ·   ·   ·   ·   ·

The tenth of October had arrived, but so far no cousins. However, that day, as the Queen and Melbourne were walking near the castle, and Melbourne remarking how cold it was, "one of my pages came running with a letter from Uncle Leopold, saying my cousins would be here very soon."

A little after seven o'clock she was standing, extremely alert, at the top of the castle staircase up which were mounting two remarkably princely looking young men, tricked out with all the fashionable adornments of whiskers, forward-brushed curls, mutiple collars, and abundant cravats. Victoria's appraising glance flicked from Albert to Ernest, from Ernest to Albert. On the instant she was almost overthrown by the brothers' appearance: so much were they "changed...embellished." The too puppylike softness of the schoolboys who had stayed at Kensington a few years back had tautened and hardened into manhood. Albert's good looks were phenomenal. Though in a portrait of Ernest his hair is very black, and his eyes, rather resembling those of a Pekinese, have a glamorous gaze, yet his pallid face, the cheeks curiously sunken for such a young man, were to prevent his gaining that acclamation from the Windsor circle which was accorded to Albert's beauty. Ernest's person was the very vial of a nineteenth-century Continental roué; and he was to become one indeed. Certainly Albert had one drawback: his voice. "Sadly disenchanting," sighed Lady Lyttelton. "His *organe*," wrote Lady Holland, "is reckoned very shrill and displeasing," and, so she continues, it was said of him "what used to be said of Mde de Coigny, 'Qu'elle n'avait qu'une voix contre elle, c'était la sienne.' " But though Victoria was sensitive in her feelings, one notices that her nerves could withstand impacts that would rasp many women, and now, her ears impervious to assault, as she and the two cousins and her mother all talked away together in her private room, her mind was filled only with Albert's attractions. ("Albert really is quite charming and so excessively handsome," she whispered the following night to her Journal, "such beautiful blue eyes, an exquisite nose, and such a pretty mouth with delicate mustachios and slight but very slight whiskers; a beautiful figure, broad in the shoulders and a fine waist.")

And on this day of his arrival, as her eyes dwelt on that youthful male magnificence ("It was with some emotion that I beheld Albert"), her whole nature came to a standstill. Young as she was, emotionally, it had been a long journey: there had been Lablache, and Lord Melbourne, and Lord Alfred Paget, and, only a short time ago, that disturbing young man from Russia; but now, as the three eager voices intermingled, and her eyes again and again sought Albert's face, the notes of *Le Gai Loisir* faded away on the castle air, faded away completely, and she realized that here, once and for all, she had come to the end of a hitherto unconscious quest.

At that moment she might have exclaimed with Bassanio, "my blood speaks to you in my veins."

2

When Albert had arrived at the castle, beneath that markedly successful exterior there had been stirring the spirit of a nervous, and at the same time slightly defiant, boy of nineteen. Before he arrived, Victoria had written to Leopold urging him to impress on her cousin that if, when he came to England, she found she did not experience "the *feeling* for him which is requisite to ensure happiness," she was "*not*" to be considered "guilty of any breach of promise for *I never gave* any." Even if she found he did please her, she could, so she said, "*make no final promise this year*, for, at the *very earliest*, any such event could not take place till *two or three years hence*." The explanation of this being the "*great* repugnance to change my present position."

It is not surprising that in response to all this unpleasant information—which was passed on to Albert by Leopold, before he set sail for England—the young Coburg Prince decided that if his evasive cousin did not now definitely make up her mind he would wait on her vagaries no longer. He confided to a friend that he was crossing the Channel with "the quiet but firm resolution to declare . . . that I, also, tired of the delay" would now withdraw "entirely." When he did arrive at Windsor his mind was filled, so he wrote to his grandmother, with the ignominiousness of his position, and for the first few days, while everything hung in the balance, he found that when he went to bed he could not sleep for anxiety. Victoria became acquainted with this fact, which she passed on to Lord Melbourne, adding "nor I either." Curiously enough—for no two faces could seem to us more dissimilar than her own bright-robin little countenance and Albert's dramatic symmetry—some of the onlookers thought that they had a strong cousinly resemblance. On the first evening of the brothers' arrival Victoria, quite drowned in admiration, positively could not resist asking Lord Melbourne "if he thought Albert like me."

"Oh! yes he is," exclaimed Melbourne, "it struck me at once."

The next day after the Coburgs' arrival, "At about ½ past 10 dancing began." Inevitably Victoria's eyes were again riveted. "It is quite a pleasure to look at Albert when he gallops and valses ... holds himself so well with that beautiful figure of his. Lord Melbourne sat near me during the intervals and during the valses." A peculiar shrouding of his personality seems to have come over her Premier that evening; a something so unusual that, so it appears, Victoria noticed it herself, and asked him if there was anything wrong, for, so she writes, "He was quite well, he assured me, and not tired."

"Just before I began the fourth quadrille, I asked him if he was going or staying."

"He said 'going.'" And if as he left the room his step was heavy Victoria would have had no suspicion of the reason. But Melbourne knew all. As he had watched Victoria watching Albert he had known that, himself, he had received his *congé*.

3

It was on a Thursday that the brothers had arrived at Windsor, and when, on Tuesday morning, they came back from hunting, Victoria was watching from a castle window. As she saw them "charge up the hill at a tremendous pace," that "same emotion" which she had experienced on first seeing the embellished Albert was now increased tenfold, for as her eyes dwelt on that splendid Apollo on his thundering horse, she was filled with the realization that within a few moments she would be imparting to him the most significant decision of her life.

It was a little after twelve o'clock when Albert, dismounting, came into the castle. Half an hour had not passed before he received a "secretly" passed-on message telling him that Victoria wished to see him, and that he was to join her in "the closet."

As he came in at the door he saw the small figure waiting for him, and alone, in the room. Then, with what he later described as "a joyous openness of manner" which "quite enchanted me," she told him, "that I thought he must be aware *why* I wished them to come here, that it would make me *too happy* if he would consent to what I wished (to marry me)."

Albert said afterward that he was "quite carried away" by what he realized was a "genuine outburst of love and affection." In one instant the mortification of his whole past position, the hideously envisaged possibility of dismissal vanished completely. From relief on one side, and thirsting love on the other, enthusiasm flew from spirit to spirit; they flung their arms around each other's necks. Victoria exclaimed that she was "quite unworthy of him."

He protested that he "would be very happy."

She impressed on him that he was making "a great sacrifice."

He would not allow it.

He was "*so* kind, *so* affectionate . . ."

The room was suffused with a golden haze. "I really felt," wrote Victoria that night, "it was the happiest brightest moment of my life."

4

The day before, Victoria had told Lord Melbourne that she had definitely decided as to the marriage. When he had come to see her at one o'clock, she had at first talked of this and of that. Then she remarked that "my cousins" were out shooting. There was "a little pause"; then "I said to Lord M. that I had made up my mind (about marrying my dearest Albert)."

"You have?" queried Melbourne. He asked when it would be.

"Not for a year, I thought."

"Too long," opined her Premier. "I think it'll be very well received . . ." he went on, "I think it is a very good thing, and you'll be much more comfortable; for a woman cannot stand alone for long, in whatever situation she is."

For the present it was to be kept secret within a minute circle; and the next day Victoria was writing with delight of "Albert's behaving so wonderfully . . . no-one could imagine that anything had taken place." But Ernest, on his part, exclaimed that "*he* couldn't bear it if he was in such a situation."

From now on Victoria and Melbourne's heads were abuzz with the organization of the great event ahead. Endlessly they discussed, discussed. Past royalties were dug up regarding questions of precedent. The list of Queen Charlotte's long-dead bridesmaids was scanned. The Peerage was gutted in the search for suitable living

ones. "I sent for the Peerage and Lord M. read through all the
Dukes." And so on, and so on. Lord Melbourne's mind indeed was
so taken up what with one thing and another that one November
evening when Victoria had sent for him from his private room
in the palace she was startled to see walking in at the door a figure
"in a strange costume . . . light white and grey striped calico trousers
with very large shoes." Victoria's reproof was merely, "I feared I
had interrupted him in his sleep."

This "he wouldn't allow; but which I think *was* the case."

All this to-do of settling and arranging was not completed without some flare-ups between Queen and Premier. They were talking
one day of the possibility of Parliament having to meet next year
as early as the ninth of January. In that case "I would *not* open
it myself," shot out Victoria.

"Oh, you must," cried Melbourne, "that would never do."

"I wouldn't, I said," and she added that she "always wished to
get out of that."

"You mustn't do that," came the charming voice "kindly and
gently."

After dinner that night, "I again teazed him about not opening
Parliament in person."

" 'Oh! you will do it,' he said earnestly, with his good kind face
expressing anxiety I should. 'Not to do so would not be right when
it is necessary for Public affairs.' "

But in the evenings, when they were most of them seated about
the familiar round table, affairs of State fled into the shadows and
all was merriment and harmony, and games, and young laughter.
Again an evening picture forms before us, one typical of many.
"I had great fun with my dear cousins after dinner," wrote Victoria
one Sunday. "I sat on the sofa with dearest Albert; Lord Melbourne sitting near me, Ernest playing at chess, and many being
seated round the table. I looked at some drawings by Stephano
della Bella and Domenichino, with Albert." Then they pushed
these on to Lord Melbourne for him to pore over. (On another
occasion, when showing Lord Melbourne some drawings, "I told
him before we began to look, some weren't quite eligible and were
tacked together.") Then Eös, Albert's greyhound and dear com-

panion, came gently padding into the room, and yawned at them all. Then, goes on Victoria, "I played 2 games of Tactics with dear Albert, and 2 at Fox and Geese. Stayed up till 20. m. p. 11. A delightful evening."

Autre temps, autre mœurs indeed.

5

During this momentous visit of the Coburg brothers, Lady Lyttelton, that lady in waiting of the virile pen, was moving about in the background and quietly forming her own conclusions. "It (a *small* party in the Castle) makes one feel more towards the Queen—more of the admiration and wonder which some parts of her character excite, more of the affection which others naturally inspire, and more, alas! of the regret and compassion, and hopelessness and helplessness which many circumstances of her education and present position and future fate fill one with."

But dear Lady Lyttelton was inclined to be overcome too quickly by a sense of hopelessness and helplessness before the characteristics of her fellow creatures if they did not happen to coincide with her own evangelical outlook. ("So many good qualities in that little body of hers," wrote Lady Palmerston—Melbourne's sister—of Victoria, "so much kindness of heart!—it is really a marvel.") Lady Lyttelton is at her best when she lets her strictures have a rest, and gives us instead swift impressions of the people coming and going around her. Sitting scribbling one day this autumn in her room at the castle, she hears Prince Ernest talking beneath her window. "There," she cries, "I hear his voice in loud laughter as he walks on the terrace." "A light figure, and a great look of spirit and eagerness," she continues approvingly; it being fortunately not revealed to her in what directions this eagerness was chiefly going to manifest itself.

When this lady in waiting is really invaluable is when she transcribes a conversation *in toto*. That, for instance, which she had with the Duke of Cambridge, who on this visit, as usual, in spite of his far-gone deafness, stunned everyone around him with his vitality and ceaseless prattle.

Windsor November 8 (1839). The Cambridges arrived yesterday, and enriched our dancing evening. Queen's headache quite gone, luckily, for it requires a sound head to listen to the Duke. . . . I was so *bestürmt* with questions, one hundred in a breath, close to my eye, by the Duke on his first arrival that I was fairly bewildered, and answered, "Yes, Ma'am."

After dinner, during the dancing, he came and sat by me, and to be sure how he did shout and cross-examine! but he never wants an answer, so it don't matter.

"Where do you *habitually* reside, Ma'am? Oh, Hagley—you *did* live there. I see, I see—your son lately married—how long? a few months? I understand. *Now* where do you mean to live? At Richmond for the winter? Oh, I see! Where have you been since your son's marriage? Leamington? Why to Leamington? Oh, your brother—I understand! Your brother Captain Spencer! I remember—I perfectly recollect. A naval man, I believe. Yes, I saw him in 1825 at your father's in the Isle of Wight. Yes, yes, I know—Frederick Spencer, to be sure! *Your* father-in-law, Mr. Poyntz? No, surely not so, Ma'am. Oh, *his* father-in-law? Oh, I see, I see," and so on for half an hour. I was quite out of breath with listening, and could hardly stick in a word in answer here and there, and all as loud as a very sonorous voice can reach.

The Cambridges [she writes next day], are gone, and the Castle is still as death for want of the Duke. . . . He shouted on to the last, singing the quadrilles while they danced, and God save the Queen while we dined rather than be silent.

She was far from being the only person to be discomposed by the Duke's irrepressible chatter. The officiating clergyman at any service at which the royal Cambridge was present, had to be prepared to hear rising loudly from the front pew the most uncalled-for comments.

"Let us pray," would come the quiet voice from the chancel, only to be met by an enthusiastic "With all my heart." One Sunday the story of Zacchaeus was in progress, but directly "Behold the half of my goods I give to the poor" fell on the Duke's ears there came the splutter "No! no! can't do that; that's too much for any man—no objection to a tenth." The congregation being asked to pray for rain—"Yes, yes, quite right, quite right; but it will never rain till the wind changes."

This unusual co-operation with the ritual, combined with, doubtless, the suppressed hilarity of the congregation, so upset a curate at the church at Kew which the Duke attended that he gave up his curacy, protesting that "he was quite unable to endure it."

CHAPTER XV
THE VICTORIA AND ALBERT LEGEND
HAS ITS BEGINNING

The marriage was to take place next February, and in November Albert and his brother went back to Germany.

Now everything began to accelerate, to rush toward the culminating event. Plans, arrangements, rearrangements, incidents, protestations, explanations, discussions, further plans, further arrangement, toppled over each other. Couriers rushed ceaselessly from Buckingham Palace to Coburg, and from Coburg to Buckingham Palace bearing letters from one of the engaged couple to the other; Victoria's being written on what she calls "picture note-paper."

"Dearest, deeply beloved Victoria," wrote Albert. "Dear splendid Victoria," he exclaimed another day, as if in prevision of the cloak of fame with which time would ultimately enwrap her. He would read with surprise the various letters she had sent on to him from the English royal family, letters so flattering to himself that he felt embarrassed. "It almost looks like making fun of me," he expostulated. He and his Aunt Kent were already on the most affectionate terms. We read in a letter of his to her this November, "You wish me to give you something I have worn. I send you the ring which you gave me at Kensington on Victoria's birthday in 1836. From that time it has never left my finger. Its very shape proclaims that it has been squeezed in the grasp of many a manly hand. . . . I beg you to wear it in remembrance of her and myself," he concludes a little strangely, considering that he and Victoria were both very much alive.

One evening at Coburg the Regatta Galop was played at a ball, and at once "the sound of it," so he wrote to Victoria, "transported me to Windsor and in my thoughts I was with you leaning against the long mirror, or flying with you through that lovely ball-room."

His gratitude to his hitherto problematical cousin for delivering him from his humiliating suspense had ricocheted him into the very semblance of a lover, and, too, Victoria's unexpected uprush of devotion had awakened an answering tenderness. Her enthusiasm over him was now the one thing that gave him a sense of security amid all the difficulties that his shrewd and pondering mind saw lying ahead. "Seymour arrived last night," he wrote to her, "and handed me your dear, dear loving letter. How happy your words make me! Such an intimate outpouring from your warm heart, your tenderness. I have to read it again and again, to see in your own words what I so love to see—that you love me." "Even in my dreams," he wrote another day, "I never imagined I should find so much love on earth."

She shone now, a reassuring star, over the confused turmoil that both inwardly and outwardly assailed him. "What a multitude of emotions," he wrote to his Aunt Kent, "What a multitude of emotions of the most diverse kind sweeps over and overwhelms me— hope, love for dear Victoria; the pain of leaving home, the parting from very dear kindred, the entrance into a new circle of relations, prospects most brilliant, the dread of being unequal to my position, the demonstrations of so much attachment on the part of the loyal Coburgers, English enthusiasm on the tiptoe of expectation, the multiplicity of duties to be fulfilled, and, to crown all, so much laudation on every side that I could sink through the earth with very shame. I am lost in bewilderment. I pack, arrange, give directions about pieces of property, settle contracts, engage servants, write an infinitude of letters, study the English Constitution, and occupy myself about my future." And there follow two terse sentences. "Ernest has left me and gone to Dresden. I shall not see him at Coburg." Abrupt sentences, but rising from a deeper layer of feeling than that roused even by the flutings that came from Buckingham Palace; for lifelong divergence of the brothers' hitherto closely shared path was now inevitable, and the realization of this weighed on Albert intolerably.

To return to the forthcoming wedding: apart from the emotional aspect the practical had to be dealt with. The choice, for instance, of Albert's gentlemen of the Household. His wish was, he said, that they should be "either of very high rank, or very rich, or very clever, or persons who have performed important services for England."

In response to this Victoria offered him as his Treasurer Lord Melbourne's secretary, Mr. Anson.

Albert had not been coached in politics by Stockmar without realizing what a mistake he would be making at the outset of his English career if he gave his patronage to any one political party. Also, as with a slight touch of sarcasm he pointed out to Victoria, he knew nothing whatever personally of Anson "except that I have seen him dance a Quadrille." "I give you to consider dearest love," he went on, "if my taking the secretary of the Prime Minister as Treasurer would not from the beginning make me a partisan in the eyes of many."

This Anson question fizzled on through several of their letters; Victoria's underlinings at times racing on for a whole paragraph. "*I am distressed to tell you what I fear you do not like*," she concluded in one letter on the subject, "but it is necessary, my dearest, most excellent Albert. Once more I tell you that you can perfectly rely on me in these matters." Most distinctly it was becoming apparent to him that if this girl with her buoyant capable mind was ardent in love, she was equally ardent in queenship. He accepted Anson.

But when it came to the incident of Victoria sending him the Garter, this time it was she who received a word of admonition. "I am very glad the Garter is coming so soon; though it might have been better if you had sent it by an Envoy; that is the general rule, and Papa is justifiably anxious lest our neighbours—especially those in Berlin—may put it down as a slight to him."

We read of Prince Albert when he came over to England as always wearing the ribbon of the Garter under his waistcoat, having put it on when he dressed for breakfast. Victoria speaks of him, the day before their marriage, coming into the room "with a little of his blue ribbon showing." At that time it was the usual thing to wear it by day, and one questions why the Prince all but concealed the ribbon. The Duke of Wellington, for instance, constantly wore his displayed over a white waistcoat.

There were some collisions both in the House of Commons and

the country over the arrangements for the marriage; over Albert's religion for instance. Lord Melbourne, in making the official announcement of the marriage in the House, had omitted to mention that the Prince was a Protestant. Instantly the malcontents in the country were crying out that Albert was "a Roman Catholic...a radical or an infidel."

The House was asked to vote an allowance for Victoria's coming husband of £50,000 a year, but would agree to no more than £30,000. When Leopold had married George IV's daughter, Charlotte being only heir-presumptive, Parliament had voted him £50,000, therefore when the news of this refusal to consent to at least the same for the reigning Queen's husband reached Belgium and Coburg, there arose great indignation. "I can only conclude by crying *shame, shame!*" exclaimed Leopold. Albert himself, already in many ways apprehensive at the step he was taking, felt it as a hostile gesture, a definite slap in the face. He was, wrote his uncle, "shocked and exasperated by the disrespect of the thing"; "very much irritated."

Over the question of Albert's precedence there had been a great stirring of parliamentary and ministerial waters, and Victoria had become worked up to a degree. "Yesterday morning," writes Greville, this January of 1840, "I met Fitzgerald...and I begged him for God's sake to find some expedient for settling *à l'aimable* the question of precedence, so as to pacify the Queen if possible, who (however unreasonable) was much excited about it." Victoria's old uncles of Sussex and Cambridge struck a friendly note by "willingly" agreeing that their niece's husband should take precedence of them: to her Cumberland uncle, now King of Hanover—and most high-handedly and successfully governing his small country— she did not apply, there being no doubt as to the violence of the refusal she would have received if she had. His jealousy of her he now extended to Albert; henceforth keeping the sharpest eye on the doings of both, and dealing out a brisk rap over the knuckles whenever an opportunity presented itself. *"My Tiara!"* came the scream from Hanover, when, at some city ceremony a few years after her marriage, Victoria wore one of the still disputed pieces of jewelry left by Queen Charlotte.

Then, after Victoria's husband had paid a visit to Coburg, "It appears," wrote the Hanoverian King to Lord Strangford, "that Pce. Albert on his late visit to Coburg... madly recommends to his Brother [Ernest by then having become Duke of Saxe-Coburg and Gotha] to take the most extraordinary step of which human mind could think, namely, that he and his Cousins, the Dukes of Altenburg and Meiningen, should proclaim themselves as Royal Highnesses in their own Dominions, and not only not satisfied with this folly, they go a step farther, giving the same title to their brothers, their sons, and even their mothers.... I could equally well take the title of Emperor of Hanover...."

He added that he had been told "that all this is owing to the advice of Prince Albert, who gives himself out, as they say, as a Great Statesman of Great Britain, and that Sir R. Peel constantly consults him upon the great and weighty interests of the Country in Foreign and Domestic Affairs. I for one do not and cannot believe this... so ridiculous that one cannot help laughing, how any man, except in Bedlam, could have imagined such a thing."

A year later King Ernest was given a delightful opportunity for castigating Albert and Victoria in conjunction. They had been paying a visit to the Continent. "The accounts I have heard concerning the visit of Queen Victoria and Prince Albert to the Rhine have mortified me much, for I hear that it was a complete failure. She was represented as being cold and uncivil, and caused much confusion by not complying with the wishes of the King and Queen of Prussia with regard to the plans which they proposed to her. She disobliged all the nobility who had assembled there to pay their respects by not condescending to speak to any of them, which you can easily conceive was not the way to render herself popular. Prince Albert was represented as being full of pretensions and totally ignorant of the common usages of the world. To give you a proof of this, the first day of his arrival, when lodged under the roof of the King of Prussia, he did not wear the insignia of the Order of the Black Eagle... this you will acknowledge *était une fière bêtise....* On another occasion he appeared at the Great Parade in the Fortress of Mayence (where Prince William of Prussia is Governor, and which, as you know, is composed of both Austrian and Prussian troops...) dressed in a great frock coat and round white hat, looking more like a tradesman or *garçon de boutique* than a prince. This act created a universal disgust in both armies. . . . I am totally at a loss to understand what could have induced him to have done this."

It was not only the King of Hanover whose bile was aroused by jealousy over Victoria. The extra attention focused on her at the time of her engagement to Prince Albert annoyed more than a few masculine minds and they took a secret revenge on the "Sceptred Child." Soon verses on her of an incredibly obscene nature were being circulated in the clubs of Pall Mall and St. James's Street. Monckton-Milnes, that ubiquitous society figure, delightedly collected these in his daybook.

You peril my reputation [his friend, Robert Monteith, wrote to him]. I receive notelets from you containing the last indecencies on the subject of Royal venery; I burn with chaste and loyal indignation, shout with laughter and end with showing the document right and left. . . . How different our own simple provincial spirit! How sincere was the mighty bonfire I raised on a hill-top . . . while you representatives of an enthusiastic people with your hearts shrivelled with meanness and envy and hate and competition and debauchery could only make bawdy charades on this solemn sowing of a new Royal tree.

This winter of 1839 to 1840 the pantomime at the Adelphi, imbued with a general spirit of vulgarity, delighted the cruder members of the audience with a skit on royal life: the performance being, writes an onlooker, "full of political jests. A courtier mounted on a *sheep* (Lord Melbourne) rides up to the gate of Windsor Castle and is received by two footmen in royal livery with a scroll 'come to dinner.' He answers 'of course,' and rides in. Another on a bird of some sort (Lord Mounteagle) has the same reception. Peel and Lyndhurst come and are driven off *à coups de bâton*. . . . But the *but* is a box inscribed 'A present from the Rhine' which, tapped by Harlequin's wand, gives out a child dressed like Albert, and another a little girl in white to represent the Queen, and they go through the form of making love on the stage, when there is brought in A Christmas Box for 1840 for the Queen, which turns out to be a cradle." This letter was written by a Mr. Archer Clive, a clergyman, to a woman friend. The same month he wrote to her again from London. "As I was coming here to write to·you I saw all the world rushing into a print shop near the opera house. I followed the crowds and found myself *en face* a picture of Prince Albert well enough painted. If he resembles it he is good-natured but decidedly soft and weak, and that won't do for such a little vixen as he is to marry."

It is not necessary here to comment on Mr. Archer Clive's supposition as to his sovereign's character. As we have seen, the venom of party politics encouraged such tart conclusions. "Some clergyman at a public meeting at Canterbury denounced the Queen as a Jezebel, and spoke of the 'orgies' of her Palace. It was a bounden duty of Christian Englishmen to pursue her and her Ministers.... Queen Adelaide again called on by the ladies of the Tory aristocracy to hold drawing-rooms, refused. None the less her health was drunk with much cheering at banquets, and the Queen's left out. It is hard for persons born in the last reign [Queen Victoria's] to imagine how lowering was its morning."

Though the Tories' opinion of the Queen was ridiculously perverse, it must be admitted that one aspect of her character, her determination, was beginning to make some of the elderly men about her uneasy. During her nearly three years on the throne, those Whig prejudices that had been inculcated in her since childhood had, owing to the Bedchamber affair, become intensified. Not only was her animus against Peel unabated, but even Wellington had come under her ban, as on the above matter, in spite of his chivalrous attitude to her personally, he had considered Peel to be in the right. This had so exasperated her that Melbourne had had the greatest difficulty in persuading her to invite the aging man to Windsor this last summer. When in the middle of this February of 1840, the Duke was seriously ill, and all London was driving up to the door of Apsley House to inquire, "the Queen alone," wrote Greville indignantly, "has never taken the slightest notice of him." "I resolved," Greville goes on, "to speak to Melbourne. Accordingly I wrote him a note begging for God's sake he would get the Q. to send and enquire and representing the injury it was to herself not to do so."

Melbourne at once summoned Greville, and explained that "He thought she *had* sent; but he had seen a paragraph in the *Morning Post* ... stating that she had not, on which He had asked her and she had owned it was true." Saying this, Melbourne then and there began scribbling a note to her.

"I suppose she will send now," remarked Greville, as he watched these proceedings.

"Oh yes, she will send now."

Greville, sitting there with his reproving face, began complaining to Melbourne that "it really was lamentable She did the things she does," but, he added, "I knew he did his utmost to keep her straight."

"By God ..." exclaimed Melbourne, "I am moving noon and night at it."

"Depend upon it," went on Greville, whose original enthusiasm for his Queen had of late turned into the most acrimonious fault-finding, "Depend upon it, she will get into a great scrape. The people of England will not endure that she should treat the D[uke] of W[ellington] with disrespect; and it is not the mere act of sending or not that will make an impression of itself, but the whole of her conduct will, and does, produce an impression of the badness of her heart and disposition. Everybody knows that her Father was the greatest rascal that ever went unhung, and they will say that it is the bad blood coming out in her."

This was too much for Melbourne. "She has none of her father's faults," he retorted.

"Certainly not, but the evil disposition which showed itself in him in one way might show itself in her in another."

Melbourne changed the subject.

Apropos of this conversation, one notes that the Duke of Bedford was one day intrigued at overhearing Melbourne, in a discussion with Victoria, suddenly cry out "with great earnestness, 'No, for God's sake, don't do that.'" And another day the Duke, who seems always to have been on the *qui vive* for any royal conversational snippets he could pick up, collected a few words of what he took to be a set-to between her and her Premier over the men's sitting on at dinner after the ladies had left the room. The Duke heard Victoria "rather angrily" exclaiming "it is a horrid custom"; and he noted that after this "when the Ladies left the room ... directions were given that the men should remain *five minutes* longer."

An unlooked-for impetus was given to Victoria's prestige by the advent of the penny postage stamp, on which, printed in black, appeared the Queen's profile. Now, with the birth of the stamp, every man, woman, or child in the country could with a penny buy their own portrait of the Queen, and realize at last what their new monarch really looked like. The stamp was hailed with "extraordinary enthusiasm." "No early fact of the last reign helped more than the Queen's head to establish a link between her and her subjects who made use of the penny post. It brought home to all minds the Queen's towering personality. What was taken from her in power by the Reform Bill was repaid in prestige and with interest by the penny stamp. In counties where the great Whig and Tory nobility resided, the Crown had been eclipsed by them; but the Queen's-head stamp gave it a moral primacy that dwarfed the great landed families.... Rowland Hill first brought home to every family that received a letter the idea of a young Queen who had come to reign on a new and better basis. A mania for postage stamps sprang up.... Louis Napoleon was so much struck in England with the increased prestige of the Crown through the penny stamp that he lost no time in having a three-halfpenny stamp struck with his profile."

In England, with the advent of the Queen's-head stamp, gummed envelopes came into being. But if the populace received these with satisfaction, many members of the old families were disgusted at this mute suggestion that the nation's saliva should co-operate with the work of the post office. For years those of the older generation would be shocked if they received a letter in an envelope, considering that the old fashion was the only well-bred fashion: that is, the sheet of writing paper carefully folded, and sealed with a drop of scalding wax, this in turn being impressed with a seal bearing the family crest or coat of arms.

2

Part of Greville's bitterness against the Queen arose from his view that her Court was, as he writes, "a scene of party and family favouritism, a few chosen individuals being her constant guests, to the almost total exclusion of anyone, however distinguished or respectable of the opposite side. Nor are her favourites ... (ex-

cept Melbourne himself) conspicuous for any superior qualities . . .
and it is with a mixture of aversion and contempt that people read
in the Court Circular of the Rt. Honble George Stevens Byng and
the Honble William Cowper dining four days a week at the royal
table, and the Ladies Eleanora and Constance Paget tagging after
the Queen, on foot, on horseback or in carriage, 6 days out of the
seven."

The Paget family was immensely favored at Buckingham Palace.
In addition to these two tagging ladies, there was their father, Lord
Uxbridge, filling the post of Lord Chamberlain; and Lord Alfred
Paget whose seductive charm has already permeated these pages.
The family of Paget greatly added to the hilarity of the Buckingham Palace evenings. "The attempt to waltz," Albert wrote back
in answer to one of Victoria's letters, "and the two Pagets tied together must really have been excruciatingly funny": for now that
she was actually engaged to Albert, the Queen felt she could valse
with him without flouting the proprieties, and was busily learning
the steps.

If others considered her willful and obstinate, she had no illusions on the subject herself. The marriage was fixed for February 10, which was a Monday, and Albert was to come over on the
Saturday; but a few days before he arrived a kind of panic rushed
through her. Was she, she asked herself, after all making a mistake? She worked herself into such a "nervous and feverish" condition over this question that those around her became convinced
she was on the point of having measles. But hers was a fever of
self-realization regarding her inner nature, a foreseeing of the difficulty she would have in ameliorating her own determined character
sufficiently to ensure a happy marriage.

"After all, this is a very hazardous experiment," she suddenly
cried out, "and how unhappy I shall be if it does not answer. I
have always had my own way," she went on with her usual candor,
"and particularly for the last two years, and suppose he should
endeavour to thwart me and oppose me in what I like, what a
dreadful thing it would be."

Though she might at moments feel anxious about the conclusive
step she was taking, at the same time she was eager that every honor
should be heaped on Albert, and most particularly that he should

be made "King Consort" by Act of Parliament. She kept urging her wish on Melbourne who, embarrassed, at first only answered her evasively. Finally, however, he exclaimed, "For God's sake, let's hear no more of it, Ma'am; for if you once get the English people into the way of making kings, you will get them into the way of unmaking them."

The night before Albert's arrival, Victoria and Melbourne sat talking together for the last time before the great event that would once for all inevitably change their relationship to each other. She confided in him that she felt "a little agitated and nervous."

"Most natural ... how could it be otherwise," came the understanding voice. "Lord Melbourne was so warm, so kind and so affectionate the whole evening, and so much touched in speaking of me and my affairs."

She began to talk of her now abandoned resolution of never marrying.

" 'Depend upon it, it's right to marry,' he said earnestly, 'if ever there was a situation that formed an exception, it was yours,' " but, he went on, "it's in human nature, it's natural to marry ... it's a great *change*—it has its inconveniences. . . .' "

Victoria remarked how thin she had grown. "You look very well," he reassured her: " 'after all,' he continued, much affected, 'how anybody in your situation can have a moment's tranquillity!— a young person cast in this situation is very unnatural.' "

And then, with his usual tender impulse to encourage her, he began to talk of what he described as "a beautiful account in a Scotch paper" of her first proroguing Parliament, in which the writer speaks of her "large searching eye, an open anxious nostril, and a firm mouth."

That a nostril should be described as "anxious" did not strike either of them as peculiar: on the contrary, "Lord Melbourne repeated this several times, looking so kindly and affectionately at me; 'A very true representation,' he said, 'can't be a finer physiognomy.' "

This talk took place on the Friday before the wedding, fixed, as already said, for February 10, and Victoria was most anxious Melbourne should come down to Windsor—where the honeymoon was to be spent—on the Thursday. So now she "begged Lord M. much to manage Thursday . . . as I said it always made me so happy to have him." "I am sure none of your friends are as fond of you as I am," she concluded; as if at this moment of the parting of their ways she were placing in his palm and gently closing his fingers over it, all the gratitude and affection that welled within her.

3

When Victoria awoke on the wedding morning her glance flew to the window. The panes were blurry with rain and, beyond, the wind twitched at the February branches. Picking up a sheet of paper, she wrote:

Dearest,—. . . How are you to-day, and have you slept well? I have rested very well, and feel very comfortable to-day. What weather! I believe, however, the rain will cease.

Send one word when you, my most dearly loved bridegroom, will be ready. Thy ever faithful

VICTORIA R.

Then she folded the sheet in *billet* form and, without putting it in an envelope (but probably either sealing it or sticking on a tiny round wafer—a mastic-colored one being *recherché*), wrote on it:

His Royal Highness the Prince
The Queen

and then had it taken to him along the corridors, he being lodged somewhere in the palace.

In spite of her assurance to Albert that she was "very comfortable," her mind, on this crucial morning, was in such a conflict of varied emotions that her eyes were becoming puffy from the tears that kept filling them. The Duchess of Kent came in and gave her "a Nosegay of Orange flowers" (having already the day before given her "a beautiful Prayer book"), while "My dearest Lehzen gave me a dear little ring." Another present of the day before had been "4 beautiful old Fans" that Albert had brought over with him. After these matutinal visits, Victoria had her breakfast, and with her usual steady continuance of daily habits wrote in her Journal.

Then a note to Melbourne. After this her hair was put up, and a wreath of orange flowers pinned on. The door opened and Albert came in "for the *last* time *alone*, as my Bridegroom."

When the young man went back to his own rooms he sat down and wrote a letter home. Since he had arrived two days ago he had, Victoria noticed, been ill at ease, in fact "agitated." ("That's very natural," commented Melbourne, "I don't wonder at it.") The discussions over his civil grant and his precedence had murked the English atmosphere for him, given the impression of a surrounding of hostility; so now, saying in this letter, "In less than three hours I shall stand before the altar with my dear bride," he concluded with, "I must end. God help me!"

At the Chapel Royal, while the rain still fell, carriages were drawing up, out of which there stepped in succession twelve young girls, the finally chosen bridesmaids. Each was a study in white: a wreath of white roses clasped each young head, similar wreaths were sprinkled about the clouds of tulle over their underskirts of rich *gros de Naples*. This flock of maidens was herded into the Queen's dressing room at St. James's Palace, and the door then locked to keep them compact and safe for the next hour and a half. Possibly they had each already received from the Queen one of the twisted rings that she had had especially made to give to her more intimate friends as a reminder of the day. In later years one of the bridesmaids, Lady Wilhelmina Stanhope, would display hers in its little cardboard box, the ring bearing a tiny medallion of the Queen and Prince Albert.

As for the political complexion of the various guests now gradually collecting in the Chapel, this determined young partisan monarch had "stuffed in a parcel of Whigs taken apparently at haphazard," for, splutters Greville, "she had been as wilful, obstinate, and wrong-headed as usual about her invitations." She ended by only admitting five Tories; one of whom was the Duke of Wellington, and there had been "a hesitation" even over inviting him. When Lord Melbourne pressed for more she had retorted, "It is MY marriage and I will only have those who can sympathize with me."

Meanwhile, at Buckingham Palace, Victoria was being turned by her eager dressers into a mass of bridal upholstery, for such was the effect: every line of her figure was gradually becoming sub-merged. Two hundred women had exerted themselves to bring into being the wedding veil of Honiton; and another two hundred had striven with the deep lace flouncings; to say nothing of the numbers who had stitched and stitched at the heavy white satin; but it is evident it was several hundreds too many, such a tasteless muddle was the final result. On top of this profusion of satin and lace were superimposed bows of ribbon, orange blossoms, the Order and Star of the Garter, "my Turkish diamond necklace...and Albert's beautiful sapphire brooch," while a large lace-edged handkerchief and a small hard knot of a bouquet, both held in her hand, added the final touch of confusion. This wedding getup marks the begin-ning of the decline of the Queen's taste in clothes. One's eye glances back regretfully at two former visions of her at the opera, her youthful person set off with infinite charm: in one of these the whole confection leads up to the fantastic gloves and exciting out-burst of enormous lace cuffs, cuffs of such ethereal froufrou that they seem more like tossed-up foam than frills of lace. In the other delineation of her the swan's-down-edged coat that outlines her figure is faintly but enchantingly reminiscent of those to be seen in oriental miniatures worn by moon-faced princesses. After marriage her discrimination as to dress seems gradually to have lapsed, and one gets the impression that finally she took little interest in it. But by then it was of no consequence; her individuality had become so paramount that it dominated any such considerations.

To return to her wedding. By now, in the crowded Chapel Royal, Albert was standing among the royal group near the altar, clasping in one hand a Bible bound in green velvet. Thickly around him clustered, in addition to his father and brother, the family into which he was marrying—Queen Adelaide, full of attentive sym-pathy for his obvious state of embarrassment, was close beside him; and so too were the Dukes of Sussex and Cambridge. The royal Duchess of Gloucester, "still very beautiful and dressed in lily white satin," was to be seen, and Princess Augusta "in pale blue with blush roses round her train." The poor Duchess of Kent's shimmering dress of white and silver with its train of blue velvet was an ironic contrast to her "disconsolate and distressed face" on which were signs of tears. Each of these successive steps in her daughter's life, first, her coronation, now her marriage, widened the distance between them, emphasized to her how she herself was receding still further into the background. A figure in the Chapel who "attracted considerable attention" was Lehzen, so arrestingly did she stand out with her inscrutable eyes, pits of darkness within a complexion now "white as marble, which appeared all the whiter by contrast with her black velvet Spanish hat which was surmounted by a white plume." An onlooker says that at this moment her face "exhibited great energy and talent"; as well it might, for, just as the Duchess felt herself sinking ever lower beneath life's waters, so the German pastor's daughter was riding ever more triumphantly on the crest of the waves. Had not Stockmar, knowing the powerful veto that was hers at Court, written to her in the most friendly fashion, indicating with circuitous tact the attitude on her part to the Queen's young husband which he considered the most advisable? "I will answer for it," ran his letter, "that after every storm he will come safely into port. You will therefore have my entire approval, if you think the best course is to leave him to his own clear head his sound feeling and excellent disposition."

In contrast to the subdued girl in her unsuccessful finery now driving toward the Chapel "her eyes much swollen with tears," the appearance of the Prince who was awaiting her was one of unsought but romantic achievement; his dress, that of a Field Marshal, instinct with legend and dignity. The Order of the Garter sloped across his swallow-tailed military tunic, on which, as well, scintillated his diamond star; a long heavily tasseled sash swung against his white knee breeches, while two great bows of white satin ribbon, one on each shoulder, struck the final notes of adornment. As Lehzen's eye took in that slightly olive countenance clustered round by the crisp auburn hair, the whole upstanding figure illumined— for the rain was over—by the expanding light that came through the windows, as she gazed, and could not but admire, did any faintest premonition cross her mind of the psychological, and, to her, completely disastrous, struggle in which she and he were shortly to become involved?

But now a flourish of trumpets with their airy ascendancy drew the divergent thoughts of everyone in the Chapel to the same point, and in a moment Lord Melbourne, carrying the Sword of State, came pacing in at the head of a slow-moving group: the Queen and her cluster of white-clad maidens. Victoria was noticeably pale, but calm. As at the coronation, not enough thought had been given to the trainbearers' difficulties. This time the Queen's train, all white satin and orange flowers, was too short for the many bridesmaids to cling to, and they were so huddled together they could barely scramble along. The Duke of Sussex, that towering figure, gave his niece away, and, as the ritualistic phrases of the service went murmuring on, he could not restrain his sobs. In his seat in the gallery Lord Fitzwilliam, too, was unashamedly weeping. Except for the low voices at the altar, the sobs of the two men, and an occasional remarkably audible comment from the irrepressible Duke of Cambridge, who was in a "decidedly gay" mood, it was so quiet in the Chapel that the wrangling voices of the waiting crowd outside could be distinctly heard. The Queen gave the responses in a voice "full of softness and music" and yet so clear that it was heard "at the most extreme corner of the Chapel," but her inner commotion was such that, so an onlooker noticed, "the orange blossoms on her head shook violently."

While the service pursues its way our thoughts travel musingly from one to another of that closely interrelated little group: Victoria and Albert, the Duchess of Kent, Lehzen, Lord Melbourne; and, as if reflected in a mirror before them, we see what is about to come to each.

Within that magnificently sculptured young figure at Victoria's side was a type of character quite new to the royal precincts, and one peculiarly alien at that time to the higher society of the country to which he was becoming affiliated. Those beribboned field marshal trappings clothed the body of a social pioneer, of a youth who, in spirit, was an adumbration of the Boy-Scout-Y.M.C.A. young man. As such he was infallibly antipathetic to the approved English gentleman of the day—hard drinking, sporting, more or less dissolute, educated on the classics, his face always turned to the traditions of the past; the chief aim of his education being to fit him socially to become an acceptable member of his own then much more exclusive group. How could men of this type feel anything but disgust for a man who drank water, went to bed early, and lived for ideals? How impossible to be at ease with a prince who enthusiastically built tenement flats in Kennington, each with its own bathroom; who, with equal eagerness, endeavored to arrange for a collection of primitives to be shown at Kensington Palace. This sort of thing upset the gentlemen of England so much that before long they began to voice objections to being asked to meet him at dinner.

Within the short span of the twenty-two years that lay before him this boy of twenty was to reveal himself as at once philosopher, statistician, agriculturist, musician, business promoter, politician, sewage expert, humanitarian, farmer, hygienist, collector of pictures; in every direction an innovator; a man whose acumen in all public matters was so penetrating that in the end his great worth was accepted by the most intelligent of his contemporaries; and has made later generations wonder as to what effect, had he lived longer, he would have had on the destinies of the country. One thing can be said with certainty: had he not died so early the Queen would never have become the national figure of legend and perpetual surmise and interest that she has; she would have retreated ever further into the background, intentionally obliterating herself so that her husband, that man of force and ideas, might shine with increasing luster. As the child-queen she had moved the nation to an unwonted tenderness; after the Prince's death, wrapped in her cloak of desolation and nostalgia, she was gradually to mature her own exceptional qualities, and finally fill the throne with a puissance of personality that was not discounted but enhanced by her quaintnesses; for, unlike the Latin races, the sense of humor of Britain is not cruel but indulgent. She has become a royal addition to the nation's arbitrarily chosen, jealously treasured picture gallery of figures: some real, some fictitious. It is these fortuitously chosen characters, injected into the very veins of the country, and thus companioning and supporting the minds of each generation, who can be assured of immortality. As for the Prince, one cannot but envisage his life, though on the surface serene and mountingly successful, as one containing the elements of tragedy. Reading of him, we see his youth, and with it his quips and rather facetious gaiety, disappear with a rapidity that can only be described as startling. Before he was twenty-six he had undergone "frightful torture" from rheumatism. By the time he was thirty-nine people were surprised to see in front of them an old man. His desire to give to his adopted country everything of worth within him, and his ceaseless efforts to that end, had constantly been met with hostility and insults most bitter to his spirit, and in consequence there remained at the back of his mind an undying ache for the country he had left: that small country of Coburg, so "lovely and friendly." Even after a marriage of seventeen years he could become "lost in the dear memories," and he did not hesitate to tell the Queen (or she to record) that nothing in his life had given him anything comparable to those pulsing days of boyhood in company with his brother. His eldest daughter, a small replica of himself with her enthusiasm for the things of the mind, and who companioned a part of his nature in a way the Queen could not, was lost to him at sixteen by her Continental marriage; each year that the Prince of Wales grew older was an added year of anxiety to his father who saw him developing just those characteristics of both his own family and of his wife's that he the most abhorred. Harmonious as the Prince's domestic life appeared, and indeed in a sense was, once the youthful physical attraction in his and Victoria's marriage became less of a feature in their lives, it is evident he did not find in her that indefinable something that might have prevented him from becoming indifferent to leaving her. She gave him her all; but her all was not enough. It was not sufficient to counterbalance the hurts of life, to provide him with such firm anchorage as would have made him immune from outside buffets. That was indeed much to ask; it would have been perhaps beyond the capacity of any one woman. One aspect of their relationship at least is clear. Those swift perceptions, those exquisitely sensitive contacts of mind with mind that make for perfect companionship did not exist between them. In later years she confided to Lady Antrim how bored she had been by the lectures that her husband found so absorbing; and, alas for her, in her anguish when the Prince lay dying she had the further grief of finding that it was not herself but their daughter Alice whom he definitely seemed to prefer having in his room. Admiration, Victoria gave him without stint, but admiration without discernment, praise that comes more from the heart than the head, can in time become enervating. Whatever the cause, when the Prince was about forty, his spirit reached that point of dejection when the inflow of life does not receive the necessary response.

Unwelcomed, the vital sources seeped away, leaving his whole being fatally open to the call of death. "I do not cling to life," he once said to the Queen. "I do not cling to life. You do; but I set no store by it.... I should be quite ready to die to-morrow.... I am sure if I had a severe illness I should give up at once; I should not struggle for life."

Searching indeed must have been the inner strains and despondencies to bring about such a complete distaste for life in a man still in his young maturity; a man at once so dowered, so needed, and whose chief satisfaction it had always been to respond to every need.

·   ·   ·   ·   ·   ·

Still exploring the mirror in which the future reveals itself, we see Victoria, Queen now for some twenty-four years, her inert figure heavily shrouded in black, looking out of one of the windows of Osborne upon the December waters of The Solent, while, away at Windsor a direful ceremony is pursuing its course: a ceremony to her so dreadful that she could not bring herself to attend it. Unspeakably forlorn and desolate—bereft now by death of Albert, of Melbourne, of her mother (whom she had grown to love), and, by disillusionment and long absence, bereft even of Lehzen herself—she bends her eyes on those slowly heaving waters, bleak as the sky above them. As she gazes those near hear her murmuring to herself, "I *will* do my duty; I will, I *will* do my duty."... "Over and over," came those despairing tones, as if by an incantation she were endeavoring to force her shrinking spirit to face what must be.

·   ·   ·   ·   ·   ·

And Melbourne? Within comparatively a few years we see him, physically a broken man, lounging, not now from indolence but from decrepitude, about the rooms of his country home, Brocket Hall. But if, as far as possession went, Brocket was his home, emotionally it was Buckingham Palace and Windsor Castle that had come to have that meaning for him. The fire to which he and Victoria used to draw up their chairs on chilly evenings had grown dear to England's Premier as a family hearth, and toward his end, his mind at times clear, at others clouded, he would indulge himself in tender reminiscent ramblings on the ardent girl who had cast such a glow across the ending of his days, bestowing on him, as he himself said, "the happiest period of his life."

He died in the autumn of 1848; his "beautiful countenance," wrote his sister, Lady Palmerston, "so calm, contented, and resigned." "The windows were open, and a soft autumn air just stirred the curtains of the room. The sun's last rays shone on the noble features and on the wasted hands that lay on the coverlet. The autumn leaves were falling. The twilight crept over the water where the swans were nestling in the reeds. The night passed; the old man lay quiet and calm. Only a sigh at six o'clock told the watchers that he had gone."

Now, while he and the Prince stand so close together in the Chapel it is irresistible to turn one's gaze from one to the other in comparison. Here, indeed, we see before us two unique figures; each of whom has made a lasting imprint on the world's wax. Physically, both are strikingly built and chiseled; in appearance, as well as in mind and character, master-men: the one representative of an era that is passing, the other of an era scarcely yet born. After the Prince's preliminary anxiety to catch the ear and impress the mind of this monolith of the Court, he was to appear to the thrusting eagerness of the Teutonically educated boy merely a lethargic old man. But Victoria's Premier possessed unusual subtleties of temperament that were not within the scope of the Prince's appreciations: his gift to the world was not only what he accomplished outwardly, but what he accomplished in himself. There was always something, some quality about him, which might be described as an overtone of splendor. The Prince Consort was one of life's efficient implements; Melbourne a musical instrument of rare quality. Two characteristics they did both possess in common: probity and chivalry. In neither was to be found a grain of corruption. Raised through their connection with the Queen each into a position of immense power, they used it solely for the advantage of her and her country.

• • • •

Curiously enough, of this closely interwoven little group of five whose destinies we are examining, it was the Duchess of Kent, at the moment the most despondent, the most depleted of the group, whose well-being was not, as with each of the others, either shortly or gradually to contract, but to expand. In the young man at the altar, at once her nephew and her son-in-law, there stood, unguessed by her, her savior. When he came to realize how fallen she was from grace he began to exert himself, and with success, to get her restored to favor. During the first years of her daughter's marriage, the Duchess, like some plant badly wilted for lack of moisture, but now plentifully besprinkled, began to show signs of recovery. Under the Prince's impulsion, his wife, who each year grew more and more to view everything with his eyes rather than with her own, became at first friendly toward, and in the end deeply fond of her mother. Rehabilitated, spruced up again by her son-in-law's patronage, the Duchess was to become—with a few most desirable and necessary alterations—much what she had been before. In the portrait of her by Winterhalter, painted a year or two after the advent of her son-in-law, we see afloat on her face unmistakable signs of triumph, of self-congratulation. There is something about Winterhalter's portrait of this redoubtable royal lady that makes the onlooker smile—not, I fear, from affection but from amusement. The way she blotted out all happiness from Feodore's young life and crushed Victoria; her bullying ingratitude to the kindly intentioned William and Adelaide choke any tender feelings that one might harbor for her; but, as one ponders on the ups and downs of an existence whose oscillations were certainly remarkable, one undeniably draws a good deal of entertainment from the spectacle. Four men in succession dominated her actions, and each, so it seems, for the time being entirely dominated her mind as well. We see her first married to Prince Leiningen; wife, mother, and *châtelaine*, bearing up under the rule of a disagreeable husband, competently dealing with the difficulties created in his small kingdom by the Napoleonic upheavals. Nothing daunted by these experiences, she passes on to the Duke of Kent, expertly playing her role as wife to a royal English Duke; whirling and twirling to his spoken or implied dictates. When she loses him, Conroy at once takes control, and within the shortest space she is made over a third time; no longer the sweet foreign Princess that Edward had brought over, all accomplished smiles and pretty phrases, but turned now into a perfect virago of tiresomeness; forever, under the guidance of her new producer, devising fresh tricks with which to torment her brother-in-law and his wife. Then comes the great collapse: the shock of a downfall she had never so much as envisaged. Even Conroy himself is finally removed, and there is the poor lady, emotionally destitute and defeated. And, in addition, completely bewildered, for there is no man to give her any sense of direction. The fourth of her producers does not appear.... And then, strangely enough, this young Apollo at Victoria's side turns out to be the very man she has been awaiting. No sooner has she recognized him as the authentic successor to the first three than she is all pliability and acquiescence, learning her new role as swiftly as possible. She is made over again. On go the Paris confections—the flounced frock, the embroidered shawl, the picture hat; and there she is facing Winterhalter's brush with all the self-assurance in the world. But she soon understands that she is cast now for a character that differs a good deal from any she has filled hitherto. Albert approves of grandmothers; and gradually it becomes evident to the Duchess that it is the grandmother aspect of herself that she is now being called on to develop to its fullest extent. It is not long before age and her son-in-law working on her together bring this about. We gaze in astonishment at the metamorphosis: so exactly the opposite is the sweet, benign, cosy old lady of Frogmore to the erstwhile viperous Duchess of Kensington Palace. In this charming country house of Frogmore, so conveniently close to Windsor Castle, sits the grandmother, forever ready with her dulcet smile to receive her daughter or her son-in-law, or this one or that one of the inmates of the rapidly filling royal nurseries. Her adoring ladies are always hovering, and adore her they do. They cannot say enough in praise of her lovely character, "the dearest old lady that ever existed," exclaims one of them, Victoria Stuart-Wortley. And in fairness to the Duchess we remember, too, how devoted old Späth and Flora Hastings had been to their royal mistress. And so, entirely nonplussed by such a chameleon, we part from her, leave her at Frogmore bending as absorbedly as ever over her embroidery frame, while on the lake at the foot of the lawn the white swans gently drift; and in the servants' part of the house special preparations are being made, for tonight Victoria and Albert are coming

THE DUCHESS OF KENT

From the portrait by F. Winterhalter

By gracious permission of H.M. The King

QUEEN VICTORIA AND PRINCE ALBERT ON THEIR RETURN FROM THEIR WEDDING
Drawn by F. Lock

to dinner, and afterward they and the Duchess will move across her drawing room to the pianoforte, and the three voices of this newly formed palace group will rise in unison.

.   .   .   .   .   .

As for Lehzen, Lehzen the exalted, the beloved; before three years have passed she is to be back in Germany, ousted from Buckingham Palace and Windsor at the Prince's wish and by his own determined efforts. Nervous, and understandably so, as to whether he could grapple with his new position, he found Lehzen—in ways known to him but not clear to us—blocking his path; and she, who so far had been equal to intricate situations that at various times had threatened her at the English Court, this time, it is obvious, failed to adapt herself. In this handsome boy who every month was gaining a still greater ascendancy over the Queen's emotions, the poor Baroness recognized by far the most dangerous rival she had yet had to face, and it seems that she lost her head. The details of this battle between the new order and the old we do not know, but it is evident that Lehzen was not pliable enough, that the partial position she might presumably still have kept she lost in the determination to keep the whole. Whether, in the final rupture, the Prince was a little too relentless is a matter for speculation only. During their mutual struggle he spoke resentfully of her "dreadful counterintrigues," ignoring the fact that those who use counterintrigues have, *ipso facto*, already been intrigued against. Altogether, whichever way one looks at it, it is a sad business. The value of the psychological support and tender affection she had given to Victoria ever since she was a tempestuous infant of five was incalculable, and yet so entirely did the Queen succumb to the Prince that she wholly accepted his view about Lehzen, and when one reads in her Journal the paragraph describing the calmness of her emotions the morning she awoke after the Baroness' departure, one cannot but be astonished. The grief that must have lain in the ex-governess's heart as she set out on the then long expedition back to Germany, leaving behind her life itself, does not seem to have penetrated the mind of either the Queen or Albert. It is, however, pleasant to record that several times when Victoria was traveling on the Continent she made a point of seeing "good old Lehzen," as she had come to call her.

We hear of one last act of self-sacrifice on Lehzen's part that is touching in its extreme of self-abnegation. The King of Hanover's resident English Chaplain, Mr. Wilkinson, who visited her one day in her rather crowded little drawing room, tells how inevitably her conversation would veer around to the subject that interested her more than anything else on earth, England's Queen; and yet, though Victoria's weekly letters to her had been her one spiritual sustenance, Lehzen herself had suggested that, busy as the Queen was, this flow of letters should be reduced to one a month.

On this visit to the little house in Bückeburg, the King of Hanover's Chaplain was amusedly surprised at discovering how Lehzen spent some of the pension the Queen gave her. At the beginning of his visit, "For an hour at least," he writes, "I did not get in a word. . . . Upon the first break of the conversation I then thought it right to make a move to go: but no, that was not to be allowed. . . . The bell was rung, coffee ordered.

"This gave time for another flow of eloquence of at least a quarter-of-an-hour. Then another move to go. Not a bit of it.

"Might she offer me a cigar with my coffee?

"I made a little demur, and cast my eye round her well-filled and elegantly furnished drawing-room. I said I was no great smoker, though I owned I did treat myself to a good cigar now and then. . . .

" 'Oh, if that were the case,' " replied Lehzen, " 'I must let her give me one of her cigars, which she flattered herself, were very good; for she could assure me they were real havanas. She imported them herself, and never offered them to her friends till they had been in her house three years!!!' "

This, thought the Chaplain, was too good an offer to be refused.

"The baroness," he continued, "went to a beautiful inlaid old cabinet, opened it with a golden key that hung from her chain, and produced a box of magnificent havanas, which regularly perfumed the room when she took off the cover. They were giants. I almost staggered at the size, and, as I ventured to say, the strength. . . .

" 'They were Regalias',' " she reassured him, " 'they were five years old . . . just in their prime; the flavour improved while their strength decreased.' . . .

"Each cigar," continues Wilkinson, "was done up separately with a blue ribbon. She examined, handled and smelt them with the eye and nose of a real connoisseuse, selected and presented me with a splendid specimen. I was more and more astonished as she herself applied the match, and I ventured to make a polite remark about fearing to taint her furniture, but I was stopped by her saying she had been used to smoke all her life, and had not the least objection to the smell.... I expected, as I blew my cloud, to see her light one of these beautiful Regalias on the opposite chair; but no, that was not to be. When she said she had been used to smoke all her life, she meant to the smell, or as she rather likes to call it, flavour."

As the Chaplain puffed away, Lehzen confided in him that "she liked to hear all that was going on in the world," and, bored at "the knitting parties of ladies . . . she formed her little scheme of the havanas to get the chief men of different professions together every week in her drawing-room." She would send round "her card to the ministers, judges, and chief men of the place" asking them in for coffee and havanas at that hour in the middle of the day when the courts and public offices were closed. Gladly they came; appreciatively they smoked and drank; delightedly poor Lehzen felt herself lifted out of the atmosphere of small town gossip into that of professionalism and administration.

Such was the sop she had provided herself with, a little to console herself for the Court life she had lost.

. . . . .

But all this is for the future. We are back now in the Chapel Royal watching those two very young things standing in front of the altar rails that glisten with their fresh coating of gilt, both at the moment overstrung with the consciousness of what each is giving up to obtain possession of the other. She, "white as a sheet," he, so "awkward from embarrassment," that the kind and watchful Adelaide has several times to bestir her purple velvets in her endeavors to help him.

In the return procession that passed through into St. James's Palace itself, the Duke of Cambridge was much to the fore "very gallantly handing the princesses down the steps" with many a shouted civility. One of the bridesmaids, Lady Jane Bouverie, wrote in later years, "I cannot recall what passages or apartments we passed through after the ceremony, but we finally found ourselves in a room with the Queen and Prince with no guests or relatives present. They were standing by a table, when an attendant brought in what looked like a plain coloured baize or cloth bag, and gave it to the Queen, who drew from it, one at a time, a little dark blue velvet case, giving one to each of us. Then she and the Prince passed out at a side door, and we saw them no more." When the bridesmaids opened their little cases they found inside a brooch which, Victoria had designed herself based on the Coburg crest—a turquoise eagle with ruby beak, and pearls within its claws. After this present giving, she and Albert drove back to Buckingham Palace and found the hall crowded with guests. "They cheered us again and again," wrote Victoria in her Journal. "The great Drawing-Room and Throne Room were full of people of rank, and numbers of children were there, Lord Melbourne and Lord Clarendon ... stood at the door of the Throne Room when we came in. I went and sat on the sofa in my dressing-room [upstairs] with Albert; and we talked together." But even as they sat down side by side on the sofa her eye flew to clock or watch, and with her usual precision she noted that the hand pointed precisely to "10 m. to 2," and that when they got up from the sofa it was then "20 m. p. 2." Then they went downstairs to face "all the Company" and the breakfast. Finally, "I went upstairs and undressed and put on a white silk gown trimmed with swansdown, and a bonnet with orange flowers. Albert went downstairs and undressed." But before they left for Windsor there was one good-by in particular that had to be said, and soon Melbourne's massive figure appeared in the doorway in his new "fine coat" over the making of which there had been much palace joking and laughter—but his thoughts at this moment could not but have worn the saddest livery. The two talked "of how well everything went off."

"Nothing could have gone off better," said Lord Melbourne.

"I begged him not to go to the party; he was a little tired; I would let him know when we arrived; I pressed his hand once more."

"God bless you, Ma'am ..." he said, "with such a kind look."

And it was all over.

Then "Dearest Albert came up and fetched me downstairs, when we took leave of Mamma and drove off at near 4; I and Albert alone."

Not much thought had been given to the impression that would be made on onlookers by the turnout in which they drove down to Windsor: "they went off in a very poor and shabby style," scolds Greville. "Instead of the new chariot in which most married people are accustomed to dash along, they were in one of the old travelling coaches, the postillions in undressed liveries, and with a small escort, three other coaches with post horses following."

But this lack of visual glamour was in no wise to affect the enthusiasm of the onlookers who along the highway from London to Windsor were clustering in thousands eager to roar their deafening approbation. All the wedding hubbub had obliterated the Flora Hastings episode from the nation's mind. Once more the little monarch was reinstated in every heart, and now as the February evening slowly dwindled, one house after another along the route leaped into a quiver of illumination; as it were a springtide of effulgence, a sudden blossoming within the gathering night. And into this fitful irradiation, amid the cries and huzzas of affection, went galloping that rather shabby little cortege down the long road that led to the castle at Windsor.

The Victoria and Albert legend had begun.

BIBLIOGRAPHY

AUTHORITIES AND WORKS CONSULTED

ACLAND, ALICE. *Caroline Norton.* 1948.

AIRLIE, MABELL, COUNTESS OF. *Lady Palmerston and her Times.* 2 vols. 1922.

ALBEMARLE, GEORGE THOMAS, EARL OF. *Fifty Years of My Life.* 2 vols. 1876.

ANONYMOUS. *La Belle Assemblée or Court and Fashionable Magazine. Containing interesting and original literature, and Records of the Beau Monde.*

The Court Doctor Dissected (Leaflet).

The Dangers of Evil Counsel: a Voice from the Grave of Lady Flora Hastings to Her most gracious Majesty the Queen (Leaflet). 1839.

The Lady Flora Hastings: Her Life and Death. With Questions for the Queen and Criticisms of her Court (Leaflet).

The Life of Queen Victoria Reproduced from "The Times." 1901.

The Palace Martyr! A Satire by the Honourable * * * (Leaflet). 1839.

The Private Life of Queen Victoria. By one of Her Majesty's Servants. 1902.

The Private Life of Edward VII. By one of His Majesty's Servants. 1910.

The Victim of Scandal: Memoir of the late Lady Flora Hastings with the Statement of the Marquis of Hastings, Entire Correspondence and a Portrait of her Ladyship. 1839.

ARETZ, GERTRUDE. *The Empress Catherine.* 1947.

ARGYLL, DUKE OF. *Autobiography and Memoirs of George Douglas, Eighth Duke of Argyll, K.G., K.T. (1823-1900).* Edited by the Dowager Duchess of Argyll. 2 vols. 1906.

ARTHUR, SIR GEORGE. *Concerning Queen Victoria and her Son.* 1943.

ASHTON, JOHN. *Gossip in the First Decade of Victoria's Reign.* 1903.

BEAVEN, ARTHUR H. *Popular Royalty.* 1897.

BELL, G. K. A., Bishop of Chichester. *Randall Davidson, Archbishop of Canterbury.* 1938.

BELLOC-LOWNDES, MRS. *The Merry Wives of Westminster.* 1946.

BESSBOROUGH, THE EARL OF, G.C.M.G., Editor; in collaboration with A. Aspinall, Ph.D. *Lady Bessborough and her Family Circle.* 1940.

BISHOP, JOHN GEORGE. *The Brighton Pavilion and its Royal Associations.* 1876.

BLOOMFIELD, GEORGIANA, BARONESS. *Reminiscences of Court and Diplomatic Life.* 2 vols. 1883.

BOLITHO, HECTOR, Editor. *The Prince Consort and his Brother.* Two hundred new letters. 1933.
Victoria, the Widow and her Son. 1934.
The Reign of Queen Victoria. 1949.

BROUGHTON, LORD. *Recollections of a Long Life, by Lord Broughton (John Cam Hobhouse), with additional Extracts from his Private Diaries.* Edited by his daughter, Lady Dorchester. 1909.

BROWNLOW, EMMA SOPHIA, COUNTESS. *The Eve of Victorianism: Reminiscences of the Years 1802 to 1834.* 1940.

CECIL, DAVID. *The Young Melbourne: and the Story of his Marriage with Caroline Lamb.* 1939.

CECIL, LADY GWENDOLEN. *Life of Robert, Marquis of Salisbury.* By his daughter. 2 vols. 1921.

CLARENDON, EARL OF. *The Life and Letters of George William Frederick, Fourth Earl of Clarendon, K.G., G.C.B.* By the Right Hon. Sir Herbert Maxwell, Bart., F.R.S., D.C.L., LL.D. 2 vols. 1913.

CLIFFORD SMITH, H. *Buckingham Palace, its Furniture, Decoration and History.* With introductory chapters on the Building and Site, by Christopher Hussey. 1931.

CLIVE, CAROLINE. *From the Diary and Family Papers of Mrs. Archie Clive (1801-1873).* Edited by Mary Clive. 1949.

COLSON, PERCY, Editor. *Lord Goschen and his Friends (The Goschen Letters).* Introduction by Sir Shane Leslie, Bart.

CRAWFORD, EMILY. *Victoria, Queen and Ruler.* By the Paris correspondent of *The Daily News and Truth.* 1903.

CREEVEY, THOMAS. *The Creevey Papers: a Selection from the Correspondence and Diaries of the late Thomas Creevey, M.P. Born*

1768—Died 1838. Edited by The Right Hon. Sir Herbert Maxwell, Bart., LL.D., F.R.S. 2 vols. 1904.

Creevey's Life and Times: a further Selection from the Correspondence of Thomas Creevey. Born 1768—Died 1838. Edited by John Gore. 1934.

CROKER, JOHN WILSON. *The Croker Papers; the Correspondence and Diaries of the late Right Honourable John Wilson Croker, LL.D., F.R.S., Secretary to the Admiralty from 1809 to 1830.* Edited by Louis J. Jennings. 3 vols. 1884.

CUST, MRS. HENRY. *Wanderers: Episodes from the Travels of Lady Emmeline Stuart-Wortley and her daughter Victoria, 1849-1855.* With a Preface by Sir Ronald Storrs. 1928.

D'ABERNON, VISCOUNTESS. *Red Cross and Berlin Embassy, 1915-1926. Extracts from the Diaries of Viscountess D'Abernon.* 1946.

DANGERFIELD, GEORGE. *Victoria's Heir: the Education of a Prince.* 1942.

DORAN, DR. *Memoir of Queen Adelaide, Consort of King William IV.* 1861.

DUFF, DAVID. *Edward of Kent: the Life Story of Queen Victoria's Father.* 1938.

DUNCKLEY, HENRY, M.A., LL.D. *Lord Melbourne.* 1890.

ELIZABETH, PRINCESS. *Letters of Princess Elizabeth of England, Daughter of King George III, and Landgravine of Hesse-Homburg.* Edited by Philip Ch. Yorke, M.A. Oxon. 1898.

ELLICE, JANE HARRIET (Lady Jane Ellice). *Some Memories of the Queen's Childhood and Marriage.* The *Cornhill Magazine,* June 1897.

ESHER, VISCOUNT, G.C.B., G.C.V.O., Editor. *The Girlhood of Queen Victoria: a Selection from Her Majesty's Diaries between the years 1832 and 1840 published by authority of His Majesty the King.* 2 vols. 1912.

FAULKNER, THOMAS. *History and Antiquities of Kensington, interspersed with Biographical Anecdotes of Royal and Distinguished Personages, and a Descriptive Catalogue of the Collection of Pictures in the Palace, from a Survey made by the late B. West, Esqr., P.R.A., by command of His Majesty.* 1820.

FIRTH, DOUGLAS, M.A., M.D. (Cantab), F.R.C.P. (Lond.), Fellow of Trinity Hall, Cambridge. *The Case of Augustus D'Este.* 1948.

FITZGERALD, PERCY. *The Royal Dukes and Princesses of the Family of George III. A View of Court Life and Manners for Seventy Years, 1760-1830.* 2 vols. 1882.

FRAMPTON, MARY. *The Journal of Mary Frampton from the year 1779 until the year 1846. Including various interesting and curious letters, anecdotes, etc., relating to events which occurred during that period.* Edited, with notes, by her niece Harriet Georgiana Mundy. 1885.

FULFORD, ROGER. *Royal Dukes. The Father and Uncles of Queen Victoria.* 1933.

The Prince Consort. By Roger Fulford. 1949.

GORDON, PRYSE LOCKHART. *Personal Memoirs; or Reminiscences of Men and Manners at Home and Abroad, during the last Half Century, etc. etc.* From the portfolio of Pryse Lockhart Gordon. 2 vols. 1830.

GOSSE, EDMUND. *The Character of Queen Victoria.* Published in the *Quarterly Review*, 1901.

GRANVILLE, HARRIET. *Letters of Harriet, Countess of Granville, 1810-1845.* Edited by her son, The Hon. H. Leveson-Gower. 2 vols. 1894.

GREVILLE, CHARLES C. F. *The Greville Memoirs: a Journal of the Reigns of King George IV and King William IV, by the late Charles C. F. Greville, Esqr., Clerk to the Council to those Sovereigns.* Edited by Henry Reeve, Registrar of the Privy Council. 3 vols. 1875.

The Greville Memoirs (Second Part): a Journal of the Reign of Queen Victoria from 1837 to 1852. 1885.

The Greville Memoirs, 1814-1860. Edited by Lytton Strachey and Roger Fulford. Vol. III, 1834-37; and Vol. IV, January 1838 to December 1841.

GREVILLE, HENRY. *Leaves from the Diary of Henry Greville.* Edited by The Viscountess Enfield. 1883.

GREY, LIEUT.-GENERAL THE HON. C. *The Early Years of His Royal Highness the Prince Consort, compiled under the direction of Her Majesty the Queen.* 1867.

GUEDALLA, PHILIP. *Palmerston.* 1926.

GURNEY, MRS. GERALD (Dorothy Francis Bloomfield). *The Childhood of Queen Victoria.* 1901.

HAMILTON, LORD FREDERICK. *The Days Before Yesterday.* 3 vols. 1920.

HANOVER, THE KING OF. *Letters of the King of Hanover to Viscountess Strangford, G.C.B.* Now in the possession of his granddaughter Mrs. Frank Russell. With an Historical Note by E. M. Cox and an Introduction by Charles Whibley, LL.D. 1925.

HARE, AUGUSTUS J. C. *The Story of My Life.* 1896.

The Story of Two Noble Lives: being Memorials of Charlotte, Countess Canning, and Louisa, Marchioness of Waterford. 3 vols. 1893.

HENDERSON, EMILY. *Recollections of the Career and Private Life of the late John Adolphus, etc. etc.* By his daughter. 1871.

HERVEY, LORD. *Memoirs of the Reign of George the Second from his Accession to the death of Queen Caroline, by John Lord Hervey.* Edited from the original manuscript at Ickworth by the Right Hon. John Wilson Croker, LL.D., F.R.S. 3 vols. 1884.

HOLDEN, LORD ANGUS. *Uncle Leopold. A Life of the First King of the Belgians.* 1936.

Four Generations of Our Royal Family. 1937.

HOLLAND, LADY ELIZABETH. *Lady Holland to her Son, 1821-1845.* Edited by the Earl of Ilchester. 1946.

HOLLAND, SIR HENRY. *Recollections of Past Life.* Bart., M.D., F.R.S., President of the Royal Institution of Great Britain: Physician in Ordinary to the Queen. 1872.

HOLMES, RICHARD R., D.G.A., Librarian to the Queen. *Queen Victoria.* 1897.

HOPKIRK, MARY. *Queen Adelaide.* 1946.

HUNT, LEIGH. *The Old Court Suburb: or Memorials of Kensington, Regal, Critical and Anecdotal.* 2 vols. 1855.

ILCHESTER, THE EARL OF, Editor. *Elizabeth Lady Holland to her Son, 1821-1845.* 1946.

JACKSON, EDITH. *Annals of Ealing. From the Twelfth Century to the Present Time, etc. etc.* With Introductory Preface by W. E. Oliver, LL.D., Vicar of Ealing. 1898.

JAGOW, KURT VON. *Königin Viktoria: die Mädchen-Jahre.*

JAMES, ADMIRAL SIR WILLIAM, G.C.B., Editor. *The Order of Release. The story of John Ruskin, Effie Gray and John Everett Mill, told for the first time in their unpublished letters.* 1947.

JENKINS, ELIZABETH. *Lady Caroline Lamb.* 1932.

JERROLD, CLARE. *The Early Court of Queen Victoria.* 1912.

KENT, WILLIAM, Editor. *An Encyclopaedia of London.* 1937.

LANCASTER, OSBERT, Editor and Translator. *The Tragedy at Clare-mont: Letters from Prince Leopold (uncle to Queen Victoria) to his sister the Gräfin Mensdorff-Pouilly, now in the possession of her grandson, Count Obersdorf.* The *Cornhill Magazine*, May 1937.

LAW, ERNEST, C.B. *Kensington Palace; Historically and critically de-

scribed and illustrated with a Guide to the State Rooms and Gardens and a Catalogue of the Pictures. 1923.

LEWIS, WYNDHAM. *Four Favourites.* 1948.

LIEVEN, PRINCESS. *Correspondence of Princess Lieven and Earl Grey.* Edited and translated by Guy le Strange. 1890.

Letters of Dorothea, Princess Lieven, during her Residence in London, 1812-1834. Edited by Lionel G. Robinson. 1902.

The Private Letters of Princess Lieven to Prince Metternich, 1820-1826. Edited with a Biographical Foreword by Peter Quennell assisted in translation by Dilys Powell. 1937.

The Lieven-Palmerston Correspondence, 1828-1856. Translated and edited by Lord Sudley. With a Preface by Sir John Squire. 1943.

LOCKER-LAMPSON, FREDERICK. *My Confidences: an Autobiographical Sketch addressed to my Descendants.*

LOFTIE, W. J. *Kensington, Picturesque and Historical.* 1888.

LORNE, THE MARQUIS OF. *V.R.I.: Queen Victoria, her Life, and Empire.* 1901.

LUCAS, E. V. *London Revisited.* 1916.

LYTTELTON, LADY. *Correspondence of Sarah Spencer, Lady Lyttelton, 1787-1870.* Edited by her great-granddaughter, The Honourable Mrs. Hugh Wyndham. 1912.

MacANDREW, DONALD. "Skittles: or Fair but Frail." *The Saturday Book.* Edited by Leonard Russell. 1948.

McCLINTOCK, MARY HOWARD. *The Queen thanks Sir Howard; The Life of Major-General Sir Howard Elphinstone, V.C., K.C.B., C.M.G.* By his daughter. 1945.

MARTIN, THEODORE. *The Life of His Royal Highness the Prince Consort.* 5 vols. 1875.

MARTIN, SIR THEODORE. *Queen Victoria as I Knew Her.* 1908.

MARTINEAU, HARRIET. *Harriet Martineau's Autobiography: with Memorials by Maria Weston Chapman.* 3 vols. 1877.

MAUROIS, ANDRÉ. *Disraeli: a Picture of the Victorian Age.* Translated by Hamish Miles. 1929.

MAXWELL, THE RIGHT HON. SIR HERBERT, Bart., F.R.S., D.C.L., LL.D. *The Life and Letters of George William Frederick, Fourth Earl of Clarendon, K.G., G.C.B.* 2 vols. 1913.

MOLLOY, FITZGERALD. *The Sailor King: William the IVth. His Court and His Subjects.* 2 vols. 1903.

MOORE, THOMAS. *Memoirs, Journal, and Correspondence of Thomas Moore.* 1853.

MUNK, WILLIAM, M.D., F.S.A. *The Life of Sir Henry Halford, Bart., G.C.H., M.D., F.R.S.* 1895.

MURRAY, CHARLES. *Three Weeks at Court: a Diary kept at Windsor by the late Sir Charles Murray. September 1837. The Cornhill Magazine,* January 1897.

NEALE, THE REV. ERSKINE. *Life of his Royal Highness Edward Duke of Kent.* 1850.

NEWMAN, BERTRAM. *Lord Melbourne.* 1930.

OWEN, ROBERT. *The Life of Robert Owen written by himself: with Selections from his Writings and Correspondence.* 2 vols. 1857-58.

PASTON, GEORGE AND QUENNELL, PETER. *"To Lord Byron": Feminine Profiles based upon unpublished letters, 1807-1824.* 1939.

PONSONBY, ARTHUR. *Henry Ponsonby, Queen Victoria's Private Secretary: His Life from his Letters.* By his son (Lord Ponsonby of Shulbrede). 1942.

PONSONBY, MAGDALEN. *Mary Ponsonby: a Memoir, Some Letters and a Journal.* Edited by her daughter. 1927.

POPE-HENNESSY, JAMES. *Monckton Milnes.* 1950.

PYNE, W. H. *The History of the Royal Residences of Windsor Castle, St. James' Palace, Carlton House, Kensington Palace, Hampton Court, Buckingham House, and Frogmore.* 3 vols. 1819.

QUEENSBERRY, THE MARQUIS OF. *Oscar Wilde and the Black Douglas.* In collaboration with Percy Colson.

ROYDE SMITH, NAOMI. *The State of Mind of Mrs. Sherwood.* A study. 1946.

RUSSELL, G. W. E. *Collections and Recollections by One Who has Kept a Diary.* 1898.

SITWELL, EDITH. *Victoria of England.* 1936.

SMITH, G. BARNETT. *Life of Queen Victoria, 1819-1901.* 1901.

STANLEY, ARTHUR PENRHYN. *The Life and Correspondence of Arthur Penrhyn Stanley, D.D., Late Dean of Westminster.* By Rowland E. Prothero, M.A., with the co-operation and sanction of the Very Rev. C. G. Bradley, D.D. 2 vols. 1893.

STOCKMAR, BARON E. VON. *Memoirs of Baron Stockmar.* By his son. Translated from the German by G. A. M. Edited by Max Müller. 2 vols. 1872.

STOKES, HUGH. *The Devonshire House Circle.* 1918.

STRACHEY, LYTTON. *Queen Victoria.* 1921.

STRONG, L. A. G. *The Minstrel Boy: a Portrait of Tom Moore.* 1937.

STUART, DOROTHY MARGARET. *The Daughters of George III.* 1939. *The Mother of Victoria: a Period Piece.* 1941.

STUART-WORTLEY, LADY EMMELINE. *Wanderers: Episodes from the Travels of Lady Emmeline Stuart-Wortley and her daughter, Victoria, 1849-1855.* By Mrs. Henry Cust. With a Preface by Sir Ronald Storrs. 1928.

SUDLEY, LORD, Editor and Translator. *The Lieven-Palmerston Correspondence, 1828-1856.* With a Preface by Sir John Squire. 1943.

THAL, HERBERT VAN. *Ernest Augustus, Duke of Cumberland and King of Hanover: a Brief Survey of the Man and his Times.* 1936.

TOOLEY, SARAH A. *The Personal Life of Queen Victoria.* 1896.

TORRENS, W. M. *Memoirs of William Lamb, Second Viscount Melbourne.*

TULLOCH, W. W., D.D., Minister of Maxwell Parish. *The Story of the Life of Queen Victoria.* Revised by Her Majesty. 1901.

VICTORIA, QUEEN. *Leaves from the Journal of Our Life in the Highlands from 1848 to 1861: to which are prefixed and added extracts from the same Journal giving an account of Earlier Visits to Scotland, and Tours in England and Ireland and Yachting Excursions.* Edited by Arthur Helps. 1863.

More Leaves from the Journal of a Life in the Highlands from 1862 to 1882. 1884.

The Letters of Queen Victoria: a Selection from Her Majesty's Correspondence between the years 1837 and 1861 published by authority of His Majesty the King. Edited by Arthur Christopher Benson, M.A., and Viscount Esher, G.C.V.O., K.C.B. 3 vols. 1908.

VILLIERS, GEORGE. *A Vanished Victorian: Being the Life of George Villiers, Fourth Earl of Clarendon, 1800-1870.* By his grandson. 1938.

VIZETELLY, HENRY. *Glances Back through Seventy Years: Autobiographical and other Reminiscences.* 2 vols. 1893.

WALISZEWSKI, K. *Autour d'un Trône: Catherine II de Russie, Ses Collaborateurs—Ses Amis—Ses Favoris.* Par K. Waliszewski.

Le Roman d'une impératrice: Catherine II de Russie d'après ses mémoires, sa correspondance, et les documents inédits des archives d'Etat. 1893.

WEBSTER, NESTA H. *Spacious Days.* An Autobiography. 1950.

WILKINSON, THE REV. C. ALLIX. *Reminiscences of the Court and Times of King Ernest of Hanover.* Allix Wilkinson, M.A., His Majesty's Resident Chaplain. 2 vols. 1886.

WYNN, FRANCIS. *Diaries by a Lady of Quality from 1797 to 1844.* Edited, with notes, by A. Hayward, Esqr., Q.C. 1864.

UNPUBLISHED AUTHORITIES

Letters of Miss Mary Davys (Extra Woman of the Bedchamber to Queen Victoria).

Extracts from the Letters of The Honorable Harriet Lister (Maid of Honor to Queen Victoria), incorporated in an article, "Queen Victoria's Extra Woman of the Bedchamber," by Miss Henrietta Tayler.

Pages from the Journal of Victoria Stuart-Wortley (Maid of Honor to the Duchess of Kent), incorporated in the script "The Poor Old Diary," 1857-63, edited by Mrs. Henry Cust.

Private information.

Letter from QUEEN VICTORIA, written in 1838 to the 5TH EARL FITZWILLIAM. (*Permission to publish this has kindly been given me by Mr. Thomas Fitzwilliam.*)

INDEX

I. The FAMILY and DESCENDANTS of

KING GEORGE III *married 1761* Charlotte
1738 - 1820

George	Frederick	William
1762 - 1830	1763 - 1827	1765 - 1837
PRINCE OF WALES	DUKE OF YORK	DUKE OF CLARENCE
KING GEORGE IV	*married*	**KING WILLIAM IV**
married	Frederica	*married*
Caroline	of Prussia	Adelaide
of Brunswick		of Saxe-Meiningen
1763 - 1821		

Augustus
1773 - 1843
DUKE OF SUSSEX
married morganatically
Lady Augusta Murray

Adolphus
1779 - 1850
DUKE OF CAMBRIDGE
married
Augusta
of Hesse-Cassel

Charlotte
1796 - 1817
married
Leopold
of Saxe-Coberg
LEOPOLD I
KING OF THE BELGIANS

Augustus d'Este
and
Emma d'Este

George
DUKE OF CAMBRIDGE
and
Mary
married
Francis
DUKE OF TECK

III. The HOUSE of COBURG - since 1826 SAXE-COBURG-GOTHA

FRANCIS of Saxe-Saalfeld-Coburg - married - Augusta of Reuss-Ebersdorf
1750 - 1806   1757 - 1831

ERNEST I	Ferdinand	Victoire Marie Louise	Leopold
Duke of Saxe-Saalfeld-Coburg	*married*	PRINCESS LEININGEN	KING OF THE BELGIANS
married	Maria da Gloria	*married*	*married 1*
Louise	Queen of Portugal	Edward	PRINCESS Charlotte OF WALES
of Saxe-Gotha-Altenburg		DUKE OF KENT	*married 2*
			Louise Marie
			daughter of
			Louis-Phillipe
			KING OF FRANCE

ERNEST II
Duke of Saxe-Coburg-Gotha

Albert - married - Queen Victoria
PRINCE CONSORT